THE GREAT PHILOSOPHERS

KARL JASPERS

THE GREAT
PHILOSOPHERS

The Disturbers

DESCARTES

PASCAL   LESSING   KIERKEGAARD   NIETZSCHE

Philosophers in Other Realms

EINSTEIN   WEBER   MARX

EDITED BY MICHAEL ERMARTH AND LEONARD H. EHRLICH

TRANSLATED BY EDITH EHRLICH AND LEONARD H. EHRLICH

FOREWORD BY MICHAEL ERMARTH

Helen and Kurt Wolff Book
Harcourt Brace & Company
New York   San Diego   London

© *R. Piper & Co. Verlag, München 1981*
English translation, Editors' Notes, and German Foreword
copyright ©1995 by Harcourt Brace & Company

Requests for permission to make copies of any part of the work should be mailed to: Permissions
Department, Harcourt Brace & Company, 6277 Sea Harbor Drive, Orlando, Florida 32887-6777.

Grateful acknowledgment is made for permission to reprint the following previously published material:

Hohlenberg, Johannes. *Søren Kierkegaard*. Translated with notes by T. H. Croaxall. Copyright
© 1954 by Pantheon Books. Reprinted by permission of Pantheon Books,
a division of Random House, Inc.

Kierkegaard, Søren. *The Journals of Søren Kierkegaard,* edited and translated by Alexander Dru.
Copyright © 1938 by Oxford University Press. Reprinted by permission of Oxford University
Press. *Kierkegaard's Concluding Unscientific Postscript.* Copyright © 1941 by Princeton University
Press. *The Sickness Unto Death.* Copyright © 1941 by Princeton University Press. *The
Concept of Anxiety.* Copyright © 1980 by Princeton University Press.
Reprinted by permission of Princeton University Press.

Pascal, Blaise. *Pascal's Pensees.* Translated by H. F. Stewart. Copyright © 1950 by Pantheon
Books. Reprinted by permission of Pantheon Books, a division of Random House, Inc.

Translation of *Die Grossen Philosophen, Nachlass 2.*

Library of Congress Cataloging-in-Publication Data
Jaspers, Karl, 1883–1969.
[Grossen Philosophen. English. Selections]
The great philosophers. Descartes, Lessing, Kierkegaard, Nietzsche, Marx, Weber,
Einstein/Karl Jaspers; edited by Michael Ermarth and Leonard H. Ehrlich;
translated by Edith Ehrlich and Leonard Ehrlich; foreword by Michael Ermarth.—1st ed.
p. cm.
"A Helen and Kurt Wolff book."
Includes bibliographical references and index.
ISBN 0-15-136943-7
1. Philosophy, Modern.   2. Philosophers, Modern.
I. Ermarth, Michael.   II. Ehrlich, Leonard H.   III. Title.
B3279.J33G762513   1994
190—dc20   93-49786

Text set in Granjon
Printed in the United States of America
First U.S. edition   A B C D E

CONTENTS

PHILOSOPHERS IN UTOPIAN POLITICAL THOUGHT   *339*

MARX   *341*

Forword

The present work is the fourth and final volume of Karl Jaspers's ambitious, unfinished project encompassing the thought of those he termed the Great Philosophers. The reader is referred to introductory remarks in this and previous volumes for the conceptual framework, broader historical context, and specific terminology of this monumental project—an endeavor that occupied much of Jaspers's long and productive life. Although the four volumes may be read separately or consulted in discrete sections, they clearly support the cardinal interpretive adage that the "whole" of a work constitutes more than the sum of its parts.

The thinkers in this final volume were especially salient for Jaspers's characteristic way of thinking, as will be readily apparent from his often impassioned observations and interpolations. These figures, especially Pascal, Kierkegaard, Nietzsche, and Weber, posed and exposed most penetratingly and urgently what Jaspers called the "radical questionability of human Existenz." Theirs was a discomfiting, peculiarly restless way of thinking, carried out in continuous movement, often in deepest dialogue with themselves as well as with their forebears and contemporaries. In its most successful employment, this dialogical element also engages the reader's deepest sense of what it means to be alive—and to be or to become oneself—in the world. This manifold "communicative dialogue" must necessarily encompass both past and present ideas and perspectives, while welding together previous, established philosophical categories with the existential truths that remain always present, even if obscurely and "cipher-like," to the reflecting mind.

Sections of Jaspers's original text show widely varying degrees of refinement: the preponderant part was finished, if not fully polished; other portions consist of random or inchoate comments and tersely abbreviated or elliptical exclamations. Sometimes he provided little more than a congeries of cross-references or clusters of quotations, some of which were quite loosely paraphrased. The text has been rendered as faithfully and fluently as possible, employing, wherever possible or traceable, standard English translations for the extensive quoted passages. Repetitions have been kept to a minimum, except to show the widening, productive "circle of interpretation" that Jaspers alludes to.

What is not (and cannot be) apparent to the reader is nonetheless deeply but invisibly etched in these volumes: they reflect the vigorous but altogether graceful touch of Helen Wolff. Her creativity, discernment, and stewardship in this project, as in many others over the years, should be acknowledged and appreciated.

—MICHAEL ERMARTH

Foreword and Acknowledgments

The preparation of this volume was made possible in part by a grant from the Division of Research Programs of the National Endowment for the Humanities, an independent federal agency. The grant made it possible for the University of Massachusetts at Amherst to grant Leonard H. Ehrlich one semester's leave to work on this and on Volume III of *The Great Philosophers.*

Our work on this book extended considerably beyond the period of the grant, and has been nothing less than a labor of love in honor of our late teacher Karl Jaspers. Our participation in this project was encouraged by the late Hannah Arendt. We received moral support from our friends and colleagues in The Karl Jaspers Society of North America. The interest in the project taken by two associates proved to be essential for its successful completion: Dr. Hans Saner (Basel), Jaspers's literary executor and editor of the German original; and Prof. Richard Wisser (Mainz). Of paramount importance was the extraordinary care with which Helen Wolff contributed to the fruition of this book; she wrote her last communication to us a few days before her death on March 27, 1994. This was the last project of "A Helen and Kurt Wolff Book" under her lone stewardship since Kurt Wolff died thirty years ago. We would like to think of the book as a fitting memorial to this grand lady of publishing.

—LEONARD H. EHRLICH
EDITH EHRLICH

The Disturbers

Editors' Note

The "Disturbers" are one of four main types of those "great philosophers" "whom all agree in terming philosophers." The others are the Seminal Founders of Philosophical Thought (Volume I of *The Great Philosophers*), the Metaphysicians (Volumes II and III), and the Creative Orderers (Volume III). Jaspers did not elaborate on a characterization of the Disturbers beyond this sketch:

"There are the disturbers and probers, the essayers and breachers, those who doubt and those who despair. There are various kinds: sophists who question and topple what is decayed; inventors of probing tools of thought, as Descartes; those whose thought anticipates the great crises of the age down to all the consequences, as Kierkegaard and Nietzsche."[1]

In his final scheme Jaspers distinguishes two subgroups of Disturbers, the "Probing Negators" and the "Great Awakeners." Both are "disturbers" in that they loosen thought configurations confirmed by convention and tradition. The first type suggests an undermining of the substance upon which human beings stand to orient themselves in reality; their "probing" marks them as "negators." In distinction thereto, the Great Awakeners are thinkers who, while exposing adhered-to conventions as defunct, are disturbers in order to recall man to his substance. Jaspers regards the Probing Negators as a type occurring in all periods of philosophy; the Awakeners as characteristic of modern times. He displays a marked affinity to the Awakeners. These two facts combine to make for a noteworthy juxtaposition in the following treatment of two contemporaries at the dawn of modernity: Descartes as the sole representative of Disturbers who are Negators and Pascal as the earliest of the Disturbers who are Awakeners.

[1] Karl Jaspers, *Weltgeschichte der Philosophie. Einleitung,* ed. by Hans Saner, Munich, Zurich, Piper, 1982, 123.

Probing Negators

DESCARTES

DESCARTES

Editors' Note

Jaspers did not leave a characterization of the type he called "Probing Negators." What he meant can be gleaned from the Introduction to the "Great Awakeners," which follows the treatment of Descartes presented here. Among the Probing Negators he counted Abelard, Duns Scotus, William of Occam, Descartes, and Hume. Only on Descartes did he leave more than notes and sketches. He had presented a fuller treatment of Descartes in response to a French invitation to contribute an essay on the occasion of the tricentenary (1937) of Descartes's "Discourse on Method."[1] Unlike this earlier essay, Descartes is treated below as representing a specific type of Great Philosopher.

The French philosopher, mathematician, and scientist René Descartes was born in 1596 in La Haye, France. He was educated at the Jesuit academy of La Flèche in the traditional Aristotelian curriculum, which stressed the qualitative, purposeful hierarchy of all being. After attaining a law degree at Poitiers in 1616, he served as a mercenary soldier in artillery units of French, Dutch, and Bavarian armies. Under the influence of pioneering developments in Dutch science and at the urging of physicist Isaac Beeckman, he began to conceive of a universal science of nature. A peripatetic period of study was followed by his move to Holland in 1628 for its settled seclusion and intellectual freedom.

Three of his most important works—*Discourse on Method* (1637), *Meditations on First Philosophy* (1641), and *Principles of Philosophy* (1644)—and others by him were placed on the Index of the Church. In addition to his writing on philosophy, he studied optics and psychology, invented a system of algebraic notation,

---

[1] Karl Jaspers, "Descartes" in *Three Essays: Leonardo, Descartes, Max Weber,* A Helen and Kurt Wolff Book, New York, Harcourt, Brace & World, 1964. See also Karl Jaspers, *Philosophical Faith and Revelation,* New York, Harper & Row, 1967, 287–89.

and became the originator of analytic geometry. He maintained an active correspondence with Princess Elizabeth of Bohemia, Constantijn Huygens, Marin Mersenne, and others interested in science. In 1649 Queen Christina of Sweden invited him to Stockholm to institutionalize the new learning. There, he died of pneumonia, on February 11, 1650. His remains were returned to Paris in 1666.

DESCARTES AND CHRISTIAN FAITH

Descartes is considered the modern philosopher who made man stand on his own feet. For him, the origin of all truth was the self-certainty of his intellect. Yet under the pressure of imminent danger from the Church, and not disposed to martyrdom, he accommodated himself to his times, and is said to have carefully concealed his thoughts and pretended to submit to ecclesiastical authority.

Doubtless his caution was related to his support of Copernican astronomy, which he considered acceptable within the framework of ecclesiastical faith and which he found uncontested even by high Church dignitaries. The outcome of Galileo's trial shocked and alarmed him. But to presuppose in him an attitude of indifference or animosity toward faith is surely false. Descartes was a pious Catholic. This fact is essential to the meaning of his entire philosophy and to the practical grounding of his life.

1. DESCARTES THE PIOUS CATHOLIC

1) Modern interpreters have found the connection between his vow to make a pilgrimage to Loretto and the inception of his philosophy disconcerting, as also the dreams, reported from the same period, that motivated him. According to his notes, Descartes was completely serious. These experiences cannot be overlooked or made light of, as though they were oddities peculiar to his times. They are an element of his life and of the attitude in which his philosophy developed.

2) Descartes's writings frequently display an explicit acceptance of ecclesiastic authority. "Above all we must impress on our memory as the highest rule that what God has revealed to us must be believed as most certain of all. Hence, no matter how clearly and convincingly the light of reason suggests something different to us, we are to trust rather

to divine authority than to our own judgment. But in matters where our faith in God does not instruct us, it does not behoove the philosopher to consider something to be true which he has not recognized as true, and to trust more to the senses, i.e., to the rash judgments of his childhood, than to mature reason" (*Principles,* I, ¶76).

After proudly explaining the certainty of his blueprint of the world, Descartes ends by saying: "Yet I am nonetheless always conscious of my weakness and do not maintain anything unconditionally but submit everything to the authority of the Catholic Church as well as to the judgment of those having greater insight. I do not want anyone to consider something to be true unless he has been convinced by clear and uncontroverted reasons" (*Principles,* IV, ¶207).

At no point is Descartes seen indignantly opposing the ecclesiastical authority that sought to pressure him not to publish a major work. His letters testify to his zeal for the Catholic religion, to his devotion to the dignitaries of the Church to which he belongs (cf. A/T, III, 259).[2] He even speaks of Galileo's judges as "persons whom I respect and whose authority has hardly less influence on my actions than does my own reason" (*Method,* 50).

Divine revelation, which forms the basis of this authority, is not God's direct proclamation at some immediate time and place, or that of individual people claiming to have heard God's voice directly, perhaps even this very day. Revelation is to be believed only on the authority of the Church. For all practical purposes, it is identical with ecclesiastical authority, which, moreover, is in a position of secular power.

Descartes's life remains grounded in authority. Since his intellectual endeavor—a matter of reason and not grounded in authority—is a personal task, and at first largely removed from practical life (even though he hopes to have a tremendous impact on the world and to establish a new Christian philosophy), the accomplishment of this task is hedged in by precautions for the author and warnings to the reader. The superior authority embodied in the encompassing ecclesiastical faith is accepted as fact.

3) Perhaps the clearest documentation of his Catholic faith is contained in his letters to Princess Elizabeth.[3] She is his closest, most understanding, most intelligent, most devoted pupil and friend. He corresponds with her about practical philosophy. Philosophy seems to be the origin sufficient for everything. Thus he speaks of a bliss "which

[2] Citations preceded by A/T refer to *Oeuvres de Descartes,* ed. Charles Adam and Paul Tannery.
[3] Daughter of Frederick V, Elector Palatine and titular King of Bohemia.

depends totally on our free will and which all men can achieve without
any outside assistance." The princess replies that "there are illnesses
which . . . rob one of the power to think." Descartes: My statement
applies only to people "who have free use of their reason." To be sure,
he says, frequently "an indisposition located in the body prevents the
will from being free." After all, we do sleep, and "the greatest philosopher . . . cannot prevent having bad dreams." But still, experience
shows that a thought frequently present while the spirit was free recurs
also when one is indisposed. Of himself, Descartes states that "my
dreams never show me anything annoying." However, we can take
absolute responsibility for ourselves only as long as we are in full possession of ourselves. It is worse to lose one's reason than to lose one's
life. For the loss of one's life is no evil: "even setting aside the doctrines
of faith, natural philosophy by itself lets us expect a happier state for
our soul after death than the one in which it finds itself at present; and
it makes us fear nothing that is worse than being bound to a body that
robs the soul completely of its freedom" (A/T, IV, 281).

Only a few weeks after these expressions of philosophic autarchy,
the Protestant princess, in a letter to Descartes of November 1645, de-
plores "the madness of one of my brothers," who converted to Catholicism. "He fell into the hands of a certain kind of people who harbor
more hatred for our house than affection for their rites. He let himself
be caught by them so that he has changed his religion in order to
become a Roman Catholic, without giving the least convincing indication that it was a matter of conscience. . . . I am forced to see him
exposed to the contempt of the world" (A/T, IV, 335–36).

Descartes replies in January 1646: "I am astonished that your Highness feels displeasure about something which the greatest part of the
world will consider good and which the others would excuse on the
basis of several strong reasons. For all adherents of the religion to
which I belong (to which, unquestionably, the greatest number of people in Europe belong) must approve even if they knew about reprehensible circumstances and motives. For we believe that God makes use of
various means in order to draw souls to Him, and that he who has
entered a monastery with bad intentions will afterwards be guided to
a holy life. One can reject the judgment of those of a different faith if
they speak ill of the matter. For always when there are several parties
it is impossible to please some without displeasing the others. If they
would consider that they would not have their religion if they or their
fathers or their ancestors had not left the Roman one, they would have
occasion neither to scoff nor to call those inconstant who leave their

religion. . . . But I do not maintain that my reasons could chase away your Highness's anger. I merely hope that time will have mitigated it before this letter reaches you, and I fear that I might rekindle it if I were to enlarge on this matter" (A/T, IV, 351–52).

4) The various reports about Descartes's death are, to be sure, not literally reliable, but are believable as a whole. He died of pneumonia. Feverish fantasies dominated his last days, but there was no confusion in his utterances. Chanut, the French ambassador in Stockholm and a friend of the philosopher, relates that Descartes said to him he had made his accounting during the night and was determined to leave this world without sorrow and with trust in God's mercy. Descartes "added firm and pious words worthy of a man who is not only a philosopher but a religious person. In his life he gave an example of purity and righteousness and . . . fulfilled the duties of a true Catholic" (A/T, V, 474).

Clerselier[4] reports: " 'My soul,' said Descartes, 'you have been imprisoned for a long time. Now is the hour when you can leave your prison and leave the confusion of this body. This dissolving must be suffered with joy and courage' " (A/T, V, 482).

He gave evidence to M. and Mme Chanut that "his subordination to the laws of God made him believe that the Master over life and death had permitted his spirit to dwell for such a long time in confusion and darkness because his deliberations were not sufficiently in harmony with the will of the Creator that he be in charge of his life. He concluded that, since God granted him the free use of his reason, He thus permitted him to follow that which reason demanded of him, with the proviso that he refrain from wanting to penetrate all too inquisitively into His secrets" (A/T, V, 491).

A few hours before his death he said good-bye to Chanut and embraced him. He then dictated a letter to his two brothers, charging them to support his nurse, for whom he had cared throughout his entire life. He turned to his confessor and for another five to six hours continued in acts of religious devotion (cf. A/T, V, 470).

5) Incidental supplementary reports: Queen Christina of Sweden testified long after Descartes's death that he had greatly contributed to her conversion and had brought her the first light. Baillet cites the testimony of one Porlier who, in Holland, wanted to spy on Descartes the atheist and was met by the devout Catholic (A/T, IV, 318ff.).

---

[4]Claude Clerselier (1614–1684) was a French philosopher who corresponded with Descartes, and published, posthumously, several of his works.

2. DESCARTES ON PHILOSOPHY AND THEOLOGY

Descartes never thought of becoming a theologian. He restricts himself exclusively to philosophy, assigns limits to it and decisively shuns theology, refusing to make judgments about theological matters or even to discuss them. He draws a circle around the domain of theology but does not enter it. This becomes especially clear in several letters to Mersenne (April 15, May 6, May 17, 1630).

A question "not touching on that which relies on revelation, which is what I mean by theology" does not seem to him "to lie outside of my profession"; rather, it "must be examined by means of human reason." But he to whom God has granted the use of reason is obliged "to use it mainly to attempt to cognize Him and know oneself" (A/T, I, 150).

Now the defense: When Mersenne speaks about God's incarnation, Descartes does not find in this any contradiction to what he is saying philosophically. But "I do not want to meddle in theology, I am even afraid to do so. You might judge that my philosophy is too impudent if it dares to express its opinion regarding such exalted subjects" (A/T, I, 150).

Hence when Mersenne raises the question whether man's eternal damnation is compatible with God's goodness, Descartes counters that this question belongs to theology. Therefore "you will have to permit me to keep altogether silent about this . . . because . . . otherwise I would do injustice to the truths that depend on faith and cannot be warranted through natural proofs, the injustice of wanting to affirm them with human and therefore debatable reasons" (A/T, I, 153).

Thus philosophy is reduced to a separate area, becoming a matter of competence, and ceding place to theology as another area.

Descartes frequently expresses the strict separation of philosophy and theology. They differ completely from each other in origin, reason, and faith. "The clarity or the enlightening power through which our will can be moved to agreement is of a twofold kind: the one proceeds from natural light, the other from divine grace." Divine grace brings about a supernatural light in the believer: "We say that faith refers to obscure things; yet that, for the sake of which we accept it, is not dark but brighter than all natural light." This supernatural light coming from God causes us "to have firm faith that what we are enjoined to believe is revealed by God Himself" (A/T, VII, 147–48).

For Descartes, this strict separation, in the tradition of the medieval doctrine of the twofold truth, is hard to carry out in actual thought.

He does not allow the contrast between the two truths to become evident, since he simply leaves theology aside in his philosophical thought, not drawing any comparisons. If the authority of the Church were to assert that such a contradiction exists, he would immediately submit, because Church and revelation have precedence.

But whenever he wants to put his philosophical proofs in the service of theology, the truths of revelation and theology are by no means a matter of indifference to him. In a letter dedicating his *Meditations* to the Sorbonne, he justifies the value of his work precisely by claiming "that in philosophy there is no task more meritorious than to collect carefully and irrevocably the best proofs of all (proofs for the existence of God and for the substantial being of the soul) and to present them so clearly outlined and so transparently that it will be established universally for the future that these are the proofs" (A/T, VII, 3).

Especially in cases where Descartes's philosophy treats essential questions of concern to theology, an ambiguity arises as to which area they belong. This ambiguity is resolved only in semblance by resorting to the theological doctrines regarding the limits of reason. (The oath of the modernists has the oath-taker confess that the existence of God can be proved by rational means—hence a faith is demanded that expects from reason that which, if reason were capable of it, would make faith superfluous.)

One example is the question of immortality. Philosophical reasoning can prove that the body and the immaterial soul are of a differing nature. It can recognize that the destruction of the spirit need not necessarily follow from the extinction of the body. But this insight can lead only as far as hope and cannot arrive at the certainty of immortality. This certainty it can gain only through revelation. Whereas the existence of God is proved, immortality is not proved. "My presumption does not go so far as to attempt to determine something merely on the strength of human reason, which solely . . . depends on the will of God." If we "leave aside what faith teaches us about this, then I confess that by natural reason alone we can, to be sure . . . have splendid *hopes* but not the least *certainty*" (*Meditations,* 3rd ed., 89–90).

According to Descartes, theology possesses its own specific area of truth, the goal of which is the salvation of souls and the content of which is supranatural revelation. But knowledge of what is necessary for the salvation of souls is just as accessible to the ignorant and the uneducated as to scholars. With them, speculation is superfluous pedantry (A/T, VI, 8).

Philosophy can be of service to theology, but not within the latter's

own area. There, theology should not aspire to offer proofs and should
be as simple as possible. We are not to submit theology to our rational
arguments, since it goes beyond human comprehension. We can and
must prove that the truths of theology do not contradict those of philosophy, but we do not need to test the former in every way. Scholastic
theology has given impetus to all sects and heretics, whereas idiots and
peasants can get to heaven just as well as we can. Saint Thomas is
responsible for Calvin (A/T, IV, 165, 176, 216; I, 584).

However, like a great many other philosophers, Descartes most
likely had the ambition to reform theology. Scholastic theology, in any
case, has to come to an end. Thereupon Cartesian philosophy—as the
only true one—will alone be compatible with faith. In contradiction to
his usual self-limitation, Descartes furnished an example by his discussion of transubstantiation (A/T, III, 295–96; IX,, 192ff.; IV, 165–70).

3. DESCARTES'S CONCEPTION OF GOD

Descartes rarely discusses God in his works but frequently does in his
letters. He is concerned with thoughts that can be followed through
without recourse to revelational faith, with thoughts subject to experience and reason. They have their place among the philosophical notions
of God, beginning with the pre-Socratics, Plato, and Aristotle. They
address man as rational man. They arrive at absolute transcendence
(that is, they find their confirmation in the Biblical God and in the God
of Jesus) but never know positively what God is and know nothing of
an incarnation of God, nothing of a Christ, a thought that they would
consider blasphemous.

Though in Descartes as in all Europeans of the last millennium the
philosophical conception of God stands within the framework of Christian tradition, this is not of essential importance for its content, which
is sustained by a much broader tradition and historic connection.

In Descartes the conception of God arose relative to the meaning
and origin of truth, to the possibilities and limits of our human cognition. Here he expresses his passionate striving for the purity of the
conception of God, including a critical illumination of the import and
the limits of all philosophizing on the part of philosophy itself.

1) *God's almighty will is not subject to any truth existing independently
of Him.* Descartes took up this thought, which had been cogitated radically since the eleventh century (Petrus Damiani) and was taken up
again later by the nominalists.

Eternal truths, like mathematical ones, are true or possible only because God cognizes them as true and possible. By no means are they cognized by God as if they were true independently of Him. Truth does not come prior to the knowledge God has of it. In God, willing and cognizing are one. Because He wants something, He cognizes it, and therefore it is true. We dare not say (that would be blasphemy) that if God were not, these truths would be true nonetheless. The existence of God is the first and most eternal of all truths. All others proceed from it.

Eternal truths are established by God like everything else created by Him. To say that truths are independent of Him would mean to subordinate God to fate.

God ordained the laws in nature as a king ordains laws in his realm. We can grasp these laws; they are innate in our spirit, as a king's laws would be imprinted on the hearts of his subjects if he had the power to do so.

God was not constrained to create these truths. He might also have made it untrue that all lines drawn from the center to the circumference of a circle are equal. God was as little constrained to create these truths as He was to create the world. These truths are bound to His nature with no more necessity than all else created by Him.

It may be argued: If God has established the truths like a king has his laws, then He can also change them. The answer: If His will can change. Descartes understands the truths to be eternal and unchanging. He thinks the same of God.

But God's will is free. His might is unfathomable. We can be certain only that God can make all that is within our comprehension, but not that He could not make what we cannot comprehend. It is presumptuous to believe that our faculty of representation extends as far as His might.

Descartes's reflection on the origin of truth impels the conception of God to a consciousness of God's grandeur, which, in the area of thought, can hardly be surpassed. Cognition surrenders the absolute sovereignty of its own origin without giving up its character as God's creation.

The conception of God comes to touch the enduring, encompassing actuality in which all cognition is situated. The sovereignty of the self-certainty of thought comprehends itself not as absolute but as created.

2) *How does God create? What is the meaning of "creation"?* It is a causality unlike any cognized by man, one that is in each case particular, yet a total causality. That is, in God volition, cognition, creation are the same. None has precedence over the other.

If we want to relate creation to the existence of things, then we could, for purposes of differentiation, speak of the pictures of eternal truth. But both are the same. Hence Descartes can also say: I know that God is the author of all things, and that truths are in some way things, and that consequently He is their author.

Creating is not a process, but a free act. Descartes says explicitly that he does not imagine the eternal truths radiating from God like the rays of the sun.

What did God do in order to bring forth things? Through the very fact that He desired and comprehended them through all eternity, He also created them.

Is "something" cognized by means of such thoughts? No. In the forms of finite thinking that alone are accessible to us, they are modes of transcending through which we do not gain knowledge applicable to the substance of a matter (for then we would again be in finitude), but through which we gain assurance. This assurance is that of philosophic faith, which cannot be forced through methodical thought but becomes clear to itself in a deepened consciousness of limits.

3) This means: *God is incomprehensible.* For the conception of God in no way implies that reason, which seeks a point of contact in the conception of God, comprehends God by way of reason. God is not the result of rational thought, but, in the last analysis, is experienced as its precondition. Reason does not arrive at God; rather, in the very constitution of reason there appears something other than reason which is the ground of reason.

Regarding God and creation, Descartes says he knows that they are but does not grasp and comprehend them. We can know that God is infinite and omnipotent although we, as finite beings, can neither cognize nor think this; just as we can, to be sure, touch a mountain with our hands but cannot embrace it.

4) Descartes desires God to be spoken of in a way more appropriate than is usually the case. Almost always He is represented as something finite. *The notion most people have of God does not fit Him.*

Men do not consider Him the infinite and unfathomable being on whom all things depend; instead, they stop at a name and think, since He corresponds to what is called *deus* in Latin, and is adored by mankind, that is all we need to know about Him.

Whoever does not have a more exalted notion of God can easily turn into an atheist. Whoever completely comprehends mathematical truths but not God's existence does not believe that the former depend on the latter. But the proper way of thinking would be: the necessity of mathematical truths does not exceed our comprehension. God, however, is a cause whose power transcends the limits of human comprehension. Therefore the former must be something less, something subordinate to this incomprehensible power.

Hence, false representations of God not only are blasphemous but also form the basis of atheism (*Meditations,* Preface, 4–5). For atheists turn against these false representations as if it were God' Himself they attacked, or possibly a being to whom human emotions are attributed; or they turn altogether against all false representations that arise through our claiming for our mind such great power and wisdom that we presume to be able to determine and comprehend all that which God could and would have to do. But none of the atheists' objections can trouble us as long as we bear in mind that we must conceive of our intellect as merely finite, but of God as incomprehensible and infinite.

In order to preserve truly and purely our consciousness of God, we must guard against overestimating the range of our cognition. This, however, occurs when we set limits to the possibilities in the world as though the power of our cognition would surpass what has actually been created by God. It further occurs when we assume that all things have been created by Him merely for our sake. And this occurs also when we believe ourselves capable of comprehending, by the power of our insight, God's purpose when He created the world.

4. THE LIMITS OF COGNITION

1) We cannot know God through Himself, that is, through an immediate illumination. An *intuitive cognition of God* is something entirely different from speculations about God with the purpose of drawing conclusions from them.

In the state of beatitude the cognition of God will be intuitive. "Intuitive cognition is an illumination of the spirit through which it sees those things in the light of God which He is pleased to reveal to it through a direct impression of divine clarity on our intellect; but the latter is seen here not as active but merely as receiving the rays of the godhead" (A/T, V, 136).

In our present state, however, all our cognition of God either grows out of thinking, which "derives it from the principles of faith, which is obscure, or it grows out of the ideas and natural concepts which are in us and which, no matter how clear, are merely crude and confused as regards such an exalted object." Thus cognition of God, gained through our intellect, starts out from the "darkness of the principles" and moves within the "uncertainty which we all experience in our thinking" (A/T, V, 137).

There is a radical difference between intuitive cognition and cognition by way of reasoning. Intellectual cognition produces "a confused and dubious perception that demands much effort on our part and is enjoyed only in the moment after we have attained it." Intuitive cognition, on the other hand, is "a light that is pure, constant, clear, certain, effortless and always present" (A/T, V, 137).

In our earthly condition we have intimations of such intuitive cognition, that is, our spirit, freed from the body, will receive such illuminations and immediate cognitions. In this body already the senses make us aware of corporeal and perceivable matters. Our souls are granted a few glimpses of the goodness of their creator, without which they would not be capable of thought. Although obscured by the body, we receive "a first, undeserved, certain cognition . . . which we reach through our spirit more trustingly than we do in regard to our eyes" (A/T, V, 137).

Such intuitive, ungrounded truth of original intuition, which is yet totally certain in the brightest light, finds expression in the statement "I think, therefore I am." "Won't you confess to me that you are less certain of the presence of the objects that you see than of the truth of this statement: I think, therefore I·am? This cognition is not the work of your reasoning, nor is it a teaching given to you by your instructors: your mind sees it, feels it and uses it. Even though your imagination, which intrudes disturbingly upon your thoughts, reduces the clarity of cognition by wanting to clothe it with its own signs, it nonetheless constitutes proof for you that our souls are capable of receiving an intuitive cognition from God" (A/T, V, 136–37).

But in this way we do not receive any intuitive cognition of God in which we would cognize God through Himself. To be sure, the statement "I think, therefore I am" is followed by: "I am, therefore God is"—but this statement says only *that* He is, not *what* He is. The cognition of God through immediate illumination by the godhead is something entirely different. "Hence confess that in this life you do not see in God and through His light that He is such; rather, you conclude this from a proposition that you have made about Him, and you draw the conclusion through the power of argumentation, a machine that is often faulty" (A/T, V, 139).

Thus we see how decisively Descartes rejects "exceeding the limits of philosophizing that I have set for myself" (ibid.).

2) Man tries in vain to focus his will to cognition in a direction where it cannot reach and where he can only become enmeshed in

deception. Descartes's pride in the indubitable certainty of clear and distinct cognition is only one trait of his basic philosophical stance. This is complemented by his consciousness of the limits of the intellect, of its weakness and vacillation, of the dependence of our life on the other. We must differentiate between the *contemplatio veritatis* and the *usus vitae* (between theory and practice). Although inaccessible to our comprehension, what we do in practice is not baseless or accidental. By what means do the practical decisions that cannot be arrived at via our intellect come about?

In the first place, the senses and the certainty of our instincts guide us when it comes to our bodily needs. These we share with the animals.

Second, since we live in time and in particular concrete circumstances calling for decisions, such decisions may have to be made without our being able to give sufficient reasons for them by means of our cognition. In the urgency of the moment we cannot wait until we have come to know everything. We must act out of origins that go beyond our always limited cognition; we must rely on opinions that appear to be the most plausible. The weakness of our cognitive nature demands the strength of decision. Here we must apply the maxim to be firm and decisive in our actions and follow even the most questionable views—once we have decided on them—with no less constancy than if they had been entirely assured.

In these decisions we are guided by the state and the customs of the country. Descartes never wishes to attack the state, the nature of the state, or current customs. He has no wish to encourage reform, much less revolution. Just as it is not sound to demolish cities in order to rebuild them in a better way, it is not sound to reconstruct the state from the base up. "It is all too difficult to set up again these tremendous structures once they have been pulled down, or even just to shore them up when they have been shaken . . . and, finally, they always prove more bearable, as it were, than would be their modification" (*Method,* 11).

Third, our limited cognition, which cannot comprehend God, is dependent on the miracle of revelation to which Descartes submits. He confesses that he believes the truths "which are revealed to us through the divinity are more certain than all cognition since the trust one has in them—as is the case in all things obscure—is not a matter of the intellect but of the will" (*Rules,* 14). Here prevails the supernatural light and the decision of ecclesiastical authority.

When Descartes turns from this threefold dependence on something other than our reason to consider his own intellectual effort as philosopher, the terms in which he speaks are extremely modest. He has attained his cognition in isolation from practical life, in solitary intellectual effort (and later on has often regretted publishing his writings, since they brought nothing but turmoil into his life). In the realm of cognition based solely on reason his procedure is different from that with regard to the state, customs, the Church. He wishes to divorce, radically, all traditional views from his conviction in order to replace them with better ones or to give them a better foundation if they were correct (cf. *Method,* 11). However, in traveling this road, he does not set himself up as an example to others; indeed, he warns against it.

This solitary cognizing, in which Descartes expects to find, and believes himself to have found, complete certainty within the limits of the intellect's range, is characterized, however, by a lack of corroboration. Neither the motive that urged the young Descartes into the world in order to prove himself in active life, nor the motive of corroboration of cognition via the mechanical arts (of which he had extravagant expectations without ever testing them himself) plays a role here. Hence the edifice of Cartesian doctrine is full of absurdities of whose correctness their author is totally convinced.

Descartes's Existenz as a whole has to be understood within the framework of his subservience to authority, of his ecclesiastical faith, as the process of a philosophizing that comprehends itself as an exception. However, after impressive starts of a truly philosophical nature, this philosophizing is bound to go astray.

5. CHARACTERIZATION OF HIS PHILOSOPHY

1) How does Descartes arrive at the revealed God from the divinity which can be felt as encompassing actuality by reason at its limit? And, from the philosophic notion of God, how does he arrive at the authority of a God in the actual world in whom one believes in obedience? In fact, Descartes does not start out from one notion and arrive at the other; for him, philosopher and pious Catholic coexist. The one cannot be derived from the other.

In no way does Descartes arrive at revelation from philosophy. Philosophic thought does not call for revelation. Revelation is simply there, present in a world that calls for it, proclaimed by men; it is promise and threat. Men of faith maintain that God Himself is speaking. This is the tremendous claim that we can either accept or reject as implausible and hence unacceptable. At the point of decision, this is beyond discussion, even though each of its actual consequences, every action emanating from it within the area of human community, every statement within the area of speech, is subject to discussion simply because it has entered the world we have in common. Descartes acknowledged this claim without questioning or doubting, acknowledged it in the form stipulated by the Church. His universal methodical doubt does not extend to revelation.

Nor does he adopt the reverse course, a philosophy growing from revelational faith (hence a theology). We have seen how strictly he abstains from any theological discussion, indeed, refuses it almost fearfully. His philosophic point of departure is independent throughout, even though with the formal premise of complete subordination to the authority of the Church. This philosophic starting point can, as such, be taken without any revelational faith and, even in Descartes, has no relation to revelational faith.

2) Descartes does not ground this obedience toward Church and revelation philosophically. This obedience is a given; in the totality of his attitude toward life it precedes his philosophy. Philosophy fills a certain space within the framework of creation. In it truth, which is, and reason, which cognizes it, have their place, but they are encompassed, limited, and controlled by the other truth, which speaks in the world through the authority of the Church.

3) If there exists an original philosophy independent of revelation and alien to it, though affected by it within the actual world, yet indifferent to it in its own depth—a philosophy such as we find in Plato, Plotinus, Spinoza, and Kant, and which in believers in revelation such as Anselm and Nicholas of Cusa could be operative in an original manner and without conflict to the very depth of their conception of God in spite of their ecclesiastical faith in Christ—then Descartes does not take part in it. Descartes is considered the co-founder of modern philosophic independence and of the independence of reason; but he is the pious Catholic, with all that entails.

4) Descartes thinks and writes with the self-awareness of the originality of his own unshakable insight. The first step of his thought based on the attempt at methodical, universal, unlimited doubt leads to *cogito ergo sum*. He takes this step without God, in pure self-certainty and independence.

Descartes takes the second step with the proposition that everything that is as clear and distinct as this first foundational thought also displays reliable truth.

The renewed possibility of doubt, namely, that an evil demon which has created us might continuously deceive us with this clarity, calls for a third step: To be sure, even this demon cannot deceive me about my thinking being. Furthermore, clear and distinct cognition is also reliable cognition, as guaranteed solely by the fact that, not an evil demon, but God has created us, who does not deceive us because He cannot will to do so.

But does God exist? According to Descartes, His existence is proved cogently by God Himself. We discover in us the idea of God as the infinite Being. We cannot have produced this idea; it must rest on the effect of this Being itself. By the certainty of my being and of that idea which I discovered within me, I deduce God's actuality with equal certainty.

This conclusion is questionable. As I think the infinite Being through my being a thinking being, I do not draw my conclusion with the same certainty as I do in regard to things in the world. For a God who is proven is not for that matter God. He has become an object.

However, the supposed proof can be a guideline for thought along which a certainty of a different origin can be attained. This origin can be perceived in the philosophic conception of God, which Descartes, standing within the great tradition, has expressed in his letters. But where Descartes establishes the reliability of clear and obvious cognition, God is demoted to a function in the assurance of all certainty of cognition. God is the ground of the clarity and distinctness of nondeceiving cognition. All further steps of cognition then happen—after God has served as guarantor—without God.

Once God has fulfilled the function of guarantor, He no longer plays any role in the entire development of Descartes's philosophy. Now cognition can base itself entirely on itself. If at the very outset of his philosophy Descartes assigns to God this totally assuring function, then it is surely no playful line of thought, which, bound to its time, would become dispensable. This role is possible because Descartes is serious about the conception of God. The God who appears here, in the system, for one moment and then disappears forever is, for Descartes, the God who created everything, even cognition.

This leads to ambiguities in the whole mood of this philosophizing.

5) In Descartes, we hear genuine philosophy in its rudiments, observe his originally philosophic acts, see the spiritual earnestness of a thinker's life.

Philosophically, the *cogito ergo sum* is an intuitive fundamental thought pregnant with something extraordinary that awaits development, but in its derivation into cogent cognition it becomes a banality.

The statement "I am, hence God is" has the character of a transcending original act of Existenz, to which I can attain. As a proof for the existence of God, however, it becomes futile finite thought, which as proof turns out to be false.

It becomes everywhere obvious that Descartes's philosophizing soon bogs down; its lines of thought become absurd and yet are considered to be absolutely certain. We perceive the loss of philosophic substance, which (in the reality of his philosopher's life, disciplined but entrapped in mere intellectual thought) this thinker can accept only because he is sheltered in ecclesiastical faith, in the actuality of authority. This did not become manifest in the quotidian, where his participation in ecclesiastical rites was minor, but at critical turning points of his life and in his dying.

6) The sovereignty of cognition, which establishes its rule in the world in an unlimited way, knows itself completely dependent on God. Up to this point we cannot speak of ambiguity, because with such statements Descartes hits on the truth of existential consciousness. They become ambiguous only in their transformation.

In Descartes the independence of reason quickly becomes the self-certainty of mere intellect. With proof for the existence of God, Descartes moves cogent certainty into an area where it is not valid. He thereby destroys cogent certainty and at the same time that which is unique to the independent speculative thinking of reason.

In practice this philosophy of the intellect may appear to have precedence over revelation; but the truth of this whole philosophy abdicates in favor of the precedence of revelation. The extraordinary self-certainty of cognition, right up to the "proof" of the existence of God, takes place within the consciousness of the limited nature of all human cognition.

Because God has guaranteed the certainty of clear and distinct cognition, there develops in Descartes the inordinate self-certainty of his philosophical system. But because this cognition is grounded in God, it bows in its entirety to revelation: the unbounded pride of reason is paired with the humility of the cognizing person. In the world he possesses the fanatical intolerance of the self-assured intellect; transcending the world, he exhibits total, unquestioning obedience.

7) The ambiguities of the thoughtful action in Descartes's philosophy would be of little moment if they derived merely from the incidental personal traits of this thinker. But they become crucially important because, throughout the modern centuries and up to the present, they give the first, prototypical, and exemplary expression to the basic character of a broad current of a manner of thought.

a) Consequently Descartes accepts mathematical natural science without any better justification than it has in itself, and without any cogent interpretation. However, since he grounds it with absolute certainty in the conception of God, he rigidifies it, contradictory to the spirit of natural science, by making absolute the world picture created by himself, a picture that is factually erroneous, indeed, absurd. In this way he opposes the spirit of the true natural scientist, for whom such cognition, precisely through its cogent methodology, and because it is unfinished and open as a whole, must be carried further into the unforeseeable. In this process even its foundations as posited at a given time, though always determined, still participate in the movement of progression.

b) Descartes establishes philosophy as scientific philosophy, which is at one with natural science. He failed to understand the true meaning of modern natural science; nor did he provide a foundation for its methods. This is evident from his criticism of Galileo, as well as in his own manner of constructive thinking, which is related to a defective—because reduced—scholasticism and not to modern science. But he interpreted modern science in a sense that, taken up time and again, hides its nature and its course, misunderstands its true greatness, and burdens it with consequences not necessarily belonging to it. Descartes's reputation as co-founder of modern natural science rests on an allegation.

In laying the foundation of a modern type of scientific philosophy, Descartes has become the undoing of most of those who followed him or recognized themselves in him.

His life and his thinking present the prototype of a modern ambiguity in philosophy. They show the "scientific" philosophy of a man faithful to the Church that takes on the appearance of an original philosophic foundation of life.

He made possible an enterprise of scientific philosophy that understood itself as similar in kind to investigation in the natural sciences and sciences in general, that is, as inquiry into facts that increasingly cognizes, if not objects, then conditions. In this claim on the part of philosophy to scientific research, with its semblance of the clarity and distinctness of the intellect, philosophy itself is lost; the truthfulness of human Existenz, which illuminates its path by philosophizing, is imperceptibly obscured and confused. Descartes was one of the first to set in motion an existentially uncommitted scientific philosophizing. Subsequently, and completely in the nineteenth century, this philosophizing had a devastating effect on authentic philosophy.

In considering Descartes to be the beginning of a whole philosophical era, that is, of the modern world, we go much too far. He represents merely a moment, and not a founding one at that, but a deceptive one. He was neither guide nor exemplar for the actual spiritual forces of the last centuries or the present, neither for the authentic sciences nor for genuine philosophy, nor for the Biblical faith searching for original ways toward its renewal. The foundering of his undertaking is not the foundering of a philosophic era but, if its meaning is understood, the end of a spiritual disaster.

In no way did Descartes lay the foundation of modern independent philosophy.

8) Original philosophy does not gravitate toward supplementation through revelation and Church, neither in Spinoza nor in Kant.

a) Further, in Descartes, his discussions, few as they are, of the grandeur of the representation of God, grow out of the tradition of original philosophy. They did not originate in revelation, but serve as the criterion of what is said about God by thinkers and theologians who believe in revelation.

In Descartes there is the semblance of an initial independence of thinking about God, as well as independence of scientific cognition. In actual fact, he did not achieve this independence, although his extraordinary influence grows from this semblance.

There are reasons for this semblance. It rests on a final ambiguity in Descartes's thinking and life as a whole. He too looks to philosophy—without revelation—as guidance for his life.

This guidance exhibits at first the aspect of a direction of life through intellect, science, and technology.

b) Descartes does not stop here. His particular philosophic form of life follows, as he says, not only insight *(raison)* but also wisdom *(sagesse)*.

This philosopher whom Descartes intends and embodies is not the human being qua human being, but the thinker detached from the world, who seeks solitude in order to actualize himself, the individual devoted, in the secret activity of his life, to the passion of thinking, to the construction of a philosophic work of cognition, to the ethos that combines skeptical suspension and provisionality with the mind-set of a stoical-humane aristocrat and culminates in the ideal of *générosité* *(magnanimitas)*.

By "study of wisdom" Descartes understands "not only cleverness in daily life . . . but a complete knowledge of all the things that a human being can cognize. . . ." For what purpose? ". . . in order to

have a rule for his life . . . in order to preserve his health . . . in order
to invent all of the arts" (*Principles,* XXXI–II). Hence rules for life,
medical science, and technology?

In fact, an extraordinary load of expectation is placed on the philosophy grounded in Descartes's principles. We shall see "up to what level
of wisdom, to what perfection of life and what happiness it can lead
us" (*Principles,* XLVII). This philosophy is "comparable to a tree whose
root is metaphysics, whose trunk is physics, and whose branches are all
other sciences that can be traced back to three main ones, i.e., medicine,
mechanics and ethics." Hence technology and also ethics. "By ethics I
understand here the highest and most perfect moral philosophy which,
by presupposing total knowledge of the other sciences, constitutes the
final and highest level of wisdom" (*Principles,* XLII).

c) It is characteristic of Descartes that he places the following on
the same level, in view of their role in practical life based on scientific
philosophy: mechanics to ease physical work, medicine for health pres-
ervation, ethics for the right conduct of life. Everything is the fruit of
philosophic cognition. Descartes does not differentiate between man-
made technical achievements brought about by scientific cognition and
that which man actualizes existentially through himself, attended,
guided, mirrored by thinking of a character radically different from
the technical thinking applied in making.

The ethos Descartes's ethics teaches has to be characterized by reference to his philosophy. It displays a threefold morality:

First, there is anticipatory morality, a reform of all of life brought
about by philosophy, just as it brings forth mechanics and medical science. It is not yet within our reach, hence cannot yet be an activating
force. For Descartes, things have not come close to reaching the point
where philosophy, owing to its cognition, can produce morality as it
can ease work and improve health. The tree has not been cultivated as
yet. Descartes is the one who wants to plant it and believes himself to
have planted it.

Second, there is morality of the present, given by authorities and
sacrosanct. Descartes has no wish to discuss matters of morality, since
it is for the rulers and their appointees to regulate other people's mores
(A/T, V, 86ff.). He has set his own rules of behavior by using his
intellect, but has no wish to set them down in writing. "For with regard to mores, each person has so many ideas about them that as many
reformers could be found as there are heads if, aside from those whom
God has set as rulers over His peoples or to whom he has given sufficient grace and zeal to be prophets, it were also permitted to others to
make the slightest changes in them" (*Method,* 51).

Until such time as philosophy will be able "to regulate our mores" (*Principles,* XXXIII), on a path which for the time being Descartes travels by himself at his own risk, the philosopher needs a provisional morality. Three rules define it: follow the mores of the country, obey the authorities, hold fast to the religion of the Church. Descartes never poses the question whether this provisional morality might not be provisional at all but meant to endure in temporal existence.

Third, Descartes developed an ethos that laid the foundation for life. Here there is no talk of authority or of methodical deduction. This ethos is rooted in the Skeptic and Stoic tradition of a self-assured French aristocrat of the seventeenth century, largely informed by Montaigne and the Stoics. It is not at all provisional, nor is it something ultimately attainable as the tree of philosophy grows; neither is it derived from Descartes's philosophy. Are we faced here with a third morality, the real ethos, something that is operative for Descartes himself and animates his life?

Indeed; for philosophy supplies the highest good, tranquillity of soul, peace of mind *(béatitude, contentement d'esprit, satisfaction intérieure),* the happiness of cognition, serenity, high-mindedness.

(1) The happiness of cognition: The "joy one finds in the contemplation of truth" is "virtually the only complete happiness in this life that is not darkened by pain" (*Rules,* 4).

The basic, really penetrating truths are, in Descartes's perception also, fundamentally differentiated from the correctness cognized by the finite intellect, though Descartes does not observe this separation. They become evident only if we do not allow the acuity of our mind to be blunted by sensory images and remain totally on our guard. Only then do we easily bear in mind "why the idea of a more perfect being than I am must necessarily proceed from a being that is, in truth, more perfect." Hence Descartes exhorts us "to linger over the contemplation of God" (*Meditations,* 39, 43).

(2) Serenity, liberation from anxiety, being content with cognition: God's existence teaches us to accept serenely all that happens to us. We learn to withdraw our intentions from worldly matters and to contemplate with detachment whatever lies within the power of fate. Cognizing the nature of our soul and its difference from the body keeps us from fearing death (especially when it is complemented by the promises of revelation). This insight into the magnitude of the universe liberates us from presumptuous prejudices, such as ambitions to participate in God's guiding council, which could only lead to unappeasable restlessness (A/T, IV, 291–92).

(3) High-mindedness: Nobility of spirit, noble pride (the *megalo-*

psychia of Aristotle, the *magnanimitas* of Cicero and later authors) consists in the risk-taking of free cognition, in mastering one's passions, in
the inclination to do great things. This manner of cognizing has its
motive in wonderment; this sovereignty over passions becomes itself
the power of passion; the will to great things keeps the high-minded
person from undertaking anything beyond his powers (*Passions*, Art.
156). It is in this condition of the soul, compatible with rational cognition but also indicative of a God-given nature (for men are not created
equal), that practical life is rooted.

No one can exist in isolation in the here and now, even though we
each lead a separate life and pursue special interests. For this reason
the interests of the whole, of which we are a part, have to take precedence over particular personal interests. We have to live together with
our great common interests in view.

This is the goal of the methodical cognition of the high-minded.
Based on certainty of principles and habituation to clear evaluation of
whatever we encounter, it may reasonably be expected that all grounds
for dissent will be obviated "so that, in this way, one becomes inclined
to kindness and concord" (*Principles*, XLV).

If everything were related to self-interest, true friendship or loyalty,
and indeed any virtue, would have no feeding ground. This realization
is the wellspring of all acts of heroism in which life is put at risk
because of the call of duty and in the belief that such acts will bring
good to others. (Contrarily, those who take life-threatening risks from
vanity or stupidity are to be deplored.) But truly heroic deeds give rise
to a satisfaction of the spirit and a sense of fulfillment which surpass
by far all the trivial ephemeral joys that depend on the senses (A/T,
IV, 293–94).

The high-minded person sets doing good to others above all else.
He is affable, courteous, and helpful toward all. He hates no one because he respects everyone. He is free of envy because he does not
consider anything whose acquisition is not dependent on him to be
particularly desirable. He is free of fear because he is secure, thanks to
his trust in his own virtue. He is free of anger because he never grants
his enemies the advantage of seeing that they have insulted him (*Passions*, Art. 156).

The high-minded person knows that he possesses nothing but absolute power over his will, that praise or blame can be apportioned to
him only according to the way he uses this power. He is animated by
the firm determination to make good use of it. "I know only one thing
that can give us sufficient grounds for self-esteem, namely, the exercise

of free will and the control of our desires. . . . This will makes us similar to God, as it were, by making us master over ourselves" (*Passions,* Arts. 152–53).

Descartes's ethos, presented as his ideal of a philosophic attitude toward life, is not the necessary outgrowth of the principles of his philosophy. It is not the morality to be expected as a future fruit on the tree of his philosophy, nor is it a transitional morality; rather, it is an ethos patched together from transmitted *loci communes,* and developed by Descartes independently of science or faith in revelation; it lacks cohesion or rootedness, and was primarily devised for Princess Elizabeth.

9) Descartes's position regarding Christian religion is one of the aspects that vitiates his philosophy. Here he is neither theologian nor philosopher, yet he constructs a philosophy facing us as a configuration of thought and conscious of itself as a method of the intellect, while he lives by a different "philosophy." On the one hand, he is an aristocratic "man of the world" with a penchant for solitude; on the other, he keeps in constant contact with a circle of thinking people.

a) He brings into being a configuration of ill-defined, faltering contours owing to an existentially ambiguous attitude, which legitimized these ambiguities for centuries: as scientific philosophy; as philosophy; as preoccupation with neutral matters, objects, or conditions, without any genuine philosophic commitment; as a pseudoscience that is neither science nor philosophy; as a philosophy without philosophy.

As a philosopher, Descartes represents a type of greatness all its own. In the pseudo-clear manner of thinking, which actually leads astray and into confusion and which from now on was called philosophy, he manifested a unique style of life, that is, that of the inimitable Descartes. This style is unconnected with the content of his scientific philosophy.

In considering his daily way of living as a Catholic Christian, the thought arises that faith in revelation has lost in him the voice of full vitality, while philosophy as an original ground of life had not yet come alive in him. Submission activated by faith in authority stands in for faith in revelation, while in philosophy Descartes's reason goes astray in the scientific dogmatism of the intellect.

For him, truth breaks apart into the cogent certainty of science (which, however, he never attains) and submission to uncomprehended authority. Through the dual restriction and inversion of what constitutes truth, which amounts to a dogmatic rigidification of knowledge as well as the defined revelational faith of the Church, Descartes silenced the primally encompassing state of faith as well as of reason. Philosophy gets lost between false science and inverted authority.

The consequence is a paralysis of human openness; caution, distancing, manipulation of relationships prevail. As the spirit of dogmatism suffuses all of life, intellect, and faith, communication is made impossible.

The ambiguity extends to the deepest ground. It is no coincidence that both the orthodox believer in Church doctrine and the atheist who fanatically rejects all authority could come close to the philosopher Descartes. The former sees the pious son of the Church and his fundamentally scholastic manner of thought. The latter sees the modern ungrounded philosopher of the intellect who had to adapt to his times and was forced to wear a mask.

Was the Church right in placing Descartes's work on the Index? It is not for us to judge in this matter. But as motivation we may assume: that Descartes in fact approaches questions of dogma unaware that he is on a collision course with Church doctrine (such as freedom and grace); that, in this context, the covenant that in the case of conflict he would subordinate himself to the Church is insufficient in its vagueness. Further, that the actual effect of his thinking was to foster independence of the intellect in relation to the Church and that it served the Church-destroying Enlightenment.

Authority poses no problem for Descartes. It exists, is acknowledged by him, and there the matter rests. He did not develop a philosophy of authority. If, as I believe, it has not been elaborated successfully to this day, Descartes did not advance it by an inch.

b) The following questions need to be asked: In what sense, in the last analysis, does the nature and condition of human life depend on the form and content of prevailing authority? In what way, taking the long view, is authority, even when the object of blind obedience, indispensable for the self-preservation of society and state? What does it mean that authorities mutually reject and exclude each other? Why cannot externally imposed authority be transmuted into an internalized, effective one? What is signified by the limit that an authority, inwardly experienced and accepted, such as that "from God," precludes the possibility of being comprehended?

Philosophy breaks down when it is transmuted into obedience, or advises, for whatever reason, obedience toward authority as an established presence. For philosophic enlightenment, however, it is imperative to pose the question and to go to the core of authority—not by way of positing a valid general concept, but by a progressive penetration of historic authority in which our own lives are grounded.

The seemingly simple solution of throwing off all authority and living by the universal intellect common to all human beings is plainly unworkable. To believe that this is the way to put everything in order is intellectually childish. To grasp the authoritative origin even in the medium of reason and to let it become actual is one of the great philosophical problems. There can be no substance in thought or life if all we draw from is empty intellect. In that way all ground is lost.

Insofar as Descartes intended the complete separation of reason and authority, there would have to be a total schism in his life. It seems to us that this is what happened. Supposedly certain knowledge opens up in him two possibilities, which are equally dangerous for science and Existenz. If this thinking considers itself to be intellectual thinking, and as such to be absolute truth, it ceases to acknowledge authority and sinks into the groundlessness of empty intellect. In comprehending its own relativity as cogent knowledge of the intellect, it comes up against an authority no longer accepted from the fount of faith as an unilluminated and unilluminable power, and sinks into irrationality. Descartes's philosophizing does not proceed from belief in its own origin; rather, he vacillates between thought that is ungrounded yet means to comprehend and uncomprehending submission.

The Great Awakeners

PASCAL

LESSING

KIERKEGAARD

NIETZSCHE

INTRODUCTION

The great awakeners do not present us with a doctrine dominating their world of ideas, they do not lead the movement of ideas in a single decisive direction. Rather, they create an unrest revealing a depth which becomes palpable as truth and actuality, beyond what they think, say, and point to.

They do not offer the security provided by knowledge, a faith, a way of life. But they lead to the awakening of what lies ready in the darkness of the possible Existenz of man. Let us delineate what these philosophers have in common.

1. Upheaval on the ground of Christianity

As a type they grew from the soil of Christianity, at the time of the breakthrough of modern science and concurrent with the experience of Europe's colonial, economic, and political expansion. The approach to this breakthrough was slow and almost imperceptible but became an overwhelming experience for Europe and the whole world. Everything that up to that period had made and supported man as the focus of knowledge and faith was suddenly put into question. The external events of history develop from inner events, first experienced by individuals and later propagated to mankind by new external conditions of existence.

The awakeners suffer, as representatives and through anticipation, the upheaval of this breakthrough. They are extremely sensitive to all the consequences of this event, boldly facing its radicality. Their philosophizing reveals to us the measure of their suffering, without, however, offering the solution of the tremendous problems that converge in the question: What is to become of man? What is he actually and potentially? Has he reached his end or is he capable of a transformation that has never been tried before?

Ever since early Christianity, and quite particularly in the Middle Ages, the relationship between faith and reason, their difference and their unity, was subjected to the most thorough theoretical study. But starting with the sixteenth century—when the sciences were first resurrected in a methodically independent form and philosophy rose again in its independent self-sufficiency, supporting the life of individuals out of its own depth—this division and relationship were experienced and thought with a different, a new passion. Philosophy, independent in antiquity, its great thinkers tied to Christianity in the Middle Ages, once more came to the fore as independent.

The origin and enduring motivations of the awakeners were derived from their Christian faith. Their thinking, therefore, is related to Christianity in a substantial way. Christianity was crucially important to them, either in order to attain to its true essence in spite of all spiritual counterforces (Pascal, Kierkegaard) or in battling against it (Nietzsche), or in striving to do it justice with a view to its future transformation (Lessing).

The incompatibility of Christian revelation—as it manifests itself in the language of the various confessions, of the churches, of dogmatics—and the modern world's positions based on verifiable knowledge, rational thought, and technological know-how has served to increase formidably the power of agnosticism over Christianity and allowed its influence to spread without restriction.

Pascal was the first to experience and to think through this situation, and did so with the greatest acuity and with radical consequences. The separation of faith and knowledge, irreconcilably effected by him, was repeated in still more radical form by Kierkegaard. The result was a Christianity subservient to the absurd, a configuration of faith in the world that is absolutely negative and negating.

Nietzsche thought the abyss no less radically, but gave it a reverse valuation and a will corresponding to it. According to him, Christianity is to be negated from its very roots in all its variations; it is the most dangerous catastrophe for humankind. But this negation of Christianity cannot itself deny its ties to Christian standards.

Lessing, too, experienced this rupture. In his open philosophizing he never abandons Christianity but nowhere shows in what, for him, the content of revelation as accepted by him consists. Yet he wanted to think the rupture—which he thought as radically as the others: "the nasty broad ditch" (13, 7), across which he cannot jump—in a manner harmless to reason and knowability if revelation were acknowledged. He did not find a conclusive formulation and knew so himself, attributing it to the nature of things. It is our portion to think and search unceasingly, we who cannot possess the truth that is God's alone.

The thoughts of the awakeners would not be possible without the violence of the rupture and indeed without the ideas of Biblical religion itself, ideas that urge us on to the ultimate.

All awakeners are critical and hence polemical, animated by a will to do spiritual battle. They find or fabricate their adversaries. The character of their thinking is dramatic. But they do not want to lose the ground on which they are based—they recoil before the void.

Pascal fought against the Jesuits but submitted to the Church; though even here he came close to the limit, so that it might be asked whether he would not have turned also against the Church had he lived longer. (As opposed to Descartes, he disapproved of the ecclesiastical decision in Galilei's trial.) His thought developed from his scientific knowledge, grounded in the most lucid modern methodical consciousness; but he bowed before his midnight experience of the God of Abraham, Isaac, and Jacob, and the prophecies and miracles of the Bible.

Lessing thought in an age in which the dissolution of the traditional configurations of faith had become commonplace. He took part in the critical questioning but did not want to sink into the void; rather, he found his grounding in the search itself, in the basic attitude of openness, in the antinomy of eternal reason and historic appearance, in the universal knowledge that becomes an element of historical consciousness. Hence his thinking moves in contradictory formulas. The fundamental questions remain unanswerable.

Kierkegaard recognized the perversion and self-deception of contemporary Christendom and Church; his radical attack on the Church had its roots in New Testament faith. On the one hand he clung to the faith of his childhood, to his father's teachings; on the other, his absolutely negative decisions were grounded in his understanding of the New Testament. He realized that he could neither teach nor preach. His thinking was intended to be a call to attention, without a program, without any prospects.

Nietzsche lived his own modern nihilism without restraints, yet tried to overcome it; he willed himself to be the Antichrist and believed in a human being yet to come; still he clung to fictions that he himself had also put in question, such as Overman, Eternal Return, Will to Power.

2. *Probing thought on the way*

To the awakeners, no thought is predominant or authoritative, no doctrine is valid or adhered to as the design of the whole.

Their thinking is carried out in movement, in the change of positions and configurations, none of which endure. It is experimental and
devoid of any formulated objectivity other than their tentative forays.
It is dialogical and dialectical.

As a result, we cannot come close to the nature of the four awakeners by assigning them presumably unique positions or one central
thought, or by characterizing their positions as unequivocal.

They want to awaken but cannot give content to that state of wake-
fulness. Their questioning challenges us, but, appearances to the contrary, they fail to present us with a clearly defined summons.

The awakening power of their truth is contained in the movement
of thought, not in its goal. In other words, the goal is not something
thinkable that can be attained by thinking; it subsists in turning
thought to existential actuality.

Their seriousness consists in unremitting thought about what truly
matters to man. Their abundant thought-experiments and positions are
not just shifting "opinions," but are immediately of gripping interest.
They themselves represent the shaking up of consciousness of being
and of self. What they think rarely leaves us indifferent.

Their greatness consists in their engagement with what truly matters, not by way of a theoretical answer to basic questions, or a solution
for inescapable problems; they recognize this solution as attainable
solely through the practice of Existenz, rather than solely through cognition or a theoretical act of faith.

Their earnestness is their unconditional will to truth. Their only
demand is magnificently uncircumscribed: truth, honesty, justice. This
demand brings about an inner action originating in the freedom of the
individual to which it speaks, independent of preliminary instruction.

The will to truth urges the awakeners everywhere to the limits, to
the ultimate. From this position, out of truthfulness, even the meaning
of truth itself is questioned.

They walk, as it were, on a path without footing and without a
location in a landscape. This fathomless movement constantly forces
them to reach for something to hold on to, but whatever they grasp is
itself merely a testing.

The endless reflection, the dialectical upheavals, the expression in
the form of paradoxes, the absence of theoretical solutions and of a

clear and unequivocal fixed attitude toward life differentiate these awakeners from the skeptics. The great skeptics of antiquity, along with Montaigne, achieved an attitude toward life complete in itself. This is rejected entirely by the awakeners. For them the skeptical attitude toward life constitutes a lack of earnestness.

The earnestness, however, that aims at knowledge and faith, but finds that all handholds give support only along an ever-continuous path, proves a challenge difficult to meet. To avoid straying into skepticism, such earnestness may succumb to the temptation of taking a handhold as the absolutely true one, a temptation to which the great awakeners might succumb for moments but never with finality.

Yet the way in which they are understood frequently displays such an interpretation. Assertions are made that, at the limits, they have slipped from awakening into prophecy. Philosophic-systematic interpretation attributes such teachings to them: the theory of the three orders of truth is imputed to Pascal; to Lessing, a philosophy of Enlightenment culminating in the philosophy of history or in pantheism; to Kierkegaard, a doctrine of stages; to Nietzsche, a doctrine of the Eternal Recurrence or a metaphysics of the Will to Power. But unjustly. Whereas it is possible and makes sense to distill and elaborate such schemes as means by which they proceed, it is wrong to present them as embodying their philosophy. Such forced unambiguities have to be countered by constantly regaining the open, infinite path they followed.

The fundamental problem that eludes solution by thought concerns the limit of thinkability itself. All thinking aims at and produces a universal. Actuality, however, is a matter of historicity. True, by way of the universal, actuality can be carried into infinity to the point of thinkability; but it is precisely in this way that actuality is realized as something that cannot be reached in thinking, as the unthinkable, as itself.

Destroying the false claim of universality would mean plunging into a bottomless abyss, even as we attempt to grasp the actual itself as a universal.

The historic, however, wherever it is actualized may, by a thinking overstepping its boundaries, be falsely interpreted and posited as a universal and therefore as universally valid.

The way around these ever-present insoluble difficulties as they were experienced and demonstrated by the awakening thinkers cannot be found by thinking alone. It is found, in practice, either through arbitrariness devoid of mooring or through an experienced and jointly realized historicity.

But if the solution is cast in universal terms, it becomes irrelevant how it is phrased; a contradiction within any such solution will always result, as, for instance, in the rule of the historic as the One and Only Universal.

To be sure, the sciences, as the universal, become an aspect of history and are themselves historic. But historicity alone is actual, can become existentially lucid, can fill and found Existenz. It cannot, however, appear as a demand on everyone, if this demand is meant to be universally valid.

The problem has been considered since time immemorial, arriving at its decisive practical significance through modern science and philosophy, and, in the latter, mainly through the awakeners.

3. *Their conception of man and its meaning*

Even though, as in all philosophy, the main concerns of the awakeners are truth and actuality, the question of man and his situation is their central preoccupation. For whatever there is, is manifest to man at the place is which he himself; there it is seen, thought, known, believed.

In no other place in philosophy but with the awakeners is the mystery of man, the wealth of his possibilities, the manifold nature of his particular secrets, brought into focus.

What they say about man and his situation grows from experience that is evident to them. Their consciousness of Being and their consciousness of self form a union. If we agree with them, we must note that there is more in what they say than a general representation of being-such, for, in the very act of thinking these aspects, faith or desperation, strength or impotence are encompassed. The powerful conviction as to what man is, is itself already an existential act that asserts its influence in the spoken word and engages in battle. There is not one but a multiplicity of ways to know about man. The will inherent in philosophizing is the precondition for gaining awareness of these aspects. A space is opened in which the directions, the ideals, and the truths for thinking manifest themselves, and the place and meaning of practical decisions become evident in their practice.

This way of knowing about the human condition is not grounded in scientific inquiry, nor does it take the form of progressive, universally valid cognition. It would be a mistake to see it as an anthropology attained via universally valid experience based on scientific investigation. Universally valid scientific knowledge of man is always specific. Man is more than he knows or can know about himself.

Scientific anthropology teaches many facts about man but does not show him what he truly is, can be, or ought to be. Becoming aware philosophically of man's position in the universe goes beyond knowledge and shows him his task and the way to be taken. This awareness grips us, since what is at stake here is all that man is, himself, capable of. The force of a truth exerts itself which, though not universally valid as knowledge, signifies for the thinking Existenz the complete clarity of its presentness.

Naming what the awakeners say about man an "image of man," and describing it as such in reproducing it, we lose the strength of faith, direction of will, and profound motivation inherent in this thinking about man.

Consequently, this philosophic self-awareness does not express itself in only one way; it sees the differences in the images of man, juxtaposes them, contrasts them. They assume the character of ideal-typical patterns which in their multiplicity and variety can become means of a scientific anthropology.

As the awakeners speak to us, they have to do it by way of such model images, and thus by comparison with images they reject. Their thinking is done in deep personal involvement, and hence is judgmental and polemical. How man thinks himself determines all his actions, his impulses, the way he deals with others.

The source of the images which the awakeners sketch does not exhaust itself. When they seem to have come to the finishing point of an image, this is always only a station along their path. They do not become prisoners of their images, which they test as they give them expression. Once the images are captured as pictures, as structural parts in a philosophical design, and are thought through as symbols, they lose the tentativeness characteristic of the awakeners. For them, the knowledge of man and his situation as contained in expressed formulations remains in flux. An illusion of absolutization may occur, however, when the reader isolates separate aspects in disregard of all the others, presuming to know in this way the totality of man's being and situation.

The inescapably evident characteristics of our human situation recur in many images, since these are not disparate, but have their point of reference in the one which remains indeterminable though it can be expressed in many ways.

Its way of expression is indicative of an attitude toward life that, by the very nature of things, has to be limited; limited, however, in such a way that we always keep within such attitudes, whether in rejection or in appropriation, in struggle or in affinity; or perhaps—as idea—in the solidarity of communication of what is substantially different, in a common space, a space that makes communication possible even between mutually repelling elements.

It is impossible to get an overview of the attitudes toward life from the outside, whether historically, that is, in the past, or biologically, the possibly causative constituent factors, or theoretically, the sketching of spiritual possibilities. The basic possibilities in man are understandable only within the context of the historic encounter in which, through speaking and informing, they rise to the level of meaning and thereby not only unfold but transform themselves.

To a greater extent than others, the awakeners transcend all limitation of knowledge about man. But no man is able to place himself, as it were, on the outside and to see, from a suprahuman vantage point, what man is.

4. Misunderstanding and misleading

The awakeners appear to be easily open to understanding. One reads them with consuming interest. Their constant concerns are matters of immediate import to human beings. They all write with verve and brilliance.

But they are difficult to understand when it comes to the ground of truth that speaks through them, for what they say immediately serves something that remains unexpressed. What motivates them can be imparted only indirectly. Kierkegaard recognized this and wanted, mistakenly, to turn this indirect communication (a concept he created) into a consciously applied method. This method develops from the nature of things at stake here and gains in truth and effectiveness in proportion to the decisiveness of the will to direct communication.

The reader becomes enmeshed in what is said directly, which leads inevitably to misunderstanding. In regard to the awakeners' writings, the reader reveals, by the way of his misunderstanding, what he is and can be.

The awakeners can become misleaders. We latecomers see all too easily the meaning of their thinking in a greatness that contradicts their deeper meaning. We let ourselves be pushed into extreme positions; we allow ourselves to be fixed in a position that the texts proclaim with tremendous force, making it tantamount to a truth that needs to be made manifest.

Conversely, we hold the movement of thought as such, the dialectics, the paradoxes, and this path in itself to be the truth, which, however, loses itself in endless reflection.

In order for their greatness to be truly effective, the awakeners must remain awakeners. If misunderstood as proclaimers of a message, they steer us—in punishment, as it were, for avoiding facing ourselves in earnest—into absurdities, acts of violence and inhumanity, into positions of finite absoluteness, or into the movement of endless nothingness.

The awakeners lose power and meaning whenever, counter to the meaning of the actuality of their thinking, they are made into bearers of doctrine, such as the doctrine of man's Existenz, or of subjugation to the Church, or of the Eternal Recurrence, or of Metempsychosis, and so on.

Each can be placed historically and biological-constitutionally: Pascal is French, Catholic, ailing, seventeenth-century—the world of absolutism; Lessing is German, Protestant, eighteenth-century—the world of Enlightenment; Kierkegaard is Danish, a man of the North, Protestant, austere even with his shattered nerves, early nineteenth-century; Nietzsche is German, Protestant, extremist, unhinged by sickness, late nineteenth-century.

But they allow no one, no party, no sect, no worldview, no century to claim them for one's own; neither Pascal for the Catholic church, Kierkegaard for the Protestant church, Nietzsche for atheism, nor Lessing for the Enlightenment. In their greatness they are unique individuals. They are not role models to be emulated, but lighthouses by whose beacons we orient ourselves.

Although no party, sect, or worldview may appropriate them, they continue to act as prods for them all in one way or another. They are there as a source for all to draw from, thereby a means toward self-discovery, support of theories ostensibly based on their thinking—like sleepers oblivious to the more profound demands of their awakening thinking.

5. *Relation to Socrates; comparisons to other types of thinkers*

Their type, growing out of Christian soil, exists nowhere else in the world, not in China or India, not among the Greeks. Asia knows wisdom and tranquillity; the Greeks know the magnificent independence of philosophy and the philosopher. But they do not know the problem of the struggle of being at odds with oneself. They do attain the depth of being human in the manifold tensions and infinite entanglements on the road leading on all sides to the ultimate.

But does not Socrates stand where they stand, and, equally, Plato's understanding of Socrates? With the exception of Pascal, all the awakeners refer back to Socrates. No other philosopher addresses them so directly. Does he not also experience an awakening through the prodding of his consciousness of self and Being? For him, too, does not the questioning movement, the clarity of not knowing take precedence over specific contents of thought? For him, too, does not the weight of absolute earnestness rest in an appeal to the free decision of the individual in practice, rather than in doctrine? Is not, for him, too, indirect communication a characteristic and the radical misunderstanding that is a concomitant to this type of philosophizing, if any direct statement is understood at its face value and indirectness is passed over? And does not the most exalted demand aimed at the individual, at his being himself, a self not covered up or preempted by direct statements, proceed from Socrates?

All this explains why the great awakeners take him as a referent. But they themselves are different. In contrast to the imperturbable Socrates—this phenomenon of perfect health in every sense—they are shaken, fragile, and most of them are also medically ill. Moreover, in Socratic-Platonic thinking the ultimate is, formally, attained in an unsurpassable manner. But this great unity could prevail because faith in revelation has no actuality and causes no problem, and because what arose in the era of revelational faith does not exist as yet: relentless self-reflection, encountered first in Augustine; the will to investigate and the will to truth, which, based on faith because demanded by the will of God, knows no limits and turns against the tenets of faith itself; the indissoluble tension; the specious consequence, disseminated among the only half-thinking masses, that Biblical faith must be abandoned.

Through the awakeners man's present situation and its possible task have become clarified. Something new arises within the horizon of Socrates and Plato, and with the help of Kant's illuminating insight, that is called for by the breaking up of all existential possibilities, the broadening of knowledge and capacities, the deepening of the infinite contents manifest in man.

Let me make a comparison with other types of philosophizing: The seminal thinkers, those who elicit creativity, seem to be closest to them—Plato, Augustine, Kant. But the difference remains great. The seminal thinkers live within their very own world, a world into which they were born and which they also helped to create; their unrest dissolves into tranquillity. Among the awakeners, however, the inconclusiveness inherent in their manner of philosophizing, that is, their breaking through limits, remains part of life's unrest. The ground itself, the Existenz which is the nurture of their thoughts, does not solidify into a personality representing the image of their Existenz. More than any other types, they seem to elude a conception of their nature as a whole. True, one can say of all men that they defy complete understanding, a sum total of their nature, a description as one or the other specific character. But here, among the awakeners, the contradictoriness is itself their nature, as though a specific character were nonexistent.

At the farthest remove are the creative orderers. The awakeners sense in them their great antagonists. By their very nature these are destroyers of systems and consider the spirit animated by the will to create a system to be ruinous for man, for his truth, for the salvation of his soul.

If what finds expression in the awakeners is the outcome of the modern breakthrough, we may expect the repetition, in many variations, of that which manifests itself in them with unique force and radicality. All that affects us in Bayle, Hamann, Dostoevsky, and many others corresponds only partially to what, in the awakeners, is greatly and wholly revealed.

6. *Their personal aspect*

Pascal died at the age of thirty-nine, Kierkegaard at forty-two, Lessing at fifty-two; Nietzsche descended into madness at forty-five. We cannot imagine their future had they lived to a riper or a very advanced old age.

Medically speaking, they are all fragile. They give the impression of discontent, of awareness of what they are not. They maintain an aloofness even in their friendships.

In the management of their mundane affairs they appear negligent, awkward, foolish.

Their inner life resembles a battlefield of many forces and possibilities.

Reduced to nothingness in confrontation with the eternal nature of the divine and consumed in its flames (Pascal), a human being on trial (Kierkegaard), a scrawl produced in testing a new pen (Nietzsche), they feel that they lack the presence of being. Their lives are not fulfilled by love, by an idea to be actualized in the here and now, by career considerations, by a bliss-promising cipher.

They give the impression of being deserters from the demands of the real world. As such, however, they appear as the type of men who in their recurring appearance are willing to risk confrontation with the abyss, who carry their questioning pursuit of the truth to that dizzying point that may well deprive one of sight and hearing, where the world may disappear—where truth may overwhelm us—a vanishing point for these exceptional spirits, whose legacy for us is reduced to a few fragments of their agony and their visions.

7. Can Lessing be counted among them?

To place Lessing among this group might be a matter for hesitation. Current perception sees him as a critic of the fine arts, a poet, a reviver of German literature, a man of the Enlightenment. All this, indeed, he is, but this would not together constitute his greatness.

Placing him among the awakeners is meant to make manifest that the enumerated roles are nothing but the medium for what qualifies him to be in the company of the awakeners: the essential inconclusiveness, the unquiet life oriented toward truth, his inability to become integrated with the world and to serve it.

But Lessing's sound health sets him apart from the others. True, the experience that all of them shared is not, as such, tied to frail health, and might have found its actualization in thought in any of them, regardless of their health.

This distinguishing endeavor, although grounded in all of them in Christianity, is itself neither Christian nor anti-Christian—hedging, as it were, in both directions. It concerns the truth which, historically, emerged solely out of Christian soil, an event most purely visible in Lessing.

He is the only one who, most naturally, without threat or coercion, effects reason in the world. It is a faith in reason which, by its very nature, eludes understanding and hence transcends itself, and exposes itself to the utmost that the awakeners will not allow to be avoided or forgotten. The question remains infinitely open, and thereby it strikes us that the utmost eludes any definite grasp, yet can become our grounding, keeping despair within bounds, and even out of the most dire calamity man can become himself in loving action in the world (Nathan saying to God: "Is your will only that I will" [3, 139]). Lessing, though as author and as person just as unquiet as the other awakeners, is distinguished from them by the exercise of self-restraint in his thinking. Reason and critical restraint applied to reflections of the intellect make him moderate. Perhaps through him we may learn to apprehend the other awakeners in a way more fitting to them.

PASCAL

I. LIFE AND WORKS

1. A brief statement on his importance

In the history of science Pascal (1623–1662) ranks as a great mathematician and as a physicist; in the history of literature, as an epoch-making man of letters. He is famous as a victorious polemicist against the Jesuits. An ardent Christian, he was consumed by his faith, immolating himself in the radical ascetic practice of a passionate Catholic piety. All that, however, was founded on his will to truth. But truth for him was no simple, easy matter. It was revealed to him in its whole depth and unattainableness. The question of what truth is he answered by way of his life and thought, with unsurpassable dedication.

2. The three phases of his life

His brief life had a span of thirty-nine years. In a more misleading than illuminating schematization, his life has been viewed as consisting of three phases: that of the scientist, of the man of the world, of the believer.

The first phase was the years of his youth, when his mathematical genius unfolded: at age seventeen he wrote a treatise on conic sections; to facilitate the work of his father, who was a tax official, he constructed a calculator.

The second phase (1652–1654) encompassed his years as man of the world in Paris society, his study of man, his reading of Montaigne, his treatise (or the treatise inspired by him) on the passions of love.

The third phase, his final eight years, was spent as a religious ascetic. All his literary and polemical writings stem from this period, establishing his unique and towering philosophic importance: the letters against the Jesuits, smaller treatises such as those on the spirit of geometry and the method of persuasion, and his most important work—left at his death as a mass of notes and preparatory work in no kind of order—on the truth of Christianity. After his death it was

published with the title *Pensées* (Thoughts) in various editions and arrangements; in complete form, not until the twentieth century.

But this schematization, in which the middle period is made to
represent the crisis in his life, obscures the fact that it is one and the
same spirit that, in contradictory manifestations, unfolds, comes up constantly against limits, founders, and at last finds its final, uncommunica-
ble peace in God.

Insofar as the main concern of this thinker's life—a man who always staked his very blood—is truth, he early anticipated these three
phases as aspects of truth, as something seamless and timeless.

3. *The three truths*

At age twenty-five, Pascal has full intellectual clarity concerning the
origins of truths and the laws of their cognition. There are three truths
(Letter to P. Noël). The first is contained in principles (axioms) clear
in themselves and in the results issuing from them as incontrovertible
conclusions. Any statement to which the method of axioms and conclusions is inapplicable is open to doubt and uncertainty. The second, of
vital importance to man, has been called "sometimes a 'vision,' sometimes a 'fancy,' at times a 'product of imagination,' occasionally an
'idea,' and at best, a 'beautiful thought.'" Pascal developed this difference more incisively in his third phase as that of the geometrical spirit
and the subtle spirit—*esprit de finesse*. Finally for the young Pascal, a
third, fully certain truth of an entirely different origin was manifest:
Only "for the secrets of faith which the Holy Spirit itself has revealed
do we reserve that subjugation of the spirit which our faith brings to
the mysteries that are hidden from the senses and from reason."

Although the three concepts of truth appear to correspond to the
three phases of Pascal's life, this can apply only in the sense of their
relative importance. His basic understanding of the origins of truth
does not change.

Pascal never questioned the complete certainty of mathematical
truth. The inventive play of his mathematical mind continued into his
last, religious, phase. In 1658, he was still making important discoveries
(the theory of the cycloid). Nor did his pleasure in technological applications ever stop. Just as, in his youth, he was the first to invent and
construct a calculating machine, at the end of his life he figured out
the organization of an omnibus company to ease Paris traffic; it was
successfully adopted.

But mathematical certainty became of little consequence for him,
since it does not affect matters truly essential for the human being.

Throughout his life it was a display of his genius, strikingly evident in his inventiveness, yet he never overestimated the value of this mental game within the context of the whole truth (Letter to Fermat).

The *esprit de finesse* attained its depth only in the middle phase. Pascal recognized that even if it seemed impossible to lay down laws and devise a method for it, its truth was of great importance for life in society, richly modulated and controlled by unwritten laws.

Pascal's knowledge and understanding of the world and of life in the world was detectable even in the very last of his notes.

Only the third truth is for him decisive, the truth of faith. The space formally and respectfully reserved for it by the youth is filled by the mature man with a passion surpassing the ardor of his earlier involvement with science and the world.

Religious questions preoccupied Pascal from an early age. A debate, at age twenty, with a member of a religious order, whom he was unable to convince, led Pascal to denounce him to the ecclesiastical authorities, forcing him to recant.

Through his father, he was introduced to Jansenist doctrine (preeminence of faith over reason, of grace over freedom). And when he lived as a man of the world, he had social contact with the men and women of Port-Royal.

But it was his crisis that first established the religious element as the one and only thing that mattered and that compelled him to deny and abandon the world. What was this crisis that led to his final conversion through a suprasensory experience?

4. *The* Mémorial

The crisis had lasted about a year when Pascal was granted, on November 23, 1654, the suprasensory experience that, for his consciousness, established a new Existenz for the rest of his life. Toward the end of 1654 or at the beginning of 1655, he joined the circle of laymen who, without taking vows, congregated around the monastery of Port-Royal. He adhered to this circle until his death eight years later. The crisis, which concluded with his experience of a certainty of suprasensory origin, divides his life into two parts.

Pascal immediately wrote a record of this experience, in the famous *Mémorial,* and then sewed a fair copy and his first draft into his clothing. He meant to preserve it safely as a remembrance and as an amulet. With the precision of an observer he noted date and time: "1654. Monday, November 23 . . . From about half past ten at night till about half past twelve . . ." What did he experience? "Fire. 'God of Abraham,

God of Isaac, God of Jacob', not of the philosophers and the learned."
How did he experience this God? "Certitude, certitude; feeling, joy,
peace . . . The world forgot and all save God" (St363–4; B71–2).[1]
This is followed by interpretations and Biblical texts. For, from the
first, this experience is accepted by Pascal as within Christian tradition
and filled by it. God is the God of Jesus Christ. He can be reached
only through the ways taught by the Gospels: complete and loving
renunciation. What was and what alone is important now is expressed
in the sentence "I departed from Him. . . . Let me never be parted
from Him." Finally there follow a few lines that are missing in the
original draft and are inserted by Pascal into the fair copy: "Total surrender to Jesus Christ and to my spiritual director" (St364; B72).

As far as we know, Pascal never again referred to this experience
of certitude, of the presence of the living God, neither to those nearest
to him nor to the ecclesiastical authorities, nor in his writings. He kept
it as his secret. The document was found only after his death.

There can be no doubt that for Pascal this event signified the
ground of his new steadfast certitude. To us it cannot have any meaning; that is his will, and the message he indirectly communicates to us.

Hence it would be a mistake to treat Pascal's singular experience as
a suprasensory actuality of validity for us too. It is the essence of this
experience that it can be neither repeated nor imparted. Methodologically aware, Pascal did not communicate it; by fixing allusive words
and sentences in writing, he made them tangible for himself, carrying
them into his further life. We, in contrast, can only place them in
the line of similar testimonies of suprasensory experiences known
from history (in the manner of William James) and, in the process, be
introduced to something unfamiliar; and, considering it in all its facets,
find that it corresponds somehow to a related experience. For someone
who has never undergone anything like it, it cannot communicate a
compelling force unless he concedes to the witness to such an experience its suprasensory character, that is, not only the psychological reality of experiencing but the suprasensory actuality of what has been
experienced.

Whoever insists on the principle that for me only that is actual
which I myself experience or which I myself could reasonably expect
to experience will not exclude the possibility of an incommunicable
suprasensory experience. He will, however, regard it as irrelevant to
his own Existenz, as astonishing psychopathological phenomena he

---

[1] References preceded by St are to *Pascal's Pensées*, trans. by H. F. Stewart. References to B are
to *Pensées: Texte de l'édition Brunschvicq*.

comes across when they are related by a man or woman willing to do so within the context of a reliably documented life.

This alternate mode of approach, relegating such experiences to the realm of psychopathological phenomena and disregarding the question of truth content or significance, cannot be applied to Pascal. Such an approach is justified only if a phenomenon is viewed and identified in the context of psychologically known realities, as part of a process. Of Pascal, however, virtually nothing is about tangible psychic phenomena, so all psychopathologically oriented debate is idle gossip applying terminologies that yield nothing and is used here in a scientifically illegitimate manner.

5. His illnesses

Pascal's life—unusual in this respect and, in Kierkegaard's sense, a case of "exception"—was determined by illnesses and eventually destroyed by a long agonizing illness.

Pascal's physical illness showed itself early. From age twenty-four, he stated, he had hardly known a pain-free day. This state continued, with ups and downs, to his death. His colics, followed by extreme weakness, were described in terms too vague to allow for a diagnosis. After his transmutation into a religious Existenz, he welcomed his ill health but accepted treatment and obeyed his physician's orders, submitting to the mischief of the medical therapy of his day. (Montaigne advised: "If you get sick, don't call a physician, otherwise you have to contend with two ills.") Suffering therapeutic mistreatment was part of the asceticism to which Pascal aspired. His obvious psychological instability is not in itself very revealing. A mental illness cannot be proven. But Pascal presents the picture of a person alienated from the natural world.

6. Stylization and veiling of his life

Immediately after Pascal's death his life was stylized by his relatives, for the sake of remembrance. Important documents, such as his bitingly sharp memoranda in the quarrel on Jansenist heresy (Pascal had retracted his signature on a form the Pope had demanded), and most of his letters to Mademoiselle de Roannez were destroyed. Thus the reality of his life is veiled at two decisive points.

Next to nothing is known about his Paris years previous to 1653—years that his sister called "the most unprofitably spent time of his

life"—when, turned toward the worldly side of life, he won the friendship of the Duke of Roannez and established a close relationship with
the Duke's sister. The possibility of a great career opened for him.
Perhaps his friendship with the Duke's sister gave him hope of a marriage leading to acceptance in the highest circles. At this time Pascal
refused to release to his sister, Jacqueline, who wanted to enter a con-
vent, her portion of their inheritance. Whether it was the dashing of
his hopes, the disappointment of the socially inferior man from the
third estate, or whether his inner development brought about the crisis
that changed his life is a matter of conjecture. In an abrupt reversal,
what had been precious to Pascal became worthless; an aversion to the
world took hold of him, turning him against a life of action, against
the pleasure-seeking crowd, against splendor and beauty.

The other veiling concerns Pascal's positions, judgments, actions or
lack of action in the Jansenist controversy.

7. The phase of religious completion

The clash of the various sources of his being got him into such difficulties on a practical level that finally he was in conflict with everyone.
He never truly resolved these conflicts intellectually.

Unquestioned acceptance of the Church's teachings as the foundation of life is not a particularity of Pascal's; rather, from the outset,
never succumbing to doubt, he shared with his milieu the ever-present
Catholic Christianity, the sacraments, the father confessor, the belief in
miracles, the unsurpassable sacred actuality of the Church. New for
Pascal in the third phase is the fact that what had been accepted by
him both practically and theoretically as a given he now chooses with
inner assent as an actuality that consumes him utterly. What was previously habitual and a matter of heritage now moves Pascal, motivated
by his will to both salvation and truth, toward consequences that remained unrealized when, devoid of a will to revolt, he unintentionally
came into conflict with the Church as well as with his friends of
Port-Royal.

In the writings of the last eight years the voice heard is that of a
man who, without having entered a monastic order, isolates himself
like a monk, receives his visitors wearing an iron-spiked garment next
to his skin, and submits himself to a spiritual director. Pascal wrestled
for the salvation of his soul, dependent on the power of the Church.
His supplication for the last sacraments, when family and friends hesitated and delayed, is an indication to what extent his faith was in need
of tangible anchors to the very end.

Pascal's faith was grounded in the ecclesiastical community as the actuality of his world, in the unique experience which immediately found an interpretation based on the Bible, and in his personal wrestling for salvation, for truth. These three origins are not identical. Pascal's thinking takes place in a space that is subject to the pressure of both certainties. Only his personal wrestling exhibits the philosophical character through which this thinking becomes accessible to our understanding. Pascal took for granted what to us appears surprising. If his thoughts seize and disturb us, it is because in what they communicate they concern us in our very humanity, and, though not simply true, they yet rouse us.

8. Keys to the following exposition

How can Pascal's thinking be presented? It is not a system, and to turn it into one would do it violence. It lacks principles allowing constructive deductions or even the means to put everything in order. I shall proceed as follows:

If we can speak of a fundamental question, it is that of the salvation of the soul, of one's own soul: the old Augustinian *quaestio mihi factus sum* — not in abstract experiment, or in calm reflection, but in the passion of being terrified to one's very core.

I will begin with Pascal's answers to the question of what man is and what he ought to be.

This will lead to the only solution possible for him: complete surrender to God in radical faith with all its consequences.

But since salvation cannot be apprehended in its truth, I shall follow with Pascal's answer to the question of what truth and science are.

For Pascal, the truth is not something to be beheld in meditation but something to be fought for in struggle with oneself and with the adversaries of truth; this battle has to be shown.

II. THE QUESTION OF WHAT MAN IS AND WHAT HE OUGHT TO BE

Pascal pursues the salvation of his soul and the certitude of faith concurrently with his passionate desire to persuade unbelievers. On this road he engages in thoughts that, quite independently of his goal, have the power to arouse in us intense agitation.

A fundamental question is posed: What is man? Pascal's command:

Man must learn to examine himself (cf. St19–20; B72). Pascal is convinced that the study of man "is man's proper study" (St19–20; B144). The first step is to become aware of man's uncertainty about himself; Pascal sharpens and deepens this awareness. By uncovering the way things stand he intends to provide proofs as a means to shake man out of his torpor. His self-scrutiny is the culmination of his ignorance about himself. The gravity of the human situation is made clear: How can one go on living an unexamined life? Only through thinking does life become something to be questioned, not only as to what it is but also where it takes us and what is all-important in it. (Pascal's answer to the last point will be discussed in the following section.) The first steps to this end must be clarity about what man is, how he finds himself in existence, his human condition. In keeping with the meaning of his question, Pascal, when he abandoned "the study of the abstract sciences" and turned to "the study of mankind" (St19), did not treat of man's nature in the form of anthropology. He makes use, instead, of diverse categories, demonstrating various aspects, all of which point to one conclusion: Man is incomprehensible to himself.

1. Man in relation to the universe

In asking how I, as a body, fit into the natural universe, the following becomes evident:

a) The universe in its magnitude: The magnitude of the world surpasses our power of comprehension. The earth is but a dot in the universe. "The whole visible world is but an imperceptible speck in the ample bosom of Nature." The cosmos appears to us (according to the ancient speculative formula) as "an infinite sphere whereof the center is everywhere, the circumference nowhere" (St19). Imagination, incapable of grasping this universe, is brought to silence by such thought, whose content is unimaginable.

Man is there in the universe, lost in this remote corner of nature. When he becomes aware of this, he learns to weigh at their true worth earth, kingdoms, towns, himself: "What is a man face to face with infinity?" (St19; B72.)

b) The universe in the minute: Now I cast my glance toward the smallest things. A mite in its minuteness has parts that are still more minute. The smallest I imagine is subdivided even further. But I do not reach the limits of minuteness in nature. A new abyss of infinity opens up: a vastness enclosed within the atom, an infinity of universes. Our human body, until now imperceptible in our universe, is now a colossus compared with the nothingness that lies beyond our reach (cf. St29–30; B72).

c) Agreement and difference between the two infinities: We stand between two infinities, that of the vastest, the universe, and that of the minutest, nothingness. It only seems that we reach the smallest more easily than the biggest: "The visible expanse of the world is visibly greater than what we can grasp, but since we are greater than small things, we believe that we are more capable of grasping them." However, our power of comprehension is equally limited in both directions. "Quite as great a capacity is needed to attain the Nothing as the All; it must be infinite for both . . . he who had grasped final principles could also manage to reach the Infinite. . . . These extremes meet and combine by the very reason of their distance apart. . . ." (St21–22; B22).

As things stand in regard to spatial reality, so too are they in regard to temporal reality. "The end of things and their principle are for man hopelessly hidden in an impenetrable secret, for he is equally unable to see the Nothingness whence he springs and the Infinite in which he is swallowed up." We are infinitely far removed from comprehending the extremes in either direction.

d) Man in the middle state: We stand in the middle between the infinites. Are we then perhaps the center of Being, relating to everything which in turn is related to us, from the vastest as well as from the most minute? Not at all. We attain to "but a glimpse of the mean of things," but not the center (St21; B72).

To be sure, we are compelled everywhere to conceive of the mode of our being as the center. Our senses are insensitive to extremes, too much noise deafens, too soft a voice becomes imperceptible, too great nearness or distance becomes invisible. Too much pleasure is tedious, a surfeit of kindness irritates us. Qualities in excess are incomprehensible to us, as if they did not exist.

It is not our true condition to rest in the safe middle. This "middle state which is our lot" has an entirely different character: "We sail over a vast expanse, ever uncertain, ever adrift. . . . To whatever point we think to fix and fasten ourselves it shifts and leaves us; and if we pursue it, it escapes our grasp." When we think we grasp a boundary line and follow it, it evades our grasp. "We had a burning desire to find a sure resting place and a final fixed basis whereon to build a tower rising to the infinite; but our whole foundation cracks and the earth yawns to the abysses." For "nothing can fix the finite between the two Infinites which enclose it and slip out of its grasp" (St25; B72).

Pascal does not present us a universe in which man would have his privileged place in the hierarchy of all beings and be the true center (as in Aristotle and the Middle Ages). Rather, he brings us a consciousness of suspension in the void with nothing to hold on to in the Infinite.

e) Summary: Man exists within the universe and has his place at midpoint between the greatest and the smallest, both fathomless to him. He has his existence in the state assigned to him by nature, between the two abysses of the Infinite, between the universe and nothingness; he is a "nothing compared with the infinite, an All compared with a mean between zero and all" (cf. St21; B72).

What we are cannot be comprehended out of nature, out of the other which we do not comprehend in its own ground.

2. *The impotence of human cognition*

That we do not comprehend our place in the universe and in relation to it is an example of the impotence of our cognition. Pascal does not deny cognition but sees its impotence as soon as it is a matter of "the nature of things" and of the "highest good." Here there are many opinions but no certainty. The reasons for man's impotence in cognizing what is essential are:

a) All the sciences are infinite in the range of research they allow. Almost all things partake of the twofold infinite of nature. We never reach the first principles (cf. St23; B72).

b) All things are cause and effect, all are linked by a natural and imperceptible bond. It is "impossible to know the parts without knowing the whole, or to know the whole without knowing the parts in detail." But man, who is only a part of the universe, cannot attain this. "How can a part possibly know the whole?" (St27; B72)

c) What completes our powerlessness to cognize is that things in themselves are simple, whereas we are composed of two opposite natures, soul and body. If we were simply corporeal, it would be impossible for us to cognize things. ". . . nothing is as inconceivable as to say that matter knows itself" (St27; B72). If we were simply corporeal, we could know nothing at all. But since we are composite, body and spirit, we are able to cognize, but not the simple things, whether they are corporeal or spiritual. For this reason we get confused and ascribe spiritual qualities to material things and material qualities to spiritual things. So it is wrong to say that bodies seek their center, flee from destruction, and fear the void; that nature has sympathies and antipathies, for all these are attributes that belong only to the spirit. And it is wrong to say that the spirit is located in space, moves from place to place. For all these qualities belong to body alone.

The blend of spirit and matter that we are is itself incomprehensible. "Man is to himself the strangest object in Nature; for he cannot conceive what body is, and, still less, what is spirit, and least of all how a body can be united to a spirit. This is man's crowning difficulty" (B72).

3. Man's self-deceptions

In addition to being lost in the universe and to the impotence of his cognition, man cannot even reach himself in his presentness, for he constantly deceives himself about himself.

That he never reaches himself is due to the structure of his temporal existence; he deceives himself through his consciousness of the future and the past. The present is almost always painful, hence we hide it from sight. We remember our past as though to check its flight. We seek to bear the present by means of the future, which we anticipate as if it came too slowly. We think of ordering things not now under our control for a time that we are not at all sure of reaching. The future alone is our goal. Thus we never live but only hope to live: always scheming to be happy, it is inevitable that we never are. Let each examine his thoughts; he will always find them occupied with the past or the future. We almost never think of the present. But what foolishness "to wander about in times that are not ours and neglect the only time that is ours . . . and let slip the only one that really is" (St457; B172).

Constant self-deception also arises because none of us can bear the truth about himself. It is the nature of the ego to love only itself and to think only of itself. The ego, however, is an object full of deficiencies and pitifulness; hence this chaos in man produces a deadly hatred of the truth, which convicts him of his deficiencies.

The human being therefore feels compelled to destroy the truth, in his own consciousness and subsequently in that of others. It is an evil to be full of faults but it is a greater evil to be unwilling to recognize them, since it leads to a collectively constructed world of illusions. The wrong kind of tact and our own advantage prevent us from telling the other what we see in him. "We hate the truth, so they hide it from us. We want to be flattered, so they flatter us. We want to be deceived, so they deceive us" (B100). This is what human society is based on—

mutual deceit. Man is only disguise, falsehood, and hypocrisy in himself and toward others (cf. St79; B100).

One source of self-deception is, after all, our vanity. Man's will to be somebody seeks to replace the life of his nothingness by a life of imagined esteem. Hence no one is satisfied unless he has gained respect among men. A soldier, a cook, a porter, each wants to have his admirers, and even the philosophers do. And those who write against vanity covet praise for having written well. "So presumptuous are we that we want to be known to all the world, and even [by] men who come after us when we are no more. And such triflers are we that the esteem of five or six of our companions delights and satisfies us" (St71; B148).

4. Man's nothingness in his contradictions

Man's lack of solid ground in the universe, the impotence of his cognition, his radical self-deception are all self-contradictory: in the universe we are small to the point of disappearing and also as great as a colossus, in the impotence of our cognition we yet cognize, in our self-deceptions we sense that they are just that. Pascal broadens his point of view to that of man's total contradiction.

We can neither cognize nor not cognize. For dogmatism, our incapacity to furnish proofs turns out to be insurmountable; for skepticism, however, our notion of truth is the insurmountable block. Hence we can be neither dogmatists nor skeptics and yet cannot escape either. We cannot be dogmatists without contradicting reason; we cannot be skeptics without contradicting nature. We are incapable of knowing with certainty and equally incapable of knowing simply nothing.

To this corresponds that both contradictories are inconceivable, and yet there is no third alternative. For example: "Inconceivable that God should exist, and inconceivable that He should not exist . . . that the world should have been created and that it should not; that there should be original sin and that there should not" (St113; B230).

We live in a state of war between our reason and our passions. There is no peace between them. "These have tried to renounce their passions and become gods; those have tried to renounce reason and become brute beasts" (St97; B413). Man cannot exist without battle. He is "always in a state of division and self-contradiction" (St95; B412). As we try to avoid the one vice, we succumb to the opposite one.

Man does the opposite of what he says. "Few speak of humility humbly, of chastity chastely, of skepticism skeptically. We are naught but lies, duplicity, contradiction" (St91; B377).

Happiness and unhappiness, each contains its opposite. The most fortunate, Solomon, recognized the vanity of pleasures. The most unfortunate, Job, recognized the truth of suffering (cf. St193; B174).

All in all: "Men are so necessarily insane that not being insane would mean insanity of another kind" (St53; B414). "What a monster then man is . . . what a chaos, what a contradiction. . . . Universal judge . . . sink of uncertainty and error: glory and scum of the universe" (St151; B434).

This is the most profound contradiction of being-human: that man's misery and his greatness are interconnected.

Man's greatness lies in his power of thought. All our dignity consists in thought. "One can imagine a man lacking hands and feet, but one cannot imagine a man lacking thought: he would be a stone or a brute" (St83; B339).

Even the minuteness of man within the universe manifests, through his thinking, his greatness as well: "By space the universe embraces me and swallows me up like an atom, by thought I embrace it" (St83; B348). "It does not need the universe to take up arms to crush man; a vapor, a drop of water, is enough to kill him. But though the universe should crush him, man would still be nobler than his destroyer, because he knows . . . that he is dying, knows that the universe has got the better of him; the universe knows nothing of that" (St83; B347).

Thus it is with all of man's misery. He is unhappy but he knows it. This knowledge intensifies his misery as well as his greatness. No being in nature other than man is conscious of its misery. Man alone experiences his misery through his greatness, his greatness out of his misery. The same serves him in proving his greatness, and in revealing his misery "in an endless circle" (St97; B416).

"Notwithstanding the sight of all our woes . . . we have an irrepressible instinct which uplifts us" (St87; B411).

5. Awakening to the human condition

Pascal's discourse is meant to awaken man. Man must know his condition so that he may react, ask himself what he truly wants, what is at stake. He is to become serious.

In many parables Pascal repeats what he sees as the human condition: "a number of people in fetters, all condemned to death, some killed daily in the sight of the rest, reading their own fate in that of their fellows, waiting their turn. They watch this in pain and hope, awaiting their turn. . . , That is a picture of man's state" (St81; B199). Or: Anyone becoming aware of his condition must be overcome by horror "like a man carried in his sleep into a dreadful desert island and roused from sleep without knowing where he is and without means of escape" (St171; B693).

Pascal confesses: "When I behold man's blindness and misery, when I see the whole universe silent and man without light, left to himself, and as it were lost in this corner of the universe, not knowing who put him there, what he has come to do there, what will happen to him at death, incapable of any kind of knowledge . . . then I wonder that despair does not overtake so miserable a condition. I see other men about me all of like nature." Some of these unhappy lost ones, looking around, "have caught sight of pleasant things, have embraced them and bound themselves thereto. But I could never embrace them . . ." (St171; B693).

Pascal looks at his fellowmen and judges them: There are two kinds of human beings "who can be called rational—those who serve God with all their hearts because they know Him, and those who seek Him wholeheartedly because they know Him not" (St111; B194). But those who choose neither of these two paths, who simply live from day to day, who do not recognize "the extent of man's misery without God," those he not only calls feebleminded, he also speaks of them with bitterness. "This carelessness in a matter which concerns themselves, their eternal fate and their all, arouses in me irritation rather than pity; it amazes and horrifies me, it is for me portentous" (St171; B693).

But precisely this is the structure of man's way of life. We lead our lives without authentic consciousness, between either restlessness or boredom. Attempting to escape both, we merely plunge from one into the other—anything to drown out awareness of our actual state. What do we concern ourselves with? What do we think about? Not of turning inward but of "dancing . . . singing, writing verses . . . fighting, making oneself King without a thought of what it means to be king or to be a man" (St83; B146). Hence the constant pressure to work and transact business, to participate in the din of the world, the concern for honors and possessions, in short, the pursuit of diversions. By means of diversion we hold the deeper unrest at bay. It keeps us from noticing the flight of time. Our attachment to external things obliterates the remembrance of our true condition. There is even pleasure in this forgetfulness.

We think we would be happy if we were rid of our cares. But

precisely this happiness would be unbearable, since it would make us think about ourselves. All those who lament their pains and perils forget that these preoccupations serve to cover up a situation unbearable in itself. Our deeper concern behind all of life's concerns is to divert thought from self. We fear self-reflection. We cannot abide staying quietly in our room. There is no comfort when we think of our condition and have no other diversion than ourselves. For this reason man hates being alone with himself more than anything else.

Thus life slips through our hands. We seek repose, fighting against obstacles, and when we have conquered them, boredom makes repose unbearable.

But boredom, which we try to escape by all sorts of diversions, instead of being the most palpable evil, becomes the greatest blessing if it motivates us to seek true healing. Diversion, however, which seems the greatest happiness to us, is actually the greatest evil, because it keeps us from finding this healing.

However, Pascal sees not just the mediocrity of human existence that, unaware, is in flight from itself; he is more horrified by the person fully aware of his condition who yet deliberately disregards his instincts prompting him to rise toward salvation and, instead, knowingly depends on himself alone. Pascal calls him an unreasonable being whom one would not care to have as a friend; for religion it is an honor to have men so bereft of reason as enemies. This is how Pascal has such a man speak: "I know not who sent me into the world nor what the world is, nor what I myself am; my ignorance of everything is appalling; I do not know what my life is, what my senses, what my soul. . . . I see the dreadful regions of the universe which encloses me, and I find myself penned in one corner of this vast expanse without knowing why I am set in this spot rather than another, nor why the little span of life granted me is assigned to this point of time rather than another of the whole eternity. . . ."

"I see nothing but infinities on every hand closing me in as if I were an atom or a shadow which lasts but a moment and returns no more. All I know is that I must shortly die, but what I know least of all about is this very death which I cannot escape.

"As I know not whence I come, neither do I know whither I am bound . . ." (cf. St105 – 06; B194).

But now Pascal lets this "unreasonable" being continue to speak, lets him express a thought that represents a sudden transition from what went before to what is specific to Pascal and not to the "unreasonable" spokesman: ". . . all I know is that when I quit this world, I fall forever either into nothingness or into the hands of an angry god, without knowing which of these two states is to be for ever my lot" (St107; B194).

The "unreasonable" being continues, without referring to this intermezzo, going on with what went before: "And it leads me to conclude that I am permitted to pass my whole life without a thought of inquiring into my future fate. Perhaps I may find some light amid my doubts; but I am not going to take the trouble to look for it, nor take one step to do so, and then, scorning those who vex themselves with such cares, I will proceed without forethought or fear to try the great venture and slip smoothly into death, uncertain as to the eternity of my future state" (cf. St107; B194).

In the carelessness of living from day to day, and especially in this conscious defiance, Pascal sees "a heart of a bad heart." Nothing is "so cowardly as to defy God" (B194).

III. THERE IS ONLY ONE SOLUTION

Pascal writes: Man's condition, if he grasps it in thought, is without hope. The more he comprehends it, the more decisively he knows there is no way out.

Knowledge itself is of no help to him. Where it is certain, it is bound to specific presuppositions, circumscribed by these and indifferent to the primary concern of man's salvation. Where knowledge would be essential, it is out of reach.

But this skeptical thinking serves a purpose. The situation cries for help. If cognition cannot furnish it, then man is dependent on something other: on God's mercy. Through despair, total skepticism forces the leap to total faith.

Pascal himself stands within faith. He has heard the witnesses of the heritage of faith, he has experienced in his own person the actuality of divine revelation in the night of November 21, 1654. The only task that still consumes him is how to actualize what this faith implies. He sees the freethinkers around him. Most people, it appears to him, live without faith, particularly among the educated upper classes. This scandalizes him and challenges him to action. He desires to help them, help through thinking, that is, by logical argument derived from modern mathematics and the sciences. This thinking, which on the surface seems to intensify unbelief, is applied by him for paving the way toward faith. The work he had planned to deal with the truth of Christianity, later titled "Apology for the Christian Religion," does not intend to defend what is weak, but to guide us toward what is infinitely strong, uniquely true, indeed Salvation itself. Those who already believe do not need his attempt at guidance to Salvation by reasoned argument. They are "rightfully convinced," since God has bestowed "religion on them by sensitivity of the heart." But those who lack this sensitivity can be given religion only by reasoning, "in the hope that God makes it felt by the heart." Without hope, thinking is of no avail; in thought alone "faith is but human" and "unavailing for Salvation." Thought can only awaken our readiness to accept Grace.

The path of this thinking demands two steps. Pascal took the first through developing the skeptical mode of thinking, by means of which reason realizes its own fragility. The second step he took through the unfolding of reason, which leads directly to faith. Even though this is done with an acuity of thought honed by mathematics and in analogy to mathematical thinking, it is informed by the passion proper to entreaty. It is utterly distinct, for example, from the gentle persuasiveness that Schleiermacher advocates for bringing religion closer to the "educated among its detractors."

Pascal's thesis runs as follows: The antagonist of faith is unreasonable because he does not comprehend the human condition and does not draw conclusions from it. Reason, however, which compels readiness for faith, ultimately compels us to surrender reason itself to faith.

1. The wager

I pass over the traditional "proofs" for the truth of Christian religion, which Pascal repeats in detail, even though they are in part simply not correct: the prophecies of the Old Testament fulfilled by the appearance of Christ; the unique traits and the perpetuity of the Jewish people; the Bible as the oldest book in the world—no other religion "has always existed on earth save only the Christian religion" (St229; B606)—the miracles, and so on. I also pass over such arguments raised against Pascal as that all other religions did not appeal to him (he, on the other hand: "I examine the [Jewish] law . . . and find it admirable" [St177; B619]); or that the many religions contradict each other; all are false save one; everyone can call himself a prophet, can claim prophecies fulfilled, but only in Christianity is this the truth (cf. St171; B693).

Peculiar to Pascal, instead, is a procedure emanating directly from the spirit of the new mathematical sciences (with analogies to the theory of probability and the concept of infinity), namely, his proposal or argument to make one's decision about faith in the form of a wager. The process of thought is presented in the form of a dispute with an unbelieving skeptic, who is to be convinced by the portrayal of life as a wager.

a) The Christians say: By natural reason, we are incapable of knowing whether God is or is not. Hence we confess that we cannot give a reason for our faith. We declare it to be folly *(stultitia)*.

b) If there are no proofs for faith, then there is no reason to accept it; that is, unless in the desperate situation in which, being human, I find myself, I recognize it as reasonable by applying my reason, and wager whether God is or is not, whether faith is true or not. What does this wager consist of? I stake my whole life on an uncertainty. My stake is my sacrifice in letting myself be consumed by the demands of faith. If God is, then I win eternal bliss.

c) In response to this seemingly mad proposal the skeptic says: Since reason can decide neither for nor against God's existence, and therefore neither alternative can be excluded, it seems reasonable to refrain from making any decision. Not only the one or the other choice seems unreasonable but any choice at all. Hence, the skeptic maintains, the right thing is not to wager.

d) Pascal confronts this argument which evades choice with our actual inescapable situation: "A game is on, at the outermost rim of the infinite chaos . . ." (B233). In reality, we are always already in the game. Therefore wager we must; there is no option but the choice on what to place your bet and to base your life, on God's being or non-being. Hence it is reasonable to make this wager since we cannot escape it. It is unavoidable anyway, even for those who bet on God's non-being.

e) Does it make sense to bet on God's being or his non-being? Only one of the two is reasonable, for if I wager that God is, then I lose nothing if I lose my bet (because this finite life is nothing in the human situation I have become conscious of). But if I win, I win all.

f) But there is always the counterargument: I stake perhaps too much—my whole life. In making my bet I am certain of losing all the pleasures of this life, of which I am certain, but I am uncertain of the winnings of this wager, since they might be nonexistent. Pascal answers: The finite becomes as nothing compared to the infinite; the same applies to our whole life: as finite life it has no value in proportion to eternity. The loss of finiteness, being nothing anyway, is countered by the possible gain of an infinity that is eternal bliss; the possible gain of the latter is countered not by infinite chances of loss, but only by the possible loss of a finite number of chances, since your stake is finite. There can be no hesitation, you must stake all.

To repeat the objection: In risking the happiness of life, what is certain is the risk, what is uncertain is the gain. This objection, says Pascal, is meaningless when the finite stands over against the infinite: every player wagers with certainty what is finite in order to win, with uncertainty, a greater finite. How much more reason, then, to risk the stake in playing the great game for eternity; for by staking the finite we are playing to win the infinite.

And again: Staking this finite life, risking the loss of this actual life which is certain as presentness, may, after all, be too great a risk. I stake everything that I have with certainty for something that is altogether uncertain. Pascal's answer repeats, first, that precisely this presentness of life, as stressed in the exposition of the human condition, is not certain. Second, however, he says that I (seemingly counter to the argument meant by him to be an act of reason) have to renounce reason, whose limits and emptiness I realize anyway. In my actual situation I have no choice but to gamble. In this situation it is more reasonable to renounce reason in order to secure possible eternity. The possible infinite gain stands over against the certain loss of a mere finitude that is a nothingness. I surrender a nothingness in order to win something infinite.

What is the consequence in my temporal, finite life if I surrender this nothingness as a stake in the game? "You will be freed from poisonous pleasures, such as ambition and luxury. . . . You will be faithful, honest, humble, grateful, beneficent . . ." (St121–22; B233).

g) The doubter seeking to avoid the choice admits all this but rejects the proposal once more, radically, using the following argument: "I am forced to wager, and I am not free," for "I am so made that I cannot believe. What am I to do?" (St121; B233). To this Pascal replies by pointing to those who have already traveled the path of faith: "Follow the way by which they began, that is, by making believe that they believed, by taking holy water, by hearing mass, etc. This will lead you quite naturally to believe and will calm you . . . will stultify you" (B233).

For our nature is to be guided by habit. Pascal sees it in everything that we are. "The soul is cast into the body where it finds number, time, extension; it reasons, and calls it Nature, necessity, and this is the absolute limit of its belief" (B233). That is, our soul has become accustomed to measure in terms of quantity, time, and motion, and believes in them. The following is in the same vein: "He who has the habit of Faith believes it and cannot fail to fear hell" (B89).

The thinking skeptic resists—instead of reassuring himself through reason—achieving faith through purposive habituation, that is, through a psychological technique, and thus reaching that extolled *stultitia* which Christians claim to derive from their faith. Rather, his reason fears this state of *stultitia*. Pascal responds: If we lose that reason which, as such, puts us in bondage and fetters us to delusion, nothing is lost.

2. *Critical discussion of the wager*

In the remarkable, decisively developed argument of the wager it is not a question of the shoddy thought of fear: Just in case, I do what is proper for faith—follow religious observances, pray, and pay church taxes, along with moderate sacrifices—then I will live well and have insured my afterlife, too. Pascal's "stake" signifies not only more but something qualitatively different: the staking of his whole finite life, its fulfillment in the world. He demands a radical turnabout of our conduct and of all value judgments. In this seriousness of Pascal's thought lies his challenge. Through its seriousness it exhibits a certain cogency. But to counter these thoughts, so impressive in their seriousness, other arguments than those Pascal has his skeptic say present themselves.

a) *The error intrinsic in Pascal's method of thought.* Pascal's mathematical analogy implies that infinity plus or minus a finite number remains infinite, does not get larger or smaller. Measured against the infinite, the finite number is nothing. Once our whole finite existence is set in proportion to God's infinity, and our own eternity in God is related as a finite number to an infinite, the result is zero. Such an analogy is deceptive, since in Pascal it ceases to be an analogy. But it is also deceptive in that we forget that there is no relation between the finite and the infinite; the finitude of my existence and the infinity of eternal bliss cannot, like two objects in this world, be treated as terms of a wager. Pascal makes one become the stake for the other. He forces onto the same level what is incommensurable or has different qualities of being.

Pascal can gloss over this objection only by ultimately surrendering, in his dialectic, reason by way of reason.

b) *The notion of decision is not applicable in this context.* Our knowledge cannot decide whether God is or is not. The statement "God is" derives its meaning not from a decision but as a cipher devolved from an all-encompassing trust on the part of my possible Existenz, a trust predating all experiences, constantly assailed by doubt engendered by thought and specific experiences and in need of unfathomable reconfirmation. If, for good reason, we want to call this basic trust, faith, then this philosophic act of faith is wrongly called an act of decision. In the here and now decisions are taken in the form of choice between finite things. Where they are serious (as decisions of possible Existenz) they presuppose faith. Faith manifests itself via concrete decisions, attains in them consciousness of itself and the actualization of what is as such eternal. Paradoxically, this means that decisions in time arise out of something that itself is not being decided but has been decided for all time. Pascal's argument concerning the wager asks for a decision that reaches into spheres inappropriate to it. He applies the concept to something that eludes decision, since it either is decided for all time or is nonexistent.

The premise for this erroneous argumentation is the alternative between eternal bliss and eternal damnation. What in its essence has nonobjective signification as indefinite cipher is forced into the realm of finite conceptions, and the infinite itself is given finite value. Eternal salvation is turned into "somewhere else," something not present here and now but present there and later.

This thinking concerning decisions also presupposes that our surrender of reason and all actualities of existence determines God's decision about our eternal salvation. Pascal identifies God's being with the demands of a historically determined revelation which, moreover, is understood in purely ascetic terms.

The consequences of such thinking are the leveling of existential (religious or philosophic) faith to the plane of choosing a religion (such as Christianity in one of its many varieties) and of the possibility of conversion.

c) *The risk of the wager is not the risk of the human being.* The wager is a risk. Is Pascal's wager perhaps a metaphor for the risk inherent in a human life, in the sense that the goal of our lives is never in our power? Or is it as with Socrates, who takes his risk on the chance of immortality and calls it a beautiful risk? Neither. Pascal's wager is a risk which, according to his theory of probability, is a risk no more; for the chances of winning are as infinity is to zero. For himself as believer, however, the risk does not exist at all. He is assured in his faith. He merely wishes to force the unbeliever, by way of the idea of the wager and through reason, to take up the challenge in order to prepare for him the way to actual faith. If I do not possess that trust of philosophic faith (unknown to Pascal), then the idea of the wager is meant to force me to place my bets on the existence of God even without this trust. What, in the Socratic metaphor of the wager, truly touched on the human condition is here equated with a game of chance. Unconditional trust becomes a calculation of probability. And the consequence of this willingness to wager reveals itself as nothing but the forming of habits that ultimately will lead to faith itself.

d) *What is present is not negligible.* The argument of the wager becomes invalid if the nullity of what is to be staked, that is, surrendered, is nonexistent. Asserting the nullity of what is to be staked implies devaluing the mode of existential actualization in fulfilled presentness on the part of other, equally serious human beings; it implies devaluing the high-minded unfolding of man's innate nobility, and the creation of works of the mind, of art, and of poetry which, in the uncertainty of ignorance, speak as the ciphers of transcendence. For those who accede to infinity by way of the finitudes of existence on earth, who can touch infinity only through these finitudes, who take hold of the supramundane only in its actualizations in the world and not outside of it or elsewhere, the surrender of this finiteness equally signifies the loss of the infinity incarnate in these so-called futilities and the irresponsible renunciation of the task given to human beings. Another seriousness confronts Pascal's. If we ask whether we want to follow the one or the other seriousness, then the answer is already there in the questioner. He need not decide at all but is already in the state of professed decidedness, which is now seen more clearly. The decisions of either side, however, distinguish them from the indecisiveness rooted in insufficient seriousness.

3. The actual human condition, in Pascal's view, can be understood only on the basis of original sin

Only the Christian faith, and no other, represents for Pascal deliverance from the hopelessness of the human condition. This faith alone, although itself beyond human comprehension, makes the situation of man and the foundering of his cognition comprehensible. To be sure, radical skepticism arising from awareness of the human situation prepares the way to faith, but only to that faith out of which we come to comprehend that it is in this intractable situation of disruptive contradictions that we find ourselves. This skepticism, first presented as the road to faith, is, instead, itself the consequence of Christian faith. Herein lies the magnificent circle.

For this faith teaches (Pascal oversimplifies and sharpens Pauline and Augustinian thoughts) that contemporary man, in the state of original sin because of Adam's fall, is a twofold creature: created in perfection and then corrupted. He preserves a dim memory of the purity attendant upon his creation and experiences the challenge originating there. But he is ensnared in the here and now. That this is the case cannot be brought into the open through philosophy; it is accessible to us solely through recognizing these two equally permanent "truths of faith: one, that man in his created state stood high above all nature, was made in the likeness of God; the other, that in his state of corruption and sin he has fallen from that state and is become a likeness of the brute beasts" (B434).

What Pascal has to say on man's condition and his nature, on the world, on politics, and so on, can be understood only if his formulations are seen against the background of belief in original sin, Christ, and God.

Pascal tirelessly confirms this truth of faith by his knowledge of actual man. His image of man, sketched out with the intention of giving an unbiased view of our present actuality, is an undeviating verification of the truth of the dogma of original sin:

"If man had never been corrupted he would in his innocence enjoy truth and happiness." Had he never been anything other than corrupt, he would have no notion of either truth or happiness. As we are, we are conscious of "an image of truth and only hold a lie" (St151; B434). We are incapable of absolute ignorance, as well as of certain knowledge. Our condition is one of "a strange reversal" (St49; B198). We are sensible to trifles and insensible to great things. But also for this reason: "Man is bored with everything . . . because he has an image of the happiness he has lost, and since he cannot find it within himself he searches for it in vain in eternal things . . . for it is . . . in God alone." Man "is plainly astray and fallen from his proper place irrecoverably. He goes seeking it on all sides, anxiously, vainly, in impenetrable darkness" (St81; B427).

Only through faith do we arrive at this insight. We do not grasp the state of glory in Adam or the nature of his sin, or our inheritance of that sin. What happens in Christ is like to what had occurred in Adam, an event that is simultaneously a cosmic process. Nature everywhere points to "a lost God" within as well as outside man. "Without Jesus Christ the world could not continue, for it must needs be destroyed or become a very hell" (St9; B556). All these are things that have occurred in the state of a nature totally different from ours. They surpass the condition of our present power of comprehension (cf. St9; B560).

But such comprehending is not what matters here. It is important to us solely so that we may understand that we are miserable, corrupt, separated from God, but are redeemed by Jesus Christ, that is, by God Himself who became man, suffered, and died on the Cross. What was lost in Adam is restored through Christ. In faith the knowledge of our corruption is joined to our deliverance from corruption. It is not enough to cognize God; neither does it suffice to recognize our human corruption. Only faith in Christ can help us. "We can indeed know God without knowing our misery, and our misery without knowing God; but we cannot know Jesus Christ without knowing both God and our misery" (St7; B556). It is the "miracle of the Christian religion that it reconciles man with himself by reconciling him with God."

I give one more summary view. First: Through the mystery of our cognition through faith, we attain understanding of ourselves; without the mystery, that is, original sin, we cannot gain any knowledge about ourselves. It is "contrary to the laws of our poor justice" and is therefore "offensive to reason." Yet "without this mystery, the most incomprehensible of all, we are incomprehensible to ourselves" (St153; B434). Second: Man must be shaken up through reason, which is powerful in its skepticism, until he comprehends that he is an incomprehensible absurdity (cf. St151; B434). But then, whoever has recognized what a paradox he is in himself has to take a further step: "Learn that man is infinitely beyond the reach of man. . . . Hearken to God" (St151; B434). Third: We can come to know ourselves "not through the proud notions of our reason, but by simple subordination of reason. . . ." It seems "that God, in his decision to render the problem of our being unintelligible to ourselves, hid the knot so high or rather so deep that we were quite incapable of reaching it" (St153; B434).

For Pascal, as for many Christians, the Christian religion is plainly unique. The doctrine just presented makes the Christian religion stand out from all the others:

No other religion has taught that man is born in sin. No other "bids man recognize that he is vile, yea, abominable" and at the same time "bids him try to be like God" (St189; B537).

Only the Christian religion frees man from falling into the "pride of philosophers who have known God but not their misery," and from the "despair of the atheists who know their misery but not their Redeemer" (St7; B556).

"The Christian religion alone makes man both lovable and happy" (St329; B542). "None is so happy as a true Christian, nor so virtuous, so lovable" (B541). Let us wait and see what being a Christian means on Pascal's terms.

Critical characterization: Pascal forcefully brought home to us that "man in a strict sense is entirely animal" (St201). But there is a rift between us and the animals no matter whether we call what makes us human beings thought, self-consciousness, consciousness of God, historical memory, or something else.

I, in contrast to Pascal, content myself with representing man's originality and the never-ending illumination of his true being.

Observing man objectively as a living being among other beings, I reject discussions on transitional stages between animals and men, because these transitions can neither be convincingly developed in the imagination nor found in reality. I can point to leaps in the biological evolution of living things which are just as incomprehensible, and simultaneously to the uniqueness of the leap to man. In the former we deal with objective assessment of the forms and functions of life; in the latter we are concerned solely with thinking, self-consciousness, history. I can understand the development of living things and the development of man as an event progressing from the lower to the higher, I can see how far this brings me in interpreting the finds of bones and other traces of past life, and I can demonstrate series and ramifications of such series in the hundreds of thousand years in which humanoid creatures existed. This fascinating research based on the idea of a natural upward development (and of progress in human history) goes astray as soon as it transforms the presuppositions of such research, productive for one aspect, into all-inclusive assertions regarding the origin of man. These explorations, while they supply significant knowledge about man, only deepen the mystery that man is to himself provided he does not close himself off from himself and hide under the cloak of the schemata of a sham knowledge. "Where does man come from?" and "What is man?"—these are the questions that remain unanswered.

But if I do not content myself with the never-concluded illumination of how and as what I find myself, if I am not content with living in existential and rational actualization, out of darkness and into darkness, or with the uncertain illumination cast by the ciphers of Being at the boundaries of obscurity, and if I want to know the unknowable, then Pascal opens up a possibility. For his Christian faith the event of being-human, in its origin and goal, and the myth of a supernatural development are based and become intelligible in the fall of man and the subsequent divine interference (as the gnostic thinkers have presented to us in detail). Out of his faith he formulates the consciousness of the radical difference between man and beast: Men and animals are in a deplorable state; but man knows himself to be wretched, animals do not. Man's condition is altogether different. He has fallen from a pure, exalted nature that was once his. Only a dethroned king considers himself wretched when he is not king. The misery of a dethroned king proves the misery of man.

This myth is indeed enthralling. But decisive is the value we give it: whether as a free-floating cipher or as firm reality. For Pascal its content is reality perceived in the actuality of faith. For the person who contents himself with the yardstick of the wholly transcendental actuality of the Biblical as well as the philosophical notions of divinity in form, this is a cipher that again suspends itself. The consequences for positive human action and attitudes are tremendous, as can be seen in the case of Pascal.

All of Pascal's judgments rest on the basis of an actuality of faith that is perverted from a cipher into reality. An impenetrable wall is raised from which everything rebounds. Whoever lives without Christian faith, or, in order to justify his actions, opposes this faith, and any objection against a formulated Christian statement of faith, is turned into new proofs of the truth of faith in Christ, which unites perdition and salvation. Thus, for Pascal, the attitude of the "godless," who live in indifference toward his religion, and the behavior of the Jews, who, according to him, are irreconcilable enemies of the Christian religion, merely serve as proofs of the truth of Christian religion.

Do we not hear in these frequent judgments the sound of an arrogance that Pascal repudiates so often and in such a humbly Christian manner? Does he forget what he had recognized with such clarity of vision, namely, that one rarely speaks humbly about humility? The Christian notion of salvation—Adam's fall, original sin, restoration through God-become-man—is not to be questioned as such. Anyone outside this faith can still perceive the gravity and depth active among the truly pious. But if, as so often, and also with Pascal, the content of this faith is transformed from a freely floating cipher into a tangible reality, as it were, and belief in it is demanded of everyone in compliance with certain features of Christian ecclesiasticism, or if eternal damnation is the sentence for those who do not share that faith, then this faith turns into inhuman nonsense. It becomes inhuman because it leads to hatred (and Pascal's hatred was fierce) and because it blinds one to the seriousness and dignity of human actualizations in the world. It turns into nonsense, since its content, counter to its claim, is not truth for everyone, because there is nothing cogent in its pronouncements and no universal credibility in its proclamations (for where it is true, it is so in its historicity and only in connection with those who belong to this historicity). Insofar as Pascal participates in this phenomenon, he represents nothing unusual and nothing new. His greatness lies in the way in which he, in relating to this faith, develops new images of man's actual state and in an honesty peculiarly his own dares to draw the most extreme consequences.

4. Faith in revelation or philosophy

Pascal most rigorously posed the following alternative: certitude of reason in ignorance, or submission in faith in obedience to the revelation embodied in the Church. After a millennium of tension and union between reason and faith, after the unity of theology and philosophy or their intermeshing, Bruno, through the tortures inflicted upon him by the Christian Church and his death on the pyre, became the martyr of original philosophy. Then came Spinoza, the most impeccable, purest philosopher of more recent times, who suffered expulsion from the synagogue by the great excommunication. It was during this period that Pascal through his thinking seemed to make the abyss between faith and reason all but unbridgeable.

Pascal did not intend to be a philosopher. His main pursuit, in which he was highly successful, was science, which he treated as neutral in itself. As a believing Christian he sought salvation by ways that allowed his thinking to express his fundamental certitude, and his faith, which is perpetually put in question by reason, to assert itself.

Philosophy as a way of life based on thought was known to him primarily through Epictetus and Montaigne, and through Descartes's thinking. In Epictetus he saw the wisdom of submitting to the will of God and of recognizing the duties of morality, but he also saw the arrogance that ascribes to one's own thinking and capability an original freedom as well as a power that they cannot claim to possess. In Montaigne he saw the truth of recognizing the impotence of reason and the misery of the human condition, but also the indifference and negligence associated with distance from God. In Descartes he saw the abstract thinker who has nothing in common with true philosophy. Authentic philosophy is actual in the power of judgment in concrete situations. This falls into the sphere of *esprit de finesse,* just as the natural sciences belong to the *esprit de géometrie.* True morality, that is, practical judgment, scoffs at theoretical morality. True philosophy scoffs at philosophy (cf. St499; B4). But then he cannot "forgive Descartes" that he "would rather not trouble God throughout his philosophy." Descartes "could not help letting Him give a fillip to get the world going." Such knowledge, which constructs the world as a machine, is uncertain and useless. If such thinking were true, the whole of natural philosophy would not be worth an hour's labor (cf. St161; B77, 78).

Excursus: On "philosophical faith" and revelation

1. Characterization of philosophical faith: knowing one's ignorance and cleaving to present reality and placing one's hope in reason and good will; experiencing origins that are present, actualizing reason with its content drawn from the possibilities of Existenz, accepting it as a gift to oneself; exposing oneself in thought to the greatest exigencies, and, should they actually occur, not veiling them.

Living in the world by means of the world, and, even in foundering, seeing what is manifest therein; not denying or overlooking the world; not treating eternity as if it were a worldly reality among other worldly realities.

2. Authority: In both philosophy and faith in revelation, authority is thinking as the process of transcending.

The question concerning transcendence of revelation and transcendence of reason is whether transcendence speaks through "revelation" which must be obeyed and whose presence is in the Church—that is, if man is dependent on a definite, sensory, temporal authority. Or whether transcendence finds its expression within each individual person and therefore whether authority is vested only in revelation and the Church. Further: whether in the last analysis, authority is a byproduct of our upbringing, be it one's way of life, be it one's parents, be it those who are our role models from childhood on, or the experiences of the great thoughts of the past, the formative links with the most substantial texts (among them the Bible). To this should be added the concretion of one's being through the historicity of one's heritage, parentage, family and friends, state and Church, all of them stripped of absolute and untrue claims.

3. The accusation of "pride" raised against allegedly high-handed philosophy wanting to dictate even to God how He is to show Himself and how to keep hidden.

Everything said about the arrogance of philosophers can be matched by pointing to the pride of the priests and theologians (pride even in their forced humility).

The contention that the very meaning of philosophy entails pride is erroneous.

Consciousness of the limits of the intellect, of finding oneself in freedom as a gift, of the limit to reason, of the position as man, of limit-situations—all this is emphasized in the philosophy that lies ready and possible in every human being.

5. The nature of Pascal's Christianity

Pascal pondered salvation from the misery of the human condition in ideas which he put into practice. His life actualized what his thinking had interpreted. Hence the power of these thoughts.

True, they are based on traditional Christian motives. But in Pascal's formulations and translation into actuality they take on a shape that has to be seen undisguised. This is the premise for any attempt to penetrate Pascal's nature.

a) *"Mystery of Jesus":* This is the essential core for Pascal: In His passion Jesus suffers tortures inflicted by men, but in His agony he suffers tortures inflicted by Himself.

What men inflict on Him culminates in Jesus's extreme loneliness at Gethsemane. At that time, the one and only time in His life, Jesus seeks comfort from His closest friends, and they are asleep. They abandon Him with utter neglect. He suffers this desertion amid the horror of darkness, left alone to face God's wrath. Only once in His life does He utter a complaint: "My soul is exceeding sorrowful, even unto death" (Matthew 26:38). Jesus is not only the sole person on earth to feel His suffering but also the only one to know it.

What He inflicts on Himself in His final agony is the shedding of His blood for the redemption of man.

Pascal knows both sufferings and relates in both to Jesus. He wants to be His most faithful disciple: "Jesus will be in agony while the world lasts: we must not sleep the while." He wants to follow Jesus: Jesus tears Himself from His disciples as He enters His death struggle. "We must tear ourselves from our nearest and dearest after His example."

To Jesus, to Him alone and to no human being, Pascal stands in a wholly personal, unique relationship. He feels personally addressed when Jesus says: "Take comfort, you would not seek Me if you had not found Me. I thought of you in My agony, I shed those drops of blood for you." Hence concretely: Those specific drops of blood were shed for Pascal. And further: "Would you wish that I should be ever shedding the blood of My human nature while you shed no tear for Me?" And finally: "I am a better friend to you than this man or that; for I have done for you more than they; they would not bear what I have borne at your hands; they would not die for you amid all your disloyalty and cruelty, as I have done" (St367ff.; B553).

At every moment Pascal feels himself addressed directly. His thought elects for himself a special position, the greatest measure of suffering in imitation of Christ and the closest proximity to Him, Who, in shedding His blood, thought of Pascal.

b) *Asceticism and perversion:* If we choose pleasure, says Pascal, we succumb to it. It is a different matter when we choose pain: ". . . we may deliberately seek pain and yield to it without that kind of degradation." For it is not pain that attracts us; we choose it voluntarily. We desire to give it empire over us so that we are the masters (St89; B160). In the pain that man himself seeks out, he yields to himself; in pleasure, however, he yields to pleasure. Hence it is no disgrace to yield to pain, while it is disgraceful to yield to pleasure.

This is Pascal's theory of active asceticism in which, in spite of his interpretation, will to power and perversion unite. He thinks of suffering only as imitation of Christ. His psychological reflections do not yet pierce to the pleasure attendant in pain, a condition that more advanced psychologists penetrated. Though without faith in Jesus, these men were torturing themselves as Pascal did but recognized the oddity of the pleasure element in suffering.

Pascal's faith in Christ found its fulfillment in his ascetic existence, which, as he neared the end of his life, he kept intensifying. He saw himself following in Jesus' footsteps and grounded divine shelteredness in his sharing in Christ's pain and agony.

c) *Lovelessness:* Love for God by way of love for Jesus Christ—this, for Pascal, is all-important, the essence of true life, salvation.

But this love, in Pascal, leads to self-hatred (the Ego is hateful; cf. St79; B455), hatred of the world, hatred of humanity. Whatever is not God is not worthy of love, since it is in a state of corruption.

What becomes of "Thou shalt love thy neighbor as thyself"? Is not the logical consequence of self-hatred "Thou shalt hate thy neighbor as thyself"? The farther he advanced in life, the more clearly Pascal understood Christian charity as love for the poor and the ailing, as the challenge to share their suffering, to alleviate it, to give to them one's possessions. And to do this inconspicuously, not as gifts to public, organized charity but quietly to one's needy neighbor, to whoever comes in one's purview. During his final illness, Pascal offered shelter and care to the poor or sick, charitable acts in imitation of Christ.

Do we have to see in Pascal's conduct nothing but the logical consequence of dogma? Or is there a predisposition in his nature, in the structure of his aspiration that enables and urges him to follow dogma as he understood it to its practical conclusion?

In his youth Pascal was capable of passionate love, discussing it, in the treatise on Passion of Love, in a psychologically acute and precise manner, and linking it with physical desire and jealousy. This love he came to reject later on.

Through all the stages of his life Pascal seems to have been unresponsive to the visible glories of creation. Nature stimulated him to scientific research but did not arouse his love. It appears that art and poetry were hardly noticed by him.

Because of his devotion to Christ it makes sense that he is lacking in love for the human race, that he comes to distrust his fellowmen more and more, and that he repudiates the potentialities in human relations. He was bound to become increasingly lonely because of that lack of earthly love which turned all his love toward Christ. Toward the end he imposed on himself a cold aloofness toward his closest relatives so as not to deprive God of any love he might lavish on them.

d) *God the Deceiver:* It is an ancient notion that God, in letting his prophets speak, deafens the hearts of the people to their veiled message, so that ultimately the people will be brought to judgment precisely because of their indifference (Isaiah 6:9–10); or that God sends false prophets with the purpose of testing men's hearts by this deception and the truth of their love for Him (Deuteronomy 13); or that God lets an impious man consult an erring prophet so that both become guilty and are destroyed (Ezekiel 14:7–10). This idea still resonates faintly in the New Testament (Matthew 24:24), where the appearance of false Christs and false prophets is predicted, aiming to deceive if possible even the elect by signs and wonders. The underlying idea here is to present God as letting His mercy and His wrath govern in an unfathomable way. The chosen ones are not deluded. God uses the truly pious as instruments of His mercy and the iniquitous as means and executors of His wrath. False prophets are his tools for deception, while simultaneously true prophets proclaim the true state of things (Spinoza, *Tractatus theologico-politicus,* Ch. 2).

Pascal gives new shape to this thought. Only recently Descartes had repudiated as fiction a deceiving God, to be dismissed out of hand. In contrast to this superficial notion, Pascal revives the deceiving God in His appalling reality. God's revelation is at the same time hidden, hence ambiguous. Only to the Church has He given visible signs "by which those who seek Him in sincerity should know Him," but "at the same time so hiding them that He can only be perceived by those who

seek Him with their whole hearts" (St101; B194). According to Pascal
it is Christian dogma that God's existence cannot be proven by anything in the visible world (hence it is opposed to all proofs, especially
the cosmological proof for the existence of God); that men live in darkness and alienation from God; that God has removed Himself from
their cognition. It is a trick of revelation that it illuminates the one and
blinds the other. It is obscure enough to deceive the profligate and clear
enough to make their error inexcusable. Reason divorced from grace is
to be misled.

e) *Death and the hour of death:* As for many Christians, death, for
Pascal, has an all-important significance obliterating everything and determining one's life. It is the fundamental view that another actuality,
an actuality beyond the world and manifesting itself after death, is the
only authentic one, by its infinity, everlastingness, incorruptibility, and
this present, ephemeral life is directed toward it. Immortality, imagined
as a being-in-time after death, carries the tremendous weight of
eternity.

Physically, the death of a human being parallels the death of animals as an agonizing process leading to the end, immeasurable suffering finding its limits only in the loss of consciousness, or in peaceable
extinction. But the dying of human beings ought to be different from
that of animals. It is indeed different by virtue of the fact that only
man knows that he is going to die. Some even wish to experience death
in full awareness, as Lessing did during a grave illness in his youth,
and also Kierkegaard; others prefer to be left ignorant of the hour of
their death.

All eras in history show that death has extraordinary meaning for
human beings. But the nature of its significance is expressed in very
divergent ways. It gains heightened significance if it is considered not
only as death, as is the case with animals, but as the self's transition
into another form of existence. For in this case the "after death" can
have a determining effect on one's life. Where the idea of a judgment
after death is added, the effect is heightened by the dual fear of physical suffering here on earth and of man's condition after death (in hell
or paradise).

Pascal lived and thought within this traditional conception. But he
saw the condition of man exclusively under the aspect of death. Hence
for him life held no meaning but the all-important one: striving for
God's mercy in the world to come. The eternal actuality of that world
after death is accessible not by way of reason or through ethical action,
but solely through God's grace bestowed on the believer. For Pascal it

is more important to believe and to know through faith, and in this way to strive, by total asceticism, for eternal life in the next world, than to pursue one's mundane life in this world.

With philosophizing, a transformation of consciousness grounded in the illumination of temporality is begun, by which all those notions of eternity vanish as realities; they are tested, appropriated or rejected as ciphers, measured by wholly different yardsticks. Essentially, eternity is not to be considered in the form of an endless temporal future after death but only as mythical cipher.

Pascal's presupposition that the time after death is genuinely and eternally actual, and hence alone important, rests on the universally familiar and traditional concept of the absolute nature of time, which is heightened speculatively by seeing time in the ground of Being itself. But Pascal's thinking remains untouched by the idea of time as appearance and by the possibility of transcendental insight into this characteristic of time (which, in variations, is discernible in the Indian philosophers, in Plato, in Augustine—although not followed through by him—in Kant, in Spinoza).

If the nature of time as appearance is actual in philosophic consciousness, if it is not merely thought abstractly but experienced concretely, then the historicity of Existenz is not only carried out in practice but is present to philosophic knowledge. The actuality of Existenz, transverse to time, as it were, is the indissoluble unity of temporal event and eternal present. What is decided in time by Existenz is, as such, eternal; that is, it goes beyond time.

The common attitude, of which Pascal partakes, is the erroneous transformation of the "transverse to time" into "future," of the eternal nature of Existenz into a state of being after death that would have the same quality of reality as present existence. True, for our capacity of imagination and of thought the idea of the future may for us who live in time be the cipher of what we are eternally, that is, for the "transverse to time." But the transformation of this cipher into a reality of future life, which, living in this life, we project in care and expectation and hope, undermines the clarity of the presence of Being. This happens to an extreme degree when, as in the case of Pascal, the capability of experiencing presentness or the awareness of actuality is diminished (perhaps in relation to a certain constitution of the organism).

The metaphysically erroneous notion of time (the correction of which, however, cannot be arrived at by the cogency of science, but only in philosophic assurance reached in transcending thought) opens the way to the second error, this one existential in nature: the notion of reward and punishment in a future eternity. The relationship of reward and punishment is erroneously carried over into eternity from the finite linkage of human affairs in time. This notion destroys the purity of moral action and the disinterestedness of actual love. What man authentically is or can be lies above the sphere of reward and punishment in time; this possibility lies transverse to historic time, is conscious of eternity in contrast to the passing of what is merely transient.

Where philosophic insight has become actuality, two theses, whose meanings have been reiterated throughout the history of philosophy, prove their validity; they have found their most authentic expression in Spinoza: (1) The sage thinks about life and not about death; (2) the reward of virtue is virtue itself. Life, as the existence grasped with the passion of existential decision in time, is eternally present as a whole. To be sure, this is beyond our capacity of thought and mode of representation, which are determined finitely, but is present as certainty in every exalted moment. This certainty supports our life, fills our consciousness of Being, is able to illuminate itself only in mythical ciphers devoid of objective reality.

For such philosophizing, the absolute importance of the hour of death vanishes, despite its decisiveness. Only when philosophic consciousness stays caught up in temporality can the hour of death, as in Pascal, command such tremendous weight, all the more tremendous if it represents the moment in which the eternity of a self is determined. Until the moment of death, what comes after is still undecided. But as of the hour of death everything becomes irrevocable. Hence the Christian overemphasis on the hour of death. Pascal's desire for the last sacraments was such torture for him because it was denied by his entourage on the premise that death was not imminent. When he finally received them—actually, immediately before his death—his final words were "May God never abandon me," meaning that he was on the threshold of another world, the hereafter. At the very last, in the hour of one's death, all may be gained or be lost, as though, at this crucial moment only, a decision could be arrived at that differed from what had been decided over a long period of time.

Pascal's position that death dominates all of existence finds expression in the following, humanly unsettling and, in our view, fundamentally untrue statement: "We are fools to rest content with the company of our peers, pitiably like ourselves, impotent as ourselves; they will give us no help; I shall die alone. We must therefore act as if we were alone" (St173; B211). These sentences mean: He who does not communicate with his fellows, who considers solitude to be the true

actuality of his Existenz (in the final analysis this applies also, for example, to Kierkegaard and Nietzsche), he who, in the lovelessness of his
inability to experience love in himself, feels the lack of being truly
loved all the more strongly; for him death becomes absolute, deepest
aloneness, becomes the culmination of all loneliness experienced in
this world.

We hesitate to consider such an actuality as even possible. But
thinking it is critically appropriate in order to address Pascal's fathomless statements.

Another meaning of Existenz might be put forward: In dying I
move in the direction of my beloved dead. Those we loved most go on
living for a while and keep alive what we once were to each other.
Death, the end of us all, unites and does not make lonely. I shall not
die alone. Never must I act as though I were abandoned.

Pascal's statements, however, are meant to imply that he dies without human bonds, relying solely on God's mercy and, excluding all
human beings, sheltered only by Him.

IV. PASCAL'S CONCEPT OF TRUTH AND SCIENCE

Up to this point our subject was the study of man in his desperate
situation and how help and salvation are bestowed upon him solely
through his faith in God become man, in Christ. But Pascal's thinking
is not confined to this circle of being-human and redemption through
faith. His questioning about man and his obedience in faith would not
affect us so deeply if the problem of truth and science had not guided
him with equal force. His search for truth is of a seriousness equal to
that for the salvation of the soul. By his powers of mathematical invention and his energy in research in the natural sciences, which went far
beyond his contemporaries, and by his will to clarity in the method of
his thinking, tremendously acute and to the point, he structured a religious thought that ultimately took precedence.

To be sure, Pascal's passionate will to know is guided by the greater
passion for letting knowledge founder on faith. Yet the former passion
never really ceases. Only that can be said to have truly and wholly
foundered which has been pursued to its ultimate possibilities. Though
he abandoned fragile reason by reason itself, to Pascal the very being
of truth was paramount; that makes him, quite apart from his prodigious abilities and achievements, great in another fashion and his life
into a Christian tragedy.

We need to discuss, first, Pascal's answer to the question of truth in relation to science, and, second, his struggle for truth in his life and within the world. In this section we shall also consider Pascal's methodological consciousness of science and truth; his struggle will be dealt with in the subsequent section.

1. The modes of truth

a) *The logic of the provable and the logic of the heart.* The statement "Truth is one" is just as immediately self-evident as the experience of thinking and cognizing seems to teach us that there are many truths, many modes (methods) of grasping the truth, and that the one truth can be reached, if at all, only by way of the many truths.

In that truth that is one, we would understand each other in a flash and be of one mind. It is Pascal's fundamental experience that we talk with each other without finding agreement, that claims are made and counterclaims, that we find ourselves in confusion verging on the arbitrary. How can this be remedied? How do we find the road to where together we cannot but see the valid truth in what we say, where it would be irrefutable to our own understanding, cogently valid for everyone?

Pascal wanted clarity about what is cogent in thinking, but also to discover the other truth and how it can be imparted convincingly and effectively.

In setting his rules for definitions, axioms, and proofs, Pascal stated: "All other precepts are useless or harmful. I know this from a long study of books, and knowledge of persons of all descriptions." He developed these rules in an extremely simple way. They are the rules of what is mathematically provable. He delighted in their certainty. But beyond mathematics "and of whatever partakes of its nature . . . no true demonstrations can be found" (P164).[2]

Thinking in proofs that proceed from axioms is limited in what it can prove. It cannot prove the axioms themselves. To be sure, this impotence of reason makes its weakness evident but does not diminish the certainty of such cognition. The skeptics are wrong. "For knowledge of first principles, such as the existence of space, time, motion, numbers, is as sound as any knowledge furnished by our reasoning" (St395; B282). But whence this certainty if it is beyond proof? It rests on the "heart" and the "intuition": "It is on the knowledge supplied by the heart and instinct that reason rests, founding thereon all its utter-

[2] References preceded by P are to *The Miscellaneous Writings of Pascal,* trans. by George Pearce.

ances" (cf. St345; B282). Principles are felt, propositions deduced. The result is certainty reached by different routes.

That means: We know truth not only through reason but also by the heart. The heart, however, not only gives us the principles of rational cognition but also raises us up to God. "It is the heart, not reason, that feels God" (St345; B278). The proofs of cognition do not reach that far.

Le coeur à ses raisons, que la raison ne connaît point. What this famous sentence expresses in its brevity defies simple translation:

1) "The heart has its reasons which reason does not know" (St343; B277) means that the reasons that point to the actuality of God cannot be grasped by reason; it omits that the heart grasps even those reasons and axioms which are the points of departure of inferential reason.

2) If we were to apply the differentiation of reason and intellect that has been operative in Germany only since Kant, we might say: "The heart has its reason, which the intellect does not know"; but then we would be thinking within the context of a philosophy alien to Pascal.

3) If we translate with seeming literalness: "The heart has its reasons, which reason does not know," the double meaning is lost. The plural *raisons* also means "grounds"; the singular does not.

4) Again literally, but in a different way: "The heart has its reasons which the intellect does not know"; but here we lose what is essential, namely, what lies in the paradox created by Pascal's choice of the word *raison*. In the simplicity of differentiating the not provable axioms from the provable consequences, the fact is lost that the thought processes in inferential thinking and the thinking of faith are by no means identical; both perhaps have different axioms. Pascal grounds the axioms themselves in the heart; however, the heart can grasp much more than these and than axioms generally. The consequence of this simplicity would be that both in theology and in mathematics conclusions would be arrived at on the basis of axioms understood by the heart. But the axioms of mathematics are clear and simple, whereas in theology there are no corresponding irrefutable evidences, but only devolutions. Axioms in theology would not be simple and clear, but would contain ambiguities which preclude the possibility of reasoned inference. We cannot follow what Pascal demanded for this kind of reasoning: to put the definition in the place of what is defined.

Pascal understood that our inferential thinking is suspended in air, as it were. We cannot prove its grounding in axioms; its goal, actuality, cannot be reached by inferential thought. If actuality is the reality of nature, then inferential thought reaches beyond logic toward experimentation. If the actuality is that of God, then thought subordinates itself to something that can be neither reached nor comprehended through thinking.

Thought merely enables us to incline the heart to receiving the actuality of God by means of thought that leads to the shipwreck of thought itself or everywhere manifests its actual foundering.

By way of radical formalization, modern logic has sought to achieve absolute certainty without an object of actuality. Its interest for philosophical thought lies in determining whether this is possible or whether the absence of contradiction is unachievable even here (cf. Gödel).

Even if a formal science free of contradiction is possible—probably in the form of an arbitrarily closed system, in which some specific acts or questions must be forbidden and the mention of infinity excluded in any sense—such science would not arrive at actuality. It would be a mental game reducible to tautologies.

Cognition of truth cannot be grounded solely in freedom from contradiction. In the discovery of reality, contradiction is merely the prod to drive this discovery forward; in the thinking of truth that is not in the nature of scientific investigation, contradiction is its inescapable form. Pascal was aware of this: "Contradiction is a poor sign of truth; much that is certain is open to contradiction; much that is false passes without contradiction. Neither is contradiction a mark of untruth, nor absence thereof a mark of truth" (St95; B384).

b) *The "art of persuasion."* Our starting point was Pascal's fundamental experience of endless discussions leading to no agreement. He sought unanimity. He suffered under its absence.

Truth is what binds us to each other. Unanimity grows from our seeing jointly the one truth.

Can we persuade each other?

1) Obviously we can when reason, or spirit *(raison, esprit),* determines our views. Here the art of persuasion consists of the unadulterated and correct use of the means of inferential knowledge. There are three:

To determine concepts by way of definitions.

To posit evident principles or axioms.

In the process of proving, always to substitute, mentally, definitions for things defined (P159).

2) But wherever it is a question of the reason of the heart—hence everywhere in daily life and in the most important moments of our

life, hence where the other truth speaks out—what then constitutes
the art of persuasion?

(a) First of all Pascal sets aside the most important, the all-encompassing truths, the divine truths. He would not "consider including
them in the subject matter of the art of persuasion; for they are infinitely superior to nature. It is by a Divine power alone that these things
find an entrance into the soul."

Not all of Pascal's thoughts that strive to guide us to God, to Christ,
to salvation, and to the authentic One Truth intend the impossible, that
is, to persuade the reader of the truth of revelation; instead, they intend
to guide him onto the road of thinking that leads to his readiness to
receive the truth of faith through divine grace.

(b) But then the entire practical question concerning almost all reciprocal associations in life arises: How does persuasion come about
where proof is impossible for the intellect following the rules presented,
where, instead, the door leads through feeling, heart, will?

(1) Principles of the will: these are the desires natural and common
to all, "such as the desire for happiness . . . together with various particular objects" which everyone chases, "and which, falling in with their
own inclination, are as powerful over the will (although, perhaps, most
pernicious in their nature) as if they were capable of constituting their
truest happiness" (P151).

"Thus we find that the art of persuasion consists as much in concili-
ating the will as in convincing the judgment; so much more are men
swayed by inclination rather than reason" (P153).

(2) For this Pascal is unable to supply us with guidelines. The "art
. . . of pleasing is, beyond comparison, more elaborate, more refined,
more useful and more interesting: the only reason why I do not attempt it is that it is beyond my power.

"Not that there are not some rules for gaining over the inclination,
as infallible as those for convincing the judgment; and anyone perfectly
skilled in them would be as certain of success in carrying with him the
favor of every class of persons—not even excepting sovereigns themselves—as of demonstrating the elements of geometry to those who
have sufficient intelligence to grasp the system. But I consider . . . that
it is impossible to attain to such a degree of skill" (P154).

(3) "The cause of this extreme difficulty is that the sources of pleasure are not fixed and permanent. They differ in different men; and
even in the same individual, they are so variable that there are no two
persons to be found equally different from each other. . . . The pleasures of the man . . . differ from those of the female; those of the rich

from the poor; the tastes of the prince, of the warrior, of the merchant, the citizen, the peasant—all differ. . . .

"There is, however, an art—and it is that now proposed to be unfolded—which exhibits the connection of truths with their principles; as well those that convince the understanding, as those that please the taste, provided the principles once avowed be firmly and consistently maintained" (P154–55).

2. The orders

Pascal founds an order in the modes of truth. In this way he has a framework available in which everything that occurs in the form of assertions, actions, inner states has its place.

Regarding the Order of the Orders (cf. St37, 321; B332, 793):

Here seems to be the center and the overview of the entirety of Pascal's thought. As so many other philosophers do, he constructs a system in which the thinker knows himself to be safe and secure, knows himself placed within an order and belonging within the meaning of a whole.

In his doctrine of orders Pascal seems to know with his understanding more than is possible for the thinking of finite beings in their fallen state.

Could we and ought we to turn Pascal's thinking into a philosophical system, consider it as fundamental? And on what basis? Perhaps founded in the doctrine of the orders, or the doctrine of man's condition?

Pascal might thus appear as the thinker capable of an encompassing overview, of a great design, who, like so many others, seemingly knows his place as an outside observer.

However, no system is able to order, ground, construct the whole; nor is it Pascal's hidden intention to create such a system.

The systematically constructed thoughts which taken singly appear to be fundamental are perverted by Pascal's commentators into a structural basis, into his main concern—suggestive by their great number.

Yet these thoughts serve a different purpose; they are meaningful precisely by virtue of their variety and even their contradictions.

In singling out one such systematic thought and placing it at the center, Pascal's movement of thought is simplified to the point of misunderstanding. The working of his thought takes many paths (in the sciences, in mathematics). What is their direction?

Pascal rejected the "scientific philosophy" represented by Descartes.

But all thinking requires a construct of concepts, without which a certain degree of unambiguousness as well as intelligibility would not be possible. Hence Pascal's thinking also displays some characteristics lending themselves to be separated out and being presented as "doctrine." After all, rejection of scientific philosophy implies a certain degree of participation in it. Among these doctrinal characteristics (besides the theory of man and that of the modes of truth), Pascal's theory of the three orders of things is the most conspicuous.

The Three Orders of Things:

the realm of material power, of the body, the flesh

the realm of spirit

the supernatural realm of divine love (cf. St321; B793).

a) *There are three orders,* that of the flesh, the spirit, the will. To the carnal realm belong the wealthy, the kings; their object is the body. Inquirers, scholars, take the spirit as their object. The object of sages is justice; wisdom is love, *charité.*

The three orders stand in relationship to the three ways of our ruin: sensuality leads to concupiscence (the evil desires); the spirit, to prying; wisdom, to pride, to vanity.

This last—wisdom (love, will)—as the seat of vanity is unavoidable: "for the contradiction cannot be reconciled that a man has grown wise and is wrong when he is praised for it, for that is right" (B460).

Hence the following demand is made of all three orders: God is to reign over everything, and everything is to refer to Him. Wisdom does not come from itself. God gives it. Therefore: "He that glorieth, let him glory in the Lord" (I Corinthians 1:31).

In their natural existence and their reason—and this applies to all three orders—human beings are left with nothing but despair and pride. Men can be liberated solely through grace, which is tendered to the despairing and lost by the proud (cf. B524).

"Great men of genius have their empire, their splendor, their greatness, their victory and have no need of earthly greatness with which they have no relation. . . .

"The saints have their empire, their splendor, their victory . . . and need no greatness of the flesh or the spirit with which they have no relation, neither adding to them nor taking from them. They are seen by God and the angels, not by bodies nor inquiring spirit: God suffices them."

Christ "stands in His order of holiness." He came "to the eyes of the heart which discern wisdom." He was poor, He made no scientific discoveries, He did not reign but "He was humble, patient, holy, holy before God, terrible to evil spirits, sinless. . . . Archimedes had no need to play the prince (prince though he was) in his books of geometry. Our Lord Jesus had no need, in order to shine in His Kingdom of holiness, to come as king; but He came in all the splendor of His order" (St323; B793).

The orders are not immutable in their schematic identity but their meaning stays unvaried.

The third order is sometimes seen as present in man, and then again as purely divine, sensed only by way of the "heart."

b) *Between the orders there is no transition, but a leap.* The distance between them is infinite. "The infinite distance between body and spirit [in the natural world] is symbolic of the infinitely more infinite distance between the spirit and love, for love is above nature" (B793).

Where there are analogies between the orders, they only serve to sharpen their utter dissimilarity. For example: In the realm of the world of bodies, the mighty are in command over their subjects; this relationship is one of force. In the order of the spirit, the lesser spirits are persuaded by the more powerful ones; this relationship is a free one.

c) *The higher orders cannot be perceived from the viewpoint of the lower ones.* "The greatness of the spiritual men is invisible to kings, the rich, the captains and all the carnal great ones. The greatness of wisdom, which is nothing if not God-given, is invisible to the carnal and to men of spirit. The saints are seen by God and the angels but not by bodies or inquisitive spirits."

"Some people can admire only earthly greatness, as though greatness of the spirit did not exist; others admire only greatness of the spirit, as though there were not in wisdom an infinitely higher order" (B793).

d) *Seen from the viewpoint of the higher orders, the lower ones lose all their luster.* "All bodies, the firmament, the stars, the earth and its kingdoms, are not comparable to the spirit at its lowest; for the spirit cognizes it all and knows itself; and bodies know naught of it. All bodies together and all spirits together and all their works are of less worth than the smallest act of love. Love is of an infinitely higher order.

"It is absurd to take offense at the lowliness of Jesus Christ, as if His lowliness were of the order of the greatness which He came to display" (B793).

e) *The higher orders are not brought forth by the lower ones.* They originate from above, not from below. "From all bodies together one cannot extract one little thought. . . . From all bodies and spirits we cannot extract a single impulse of true love" (B793).

Now follows a final, crucial, aspect of Pascal's doctrine of orders:

f) *The higher orders do not need the lower ones.* "Great men of genius have their empire . . . and need no carnal greatness with which they have no relation. . . . The saints . . . need no greatness of the flesh or the spirit with which they have no relation, neither adding to them nor taking from them. . . . God suffices them" (B793).

The higher orders have no need of the lower ones because they have their ineradicable being for themselves. They do not need to conform to the lower ones and do not need to gain actuality by embodying themselves in them. Pascal believes that the higher orders can have independent, separate being.

Pascal does not seem to address the question concerning the manner in which the higher orders appear among the lower ones, except in one instance: they are not intuited, do not matter, are destroyed insofar as, measured against the lower order's yardstick of reality, they lose their existence. Such an answer is possible because Pascal in his rejection of the world maintains the supranatural existence without the prop of natural existence, the dissociation of the orders, their lack of interlocking relationship.

g) *The consequences of the proposition in f.* Pascal, however, does not rest content with this split. The situation within the world is compelling. As reality it cannot be ignored but has to be comprehended and interpreted in its full scope. Pascal does both. In this way his political thinking comes into being.

Within the world, as existence in the world, everything is subject to conditions of power and brute force. True, these are unproductive forces, able to destroy or allow room for everything. Power and brute force encroach, not, to be sure, on the true meaning, but on the visible manifestation of the higher orders.

1) An example: "On the Condition of the Great."

(a) "You owe to a multitude of chances not only that you are the son of a duke but that you are born into this world at all. . . . You hold, you will say, your revenues from your ancestors; but is it not the result of numberless accidents that your ancestors acquired, and have retained, the possession of them?"

(b) "That order is founded alone on legislative enactments originating, perhaps, in the soundest reasons, but none of which assume any natural right on your part to these things. Had our forefathers thought fit to enact that the possessions . . . should revert to the commonwealth after their death, you would have had no ground for complaint.

"Thus, then, the whole title . . . is not one conferred by natural right, but by human regulation. . . ."

(c) "I say not that they do not belong legitimately to you. . . . God . . . has permitted societies to make laws . . . and once these laws are enacted it becomes a crime to violate them."

(d) The right by which you possess power and wealth is not founded in any "qualification or merit in yourself. . . . Your soul and your body might have been, indifferently, those of a sailor or of a duke."

(e) What follows from this? "That you ought . . . to entertain a *double* habit of thought; and that, if among men you comport yourself in a manner conformable to your rank, a deeper, but no less true conviction should suggest that by nature you possess no advantages over them. If the avowed thought elevate you above the generality of mankind, let the inward reflection humble you, by showing you the perfect equality . . . between yourself and all your fellow-men."

(f) "The people who admire you know perhaps nothing of the secret. They regard the great as almost of a different species. . . . Do not dispossess them of this illusion, but . . . abuse not your elevation to arrogance and, especially, do not mistake yourself. . . .

"Most important is this caution! . . . All the excesses, all the follies, all the outrages of the great arise out of their ignorance of what they really are" (P263–67).

(g) The two orders: "There are in the world two kinds of greatness . . . greatness due to institutions and natural greatness." Greatness due to institutions grants distinction to certain conditions—that of aristocrat or of commoner, of the elder of a house or the younger.

"The matter was, perhaps, one of indifference before the institutions arose; afterwards it became a right and cannot be violated without injustice."

Natural greatness, independent of man's whims, ". . . consists in real and effective qualities of the soul or of the body, such as intelligence, virtue, health, strength."

(h) "We all owe some consideration to one or the other of these descriptions of greatness. . . . To external greatness we owe the marks of external respect: that is, certain ceremonial observances . . . properly accompanied with an external conviction of the fitness of the tribute. . . . The sovereign is addressed on bended knees, we stand in the chamber of princes. It is a mark of folly and baseness of spirit to with-hold from them these distinctions.

"But natural and intrinsic reverence is the due only of natural greatness: on the other hand, we justly feel contempt and aversion toward qualities opposed to this native superiority."

(i) The distinctions: "It is not incumbent upon me, because you are a duke, to esteem you; but it is incumbent upon me to offer you the most respectful salutations. If I see you to be both a duke and a good man, then I render my dues to you in both these characters. . . . But if you were a duke and not a good man, still I would give you your dues; for . . . I may still retain that inward contempt which the unworthiness of your character has incurred from me."

(j) The "abuse consists in attaching internal reverence to accidental distinctions; or in claiming adventitious ceremonies as the due of natural eminence. M. N. is a greater geometrician than myself; in that capacity he desires to take precedence of me. I tell him, he understands nothing about the matter. Geometry is an accomplishment of our nature: it demands the tribute of our respect; but men have not attached to it any external distinctions. Then I am entitled, in society, to precedence over him, but I hold him superior to me as a geometrician. In the same way if you, because you are a duke . . . would not be contented with my standing bareheaded before you but insisted on my esteeming you, I should ask you to show me those qualities for which you claim respect. But if you could not do so, the injustice would be on your side and assuredly you would not obtain your demand . . ." (P267 – 70).

(k) What is dominion? "My endeavor is to make you acquainted with your true condition in the world." All wish and hope "by means of the services and deference they render you to obtain some share of the benefits they seek and of which you . . . have the bestowal. . . . You then are . . . but the sovereign of evil desires . . . which constitute your power, that is, the possession of those things which the cupidity of men most affects. . . . Conscious of your true condition, improve the means it puts in your power and aim not at another dominion than that it confers upon you.

"Lay yourself out to satisfy their reasonable desires, alleviate their needs, derive your pleasure from beneficence; promote in every way their welfare . . ." (P270 – 72).

(1) But this course, open to you, does not amount to very much. "If you stop there, you will be a *lost* man! But your ruin will be, at least, not unattended with a measure of repute." You may not stop at this

stage in life. "You should despise both evil desires and the sovereignty it confers on you; and aspire to the domain of the love of God. . . . I leave it to others to point you to her paths."

Auerbach writes: "Being well dressed means showing one's power . . . the people have a healthy instinct when they respect power and its outward signs, even though they are in error regarding the motives of their respect; they believe they have to respect power because it is just; this is a mistake. Power is to be respected not because it is just but in itself, because it exists; however, it is dangerous to enlighten the people regarding this mistake of theirs" (A61).[3]

(2) Tyranny: Pascal's descriptions of this condition can be summarized in a principle.

The state of tyranny consists in the encroachment of the lower orders upon the higher ones. Pascal calls this tyranny and speaks of an "ought." "Tyranny is the desire to dominate everywhere, even beyond one's domain."

Different great families, "strong, noble, good souls and pious, each master in his own house and nowhere else; and sometimes they meet in battle, and the strong and the noble fight—fools that they are—to see who is master; for their mastery is of different kinds. They cannot agree, and their mistake is to try to lord it everywhere. That is impossible even for might; in the kingdom of wisdom, might is powerless; might is only master of external action . . ." (cf. St37–39).

"So such expressions as 'I am beautiful, therefore I must be feared' and 'I am strong, therefore I must be loved' are untrue and tyrannical.

"To try to gain one way what can only be had in another way—that is tyranny. Different homage is due to different merit—homage of love to charm, of fear to might, of belief to knowledge. . . ."

It is equally untrue and tyrannical to say: "He is not mighty, so I will not esteem him; he is not clever, therefore I do not fear him" (B332).

The meaning of might (force) and right in Fragment B298; the condition of tyranny:

"It is right that what is right should be obeyed.

"It is imperative that what is mightier should be obeyed.

"Right without force is impotent.

"Force without right is tyrannical.

"Right without force is flouted, because there is never any lack of delinquents.

---

[3] References preceded by A are to Auerbach.

"Force without right is condemned.

"Right and force must therefore combine, and to this end what is right must be made mighty, or what is mighty made right.

"Right lies open to dispute.

"Might is easy to recognize and is undisputed.

"So we cannot wed might to right, because might resists right, saying that right lies with her.

"And so, unable to bring it about that what is right should be mighty, we have made the mighty right" (B298).

(3) Nature and original sin: Concerning Pascal's belief in original sin, this doctrine is just in its injustice. For through the Fall of Man we have lost our authentic nature.

The radical difference from Montaigne: in Montaigne, "custom" is foremost. The customs that are becoming and have become traditional "become strong and noble as they flow along, just like our rivers." In Pascal, customs follow from arbitrary acts of might, the whim of the lawmakers. Auerbach: "Might could, at any time, repeat this arbitrary act and bring down custom." Pure might arbitrarily shapes customs to suit its purposes; it has "the capacity freely to create right." And this happens rightfully for there is no other right than that established by might (A54).

Quarrels cannot be decided according to merit and right: "Which one of us has precedence, you or I? You have four lackeys, I have one: the situation is unequivocal, one merely needs to count" (A54).

On corruption of human nature Montaigne says on occasion "that we have lost our nature and that only art and custom have remained— but yet man relies on this nature or . . . on this nature reshaped by tradition into custom—he lets himself be guided by custom as he lets himself be guided by nature—the current of historical life embraces him, and he willingly lets himself be embraced by it . . ." (A55).

Pascal: The world is "fundamentally and necessarily evil" in sharpest contrast to the kingdom of God: choosing whether one wants to follow the latter or the former.

(4) Summary of Pascal's Basic Attitude: Three ideas on Pascal's political theory:

"His hatred of human nature (and hence of his own); his unmasking of existing right as merely posited and wrongful; and his acknowledging this wrongful right as the only one that rightfully exists" (A57).

This condition is just in its injustice.

Auerbach: "*Folie* means folly as well as madness; hence I do only little violence to Pascal, I exaggerate only slightly if I summarize his idea as follows:

"The arrangement of the world is madness and violence;

"The Christian has to submit to the madness, must not move a finger in order to improve it; for it is God's will that madness and force rule, it is the true justice we deserve; the triumph of madness and force, the triumph of evil on earth is willed by God.

"Not many will be found wanting to live under such a paradox and remain Christians; but Pascal also says . . . the Christian religion is *la seule religion contre la nature, contre le sens commun* . . ." (A64).

(5) Pascal's truth and Augustine's thought: Although this denial of the world amounts to an incalculable loss to philosophic consciousness, it also directs a positive light on all that is eliminated when our being is turned exclusively toward existence. Pascal thinks the thought by which man's shipwreck, the annihilation of existence, the vanishing and obliteration of existential possibilities are not simply brushed off as nothingness but are named and acknowledged. Thought expresses the eternal nature of each act of love, in contradistinction to the fleetingness of mere acts of existence. But these acts of love are solely those of the love of God.

This is an intensification of the Augustinian thought. Augustine: *uti—frui:* to love creatures not for their own sake but for the sake of their creator: to them we owe *amor transitorius,* not *mansorius* (cf. A57).

"It is reported of Pascal that toward the end he behaved to those closest to him with a certain coldness, warding off the affection they showed him since it meant depriving God" (A57).

Expressed radically: "that love for creatures necessarily leads to disappointment, even despair. For in this case the object of love is transitory, as a whole as well as in its individual qualities for which it is loved. The idea of the transitory nature of what is loved was unbearable to him . . . an abomination. Whatever is transitory, whatever must return to the void, for Pascal is nothingness: Heaven and earth, family and friends, one's spirit and one's body; God alone endures . . . God alone is worthy of our love . . . the fleetingness of human beings . . . all this is the consequence of original sin . . ." (A57–58).

h) *Concluding remarks.*

1) Generally there was no political thinking in Port-Royal, only in Pascal. In Port-Royal there was no political theory, only instruction regarding the attitude of the Christian vis-à-vis the world; detachment from it and submission to it, the former internally, the latter externally.

External detachment is linked to internal cloistral seclusion (following the will of God as shown in circumstances and signs; cf. A55).

But even "within the world detachment can be practiced by averting one's heart and participation from its pleasures and desires but sharing in its cares and suffering, for suffering is the strongest bond that binds us to Christ" (ibid.).

The evil in the world is given scope as the rightful punishment and penance. "Port-Royal did not think about political theory." Pascal experienced the terrible crisis of Port-Royal: "In these years the problem of right and might became relevant for him" (A56, 57). Theory of current right as mere custom (Montaigne) with the Augustinian theory of the world as the kingdom of evil: custom as product of might, nothing but the arbitrary will of evil.

2) "Three Discourses on the Condition of the Great."

Submission and simultaneously extremely revolutionary thinking if God and the dogmatics of original sin, or even only the latter, were omitted. The accidental nature of right, of rank.

3) Pascal's historical position within the series of doctrines of orders: His theory of orders, not systematically thought through but posited and applied as though self-evident, belongs within the series of doctrines of orders that run through the history of philosophy. Such doctrines are formulated in a variety of modes, from expressing existential forces to classification of subject areas of research. Kierkegaard's doctrine of stages demonstrates the reversion of Existenz in the leap of decision and eludes objectivization. The doctrine of levels of soul, body, of beings as such, makes cognitive consciousness aware of specific realms of objects. Realms of Being can be called to mind which are characterized by their manner of encompassing the subject-object dichotomy (I-object, existence-environment, spirit-idea, Existenz-transcendence). But the manner has to be such that living within them is the condition for being able to understand them. All orders entail series of higher and lower levels.

With regard to full development and clarity Pascal's doctrine of orders cannot bear comparison to the great orders of Aristotle, Plotinus, Thomas, Dante, or with that of Kierkegaard. But it shares with Kierkegaard as essential trait that primacy is given not to theoretical teaching (reducing knowledge to schemata of objectively cognized levels of Being) but to its power to awaken. Pascal and Kierkegaard do not satisfy a desire to know but stimulate the unrest that urges on to decision.

3. Science

Science has its place in the order of the spirit. In his youth Pascal had turned to it with all his passion and did not relinquish it later on when it assumed the character of a subordinate mental game.

a) *The method of the new natural science.* Pascal clearly discerned the new natural science, seeing it as based on the combination of the cogent method of the geometric mind-set with experimentation. He applied this method himself by taking comparative measurements of the height of a column of mercury in a barometer on a mountaintop and on the plain. In constructing his calculator, he acted in the spirit of technology, and likewise in the calculating organizational spirit as he mapped out routes for an omnibus service in Paris (in his will he even disposed of his income from the latter). All these matters functioned practically and appropriately.

Pascal grasped the progress characteristic of natural science. "Is not this treating with indignity the reason of man and putting it on a par with mere animal instinct? We annihilate the main difference between the two; which is that the acquisitions of reason are incessantly accumulating, while instinct remains ever stationary. The cell of the bee was exactly constructed a thousand years ago as at this day. . . . Nature conceals her mysteries . . . although always alike and unchanged, her operations are not always equally known. The insight into these secrets through experimentation . . . is continually augmenting; and as this furnishes the groundwork of physical science, the results . . . multiply in proportion. . . . Compared to us the Ancients were in the state of infancy. Our eyes see farther . . . we see more . . . than they" (cf. P114–15).

In science, authority does not count, nor do books. Truth must always take precedence "even though newly brought to light. Truth is in herself more ancient than any conjectures that were ever formed concerning her; and it would be to know little of her nature to suppose that she *began to be* only at the time when she began to be known" (P 114–19). In physics the boldness to invent something new is appropriate, whereas in theology this is presumption. Each person begins work on the level reached by his predecessors and surpasses it, and the same will be true of those who come after him. The progress of inventions knows neither end nor interruption.

Pascal thought entirely along the lines of modern mathematical natural science. This manner of thinking turned him into an opponent of Descartes. He rejected Descartes's precipitate system as entirely wrong, since it proceeds by speculative construction instead of verifying experiment. As a consequence of Cartesian thinking, the idea of progress ends up in the fundamental cognition of the whole, a cognition that knows progress only in the particular, in completion and confirmation. This, however, does not conform to the new science but in a general sense to past forms of philosophy. Pascal's criticism has two motives. In the first place he recognizes in line with exact natural science the superficiality of mere theory unsupported by experimental verification. Second, he rejects the grounding of philosophical thought in scientific knowledge. For him, such purely rational thinking is not the basis of philosophy but only of the inferential sciences. For the same reason he also shuns the road of Malebranche, who, in contrast to Descartes and deeply affected by transcendence, invented a harmonious philosophical system using Cartesian means. Counter to all such philosophizing, Pascal experienced the human condition in his own way, in the passion of despair, and found his salvation in faith of such radical nature that it bears no comparison to the faith of Descartes or of Malebranche.

b) *Pascal cannot be claimed as a witness to modern scientific attitude.* Even if Pascal, in contrast to Descartes, is closer to modern science, grasping it in its method, its open-endedness in its unforeseeable progress, its independence, its unphilosophic character, he still by no means can be claimed as witness to the modern scientific attitude. Limited to the mathematical, experimental, and mechanical methods, he did not penetrate to truly scientific thinking itself. He did not have a sense of the universality of the scientific attitude that, by the variety of its methods and in a process that is endless, makes accessible—though never completely—whatever becomes an object for its universally valid and cogent insight. It is astonishing how uncritical Pascal can be in specific cases, though comprehending the logic of proof and of the cognition of nature.

To be sure, in his cosmology he gives reasons why the correctness of Galilei's theses (and therefore also those of Copernicus) cannot be decided on the basis of papal bulls. But contrary to the insights already gained by Kepler and Galilei he sticks to the worldview of Tycho Brahe: "It is right in my opinion not to probe the mind of Copernicus . . ." (St81; B218).

The methods of historical and philological-hermeneutic research are far from his mind. He accepts the allegorical interpretation of the Bible without the slightest misgivings regarding the matter of proof. The prophecies and miracles of the Bible he treats as facts that serve him as evidence. Even in that which is most specifically his own, namely, the relentless illumination of human self-deceptions, and in his attack on the ways of skepticism which put in question man's state and his cognition, Pascal's sense of truth is limited by the passion with which he shows us only what is hopeless and unbearable. Through total hatred of the world and of self he opens up, to be sure, grandiose vistas that others keep hidden. But by absolutizing these vistas into a cognized whole—grounded not in scientific certainty but in faith—his insight, owing to its lack of independence, becomes untrue.

c) *Natural science and common misunderstanding of its respective steps and of its results,* its perversion and its meaning:

1) As stated at the beginning, the ways of thinking that are modern in their development and their particular forms of expression are grounded in the seventeenth century: in the natural sciences, in science generally, in political thought, in the philosophy of Existenz, in the new open-ended universality, in the complete openness in experience and thinking, in the vast possibilities of actualization and total ruination.

2) What gives the study of all this its paramount importance is the confrontation, from the very beginning, with truth and its reversal, with the new together with the utterly ancient.

What we are used to calling the "modern age" in contrast to earlier ages, conceived as something clearly set off, whole and new in its nature, may in fact not exist at all.

The modern age is more often characterized by new reversals than by the new great experiences, achievements, and possibilities, which make penetrating minds prefer life today to that in any other age, to feel fortunate to be men of their time.

I have attempted to demonstrate this reversal in Descartes as much more of a beginning and model of modern ruination than as a witness and cocreator of the truths of our age as they have recently become evident. With this I have touched upon the fact that Bacon's mechanism (with which Descartes was in complete agreement) did not lay the foundation of modern natural science and technology, but, rather, of the attendant erroneous attitude and corruption in their ways of comprehending truth, which by no means necessarily attach to modern natural science and technology.

4. Pascal's thinking in science, philosophy, theology

Pascal's essential thinking ranges between science, philosophy, and knowledge of faith—in all three of which he participated.

a) *The indifference of natural science,* in which Pascal participates as investigator: He was one of the first to recognize the limits of science, since its results and methods have no bearing on the salvation of the soul. They are unable to provide experience and evidence for something that replies to core questions of human beings who expect to be enlightened about the road to salvation.

Pascal considers mathematics "to be the highest exercise of the mind but [I] see in it at the same time something so useless that I prefer a skilled artisan to a man who is nothing but a mathematician. I consider it to be the most beautiful occupation there is, but ultimately it is only an occupation, and I have said frequently that it is, to be sure, the greatest test but not the fulfilment of our powers; hence I would not take two steps for the sake of mathematics, and I am certain that you are totally in accord with me."

Considering Pascal's radicalness this indifference is possible only because he lacks the true motives for universal research, which are grounded in a fundamental attitude toward the actuality of the world and of nature.

Pascal lacks the attitude of the inquiring scientist, his passionate urge to orient himself in the world in every direction. He is ignorant of an inquiring spirit ranging into the infinite, and in this way realizing itself as it observes and invents.

Because for Pascal nature is seen only in the form of a mathematical-mechanical structure, and therefore is perceived as a reality that stands in no relation to him, he tellingly formulates his complete alienation: "The eternal silence of these infinite spaces fills me with fear" (St173; B206).

Pascal is incapable of adopting a basic attitude that allows human beings confronting the universe to admire its order, secure in the thought of its unknown guide, and finding a singular gratification in replicating the thoughts by which it has this order. He is ignorant of the structure that supports the grandiose philosophic consciousness of the Chinese, of having their being within the whole of the universe, a fundamental attitude shared, in a different mode, by Plato (in *Timaeus*); in another variation it is actualized by Giordano Bruno, and finds a voice in a multitude of poets and artists throughout the millennia before Christ and in the West as well. Pascal reacts like the sick man who states: I see the sun shining, but I don't feel it shining. But in Pascal this is not the lament of melancholia but the dread of a seeker after God for whom nature has no relevance. He rejects closeness to nature in favor of listening exclusively for God's voice, which is audible nowhere but on the road of revelational faith. He does not find rest in his grasp of the boundaries set to all our objective cognition, boundaries that are fixed in the limitation of this cognition and imposed by the forms of our consciousness-as-such, by its restriction to appearance, by foundering on the infinite. Rather, out of a desire for knowledge that for the measure of man is presumptuous, he basically postulates the alternative: all or nothing. In the light of an absolute and total knowledge, which is denied to man but is thinkable for him as a thought at the limit, he sees all our factual knowledge not only as insufficient but also as irrelevant and even reprehensible. Thus he finds himself in the position of wanting to lead by means of reason to the destruction of reason in order to see Christ appearing out of the abyss as the only salvation. So, science fades away for him.

Because for Pascal all scientific investigation sinks into triviality when measured against the idea of absolute cognition and its value for eternal salvation, he can reject scientific work as such. "Failing to perceive these two infinities, men have rashly plunged into an examination of Nature, as though they were in proportion to it." They tried what was impossible for them: to grasp the principles of things and from there to go on to know the whole. But you cannot embark on this without infinite presumption or infinite ability—infinite as nature herself. When, however, man becomes conscious of the never-to-be-transcended limits of his cognition, when he realizes that he will never be able to cognize the beginning or the end of things, then he will tremble, his curiosity will change into admiration. He will "rather gaze in silence beholding these marvels than dare to question them" (St21, 23; B72).

b) *The resistance to philosophy,* to which Pascal constantly reverts. He comprehended accurately the originally different ways of cognition, which he called the spirit of geometry, the *esprit de finesse,* and the *logique du coeur.* They all are ways of thinking. But Pascal did not rise to the consciousness of the logic of philosophic thinking which, by comprehending those three ways, includes them in its own activity, goes beyond them, and matures to a self-understanding without becoming *mathesis universalis.* Hence Pascal never arrived at primal philosophy.

Together with the spirit of research inherent in modern scientific endeavor and with a primal relation to nature, the philosophic attitude of thought is once more lost to Pascal. He misses the philosophical way which at the limits and through the limits awakens the reason of a possible Existenz to its own reality, so that—plunged in the darkness that is illuminated by ambiguous ciphers—it actualizes itself in the world in relation to transcendence. Whoever risks such philosophizing knows that in his freedom transcendence has been granted him as a gift; thus this whole world of appearance seems to become transparent and the consciousness of Being is given fulfillment from the ground of Being.

Ultimately Pascal rejects philosophy altogether. He sees it either merely as science, in which capacity it indeed does not accomplish anything, or as philosophy, of a kind whose thinking is completely wrong and leads to arrogance. In place of philosophy, only devoutly Christian certainty is acknowledged as valid.

c) *Pascal's inability to grasp theology,* which he approached with theological thinking. For him something beyond science and philosophy became all-important. Since he longed only for an absolute and all-embracing knowledge which entails the eternal salvation of the soul, authentic knowledge could consist only of knowledge through faith. This, however, he neither developed nor renewed. He based himself solely on traditional material. And as one reads the works of theologians, one gathers the impression that Pascal's theology is a poor theology. But then, he did not intend it to be theology.

5. *Conclusion*

Pascal's intermediate position in its productive rather than obscuring effect:

He leads us to the limits. By his clarity he makes the most profound contradiction accessible and enables us to follow his thought.

This is what makes his thinking so stimulating. Though it does not find a secure foothold anywhere (in order to see him as an extraordinary Christian, we have to adopt his sharply defined standards and to take into account his clearly stated intention and his self-abasement to be the ultimate meaning of his actions) his thinking, in its clarity and acuity, makes it possible to put the actuality of his life into words, a life that should concern us. This he achieves not by advancing his own doctrine but through the power of awakening, and ultimately through the Christian tragedy into which his life was transformed.

V. PASCAL'S STRUGGLE FOR TRUTH

Our presentation of Pascal's philosophy has demonstrated two aspects in turn: first, the circle of the desperate human situation and the liberation through faith in Christ's revelation. Second, the concern with knowledge and truth.

These belong together. The "theory" of truth and its orders shows the boundaries of our thinking, in which reason forces itself to self-sacrifice. Within this theoretically conceived framework evolves the circle that in Pascal may find its conclusion in the silence of the certainty of faith.

These aspects do not, however, unequivocally aim at the same central point. To be sure, Pascal's movement toward the obedience of faith and his wrestling for the truth were intended to find their identity through Christ in God. That is possible provided faith in revelation did not lay claim, in the world, to absolute authority via the agency of the Church which wields temporal power. Because Pascal acknowledged this claim, because Christ's revelation was present for him only in the Church, his relation with the Church became one of tension, and finally one of conflict even though, according to his own belief and thinking, such conflict was impossible. Death finally relieved him of settling this conflict, whether in favor of obedience or in revolt against the Church. In Pascal's case both seem impossible. His interpreters give conflicting answers, according to their respective faith. Those of Catholic persuasion base themselves on questionable documents intended to prove his obedience. Protestants see in him a "protestant" who in actual life did not get around to accomplishing the protestant act. We must content ourselves with the *non liquet*.

However, the events of the struggle and Pascal's statements may fairly be presented.

Pascal's struggle for the truth attains to greatness only with his crisis of 1653–54. Earlier, as mathematician and natural scientist, he had striven for that determinate truth whose limit and meaning were elucidated only later in his encompassing notion of the truth. The latter truth seeks not merely the correctness of specific cognition but a greater truth of all-important relevance to us since the eternal salvation of the soul depends on it. Even though, for Pascal, the receptacle of this one and only truth was Christian faith, it not only had to be grasped as doctrine of the Faith (*vide* his threefold conversion) but also had to bear witness in concrete situations, had to be regained in confrontation with unbelief and taught to the unbelieving. For this truth is not sufficient to itself; it needs to be imparted to everybody. It finds itself confronted with other truths, which it knows to be false. As it seeks to impart itself, it becomes involved in battle.

1. Reason and obedience to faith

Something on the surface, very simple, is at the core of the tension that Pascal, owing to the nature of the matter, was never able to overcome. True, his will to truth, his struggle for truth, takes place under Christian obedience to faith; but it has its own origin in Pascal's longing to experience this truth himself, in the way it has been granted to him: in science, in his outstanding discoveries; in faith, in his singular nocturnal experience of the certainty of God. Inwardly supported by both certainties, truth means to him—considering man's lost state—the dignity of being able to think out of the now hidden origin of the first creation. This became the origin of his practical difficulties with the ecclesiastical authorities, which deeply disturbed him.

The difficulty did not lie in Pascal's postulate of obedience to faith. What mattered to him was not only that the truth of the need for persuasive thinking and the truth of obedience to revelation were not mutually exclusive. He declared himself explicitly for obedience to faith and for obedience to the spiritual director representing the Church. "We know that all virtues, martyrdom, hardships and all good works are useless outside the Church and outside the community with the leader of the Church who is the Pope. I shall never separate myself from his community, at least I ask God to be merciful to me in this respect; without this I would be lost for ever."

This is Pascal's way of expressing the ancient shelteredness in faith that evidently dispensed infinite bliss, promising security for all eternity, which is anchored in the physical presence of this Church. Here he follows Augustine, who said he would not give credence to the Gospel were it not for the tangible presence of the Church. In this faith based on the Church, the earthly existence of a hierarchy, of rites, priests, and sacraments partakes of the nature of the divine and becomes the presence of God, separate from all other worldliness.

The philosopher cannot share in this fundamental experience. An actuality seems to be involved here comparable to that of objects in space and time. In Kantian philosophy space and time are conceived as conditions of all experience of reality and cannot be transcended by us. Similarly, the ecclesiastical, physically all-encompassing reality (though itself situated also in space and time) would have to be understood as the conditions of faith in God and everything which then results as absolutely essential for human beings. True, regarded from the standpoint of philosophy, this experience of truth in faith can be neither contested nor substantiated but is absolutely alien to philosophical thought. Its tendency is to raise a barrier between those having this experience and all others. It can have consequences in existence, in human actions, in the ethical realm of human solidarity based on unreserved communication, consequences justifiably open to radical spiritual criticism from philosophical quarters.

For ecclesiastical faith and philosophic faith encounter each other in space and time. And the believer in revelation as professed by the Church is himself subject to the reality of the Church as it is presently active in space and time. What happens when the content of revelational faith and ecclesiastical action—realized as it is by human beings in space and time—is contradictory in the view of the believing individual?

The argument for obedience to the Church rests in the fact that reason is never sufficient unto itself. "The last step that reason takes is to recognize that there is an infinity of things that lie beyond it" (St31; B267). Hence: "Nothing is so conformable to reason as this repudiation of reason." Pascal based himself on Augustine: "Reason would never surrender if it did not consider that there are moments when it must" (St357; B272, 270; cf. Augustine, *Ep.* 120, 3). But this subordination is by no means a repudiation of reason; instead, it acknowledges its limit: "If we surrender everything to reason, our religion will lose all mystery and the supernatural. If we offend against the principles of reason, our religion will be absurd and ridiculous" (St357; B273). Pascal never declared the absurd to be the sign of the truth of faith, nor did he ever accept the *credo quia absurdum*.

There is a distinct origin of truth which, in obedience to the ecclesiastical authorities in the world, in turn subordinates this obedience to the conditions of revelatory truth. Pascal did not formulate this ultimate origin in any explicit statement. In the world of reality this ultimate truth was what he suffered for. How this did happen and how he responded in such circumstances has to be related.

2. Sacrifice or rebellion

Papal authority demanded assent to the condemnation of five Jansenist theses denounced as heretical. Pascal advised against signing such a declaration. Almost everyone within the circle of Port-Royal was willing to sign; Pascal passionately argued against it. He rejected the evasive interpretation that differentiated between the question of truth and the question of fact (that is, whether the theses were heretical and whether they were traceable in Jansen's teaching; the first was to be admitted but not the second), even though he himself had raised the issue earlier. The papal declaration, he wrote, condemned the Jansenist concept of Grace. To sign it would signify betraying the faith. Since Pascal's pertinent memoranda were destroyed, his radicalism is deducible only from the replies he elicited. This was Pascal's last word on the subject; nothing further was added by him.

The Church's conduct toward Port-Royal and thus toward Pascal forms part of the series of shameful deeds committed by ecclesiastical authority (Bruno, Galilei, and innumerable others from the very beginning come to mind); moreover, it belongs to the worst among such deeds—those by means of which the adversary is not destroyed in body but is broken by means of his belief in the Church, by his very faith. The Church exerts her authority in demanding of him, in the denial of evident truth and evident justice, the forcible subjugation of his will-to-truth. He is coerced into doing this by his belief that outside the Church there is no salvation and hence God would be lost to him. A neutral observer might think that in such a confrontation the Church might appear to the believer as a grotesque human distortion when measured against the object of his faith. But this does not seem to have been the case.

Obedience to the Church, identified with the obedience of faith, with the subjugation of reason as well as with obedience to God, has forced man—but only in the world of Biblical religions—to an agonizing denial of one's own experienced objective necessities of thought as well as actualities of truths of faith. Hence submission to the Church was understood as a sacrifice, and its refusal as rebellion. For Saint Francis of Assisi, his submissive obedience caused immense suffering. Luther took the risk of breaking with the Church, at first reluctantly and finally in savage indignation, but nevertheless establishing immediately a new version of similar obedience. Throughout his entire life, Lessing opposed the halfheartedness and dishonesty he discerned in Enlightenment theology, but he engaged only briefly in his pitiless polemics against the pitiless form of orthodoxy of Chief Pastor Goeze, a battle that to him meant little more than a "farce" and a "squabble." Kierkegaard reserved his devastating exposure of the Church to the last months of his life, in complete independence. Referring himself to the New Testament, all he called for was honesty, not a following. Nietzsche merely indulged in a wild rampage against all of Christianity and its consequences, with no defined contemporary adversary. Prominent Catholic scholars of the nineteenth century have complied with the coerced recantation, remaining silent about their having been broken.

In comparison, Pascal appears to us in a different light. He died without recanting, shortly after having been drawn into the insoluble conflict between self-experienced truth and obedience to a papal decision and following the expression of his indignant dissent, couched in radical, uncompromising form. The conflict which, considering Pascal's faith and will, was ruled out as a possibility (truth being unable to stand in conflict with truth) actually remained unreconciled.

For Pascal, there was no way out: on one side was the authoritative dictum of the Church; on the other, the opportunistic humility of his Port-Royal friends. For as long as he could speak out, he continued the battle. For him, there was no possible compromise of the truth with an authoritarian dictum whose substance he considered untrue. When his illness sapped his strength for battle, he chose silence. Shortly before his death he desired and experienced the power of the Last Sacrament. No one will ever know what went on in his mind and heart throughout his mortal illness. Pascal's silence accompanied his bodily extinction. There is no indication allowing, with any degree of probability, assumption of a hidden meaning in his silence. (On the other hand, see Romano Guardini, *Christliches Bewusstsein, Versuch über Pascal.* Leipzig, 1935, 296ff.).

For Pascal, there were two fixed points: first, the cogent insight of mathematics and proof reached by experiment; second, the religious experience through the presence of the Church, through Christ and God in Biblical revelation, through those nocturnal hours (in November 1654) of absolute certainty whose meaning he set down in the *Mémorial.* He reflected on the origin and consequences of what he grasped on both paths; but next to the second, the first path shrank to a matter of indifference, though never something to be denied.

The meaning of his thought can be claimed by neither the Catholic nor the Protestant denomination. He did not join the Reformers, since he did not want to break with the Church. Nor was he an apologist for the Church, but, instead, for the Christian faith (even if he never made a distinction between Christian and Catholic faith). Pascal's faith came from a depth of experience whose meaning has precedence over the quarrels and battles of the denominations.

When his obedience in faith to the Church and his self-persuasive faith and urge to think came into conflict, Pascal was faced with an unsolvable dilemma. His relationship to Church and state (which in those days was the servant of the Church) became strained, but only in actual fact, not in his reflections on his faith. It is not known how it would have turned out had Pascal been confronted by the ecclesiastical powers with the problem of having to make a choice.

But in the study of his writings he comes close to us in a way that differs from our approach to theological writers. Whoever, by making the *sacrificium intellectus,* submits to the dogmatically formulated word of the Church has for the rest of us lost our trust in what he has to say about truth. It is impossible to decide whether or where that person speaks out of genuine conviction. We expect and find in such writings instances of bending the truth, of accommodation and sophistry that reveal suffering and defiance of the freedom that must now be hateful. Such obedience is rendered not only to the Catholic Church but also to modern totalitarianisms, as well as—unconsciously and chaotically— to the interests of groups, nations, parties. Whenever the suspicion of such obedience arises, our interest in listening soon comes to an end. But we never lose our trust in Pascal. No matter where his road diverges from ours, where we think we can discern his errors, there always remains the persuasiveness of his will to truth, a will that is relentless but also goes to the very limits, where it might turn a somersault. Let us look further into this process.

3. Pascal's battle

For Pascal the will to truth—for as long as he is able to speak out— equals the will to do battle.

He battles against the Jesuits (in regard to their morals), against Descartes (challenging his claim to being scientific), against Montaigne (questioning his approach to life), and against his own Port-Royal friends (with regard to the expediency of a subordination that goes counter to truth). He battles against the multitude of anonymous adversaries, the unbelievers. He seems to battle against all sides on ever-shifting fronts. It is a battle of the spirit, waged always on the level of absolute truth, a battle waged with bitterness, outrage, horror, contempt.

Pascal was not above accommodating himself to the pressures of his times, to seek effective cover for his criticism of Jesuits and Thomists under a pseudonym ("Montalte"), not without explaining repeatedly the reason for this subterfuge, stating, contrary to the truth, that he stood in no relation to the Jansenists. In his eighteen provincial Letters, which appeared singly and successively and caused a tremendous stir, he created the fiction of a neutral outsider with friends in all parties, who visits them, questions them, and reports their opinions. This he does for no other reason than love for the truth, in order to uncover what was really going on behind those excited discussions, behind the papal bulls and the censorship imposed by the Sorbonne. In the process he compromised everyone except the Jansenists. He achieved this through these letters, a masterpiece of great polemics, reverberating to this day. But surprisingly, the modern reader—so it seems to me—if he reads them not for the literary pleasure of their intrinsic artistry, but out of his own interest in truth, ultimately does not find himself satisfied. Of course Pascal is right in exposing theological arguments as sophisms of *distinguendum est* used for justifying anything whatever by the subterfuge of constant shifting; right in baring the will to power of the great orders and their opportunism, the technique of silence and of the mysterious, the claim to authority based solely on learning in cases where truth itself and established historical facts are at stake, in a style that recklessly piles on invective and abusive language (for instance, when the Jesuits denounce as insolent, blasphemous, damnable, and heretical a statement that can be found in Augustine and other Church Fathers), and the manipulation of the mood of the masses and majority opinion. But what also affects us is that Pascal in the heat of battle does not scruple to deploy eminently effective exaggerations and sweeping denunciation. His method does not confine itself to justified attacks on individuals or predominant trends, but aims at the very essence of the Jesuit order. What may appear proper at the height of a battle of minds in which one adversary has all the advantages of material might and power strikes us, when taken out of its historical context, as towering injustice.

In his battles Pascal insists on clear decisions. But we notice here a striking limitation: Whenever, in whatever context, he touches on the Creed, on obedience to the Church, he immediately ceases to interest us because of his perseverance in tradition and convention. He reveals to us that decisions of this kind are not truly existential. Existential "decisions" are resolutions that are not based on choice, but arise only in response to specific situations and with regard to determinable things. Pascal confronts us with decisions that are not decisions at all.

In the realm of reason Pascal described the battle between dogmatists and skeptics: The former maintain that you cannot doubt natural principles; the skeptics maintain the uncertainty of our origin, which includes the uncertainty of everything. And with this begins a war in which everyone must choose sides. For if you hope to stay neutral, you will be a skeptic as a result. Therefore he who is not against the skeptics joins their ranks. For the skeptics "are neutral, impartial, of two minds about everything including themselves" (cf. St149; B434). But this too is impossible. One cannot doubt everything, as, for example, whether one exists. Hence there has never been a perfect skeptic. "Nature comes to the help of impotent reason and prevents it from going so far astray" (St151; B434). But by no means is reason, as a result, in safe possession of truth. The most complete skepticism as well as the impossibility of complete skepticism is the road and the turning toward faith. From the position of faith arises the new battle, that of faith against unfaith.

If for him the sole fixed point is the certainty of faith and within it the love of God, then these appear in him as passion and not at all as unequivocal attitude. They are themselves in motion, in contradistinction to their always apodictic formulation.

Pascal's life demonstrates the drastic steps he took, an ultimate in ascetic self-torture, but does not manifest the serenity of a life grounded in decision. His thinking affects us deeply by its unrest, which not only *knows* about the earnestness of actualized Existenz but also continues to struggle in independence.

To a large extent Pascal's external battle is also a battle with himself. In the adversary he recognizes what he knows to be within himself. The ferocity of his battle with the others is conditioned by his constant struggle with the ego that he finds hateful. Seeming inwardly uncertain, he frantically clings to the certainty that he will attain someday by the many uses of reason, a certainty that transcends reason. Saturated with all skeptical motives, he finds truth only through revelation, in obedience. But he needs to elaborate by thinking the faith gained in this manner, to ground and to justify it. For him, it is not a tranquil presence except in moments of extreme enthusiasm; but in the state of rapture, it misses out on serenity.

4. Pascal's questioning of the battling stance

If Pascal's spiritual life is seen as a constant battle and his work as permeated by polemics, it might appear as though the battle itself was his main concern. We sense his pleasure in his superior powers, in his high-spirited sallies which badger the opponent, particularly the non-believer, with intellectual feats of supposedly cogent force. The intensity of his inspired passion for the truth combines with his combative spirit. This, however, alarmed him. He sensed his pride.

Hence, by means of his will to truth, he wanted to gain mastery over his pleasure in this truth—the pleasure that manifested itself in polemical form. "Even out of truth one creates an idol for oneself." For truth remains truth in love for God. Truth outside love of God is, as an image of God, an idol that one should neither love nor revere.

For Pascal, the battle for truth was not in itself an unalloyed satisfaction. It intoxicated and tormented him simultaneously. It did not
lead to his goal. Battling was understood by him as unavoidable, an
obligation as well as a new guilt.

In counterbalance to the actuality of his own polemics, Pascal advocated patience and humility in the battle for truth. For it is obvious
"that the same Providence which has enlightened the mind of one has
withheld that advantage from another." Yet the power that awakens
piety is not different from that which strengthens its adversary. In the
"spirit of self-affirmation" it may seem to us that the adversary serves
a God different from the one causing his resistance to us.

What is the spirit of self-affirmation? When we seek the success of
a cause by our own efforts only, we become irritated by opposition; we
feel a different principle governing our actions than these obstacles. Yet
the "spirit of humility" bids us be patient. But when "it is really God
who is the principle of our actions, we encounter nothing externally
that does not spring from the same principle which influences ourselves. . . . He who is the author of *our* conduct is the author of that
of our opponents, or, at least, permits the resistance they offer us." The
resistance, and the suffering it causes us, have their origin in God. "It
is far more certain that God permits this evil . . . than that he (and not
any other secret mover) does not produce the good in ourselves." We
are merely ". . . justified in a humble hope" that God elicits that passion
in us with which we believe we are battling for what is true.

"We act as if our own mission was to ensure triumphs to the truth,
instead of its being one only to contend for it." Our love of victory and
self-assertion seduces us: "We think we are aiming at the glory of God
when, in fact, we are only seeking our own" (P39–41). We confuse
victory with truth.

Pascal revolts against those who wish us to believe the truth by
proofs they themselves furnish, recognizing admirably the confusions
intrinsic in spiritual battle, and in the last year of his life he expressed
them with simplicity. With bitterness he opposed the bitterness that he
rejected in his opponents as well as in himself (a paradox he was unable
to overcome). Again we see the grandeur of honesty in his struggle. But
even Pascal cannot find a viable way out of the antinomy of contest—a
struggle fueled by the vainglorious passion of self-assertion as against a
struggle out of suffering, undertaken humbly in passionate devotion to
the truth; or struggle as an end in itself as against struggle as a role
imposed; or destructive struggle as against loving struggle. Pascal gives
free rein to the battle on the lower level of the hierarchy of orders but

cannot really change the nature of the battle itself, even though he comes close to it in some passages of this late letter.

Though it is one of his last statements preceding his final silence, Pascal's call to humility in battle cannot be taken as conclusive. The existential question remains open and the battle continues to be necessary. Even less do we find anything in the nature of subordination to the papal decree of recantation of his attack on the Jesuits. Rather, his divinely willed task remains unchanged: to fight for the truth that a human being is capable of perceiving. What matters solely is our inner attitude while doing battle and God who stands above all the truth we claim to be absolute, in a battle that may deteriorate into arrogance and presumption even though waged in the name of faith in revelation. This letter formulates one of the earliest gropings by one of the greatest polemicists toward transforming the fighting spirit, a transformation that remained elusive to him.

5. Final critical observations

Pascal's writings represent a grand example of polemics, not only because he engages in them but because he does so in full awareness and ceaseless searching for their meaning. They are part of the chain of writings in which thinkers experience spiritual battle as an existential problem. The question arises: Is it a battle fought on the basis of a common ground, objectively explorative and critical, or is it a destructive battle rejecting what is alien and denying its right to existence, or is it a loving struggle, an encounter between forces of truth in which each realizes itself without becoming one.

Nothing in Pascal speaks of loving struggle, and there is barely a striving for communication with forces that are and remain strangers to each other.

Though aspiring to ground all truth in the love of God, Pascal appears deficient in communication and love. This love of God is a love wholly different from love for human beings and the forces that speak to us in them. This love of God is compatible with the boundless egocentricity of a supposedly personal salvation of the soul, apart and separated from all other human beings in accordance with Pascal's dictum "Man dies alone." This retreat from a totally negated world to oneself as the singular one, the absolute point existing by the grace of God, in Pascal combines with passionate struggle in the visible world, which, owing to his intellectual honesty, ends in terrifying him.

VI. CHARACTERIZATION AND CRITICISM

a) Pascal proceeds everywhere to the ultimate, and it is the standpoint from which he sees everything. Thus he reduces the finite to nothingness before infinity. In the face of eternal perpetuity, in the face of infinity, even in the face of nature with its endlessly repeated sameness, Pascal makes all our existence disappear into absolute nullity and insignificance: The duration of our life in eternity is so infinitely far removed from the duration of our earthly life that ten more years of life on earth are of no import. Thus he argues against those to whom each day of loving companionship, of productive activity is precious. Since man in spite of all his research remains at infinite remove from perfect cognition, "does it matter if a person has a little more insight into things?" (B72). Thus he argues against the inquiring spirit which, in progressing and consciously creating a further step for those who will follow, is blissfully confident in the idea that there ought to be knowledge.

Pascal appears to be a soul in constant torment, inexorably pushed to the extreme limit. We notice the absence of cheer, of the relaxation that grows from deep trust, of humor. All-pervading terror and a passionate fighting spirit are evident in his wrestling within his inward self, informing his objective expositions, and cannot be ignored. This was forced on him by the vastness of his vision, which put him in constant combat with his total skepticism manifesting itself as despair and lack of faith, his pleasure in scientific knowledge eventually repudiated as useless, and his attacks on the moral impurity of the Jesuits, which he opposed because he had to overpower it in himself. He realized that the struggle itself leads to pride, and that combatting this pride by humility in turn makes humility proud. This vicious circling gave rise to his violence in his suppression of self as well as his thought processes; it was a temperamental violence which made him want to

b) It was Pascal's passion to unmask unreason in reason, to force reason to relinquish itself by reason. Hence his never-ending pleasure in paradoxes. In tune with ancient philosophical tradition, he successfully used paradox to point out the limits set to thought and to concrete knowledge; hence the element of truth. But by relentlessly playing with paradox as a forcibly imposed avenue to the grace of Christ is inappropriate to paradox and sinks to tendentious misuse. As a result, Pascal attains not only to the purity of dialectical transcendence but to the impurity of pretense. Because this occurs in an aura of strict conceptuality, clothed in language of pounding precision, the effect might be all the more repelling.

c) The energy of his mind was directed toward a truth that can be attained by force. To be sure, the insights he experienced in mathematical knowledge were not applicable to any other knowledge, but he wanted to bring about by virtually coercive means the cognition of faith through reason. In the service of a faith that itself is prey to doubt, the soul is to be conditioned by operations of thought to seek salvation through faith by the grace of God. Pascal's methodological writings display his passion for presenting clear, unambiguous, forcibly persuasive rules and their application. Such a stance is valid, however, only if one presupposes a universally valid truth, in faith as in mathematics and the natural sciences. He seems blind to the possibility of communication which, in questioning and loving encounter, strives toward clarification of what can never be the one and whole and all-encompassing truth. The true concern of Existenz is made subject to Pascal's verdict: "We should seek truth without faltering; and if we refuse, we show that we set more store on the esteem of men than on the search for truth" (St173; B211).

d) His life was governed by "negative decision." To love the world and to actualize this love in the world was beyond Pascal's capacity and temperament, as becomes evident in his thinking. Though not originally willed by him, solitude and lack of communication were the underlying principles of his thought. Bitterness and outrage at the unbelievers he addressed overwhelmed him—unbelievers by the light of his own Christian interpretation. The same principle implies a missing sense of historicity.

What is a sense of historicity? It means finding, within our earthly being and in relation to transcendence, existential certitude in loving and beloved communication. It means, because the unconditional speaks in us and sustains us, being able to content ourselves with what can be known and beyond that with knowing ignorance. It means being boundlessly fulfilled through actualization in time as cipher of eternity. Lacking a sense of historicity, we seek an analogue from which the possible historicity in our truth can no longer be seen. In solitude, not risking trust in anything in this world, focusing realistically on all that is evil, rotten, perverted, chaotic, using it as our source of information, we cleave, in our faith, to what is not of the world but utterly other, a kingdom of God without world, an eternal bliss, into which we can enter only after death. Become impersonal but still attached to human life, filled with self-hatred, devoid of love, fundamentally contemptuous of our own person and of all fellow beings and the world, our next step becomes denial of the world. This may take the form of ascetic practice, as in Pascal, or, as with others, in a dissolute life.

Historicity and actualization in history are destroyed by the sheer force of placing ourselves outside the world while being in it. Instead of a grounding in historicity in the here and now, exclusive validity is given to an incorruptible phantom—the absolute.

In Pascal we observe a persistent hatred, rooted in his faith and psychologically actualized: "The ego is hateful" (St79; B455). It is palpably evident in the unequivocal way in which he denigrates man, in the gleeful abandon with which he fostered his skepticism regarding world and reason, in his polemics.

An aura of loneliness envelops his thinking and his activities. Love *(charité),* so persistently in the foreground of his mind and considered by him as the highest good, appears to us as an abstraction manifested in extremes, in studied humility, in asceticism, in instances of self-abasement, in largesse to the poor. Even his doctrine of love suggests lovelessness. He was unresponsive to nature, applying to it merely a mathematically abstract and experimental understanding; he had no love for nature and no love for beauty, no appreciation for art or poetry. What he did have was a gift for the brilliant form of literary expression inaugurated by him. His nature and temperament had a tinge of illiberal inhumanity.

The human world for him denoted passion, physical love *(amour),* ambition, represented by society and its vanities. But for years he was in close touch with it and could not have moved in it without respecting its rules and manners.

e) Pascal disparaged all love directed toward him as well as toward the other. He consistently denied the possibility of self-being in this world: "What is the ego?" What is man that he should be loved? Neither the visible body, nor beauty (smallpox destroys it, but does not destroy the person, who is no longer loved), nor my judgment and my memory (I can lose these qualities without losing my ego), says Pascal, and asks further: "Where then is this *I* if it resides in neither the body nor the soul?" And why does one love both? Only because of "these qualities which do not make the 'I' since they are doomed to perish." Pascal concludes, "So we never loved anyone but only qualities." It is impossible to love "the soul of a person in the abstract, irrespective of the qualities." And he draws the conclusion: "Cease then to sneer at those who get honor from rank and office, for we love no one but for borrowed qualities" (St337, 339; B323).

If that is the case, the only true virtue is "self-hatred . . . and the search for a truly lovable being to love. But as we cannot love what is outside ourselves, we must love a being within us, who is not our self, and this is true of each and every man. Now only the Universal Being (*Être universel*) is of such kind. The kingdom of God is within us: the universal good is within us, is our self and yet not ourself" (St325–27; B485).

But my nature, as it was originally created—prior to Adam's fall—serves as a measure of what I want to be and never am, wherefore I must always hate myself, and this hatred is my virtue. I am reminded of my original nature in traces that suffice to make me conscious of my lowliness and my odiousness.

f) Pascal's half-mathematical, half-psychological formulations appear to hit the target; postulating them as absolutes, however, makes them untrue; lacking in love for himself and for others, he fails to see, in what he perceives as signs of deception, delusion, baseness, an essential possibility: In man's bid for recognition Pascal misses the loving bend of self toward self, in which each comes to itself in relation to the other; in finitude Pascal does not perceive historicity as the unique moment that joins time to eternity; in the unfathomable center, he fails to see each individual's historic origin in community and communication at this time and place, nor their fulfillment from their ground.

For when the "center" is unfathomable and as a result unstable, fluctuating, and when measured against the absolute—be it abstract or, as in miracles, concrete—everything becomes vain and indifferent, then the space is lost in which each thinking existence may arrive at the historicity of its possible Existenz.

To establish yourself at the center of your historicity does not necessarily demand a compromise with radical extremes or reduce itself to a comfortable retreat into the privacy of your garden, as long as the garden, along with your person, is not invaded and ravaged. Instead, there is at stake here another unconditionality, fulfillment and passionate engagement, enlisting the service of universality, existence, and spirit. All this, in our consciousness, is overarched and suffused by the concreteness of the eternal historic ground, unknown and unknowable by anyone, but becoming visible within the realization of the historic center, rather than in extremes of annihilating infinities.

g) Pascal's greatness does not rest on a single completed work. Others have proven themselves as creators of systems, as purveyors of valid insights and useful discoveries, in the continuity of man's shaping the world and actualization within the world. Pascal, by contrast, sees his

human fate in relinquishing his ground, as it were, to become the beacon of truth, forgoing any possibility of successors. He opens himself
without any safeguard to the void in which Christ brings him peace,
to the solitude out of which he is able to see and think; for this we are
indebted to him. Pascal is not a well-wrought person, naturally aiming
toward his perfection, he is not endowed with personal greatness, he is
not "a beautiful soul," but a man of the highest spiritual power, with a
consuming passion for truth.

h) Pascal bears the hallmarks of the true "exception"; he is exceptional not only because of the commanding level of his spirit, not only
on account of his willpower and the stern demands on himself, but also
as an unintended sacrifice for a meaning that is in no way generally
comprehensible. Nothing of universal import is actualized by him, he
does not point the way, he is consumed by negativism, lives the life of
an invalid, and dies virtually deserted.

The structure of his personality may be outlined as follows: Psychologically, Pascal experienced an incapacity of fulfilled presentness (a
condition Janet describes in his case histories of psychasthenics).[4] Philosophically, this signifies his unreadiness to immerse himself in the historic moment. Both these phenomena lead to his desperate seeking and
grasping at something altogether other that is perceived as absolute,
that is neither world nor "I" but is nonetheless real though in a future
after death, that is somewhere in eternity and yet actual like things in
the world. But since this is pursued in temporal worldly existence and
meant to bring tranquillity, it is imposed forcibly with world-obliterat-
ing violence, by means of asceticism, solitude, self-denial, and yet
achieves nothing. To the neutral observer it appears as unrelieved torment, yet to him it brought incommunicable bliss and certitude.

i) Pascal was great in being exceptional by refusing any form of
evasion. He did not keep for himself any reserve of harmony, sought
no refuge in a world the permanence of which held its own truth, nor
in the tranquillity of the simple, single-minded asceticism of a monk.
Pascal's was the fate of the person who lives ungrounded, who chooses
to face all that is terrifying, unbearable, monstrous, depressing, as a
way to experience grace in the faith of Christ.

We should not oversimplify Pascal's personal solution as obedience
to the authority of the Church. This obedience was only one aspect,
and did not prevail over his radical sense of truth when it came to the
test of a concrete situation. The highest authority remained a Christian

---

[4] See Pierre Janet, *Les obsessions et la psychasthenie.* Paris, 1908 – 11.

faith which he conceived in his own way, unfathomable for us when he gives it word.

VII. PASCAL'S INFLUENCE

a) Pascal was not an objective example affecting the history of mankind. He was neither a reformer nor the founder of a school. He was a singular individual, an "exception," someone outside the mainstream, affecting single individuals and creating unrest. This awakening power continues to the present. He cannot be sidestepped; he has to be confronted. It is of no use to do what had been done from the beginning: to diminish him, to muffle him, to bend him into shape, to rectify him with the purpose of claiming him for one's own cause—as though he were part and parcel of the Catholic community or, on the other hand, had been motivated by reformative tendencies not worked out to the end but on the point of being revived. It is a fallacy to make Pascal a secret sharer in the reformatory movement.

Pascal is renowned for his battle against the Jesuits. Indeed, his effect was such that the Jesuits never were able to shake the image in world opinion exposed by Pascal as "Jesuitical." He saw something that was true, and this insight remains ineradicable, but does not do justice to the substance and achievements of the Jesuit order.

b) True, Pascal was renowned during his lifetime. But the philosophers shunted him aside as a writer of aphorisms and an enthusiast. His scattered admirers understood him as the great stylist whose works it is a pleasure to read, or as the magnificent skeptic whose shift to Christian superstition can be ignored, or as the believer who strengthens the Christian soul.

Not Pascal, but Descartes had a great effect on philosophy. In the *cogito ergo sum*—I think, therefore I am—Descartes elevated the self-consciousness of thinking to the point of departure of philosophy, and thus founded a broad current within modern thought that is sure of itself. Pascal too takes the human being as his point of departure, but with an entirely different interpretation. Whereas Descartes, following his methodological doubt, erects a system based on the absolute certainty of the *cogito ergo sum,* Pascal sees the questionable nature inherent in this self-consciousness. What for Descartes was unquestioned becomes questionable for Pascal.

c) We saw how Pascal, based on Christian dogmatics, found intelligibility in the incomprehensibility of man's state—man torn by his contradictions and existent only in a paradoxical unity; this he arrived at via the incomprehensibility of the Pauline-Christian doctrine of original sin, accessible only in faith. Pascal's impact rests not on this ancient proposition but on his way of presenting it and making it acceptable to reason. Before his Fall man was a perfectly created being. Now his nature is dual: he presents a dim memory of what he ought to be, stemming from his origin, which makes him aware of his corruption; it is in this corruption that he now lives. Man is an interweaving of the two modes of being-human, before and after the Fall. Pascal brings this element of the Pauline conception of man to our consciousness in an entirely new way, namely, as an image of man which even to the still unbelieving appears true exactly as presented. Pascal succeeded in this to an astounding degree.

But only in the twentieth century has his influence widened. Only then was there a call for scholarly and complete editions of his writings. He could be seen as the pitiable despairing invalid in a world all of the aspects of which he found unsatisfying; he could be found repulsive as the negator and poisoner of man and the world: but the fascination was there. Pascal's recent great influence was based on his notion of man. Owing to the dire personal fate of a great many people, their witnessing the events which forced us all into their vortex, and experiencing the hideous actions committed by human beings against their own kind, a mood developed that wanted to place present calamity into the very ground of events and of Being itself. To this century Pascal's language sounded familiar. There is a tendency, in such times, to surrender totally to our sense of outrage over all that is horrible, to our consciousness of not knowing where to turn, to the glorification of suffering; or again to revel in the cynically enjoyed rapture of the ephemeral moment of nothingness, in the perverse rage of destroying and letting ourselves be destroyed, in a nihilistic way of feeling and thinking.

What lends such tremendous impact to Pascal today is not his Christian faith but his relentless description of an existence alienated from God: the boredom (ennui), the disgust (*dégoût*), the rejection of the world because of a total lack of love. It is a mood of hatefulness that defiantly denies any alleged, yet now proved deceptive, grounds uniting human beings in their actualization and in their very humanity. Everything "of this world" is seen as rotten at its very core. The ferocity of Pascal's polemics, his total mistrust coupled with the energy of his intelligence and spirituality, appeal to this modern nihilism much as do brute force and athletic feats. It is the desperate exultation of nothingness which can feed on Pascal.

This modern consciousness, however, which loudly proclaims its desperately cynical sense of profound dissatisfaction, is by no means that of humanity as a whole; quite probably it engulfs only a minority in our contemporary world, especially among intellectuals.

d) Most important in this basic mood of Pascal's was that it was meant to be the way to Christ both for himself and for the unbelievers. This applies even today, when theologians appropriate his thoughts. Considering their origin, they have their rightful place in theology. For this picture of man is the result of Christian dogmatic teaching, as Pascal himself understood it when he stated that complete insight into human perdition was only possible to the Christian believer. Because of ideas he gleaned from the New Testament—which had been interpreted by Augustine and were to find further interpretation in Kierkegaard—Pascal stands as one of the creators of an image of man that today is considered by some theologians to be the result of scientific philosophy. They use this image as the basis for their theology, as the presumed universally valid correct analysis of the human situation and of being-human itself. They forget that they are moving within the circle of their own world of ideas; they attach value to certain philosophical thoughts because these thoughts can be traced to the New Testament.

Many of Pascal's propositions lend themselves to appropriation in a sense that is not his own: "Man's misery without God" (St13; B60); such a statement and many others may also be ours if we leave aside the meaning they had for Pascal, that is, man's misery without the grace of salvation through Christ.

e) Whoever makes Pascal's image of man his own but eliminates Christ has to be reminded that this image by no means represents being-human at large, a being-human that could understand itself collectively and unanimously in this portrait. What Pascal shows us is only one aspect, which is important for all philosophizing to see, to know, and to examine.

But it could be that it is a condition of independent philosophizing to contradict this picture out of the depth of our own substance. Such philosophizing proceeds out of natural self-consciousness, received as a gift from transcendence, in a life fulfilled in its historicity and embedded in the one stream of great millennial philosophy (in which Thomistic Church philosophy and the world-philosophy of Spinoza or Hegel meet). This philosophy is thoroughly recalcitrant where it is meant to make way for unphilosophical zealotry, as was done by Pascal, at least in intention if not in actuality.

It is necessary further to see what in Pascal's picture of man is particular and by no means universally valid, so as to counter the tendency flowing from this picture, be it in Pascal himself or in a modern version: the tendency to use this aura of negativism as a springboard for submission of faith to authority, to see in such a submission the promised salvation, whether, as in Pascal, in faith centered in a Church, or, as often today, in a totalitarian ideology, or jointly in both. Pascal chose subordination to faith. Assuming that his influence also produced the opposite, then we owe it to his way of thinking that this opposite is urged on to another obedience once it has shaken off Pascal's faith.

f) The "exception" brings a truth to visibility that is not in the nature of dogma, nor is it the truth of a path shown to us, but is truth solely by its awakening effect. Such a shaking up only happens to someone who goes to the outermost limit. But this also implies that this truth appears in the guise of impossibility, which, while seductive, to be sure, is in fact destructive. This truth confounds and misleads us if we fail to apprehend it as an indirect communication of which the author is unaware, that is, if we accept it at face value. Whomever Pascal arouses from somnolence has to come to what he can be by himself. If he follows him to the letter, he will be lost.

LESSING

Editors' Note

Jaspers's references to Lessing's works are to *Gotthold Ephraim Lessings Sämtliche Schriften,* edited by Karl Lachmann. 3rd edition, 23 vols., Stuttgart/Leipzig/Berlin: Göschen, 1886–1924.

He also used *Lessing: Geschichte seines Lebens und seiner Schriften,* edited by Erich Schmidt. 4th edition, Berlin: Weidmann, 1924.

LIFE AND WORKS

1. Life

Lessing was born in 1729 in Kamenz, Saxony. From 1741 to 1746 he attended St. Afra, a ducal school in Meissen, where he received a boarding-school education. He started his university studies in Leipzig in 1746, beginning with theology and philology; in 1748 he briefly studied medicine in Wittenberg.

He lived in Berlin over a number of years, from November 1748 to 1751, then in 1752–55, 1758–60, and 1765–67; in this period he spent only nine years away from this city. In 1751–52 he studied in Wittenberg, where he got his master's degree. From 1755 to 1758 he was in Leipzig, where for five months in 1756 he was engaged by a wealthy young man as travel companion, getting as far as Amsterdam; this tour was interrupted by the outbreak of the Seven Years' War. In 1760–65 he was in Breslau as secretary to General Tauentzien.[1] Traveling by way of Pyrmont, Göttingen, Kassel, and Halberstadt, he briefly returned to Berlin. From 1767 to 1770 he acted as dramaturgist at the German National Theater, Hamburg, which was founded and later failed there; and then, to his death in 1781, he held the office of ducal librarian at Wolfenbüttel.

[1] Friedrich Bogislaw Tauentzien (1710–1791), army general and governor of the fortress at Breslau.

This sketch of Lessing's life depicts a man who did not pursue a normal career. He lived the life of a free-lance writer, and in order to support himself grasped at opportunities as chance presented them. Only the last decade of his life had some stability, owing to his appointment as ducal librarian.

Lessing's father was a minister; his mother, the daughter of a minister. The atmosphere in the home was moderately orthodox and morally serious and joyless. His education was strict, and his life was one of poverty and hardship.

At age twelve he had entered boarding school in Meissen, one of three famous ducal schools. A disciplined life of study stretching his powers to the utmost and allowing virtually no vacations had equipped him with a solid foundation in classical languages and literature; throughout his life Lessing read Greek and Latin with the same facility as German, French, and English.

In his student years, Lessing faithfully attended courses and would, in later life, mention some of his teachers in grateful recollection. But his main intellectual stimulation came from another field. Through Christlob Mylius—a highly talented but unstable journalist with a steady output, and the publisher of several journals—he was introduced to the circle of Leipzig's literary and theatrical life. He admired the great artistry of the actress Karoline Neuber, started to write comedies, and saw his play *The Young Scholar* successfully performed. For him this was a liberating opening to a wider world, to shedding of his inhibitions, and to truth.

The life led by the young student was a source of anxiety to his parents. Living among actors and free spirits, neglecting his studies, writing plays, associating with wicked people such as Mylius was bound to ruin their son. In January 1748 Lessing's father summoned him back to Kamenz. Lessing obeyed, even though his *Young Scholar* was having a very successful run on the stage. His parents were relieved to find that he was in good health, well behaved, and knowledgeable in the sciences. After three months, they permitted him to return to Leipzig.

For a while he switched to medical studies, as something to fall back upon in his unremunerative intellectual life. But he paid only fleeting attention to the subjects of his field, for example, obstetrics. Instead, for him the main attraction was again the theater. Truth here manifested itself in comedy or tragedy, here Frau Neuber's performing artistry enthralled the audience in a hundred roles. Here Lessing had a vision of Germany: its dramatic arts were to be purified.

But this glorious state of affairs came to a rapid end. The theatrical company went bankrupt and broke up. The actors scattered. Lessing remained without funds, burdened by sureties he had given for friends who now had disappeared. In June 1748 he himself left for Berlin to escape his creditors, but he became seriously ill and had to interrupt his journey in Wittenberg. After regaining his health, he registered there as a medical student; but November saw him again in Berlin, destitute, in threadbare clothes. In a memorable letter to his mother (January 20, 1749), he summed up his life and stated his decision to continue his life in freedom, not in academic bounds:

"I left the schools at an early age, fully convinced that all my happiness could be found in books. I arrived at Leipzig . . . where the whole world can be seen in miniature. The first few months I lived in much greater seclusion than in Meissen. Always at my books, centered exclusively on myself, I thought about others about as rarely as I did about God. . . . My only comfort is that nothing worse than my diligence made me so insane. But before long my eyes were opened. . . . I learned to realize that books would indeed make me into a scholar but never into a human being. I ventured out of my chamber to mingle with my peers. Good God! what a disparity I discovered between me and the others. A rustic shyness, a neglected and awkward body, complete ignorance about manners and behavior . . . I felt embarrassed as never before. And the effect of all this was the firm decision to improve myself on this score no matter what the cost. . . . I learned to dance, fence, vault on horseback. . . . I improved to such a degree in these exercises that those . . . who at first disbelieved in my capacity for such skills, ended by giving me some credit. This promising start encouraged me. . . . My body had become somewhat more skilful and I looked for company so that I could now also learn to live" (17, 7–8). "For a while" he tossed "aside the serious books." "I got hold first of the comedies . . . they rendered me very great service. From them I learned to differentiate mannerly from awkward, and crude from natural conduct. They acquainted me with genuine and false virtues and taught me to eschew vice, as much for its ridiculousness as for its vileness. . . . But I almost forgot the most important benefit I owe to the comedies. I came to know myself, and surely have laughed and scoffed at no one more than at myself since then." This led to the decision "to write comedies myself. . . . When these were performed, I was assured that I am not inept at it" (17, 8).

But all this came to a sudden end when he was summoned home. He was upbraided for associating with a certain type of people, for his debts, and for his vacillation in determining which discipline to choose. When he was again permitted to return to academic studies, he "chose Berlin," because it was less expensive, but he fell ill in Wittenberg. "I was never a more unbearable burden to myself than at that time" (17, 9).

Now, in Berlin, his clothing was in a state of such neglect that he could not go among people. He would have liked to obey when his parents requested that he leave the city. But: "I am not coming home. I am not going to attend any university at this time, either. . . . I shall most certainly go to Vienna, Hamburg or Hannover. . . . At all three places I shall find acquaintances and very dear friends of mine. And if nothing else, my wanderings will teach me how to adapt to the world. That is profit enough! Surely I shall yet arrive at a place where they need a tinkerer like me" (17, 10–11).

The parents' worries and recriminations did not cease. Finally (May 30, 1749) Lessing protested to his father: "Time will tell whether I honor my elders, believe in my religion, and ethically conduct my life. Time will tell who is a better Christian—he who has memorized the principles of Christian doctrine and frequently mouths them without understanding them, and goes to church . . . or he who started by prudently doubting them and has arrived at his conviction by way of examination, or at the least strives to arrive there" (17, 17–18).

We see reflected here the feelings of a young man who, though brought up in narrow, limited circumstances, was also formed by a committed ethical-religious life and an education based, as a matter of course, on the classics, the Bible, and theology, and who now enters the world with no other desire but to lead a true life, a life permeated by spirit.

We see the approach of such a young man to his studies, one who harbors no trace of philistinism or hedonism or is exclusively career- or exam-oriented, intent on making the right contacts with a view to future success, and, for the rest, looking for diversions. A genuine student is a student only once and in his own way, guided by his very own daimon. Lessing cannot be imitated, but his example encourages young people who follow after him to search, in their different world and in a different way, for their own unpredictable path, unimpeded by the rules of academe, by examinations and the suffocating mediocrities with which mass society inescapably tries to overwhelm us.

Throughout his life, Lessing regarded his father, who had made things so difficult for him, with reverence. A few examples:

In 1768, on the occasion of his father's fiftieth anniversary in the ministry, he placed the following announcement in the *Hamburgische Zeitung*: "This worthy old man, now 75 years of age, still has an excellent memory and a cheerful face" (10, 225).

In 1771, at his father's death, Lessing assumed responsibility for all outstanding debts (whenever Lessing had had the means, he had regularly assisted his parents and siblings). The creditors had to wait a while, since he was unable to pay immediately (cf. 17, 391–92).

He had intended to write an obituary notice for his father, not one that is conventional and soon forgotten, but the kind that is more lasting and effective. He never got around to it.

An instance from a later date goes to show how vividly his father's image lived on in him:

When, in 1778, Lessing received a letter from his government ordering him to discontinue printing his *Anti-Goeze*, he vented his anger in a note written at night so as to regain his calm and not ruin his sleep: "Well, go ahead," he addressed his anger, "my dear irascibility! . . . just burst forth! . . . rascal! Well now, you merely wish to catch me by surprise? . . . Go ahead, do what you will, gnash my teeth . . . bite my lower lip! And as I actually do this, there he stands before me . . . my father. . . . That was his habit when something riled him. . . . All right, old boy, all right. I understand you. You were such a good man and also such a hothead. How often you yourself complained to me, with a manly tear in your eye, that you got excited so easily, that in your excitement you got carried away. How often you said to me: 'Gotthold! I beg you, learn a lesson from me: watch out. . . . I wish to improve at least in you.' Yes sir, old man, yes sir. I still feel it often enough" (16, 422–23).

In Berlin, in the circle of journalists and their journals, Lessing had attained a position of intellectual leadership, had friends, among them Mendelssohn, Nicolai, and Ramler,[2] earned royalties, and lived modestly but without pressure. In 1760, to everyone's surprise, he left Berlin for Breslau, accepting a position as secretary to General Tauentzien, a high governmental administrator, a position his recently deceased friend von Kleist[3] had mediated.

Why did Lessing go to Breslau? After a year when he had much to complain about, he described in a letter to Ramler (December 6, 1760) how he argued with himself: "But was not all this your free will?

---

[2] Moses Mendelssohn (1729–1786) was a German Jewish religious philosopher; Christoph Friedrich Nicolai (1733–1811), a bookseller and writer; Karl Wilhelm Ramler (1725–1798), a poet, translator, and theater director.

[3] Ewald Christian von Kleist (1715–1759), poet and Prussian officer, was mortally wounded in the Seven Years' War.

Were you not tired of Berlin? Did you not believe that your friends must be tired of you? that the time had come again to live more among people than among books?" (17, 179).

In his important new position, Lessing now had a high income. He spent it freely. He lived in a wartime atmosphere, mixing with officers in the taverns. In his correspondence he called himself a drinker and gambler. Goethe, in *Dichtung und Wahrheit,* wrote: "Lessing, unlike Klopstock and Gleim, did not mind discarding his personal dignity because he was confident of his ability to resume it again at any moment. He took pleasure in the distractions of a life in the tavern and the world at large since the mighty workings of his inner self constantly required a powerful counterbalance; and thus he joined the retinue of General Tauentzien."[4]

During these years Lessing gained intimate knowledge of the men who lived a soldier's life. He accompanied Tauentzien to the front and took part in the siege of Schweidnitz. His function was to draft Tauentzien's many letters, addressed to the King, to government authorities and others. Some of these letters can be found in Lessing's published works. The people of Breslau would later express their gratitude to him for exerting the influence of his office on their behalf. Without all these practical experiences Lessing could not have written his play *Minna von Barnhelm.*

He was full of the joy of life, in spite of his many complaints about disagreements. He used his income also to acquire a library, and placed orders at auctions, finally owning some six thousand volumes. It was during this period that he studied Spinoza and the Church Fathers.

Two years after the end of the war, the fetters imposed by his official position became unbearable to him. Again he returned to Berlin. To his father he had written: "I shall most certainly leave Breslau. What will happen then is my least concern. Whoever is healthy and willing to work has nothing to fear in the world" (17, 208).

There were recurrent adversities in Lessing's life. The repeated discontinuities brought about by his own free will were only one cause of calamity in his life. From his student days on, he struggled with financial difficulties. Only in his five years with General Tauentzien was he financially well off. In his last ten years he subsisted on the modest, barely sufficient salary of a librarian; the state had to pay for his funeral. Many of his ventures failed, most important of which was the Hamburg Theater, and also his negotiations for positions in Mannheim and Vienna. Frederick the Great took no notice of him.

[4] Goethe, *From My Life, Poetry and Truth,* trans. by Robert H. Heitner. New York, Suhrkamp Publishers, 1987.

In spite of his great success as critic, author, and dramatist, in spite of his position in German intellectual life as the well-nigh supreme arbiter in matters of writing and the theater, in spite of his fame, fate denied him happiness.

He was not the forceful individual striving purposefully, attaining and holding fast to success; he refused utilitarian byways if they ran counter to his pride. He lacked Goethe's good fortune. But though, being highly sensitive, he was easily upset and outraged, he quickly regained his balance, and no distress could make him despair. He persisted in his intellectual endeavors with passionate intensity, but always with that grain of self-irony that preserved him from becoming maudlin. He was modest, solid in his achievements, healthy, honest in all circumstances; he did not hide from actuality, admitted to himself what happened to him and where he went astray; he persevered in his creative work as long as it was granted to him to do so, with an energy that seemed to increase with calamity. He conquered himself.

Nothing came easily. He worked hard for what he became. He broke through the constraints of narrowness in every sense but without attaining the tranquillity of material freedom or the natural joy in existing.

A different kind of joy must be credited as the source of his high-spiritedness in all suffering—the satisfaction inherent in proceeding incorruptibly on the way of truth.

The greatest calamity he suffered was the death of his wife after two years of marriage.

Eva König, born in Heidelberg, was the wife of a Hamburg merchant. König operated on a large scale, expanding his business throughout Germany, Austria, and Italy. Still at an early age, he died suddenly in Venice in 1769. Eva was widowed at age thirty-three, left with the care of a daughter and three sons. As he was leaving on his business trip to Italy, König had told Lessing, who was a friend of the family: "If anything should happen to me, take care of my children!" (Schmidt, II, 118).

The development of Lessing's relationship with Eva König can be traced in their letters. They became engaged in 1771, but did not marry until 1776. The reason for this five-year waiting period, accepted by Lessing under protest, was Eva's task of liquidating her husband's complicated business enterprise in order to save whatever possible for her children. This task kept the courageous and able woman busy and on the road for years. Lessing's financial position did not ease until 1776, when he at last secured an apartment suitable for a family. The infinite happiness of living "with a sensible woman" (18, 284) did not last long.

In December 1777 their son died after a forceps delivery; in January 1778 the mother died while still in childbed.

Lessing's short letters from those days show how he took this calamity. December 31, 1977, to Eschenburg:[5] "My joy was only short-lived: And I was so loath to lose him, this son! For he had so much sense! So much sense!—Don't believe that the few hours of my father-hood made me into a doting father! I know what I am saying.—Did he not show good sense by having to be dragged into the world with iron pincers? by smelling a rat so soon?—Was he not sensible in tak-ing advantage of the first opportunity to clear out?—However, the little curlyhead is dragging his mother along with him!—For there is still little hope that I shall keep her.—Just for once I wanted to be as happy as other people. But it did not agree with me" (18, 259).

January 5, 1778, to his brother: "I have just experienced the saddest fortnight of my life. I was in danger of losing my wife, a loss which would have made the rest of my life very bitter. She was delivered and made me the father of a very pretty boy who was healthy and lively. But he remained with us only twenty-four hours and then fell victim to the cruel way in which he had to be pulled into the world. Or perhaps he did not think very highly of the meal to which he was invited so forcibly, and stole away again on his own? In short, I hardly know that I have been a father. The joy was so brief, and the sadness was so drowned out by the greatest worry! For the mother lay for a whole nine or ten days without consciousness, and every day, every night I was repeatedly chased from her bed and told that I am only making her last moments more difficult. For she recognized me in spite of all her unconsciousness. At last the illness took a sudden turn, and for three days now I have the certain hope that I may still keep her this time, she whose companionship, even in her present condition, becomes more indispensable to me by the hour" (18, 260-61).

January 3, 1778, to Eschenburg: "As of yesterday the doctor assures me that I shall most likely keep my wife this time. How calm this news has made me you can see from the fact that I am once more beginning to think of my theological skirmishes" (18, 260).

January 7, 1778: "The hope that my wife is improving has again diminished; and actually my only hope now is to be allowed soon to hope again" (18, 161).

January 10, 1778, to Eschenburg: "My wife is dead; this I have now

<hr>

[5] Johann Joachim Eschenburg (1743–1820) was an esthetician and literary critic.

experienced also. I take comfort in the thought that there are not many such experiences ahead of me; and feel quite relieved."

January 12, 1778, to his brother: "If only you had known her!— But it is said that praising one's wife is praising oneself. All right, I will say no more about her. But if you had known her! I am afraid you will never again see me the way our friend Moses did: so tranquil, so content, in my four walls!" (18, 262).

January 13, 1778, to Eschenburg: "It remains to me to begin dreaming along on my path by myself. A good supply of the laudanum of literary and theological diversions will help me to live tolerably one day at a time" (18, 263).

Lessing's marriage was not the fruit of an early love, which, in its origin, seems to merge with life itself and hence to endure a lifetime— the only conceivable actuality, not allowing the possibility of another love. The love uniting Lessing and Eva König was that of two independent, mature people, drawn to each other at the wellspring of reason and humanity. Lessing experienced his love as unique, as though he had never loved before. It allowed him, the vagabond, for the first time to put down roots, as it were, in the world. Existence as such, day-to-day reality, becomes shelteredness.

What took place in Lessing upon the death of his wife can be sensed only indirectly.

It was not despair. Eschenburg had misinterpreted the letter of December 31. Lessing replied on January 7: "I can hardly remember what a tragic letter that might have been which I am supposed to have written to you. I would be truly ashamed if it were to betray the tiniest trace of despair. Also, my failing is not despair but light-headedness which expresses itself at times in a somewhat bitter and misanthropic manner. In the future my friends will have to put up with me the way I am" (18, 261).

At that very time the first essay by Chief Pastor Goeze[6] against Lessing appeared. This constituted a turning point in the theological polemics, begun a few months previously, based on the fragments of an anonym published by Lessing. On January 7, 1778, in the same letter in which Lessing told Eschenburg that his hopes were again waning, he wrote: "I thank you for the copy of Goeze's article. These matters are now truly the only ones that can distract me" (18, 260). Despite the great emotional stress caused by the death of his wife, Lessing continued his work immediately.

---

[6] Johann Melchior Goeze (1717–1786) was a German Lutheran theologian.

In the three years left to Lessing after Eva König's death he occupied himself with the same matters that were important to him throughout life. But now everything seemed suffused by a new strength drawn from his very depth, a new voice from the soul.

Though developing the most powerful polemics against the vileness of Pastor Goeze's attack, he saw the whole matter as merely a farce. In *Nathan the Wise* he bears witness to another world that is actual to him, a world, originating in the power of love, of reason, of communication, that has overcome the tragic.

He dared to express his faith in ciphers. He kept his expression fluid, but thereby intensified the impact of its substance, in *Education of the Human Race,* in *Gravity and Levity,* and finally in the conversation with Jacobi. The last, however, became known only after Lessing's death through the deceptive mirror of his interlocutor's account. In all these documents we find a sovereignty that seems to issue from another sphere but is wholly of this world. What he produced in this period is philosophically the most impressive in his work, growing as it does out of the continuing effect of the emotional upheaval caused by Eva's death. Yet nowhere does he refer to her explicitly. Lessing's legacy to the Germans, to the West, to the world, is the fruit of a love that, in happiness and calamity, timeless in time, led to an articulation of something that may have been expressed abstractly before but could only now find its truth.

In the three years between Eva's death and his own, Lessing's irremediable misfortune was poisoned by slander. His position as librarian was threatened by Goeze's attacks. His urge toward freedom again put his material existence at risk. The magnificent vision of the peace of a world of humanity and truth was created by a man who, when it came to his own existence, skirted the edge of the abyss.

Here are examples of Lessing's state of mind in those years:

Elise Reimarus[7] had, on August 5, 1778, advised him to stay on in Wolfenbüttel and not, in an hour of bitter weariness, "to tender a resignation that can give pleasure only to your enemies!" (21, 223). On August 9, Lessing replied: "Ah, if he knew, this wretched enemy, how much more I suffer if I continue here just to spite him!—But I am too proud to think of myself as suffering—just grit my teeth—and let my boat drift with wind and waves. Enough that I do not myself want to capsize it!—" Not once in his life did Lessing contemplate suicide.

---

[7] Widow of H. S. Reimarus (see footnote 8), she was the daughter of J. A. Fabricius.

The letter continues: "I am left completely on my own here. There is not a single friend here in whom I could confide completely. . . . How often am I tempted to curse my wanting to be, just for once, as happy as other people! How often do I wish to return in a trice to my former isolated state; to be nothing, to want nothing, to do nothing other than what the present moment brings with it!" (18, 284).

Elise Reimarus had written him about a rumor making the rounds in Hamburg alleging that Lessing was in love with his stepdaughter, who kept house for him, and for this reason refused to part from her. On May 7, 1780, Lessing replied: ". . . It would have almost amounted to turning her out of the house had I wanted to abandon her straightaway to what her relatives proposed so coldly! . . . I do not want her to offer herself to any of these people; and I certainly do not want to be the one forcing her to throw herself into the arms of complete strangers. . . . Whoever wants to call this attitude on my part love, can use his words as he wishes! And it is, admittedly, love, and I gladly confess that this girl returns this love in all the ways I might wish" (18, 339–40). Her domestic virtues, writes Lessing, make "my life, which alas I must continue to lead in this way, just bearable. . . . I could have added . . . that I tremble at the thought of the moment that will take her away from me. . . . For I shall fall back into a terrible loneliness to which I will hardly be able to adjust as well as I did before; and to escape it I might easily go all the way in the contrary direction, concluding my life the way it had started, namely as a vagabond, only in a much worse state than before. For the desire to study would not keep me as long in one place as it did in my youth, when curiosity and ambition held complete sway over me" (18, 340).

On the night of February 3, 1781, while at his club, he suffered a stroke. Intermittently he was unable to speak. He coughed blood. He knew that it was his turn now. His clouded consciousness cleared up time and again. On February 15 he was able to leave his room one more time. On his return he leaned against the doorpost, sweating profusely, and said to his stepdaughter, who was taking care of him: "Be calm, Malchen!," went back to bed, submitted to one more bloodletting, and died with a smile on his face (cf. Schmidt, II, 617–18).

2. Works

As we look at Lessing's works we find them confusing in their multiplicity, diversity, and amplitude. If we were to pick out those that are still important today, the following, perhaps, suggest themselves:

Dramas: *Minna von Barnhelm, Emilia Galotti, Nathan the Wise;*

Art criticism: *Laokoon, Hamburgische Dramaturgie;*

Theological and philosophical writings: numerous from his youth on and always brief; famous for their dramatic high point, the publication of *Fragments of an Anonym* (written by Reimarus[8]) and the ensuing unique polemics.

Hence it can be asserted Lessing was simultaneously poet, critic, theologian. All this might be fitted into a few volumes. But to this has to be added a host of other writings and fragments, poems, fables, epigrams; critiques of individual books and literary criticism generally; the "rescue" *(Rettungen)* of misunderstood personalities; philological essays; miscellany that bear witness to the scope and versatility of his interests, which led to constant note-taking; and his letters. Lessing is not only poet, critic, theologian, but also philologist and polyhistorian. A valuable part of his work is contained in his extensive literary estate, published posthumously and constantly supplemented up to the present.

In an ironic vein, focusing only on externals, Lessing characterized his approach in a preface to a planned compilation: "Imagine a person of unlimited curiosity, without bent for a specific science. Incapable of giving firm direction to his mind, he will, in order to satisfy it, roam through all the fields of erudition, gape at everything, aspire to know everything and get tired of everything. If he does not lack genius altogether, he will take note of much but substantiate little; he will get onto many a trail but follow none; he will make more strange than useful discoveries; point to a view but in regions which often are hardly worth looking at" (Schmidt, I, 450).

Reading Lessing does not help us to know beautiful, perfected, classical literary works that have their place in world literature, nor does it introduce us to a philosophic whole, an intellectual masterpiece, to seminal thinking, adding up to a lasting orientation for all philosophizing; nor are we enchanted by the beauty of his language. This language satisfies us through its magnificent clarity and the vivid immediacy to the matter at hand. Reading Lessing does not lead to a state of wisdom which, supported by comprehensive tradition and assured vision, would enable us to pass true judgments with penetration and finality. Nor does it convey the happiness of a frame of mind engendered by wealth, talent, appropriate conduct, and, simply, a world which could evoke in the reader the joy of participation. What then is left?

Lessing was passionately devoted to the theater from an early age.

[8]Hermann Samuel Reimarus (1694–1768) was a German philosopher, orientalist, and theologian.

In the freedom of the play he was gripped by the truth of man's ethical substance which, arising from a timeless world, is brought to bear on situations, people, and audience.

In his criticism, he brought clarity, occasioned by specific works of literature and art which he illuminated by differentiating in principle the relevant categories.

In his philosophic thought about theology, he puts diverse positions on the stage and shows opponents battling each other; here again he demands clarity. He becomes a fighter for justice (as he does in the many "rescues"), for humanism and tolerance, for truthfulness in faith.

In everything the ethical-religious substance is what counts, what determines his judgment and commands our interest. It is visible in him from the very beginning and reaches its summit in his final years.

Lessing does not pursue the many areas of his research, thought, and creativity along separate tracks. They are not distinct fields, explored by a man of many parts. It is, rather, the unitary will to truth which plunges headlong into everything. Everywhere he finds the vehicle for his experience and his responsibility.

Whatever he encounters belongs not to a beyond but to this world, sustained and illuminated, however, by something beyond it. Hence he is not caught up in worldliness or in the world.

His thinking does not derive from a higher inspiration, it bears no trace of mystical experience. It is not bound by ecclesiastical certainty of faith. It does not urge on to revelation as experience and guarantee. Yet it is aimed with equal force of existential earnestness at the thing that alone matters, not, however, as something to be appropriated or proclaimed. It is not a having but a being, a being in the temporal appearance of moving toward it. The certainty of such thinking lies in not-knowing.

This thinking is an awakening, not a fulfilling thinking. Fulfillment rests in the one who is awakened by it. This is, if you will, the poverty but also the unique strength of this thinking.

If we attempt to find a development in the chronology of Lessing's life, the steps taken toward something new, a turnaround or an intensification, we are left, in the end, with our first impression: What matters most to Lessing remains basically the same.

It is therefore relatively unimportant that in his philosophizing Lessing in his youth thought in the categories of Wolffian philosophy, from there proceeded to the study of Spinoza and of the Church Fathers, and from approximately 1770 became familiar with Leibniz from the source material in Wolfenbüttel.

The superficially meaningful division of his life into the time before the outbreak of the Seven Years' War (1756), followed by the time in Berlin, Breslau, and Hamburg (1756–1770), and finally by the years in Wolfenbüttel has no intellectually significant import.

3. Literary output

In the history of literature Lessing takes his place as creative writer. In interpreting him as an "awakener" among the philosophers, I believe that his greatness does not primarily lie in his works of fiction. However, the place of Lessing's poetic output within his work must be kept in mind from the outset.

a) *Early poetic writings:* Lessing started writing poetry as a boy. As a student he had filled many pages with poems entitled "Wine and Love." His parents were horrified; his sister burned most of the manuscripts. He, however, wrote (April 28, 1749): "They are free imitations of Anacreon . . . one cannot know me well if one believes that my feelings harmonize in the least with this." They show "nothing other than my inclination to try my hand at all kinds of poetry" (17, 15–16).

This, then, is the nature of his early poetic attempts: they are not elemental creations of a young genius, but are imitative games, attempts in analogy to what already exists, on the part of a practicing, highly gifted mind and heart. He writes dramas following the French model, with, as his example, Voltaire, whom he at that time still considered "divine" (cf. Schmidt, I, 73); he was still influenced by the school of Gottsched. He wrote fables like Gellert, and in the fashion of his time crafted epigrams, as did Kästner; he attempted didactic poetry in Haller's manner, wrote lyrical poetry in the style of Hagedorn and Gleim.[9]

He was driven by his pleasure in his many-sided ability, and his openly admitted ambition: "One needs to praise me only in one field of endeavor in order to make me pursue it with increased seriousness. Hence I thought day and night how I might show strength in one area in which, as I believed, no other German had excelled so far" (17, 8).

He was on the lookout for something that was out-of-the-ordinary in Germany. "It is very difficult to make a name for oneself in a science

[9] Johann Christoph Gottsched (1700–1766) was a German scholar and author; Christian Fürchtegott Gellert (1715–1769), a German man of letters; Abraham Gotthelf Kästner (1719–1800), a German mathematician and poet; Albrecht von Haller (1708–1777), a Swiss natural scientist, physician, and poet; Friedrich von Hagedorn (1708–1754) and Johann Wilhelm Ludwig Gleim (1719–1803), both German poets.

in which all-too-many have excelled already. Did I do so very wrong, then, to have chosen for my youthful endeavors something in which very few of my compatriots have tried their powers so far?"

He recognized the dubious nature of his ambition: "If one could rightfully bestow upon me the title of a German Molière, then I could certainly be assured of lasting fame. To tell the truth, I long to earn it, but its compass and my impotence are two factors that can smother even the greatest desire" (17, 16).

But notwithstanding their playful character, even his earliest poetic efforts exhibit the motifs which would endure to the end of his life. In his youthful comedies certain basic situations stand out clearly: in *The Young Scholar* the rejection of the world of abstract knowledge in favor of actual life, in *The Freethinker* the questionable character of mere intellect, in *The Jews* the struggle against the greatest injustice and failure of love in the Christian world.

b) *Understanding of himself as poet:* We possess Lessing's own evaluations of his literary activity from all periods of his life. They all concern the relationship of reflection and poetry in his work. The two are inseparable, but reflective thought is primary.

In 1759 he published *Essays on the Nature of the Fable,* having published many fables in the preceding years. In his preface he casts a "critical glance" over his literary output. In his "initial displeasure," he writes, he was tempted to discard his earlier writings altogether, in the belief "that I could now atone for my youthful indiscretions by going on to better things, and might, in the end, even consign them to oblivion." But then he gives thought to his "well-disposed readers." Ought he to expose them to the judgment that their approbation had been wasted on something wholly unworthy? "Your indulgent encouragement expects of me that I strive to vindicate your judgment by putting enough that is genuinely worthy into my writings, phrased so felicitously that they might have noticed the inherent promise. And so I resolved rather to improve as much as possible than follow my initial urge to discard" (7, 415).

He gleaned a large number of fables from his earlier writings. "I liked it at this border common to both poetry and morality." He had read all the old and new fables and given thought to the theory of the fable, which "led to his writing the present work." He started by putting down "notes as one does in one's studies, since one mistrusts one's memory; thoughts that one is satisfied merely to think, without giving them the requisite verbal precision; sketches attempted for the sake of practice." At this stage "a great deal is still lacking for the making of a true book" (7, 416). Then Lessing proceeds to show his readers how it turned out in the end, namely, as a collection of fables accompanied by essays.

He asks his readers "not to judge the fables without the essays. For even though I neither wrote the former to further the latter nor the latter to further the former, both of them—as things that came to be at one time in one head—borrow too much from each other to remain unaffected individually and separately."

Should the reader "in the process of reading discover that my rules do not at all times accord with my execution," he declares himself willing to jettison those fables without hesitation. For, he asserts, the reader "knows that genius is stubborn; that it rarely follows the rules on purpose; and that these rules are meant, to be sure, to prune excesses, but not to inhibit. Therefore let him examine his taste in the fables, and my reasoning in the essays" (7, 416).

Lessing would like to apply in time the same treatment he used on his fables to the other categories of his writings. He means to reconsider, justify, and correct what he has so far produced and will produce in the future. His working experience he describes as follows: "As long as the virtuoso plans attacks, collects, selects, and orders ideas, and divides them into projects, he delights in the rewarding raptures of conception. But as soon as he takes the further step and starts to put his creative ideas into words, the birth pangs set in, which he rarely is ready to endure without encouragement" (7, 417).

In *Hamburg Dramaturgy* (1769), Lessing starts with "a word about myself": "I am neither actor nor poet." He tried to write plays. "The earliest of these attempts were written at a time when one tends to take joy and lightness to be genius. I am fully aware that whatever is acceptable in my more recent plays I owe uniquely to criticism. I do not feel within me the living spring propelled upward by its own power, gushing forth in such rich, such fresh, such pure jets: I have to squeeze myself mightily to put pressure into the pipes. I would be very poor, very cold, very nearsighted had I not learned, after a fashion, humbly to borrow from others' treasures, to warm myself at others' fires" (10, 209).

Lessing's awareness of his debt to criticism made him "irritable" when criticism was accused of smothering genius. "I am lame myself, and therefore a diatribe against crutches cannot possibly edify me" (10, 210).

c) *Criticism and poetic imagination:* For Lessing, criticism is in itself of the highest order. ". . . I flattered myself that I derived from it something that closely approaches genius." That which makes him a slow worker, the constant critical reflection which urges him to surpass himself ("My first thoughts surely are not an iota better than the first thoughts of everyman; and with everyman's thoughts one best stays at home" [10, 210–11]) has its own inescapable significance and value. It was the purpose of the sheets later collected in *Hamburg Dramaturgy* to give criticism as such a more developed and useful role.

About this role of criticism Lessing states: "Everyone has the right to pride himself on his diligence: I may say that I have carefully examined the art of playwriting. . . . I have also practiced it sufficiently to be allowed my say in the matter. . . . Concerning things I myself am not capable of doing, I still am able to judge whether they can be done."

What assures Lessing that he does not study his way into error "is the fact that my understanding is wholly in accord with Aristotle's abstractions from the innumerable masterpieces of the Greek stage . . . that I consider [his *Rhetoric*] to be just as infallible as are Euclid's Elements . . . just as true and certain, but, to be sure, not as comprehensible. . . . In particular I consider myself capable . . . of proving conclusively [in regard to tragedy] that it cannot move away a single step from Aristotle's guidelines without moving away an equal distance from perfection" (10, 214).

This insight had the most radical consequences for Lessing's understanding and evaluation of the tragedies under discussion.

Running counter to "our feeling," the preconceived notion that French tragedy was constructed according to Aristotle's rules could not last forever. "A few English plays aroused us from our slumber."

"But blinded by this sudden ray of truth we rebounded against the rim of another abyss. The English plays lacked . . . certain rules. . . . What conclusions were drawn from this? . . . That the aim of tragedy can be attained even without these rules. . . . But once started with these rules one began to muddle up all rules and to denounce as pedantry that genius should be told what it must do and what it need not do" (10, 215).

Lessing demonstrated that no nation had misunderstood the laws of ancient drama as severely as the French, that they had taken some external features in Aristotle's dramaturgic theory to be its essence, and in turn weakened the essential elements.

There are rules. Lessing thinks himself capable of improving each play of the great Corneille (cf. 10, 216). But he does not deny genius its own originality. The rules of drama are not to be learned from

Aristotle only but can be gleaned from the creativity of genius which itself brings forth the rules.

Lessing pushed French tragedy off the absolute throne it had hitherto occupied. He discovered Shakespeare.

d) *Plays:* Three of Lessing's plays continue to be performed and impress us even today. The truly great poet conceives of his work as mirror of the world. Boundlessly ingenuous in his creative vision, he sees all things and transposes them into a realm of all-embracing truth, into an infinity that eludes definition or structure. Yet in Lessing this truth is circumscribed and structured.

Thus in *Minna von Barnhelm,* Lessing points to the morality in a world of war and selfish concerns. In *Emilia Galotti,* Lessing presents an aesthetically deliberate construction of a tragedy via a traditional theme, as prescribed according to rules. In *Nathan the Wise,* we see the construct of an ideal world in which truth and humanity and communicative reason prevail, actualizing themselves within a setting of adversity and turmoil.

There is no denying that Lessing is also a poet, an innovator, a master of dramatic and pointed dialogue. This, however, does not make him a great poet. In spite of all its freedom, the poetic work becomes, in Lessing, the instrument of a different intention. In him there is always a mind-set at work which, compared to the breadth of ancient tragedians or of Shakespeare, strikes us as limiting. It is not poetry but the thought which is the preferred instrument of what Lessing really means to say.

This explains the fluctuations in the evaluation of his dramas:

Minna von Barnhelm is falsely interpreted as the patriotic glorification of Prussian character; correctly understood, the play celebrates good will and reason correcting self-induced excesses and a blinkered vision not immediately recognized as such.

Emilia Galotti was dismissed by the Romantic poets as algebra in dramatic guise, a play produced in sweat and pain, the child of unadulterated prosaic rationality. Even Goethe considered it "merely the product of thought." Lessing himself, owing to his implacable awareness of the aesthetic norms of tragedy, knew that it was labored rather than created. Though he was praised for the impeccable execution of his product, he commented: "I do not intend it to stand as my best play" (cf. Schmidt, II, 48).

Lessing tells us that *Nathan* served to express his own convictions indirectly when the censorship imposed on him during his theological battles prevented his voicing them directly. He chose the stage as his platform when the publication of his ideas was closed to him. In a projected preface to *Nathan* (among his posthumously published writings), he wrote in 1779: "If, in the end, people will say that a play of such singular tendency is not richly enough endowed with corresponding beauty:—I will keep silent but I will not be ashamed. I am conscious of a goal that could be pursued much farther and still with all honors" (16, 445).

After this introductory preparation—the exposition of Lessing's life, a survey of his works, an interpretation of the meaning of his poetic endeavors—we now come to the Lessing whose greatness we see in the awakening power of his thinking.

First, we shall treat of Lessing's philosophical thought; second, of his theological thinking; third, of the merging of both in the unique polemics against Pastor Goeze, in *Nathan the Wise* and in *Education of the Human Race.*

LESSING'S PHILOSOPHIZING

1. *Theoretical philosophy*

A. *Lessing's point of departure*

What Lessing wanted as a young student was not a life lived through books but life itself, not a turning inward but openness to the world. At that time he said, "Books would make me into a scholar but never into a human being" (17, 7). And even late in life he reiterated: "I do not wish to be erudite. . . . All that I in some small way strove for was the ability to make use, whenever necessary, of others' learned works. . . . The wealth of experience garnered by others and acquired from books is erudition, personal experience is wisdom. The smallest capital of the latter is worth more than millions of the former" (16, 535).

Doubt: Erudition may properly be used as a tool; as such it is not to be despised. But false knowledge, and dogmatic structures, Lessing considers absolutely pernicious: "Damned book learning!" (1, 257). Because of the latter he almost lost himself and wasted his time. "Foolish sages" keep forgetting that "human knowing is mere supposing." They "taught us arrogance." Obstinately protective of their dogmatic structures, they cannot abide "vigilant doubting." For such arrogance inquiry is "poison," "stubbornness its fame"; "from the heights of

piled-up lies" they pretend to see "nature and spirit and God . . . un-
veiled to their view" (1, 258).

This becomes evident, for example, in regard to the question of
immortality. Wisdom itself remains silent, ". . . her fingers ever on her
lips." Her disciples, by contrast, "tell us more than wisdom teaches."
Simplemindedness listens in the belief that it hears God speaking. It
places its trust "in God's word." I, too, writes Lessing,

> " . . .
>
> succumbed to pride, seduced,
> took philosophic ravings for God's truth,
> where maddened minds outrageous marvels think
> dream up a kingdom, give their dreams for naught.
> . . .
>
> Until a cruel doctor rends their ravings—
> he now is sane and poor who first was sick and rich."

First he was poor and wretched. And now?

> "Who comes and teaches me what I believed I knew,
> Before the light of day took God, world, and myself
> away from me"　(I, 258).

What has been toppled cannot be righted again. But doubt affects
only knowledge, dogma, "God's word," arrogance. He does not despair,
for he goes on for the rest of his life philosophizing in this state of not-
knowing; he will allow himself to be moved by the substance of tradition, will examine, think, appropriate, possess a trust whose ground he
can neither prove nor lose.

B. Lessing's question concerning philosophy

1) Early on, the young Lessing glimpsed the nature of philosophy in
its history—as he understood it.

In 1750, aged twenty-one, he put his "thoughts about the Herrnhuter" into writing.[10] In this fragment, of which only the beginning
exists, he treats of philosophers whose path can be compared with that
of religion.

"Man was created for action and not for hairsplitting." There was
a time when all wisdom consisted in concise rules for living. The most
virtuous person was taken to be the most knowledgeable. But pupils of

---

[10] The Herrnhuter were members of an eighteenth-century Pietistic Moravian sect whose set-
tlement "Herrnhut" (Protection of the Lord) was located near Dresden in Saxony.

the seven wise men defected. They desired knowledge but forgot about practice. "Truths that everyone can grasp but not everyone can practice were an all-too-insubstantial nourishment for their curiosity." They wanted more. "The heavens, previously the object of their admiration, became the field for their conjectures. The numbers opened up to them a labyrinth of secrets. . . . The wisest among men," Socrates, "wanted to summon their quest for doctrines away from this daredevil flight." ". . . what is above you is not for you! Turn your eyes inward! . . . Here understand and master the only thing you are to understand and master: yourselves!" (14, 155–56).

Against this the Sophist shouted: "Blasphemer of our gods! Seducer of the people! Plague of our young men! Enemy of the fatherland! . . . What is the aim of your eccentric teachings? Seducing our pupils? Denying us our teaching posts? Abandoning us to contempt and poverty?" (14, 156).

However, can malice force a wise man to deny the truth? It can take from him nothing but his life.

"Only a few of his disciples took the path he had shown them." Plato began to dream, Aristotle to draw inferences. Throughout the long tradition of philosophy that has come down to us, sometimes the one, sometimes the other predominated. Then Descartes appeared. "In his hands truth seemed to take on a new shape; the more deceptive the more it sparkled." The new philosophy was to be subjected to the art of measurement. "A science barely glimpsed in classical antiquity guided it with firm steps to the most hidden secrets of nature. They seemed to have caught it in the act." The disciples of this new science "are inexhaustible in their discovery of new truths. In the smallest space, they can, with the aid of a few numbers connected by signs, clarify mysteries for which Aristotle would have needed a forbidding number of volumes" (14, 156–57).

But when it comes to man, admiration for the new accomplishments cannot forestall the following judgment: "They fill the head but the heart remains empty. They lead the intellect into the farthest heavens, while feeling, because of its passions, is reduced to below the level of brute beasts" (14, 157–58).

Next, Lessing sketches his vision of the philosopher of the future: "Let us imagine a man arising who from the height of his perception were to look down on the principal labors of our men of learning, who with Socratic acuity would discern the ridiculous aspects of our so highly praised sages, and would dare to proclaim in complete confidence:

"Alas! Your science is still wisdom's infancy,
   A game for the adept, a balm for blinded pride!"

"Suppose . . . that he would teach us relentlessness toward ourselves, indulgence toward others; teach us to value merit highly, even if ill fortune and disgrace are heaped on it, and to defend it against almighty stupidity . . . teach us not just faith in God but—most excellent—love for him; and teach us, in the end, to meet death fearlessly and, by a willing exit from this stage, bear witness to our firm belief that wisdom would not ask us to remove our mask had we not played our role to the very end" (14, 160).

"Further, let us imagine that this man commanded none of the knowledge that is the less useful the more it boasts. Let him be innocent of either histories or languages. Of the beauties and marvels of nature let him know only enough to recognize them as the surest proofs of their mighty creator. A man who left unexamined all of which he can say: I don't know it, I cannot make sense of it" (14, 160–61).

"Yet this man would lay claim to the title of philosopher. Equally he would have the courage to deny this title to people officially granted the right to this dazzling designation because of the public office they occupy. If he were to venture tearing off the mask of false wisdom in whatever company he found it, thereby causing their lecture halls to become, if not empty, then at least less crowded . . . what would our philosophers do with such a man?" (14, 161).

A "proud algebraist" would deny him the title of philosopher: He cannot even "differentiate an exponential quantity." The astronomer says: Without knowledge of algebra you cannot have a better lunar theory than mine. A metaphysician queries: "You do believe in monads? Yes. Another shouts: You do reject monads? Yes. How is this—you believe and you don't believe in them at the same time?" (14, 161).

"In vain . . . would he submit to his scoffers other important questions. In vain would he even prove that there was more to his questions than to theirs . . . should one not exercise one's reason on something better than on the unknowable? You are a dreamer! they would cry as with one voice. A fool escaped from the madhouse! But we shall see to it that you return there."

"Thank God," Lessing concludes, "that such a foolhardy friend of laymen has not risen up as yet and would not rise up in our time: the gentlemen so engrossed in the reality of things will see to it that my imagination never arrives at reality" (14, 162).

In this youthful pronouncement, which for Lessing constitutes an undeviating orientation for his life as a thinker, we find an analogy to Pascal, Kierkegaard, Nietzsche: all of them understand modern science in their own way, affirm it as such, do not despise it. They participate in it actively; Pascal in the natural sciences, Lessing and Nietzsche in philology and history. But they understand that the truth all-important for human beings is not to be found there.

But about the other truth? Can Lessing be said to scorn philosophy?

Is it his intention to abandon philosophical thought to feeling and enthusiasm? Not in the least. Not only does he consider Leibniz and Spinoza to be great men, but he acknowledges their thinking as cognition. Following their thinking requires clarity, differentiation, and depth.

2) The same youthful Lessing who sketched the future philosopher provides us with *an example of this mode of philosophic thought.*

Lessing belittles neither the sciences nor systematic and metaphysical philosophy. All he asks for is to see them carried out properly and not confused with each other.

At age twenty-six (with Mendelssohn, to whom he most likely owes his information about Leibniz and Spinoza), in the essay "Pope a Metaphysician!" he attacks the Prussian Academy of Sciences for phrasing the problem set for a prize competition in a form confusing philosophy and poetry; it further lacked the required acuity of philosophic thinking. His way of interpreting Pope,[11] his comparing him with Leibniz, his critique of him, and his examination of Pope's propositions are evidence of his systematic thinking in this area.

a) A poem is "perfect, sensual speech" (6, 414). Everything a poet utters "ought to make an immediate strong impression; each of his truths ought to move as well as convince us. To achieve this, the poet has no other means than to express one truth in accordance with one system, and another truth in accordance with another system. Here he speaks according to Epicurus . . . there according to the Stoics . . ." (6, 416–17).

A system of metaphysical truths is an altogether different matter. The metaphysician has to make clear the meaning of words he wants to use, never stray from this meaning; his thinking must be internally consistent.

Poet and philosopher may be consonant. "However, a philosophic

---

[11] The English poet Alexander Pope (1688–1744).

poet is still no philosopher and being a poetic philosopher still does not make him a poet" (6, 415).

b) Lessing extracts from Pope's verses everything that, brought together, can constitute something like a philosophical system:

Of all possible world systems, God must have created the best. In this best system everything has to hang together, or it will fall apart. The connection lies in a hierarchy of perfection in which all beings have their place. This great chain extends from infinity to man and from man to the void. In this chain of unchangeable beings man has his appointed place. To ask of him that he be more perfect than he is is just as ludicrous as it would be for the hand to demand that it be the head and not an instrument of the mind. The question of why man was not created perfect is the same as asking why man is not God and earth not heaven. "The happiness of each creature is found in the condition that is tailored to his nature" (6, 420), that is proper for his nature and his degree of perfection. Man is as perfect as he can be.

c) Lessing compares the content of Pope's verses with Leibniz, Shaftesbury, and others. He detects in Pope inaccuracies, superficialities, contradictions, and exposes them with great acuity. But he finds these understandable. As a true poet, Pope was more concerned with "gleaning the sensuously beautiful from all systems and using it to embellish his poems rather than creating a system of his own . . ." (6, 432). "He had first read one or the other writer who dealt with the same subject matter and, without examining it according to his own basic principles, garnered from each what he thought most conducive to expression in euphonious verse" (6, 438). Lessing proves that the metaphysical part of Pope's material had been more borrowed than thought out by him.

Pope himself was aware of this, as many passages in his letters document. Someone came to his defense, countered these accusations, and expressed himself in his favor. Pope wrote to him: ". . . You have expressed my system as clearly as I ought to have done and could not. . . . You express me better than I was able to" (6, 438–39). But decisive for the meaning Pope attaches to the philosophical thoughts in his verse is this sentence addressed to Swift: "Permit me to wear the beard of a Philosopher till I pluck it out and make a jest of it myself." To this Lessing remarks: "That says a lot! How astonished he would be once he discovers that a noted academy had considered this false beard worthy of serious examination" (6, 445).

d) The contest topic, in the way it is formulated, in the last analysis rests on a false premise. It asks for an "examination of Pope's system contained in the proposition that ultimately all is good" (6, 411). But this is precisely what Pope did not maintain. He concedes that nature allows many an evil to befall us (cf. 6, 426). Hence he could not possibly say that everything was "good." But he could say that, in the scheme of things, everything was "right." Hence he states: "Whatever is, is right" (6, 425). The academy had been led astray by the French translation *tout est bien.*

e) Lessing rescues and defends what matters most in philosophy against both sides: against scientific research, which wants to take the place of philosophy, and against the confusion of arbitrary, haphazard, unsystematic argumentation. These antagonistic parties occupy academic chairs and are members of academies.

But does Lessing clarify what he rescues and defends? Obviously not by either of the aforementioned methods—scientific truth or the muddle of uncritical, arbitrary, inconclusive thought. But then, by what other method? As philosopher, Lessing is an awakener, his thinking is illuminating and unsettling, but it does not specify the truth which will offer tranquillity and a safe harbor. On the contrary, he realizes that such a goal is unattainable; all we can do is remain on the way.

This accounts for Lessing's affinity with philosophers such as Leibniz and Spinoza, and his admiration for them.

He is able to think in a systematically strict manner. On a limited scale, he tries to outline systems. But he is not the creator of any system. The only time he comes close to it is toward the end of *Education of The Human Race.* There, his philosophical and theological insights seem to arrive at a synthesis; but the whole remains in suspension and he ends with questions.

The attempts to organize philosophy in systems are recognized by him as distinct areas of human cognition. But he resists wherever a configuration, or a system, posits itself as absolute.

For philosophical criticism in the arts, he draws his ideas from Aristotle; for his basic views his preference points to Leibniz and Spinoza.

C. Lessing's mode of thinking

Lessing's thoughts differentiate, narrow, push to extremes; they force us to ask our questions clearly; results pertain to specifics, not to totalities. Whatever the circumstances, thought opens up to further thought, deeper penetration, greater emphasis until we see clearly what is at stake when one arrives at faith.

Formally, reading Lessing is an exercise in clear thinking, in precise expression, in following a sequence of ideas that is clear and eschews what is extraneous. But he also brings us integrity of content, seriousness of truth, freedom of communication, sovereignty of expression.

This thinking is experimental: it experiments with consequences; it conveys immediacy through the calculated evocation of feeling; it questions what had seemed sacred and inviolable; it risks the loss of a ground in which one's life is rooted; it ends in questions. It is an experiment with concepts, with real actions, with oneself. It is the risk which human beings take upon themselves in being human, that is, a being that thinks.

This thinking blazes trails and is liberating in the search for truth.

In the realm of theory, experimental thinking is hypothetical thinking: if this is true, then that will follow.

Clarity of thought calls for decisive expression. This clarity, however, signifies that it is no more than experimentation. Such experimental thinking cannot find in the substance of its thought the ground on which—because it is absolute—it would be possible from now on to base oneself for all time to come.

". . . precisely these propositions, which I present as possible points of view able to secure the peace of mind of those desirous to rest content with a Christianity doing without theology . . . precisely these propositions Herr Mascho [12] turns into postulates, not of Christianity but of theology" (13, 146).

The Bible contains revelation but is not revelation as such—distinction between letter and spirit. Religion existed before there was a Bible (cf. 13, 145).

Lessing therefore has no "system." But he takes hold of systems, designs systems, and may even in a particular context speak of "my system." All systems are experiments, subject to both acceptance and rejection. Lessing understands systems and constantly practices systematic thinking. But he does not give preference to one system over another and does not follow any of them. Since his conception of truth excludes systems, and since thinking as such is systematic and, if it is developed in the form of a system, demands postulates, systems for him become transformed into a multitude of designs, of possibilities. At the end we find not a system but a question.

In this world the philosopher operates within the means granted him as a human being. Consequently he relinquishes revelation. But, thinking and restless, he confronts the claim of revelation. At this point

---

[12] Friedrich Wilhelm Mascho (died 1784) was an independent scholar, author of *In Defense of the Revealed Christian Religion.*

Lessing's thought achieves its height and breadth. A philosopher is a "man who saw and acted solely in the light of nature, let himself be wholly contented with this light, and sought to make and maintain this light as pure and bright as possible" (16, 424).

Lessing's mode of thinking is polemical. It challenges and wards off. It is antidogmatic: whatever claims to be absolute theory, creed, or to be unquestionable is by its very nature untrue for him. His thinking is ironical; thus even his own pronouncements are immediately suspended.

This kind of approach is characteristic of the literati. Lessing is a leader of the literati just as Socrates was of the Sophists. But Socrates and Lessing think polemically, not destructively. The distinction here lies in whether one proceeds in an arbitrary fashion, exhibiting one's intellectual brilliance in whatever situation, or whether proceeding from belief, one proclaims through such forms something positive in an indirect way because it cannot be said directly without becoming lost in what is said and in the speaker. What does such oppositional thinking, which is antidogmatic and ironic, stand for and what is affirmed in it?

Nicolai said of Lessing that he is "dogmatic in his principles but skeptical in his investigations." Nicolai is right on the mark, but errs in the use of "dogmatic." If "dogmatic" character is ascribed to Lessing's principles, they defy formulation. But they are precisely the means by which the polemic, antidogmatic, experimental, ironic language avoids becoming arbitrary in character and transmits to us a faith which is unitary. Such integral thinking is supported by one basic frame of mind.

This frame of mind is manifested directly in practice and in the thinking related to practice.

2. *Philosophy in relation to practice*

Lessing realizes an idea of humanity, one that is not primarily a humanism informing education, nor does it hark back to the ideals of classical antiquity. Nor does his idea of humanity lie in a flourishing spirituality; it means realizing a modern humanity which presents the following features:

The idea of tolerance; a disposition for communication, discussion, and polemics; a way to judge greatness in human beings, and evaluate justice; the degree of humaneness possible in the state.

Lessing was the first to recognize, with great indignation and fundamental clarity, the inhumanity with which the Jews among us in the Western world of Christendom are judged and treated. One of his earliest plays, *The Jews* (1749), deals with this problem; in his last great dramatic poem, *Nathan the Wise,* he chose a Jew to represent greatness in faith, reason, and humanity.

In a later preface to *The Jews,* he wrote about "the disgraceful oppression under which a people must suffer which a Christian, I would think, cannot regard without a kind of veneration. From among this people, it seems to me, a great number of heroes and prophets had issued in the past, and now should people doubt whether an honest man can be found among them" (5, 270)?

The significance of Lessing's attitude needs to be clarified by way of comparison. For a long time individual Jews had been acknowledged to be decent. But among Christians it was taken for granted that, by and large, Jews still were the evil people, the usurers, the swindlers. The poet Gellert thought that "perhaps many among this nation would have a better heart if we did not make them even more vile and deceitful by our contempt and crafty brutality and did not . . . force them, by our own conduct, to hate our religion" (Schmidt, I, 149).

Lessing was the first to see the Jews, without any reservation, as human beings, not as alien, in no way inferior. And he did not ask (as would happen in the course of the so-called assimilation) that they cease to be Jews. He not only went beyond earlier humane pronouncements, but also transformed them fundamentally.

He may have been the first person in the Western world entirely free of anti-Semitic thoughts and feelings who made his stand (as clearly as, before him, Balthasar Bekker[13] did against the madness of belief in and persecution of witches) against the madness of hatred for Jews, of antipathy and persecution.

We would do him an injustice if we were to label him a philo-Semite—who is merely a counterpart of an anti-Semite. This contra position evaporates in the pure air of humanity.

Around 1753 Lessing came to know Moses Mendelssohn, his best friend. But long before meeting him, Lessing had already clarified his own position with regard to the Jewish question. In 1754 he describes his new friend enthusiastically in a letter: "His honesty and his philosophic spirit predispose me to consider him a second Spinoza who will lack nothing to be Spinoza's equal except his errors" (17, 40).

Lessing already had been exposed to the defamation which became the lot of many Germans who stood up publicly for Jews. In 1778 a

---

[13] Balthasar Bekker (1634–1698) was a Dutch Reform theologian.

rumor was current that, in recognition of his attack on Christianity (though there was no such attack except in the eyes of some orthodox), the Jews of Amsterdam had made him a gift of one thousand ducats.

Let me digress briefly by speaking about the last classical age of the German spirit. It was with Lessing and Mendelssohn that the spiritually great era of the indissoluble union between Germans and Jews began. Ever since, there have been Jewish Germans or German Jews, which, in the original meaning, amounts to the same thing. They lived and created in the German language and considered themselves rightly to be Germans without having to abandon their Jewishness (a perversion that arose early).

Since that step was taken, the spirit of humanitarianism, impartiality, openness, and freedom itself cannot tolerate anti-Semitism within its purlieu. Anti-Semitism is not only indecent but also a threat to freedom itself. Wherever anti-Semitism arises there begins the self-destruction of truthfulness, of reason, of justice, of the love of mankind—as was to happen in wide circles among the Romantics, for example, in the anti-Semite Fichte, the pernicious prophet of a false German nationalism. When Treitschke, in Overbeck's phrase, made anti-Semitism "housebroken" *(stubenrein)* and when in the world of German culture one could make anti-Semitic remarks without being despised for it, the downfall of spirit itself had its inception. Even the tinge of anti-Semitism in Jacob Burckhardt, the uniquely great historical thinker, opens the door to the question of human limitations in conceptions of history.[14] It throws a slight shadow on the depth of his insights.

No matter how great the distance between the prevalent anti-Semitism and the murder of the Jews in Germany, without the anti-Semitism this murder would not have been possible. It brought to an end that German spiritual epoch and has produced the present total emptiness. Its symbol was the spiritual collapse of our philosophical seminars after 1933, when German Jews were absent.

LESSING'S THEOLOGICAL THOUGHT

1. Biographical perspective prior to publication of Fragments of Anonym

The polemics of 1777–78 that followed the publication of excerpts from the papers of "Anonym" are famous. In Lessing's thinking,

[14] Johann Gottlieb Fichte (1762–1814) was a German philosopher and early proponent of German idealism; Heinrich von Treitschke (1834–1896), a German historian and publicist; Franz Overbeck (1837–1905), a Russian-born Protestant theologian; Jakob Burckhardt (1818–1897), a Swiss cultural historian.

however, they constitute the high point of public debate on questions that occupied him from the outset and continued to do so. In these writings—many minor ones published only posthumously, others occasionally, but only incidentally, alongside poetical and critical works that at first glance were much more impressive—Lessing documented consistently what was of major importance for him.

a) *The youth:* Two poetical pieces—"From a Poem on Human Happiness," 1748 (I, 237ff.) and "Religion," 1751 (I, 255ff.), both fragments—testify to what the twenty-year-old experienced and thought on a philosophic-religious level.

He poses questions about his existence: "Why? . . . For happiness. Who? . . . A human being.—Where? . . . On Earth" (I, 258). These three answers—"Information without illumination"—may satisfy children. He must question beyond them.

> "What is man? His happiness? The earth on which he errs?
> Explain whatever you name."

No answer is forthcoming. The questioning turns to the future:

> ". . . and tell us also what he will become.
> Once the clock stops that thinks and feels in him.
> What stays of him when worms assault his corpse,
> Fatten on him and soon will rot on him?
> Are worm and man alike, laid out sans hope,
> Does man stay dust in dust? Or will new life
> Rise at the Almighty's signal from his ashes?"

The situation is desperate.

> "Examine, mortals all, life's short expanse!
> What is to come is Night. What lies behind is Dream.
> The point of presence is too short for joy,
> And yet, short as it is, too long for pain."

Lessing prefaces these skeptical aspects of his poem:

"The first canto addresses specifically those doubts that can be raised against all that is divine, occasioned by the internal and external wretchedness of man." It is a "soliloquy . . . silently put into words on a lonely day of trouble. One should not think that the poet loses sight of his subject when he appears to lose himself in the labyrinths of self-knowledge. Self-knowledge always was the shortest path to religion and, I might add, the surest" (I, 255).

His motive was not to play skeptical intellectual games, was not ill humor, a whim, disgust or ennui. He thirsted for truth. He searched for it in thought by searching for himself:

> "Apart from world and joy, in hours unwatched,
> I tied fugitive thought to its own self,
> And since my cries for help were left unknown
> I blithely undertook myself to know."

To no avail . . .

> "Lost in myself, I neither saw, heard, felt,
> Hoping for light of day I was plunged into night
> I've lived now twenty years, and still no I in sight."

The immediate result—perplexity:

> "What of myself I thought is false, ridiculous.
> I doubt my very being, so unknown to my mind" (I, 257).

In his introduction to the poem Lessing developed the dreary picture we are faced with when investigating the nature of man:

"Let us look back on the first day of our life. What do we find? A birth process that we have in common with the animals . . . an even worse one, followed by mindless, unfeeling years; the first proof of our humanity we give in the vices we find implanted in us, and implanted more powerfully than the virtues. . . . Our vices alternate with our betterment; a betterment brought about by the passage of years, grounded in the changes of our humors" (I, 255–56). Not even the wisest is exempt. "In him vices exert their rule in more attractive guise and owing to the nature of their motives are less harmful, though just as compelling as those planted in the most depraved soul among the rabble.

"What a sight! To find, within the whole confines of the heart, nothing but vice! And this comes from God? Comes from an omnipotent, wise God? Torturing doubts!

"But perhaps our mind is all the more divine. Perhaps we were created for truth since we are not made for virtue. For truth? How multifarious is it? Everyone thinks he possesses it, and everyone possesses it differently. No, only error is our share and illusion our science.

"Add to this pitiful picture of our noblest part also a depiction of the less noble—of the body. It is a combination of mechanical miracles that testifies to an eternal artist. But the body is also a combination of loathsome illnesses, illnesses inherent in its structure which betray the hand of an incompetent" (I, 256).

All this persuades the doubting poet to draw the conclusion:

"Whence man?
Too bad to be from God;
Too good to be by chance."

All these objections, says Lessing, "will be refuted in the cantos to follow." "Even the misery just described" must "become the guidepost to religion" (I, 256). These cantos, however, were never written. But even earlier, and throughout his life, Lessing expressed what would have been their content.

There is another aspect to man:

"That which inhabits me, which feels and thinks in me,
. . .
That knows itself and tells itself: I am;
. . .
By power invisible propelled from day to day,
And with encompassing sight foresees tomorrow
And lifts me, creature not endowed with wings
From dust below to flights in heavens above.
. . .
By which man becomes man, and challenged as a human:
That is the clockwork's force, which beats within the brain . . ."

This, which is actual, of which I assure myself when I become conscious of myself, can it be explained on the basis of nature? No. Lessing exclaims:

"Speak then, you clever fool, if that which bodies make,
Be so much clearer than the spirit's work.
You clarify dilemma through dilemmas . . ." (I, 240).

What is man? This question is inseparable from *Is there a God? Why?*

"Yes, I believe in God,
Denying God, yourself you must deny.
If I am, so is God. He can depart from me,
But not so I from Him. He is if I were not.
And something speaks in me that says, He is."

But what if there's no God?

"Woe to him who, not feeling this, wants bliss,
Drives God from Heaven, looks for Him on earth.
O wretched world that its creator lacks,

. . .

Is Chance the thing that toys with me and you?
Am I become a man begotten only . . . ?"

Then it would be best to die immediately:

"Die then, since all your toiling serves no purpose,
Tossed between joy and pain, plaything of puckish chance,

. . .

The sage disdains a game controlled by chance alone
Where brightness does not win nor dimness lose.

. . .

I am not pleased by luck that also serves the fools,
Die, leave the world, prototype of such games."

These thoughts are only God-forsaken straying:

"But why am I so wroth? God is, my fate stands firm,
Time, pain, reversals cannot change my bliss" (I, 239).

These are simple, basic philosophic ideas which, grounded in the primal experience of existence, issue from the logic of ignorance.

But this is not enough. It must be thought through, must prove itself in thinking as faith, must as faith be within the community of its origin.

Here Biblical revelation offers itself. Does it give us this truth? It is the presupposition of the truth of faith that it does not permit untruth, does not contain false assertions about any reality. We must see and recognize, out of the motives of faith itself—a faith that unconditionally wants the truth—how revelation appears in the world as reality.

Hence Lessing's research into the Bible, into church history, into the realities of faith that appear to be secular. Their high point falls within his stay in Breslau.

b) *His time in Breslau:* Lessing studies the Church Fathers. He turns toward the realities of church history: the Elpistics (14, 197ff.); the rise of revealed religion (14, 312–13); the manner of transmission and propagation of the Christian religion (14, 314ff.).

At the outset of his research into the propagation of the Christian religion, he tells himself what he intends to do: "Carry out this investigation with all honesty. Look everywhere with your own eyes. Do not exacerbate: do not extenuate. Let the conclusions flow where they will. Do not inhibit the current; do not change its course" (14, 315).

Here are some examples of what he asks and examines, presupposes and maintains:

1) The propagation of Christianity is based on natural causes and is to be understood through them.

2) The first Christians had an esoteric as well as an exoteric doctrine.

3) Rome's persecutions of the Christians were the necessary consequence of the Roman idea of the state. The Christians broke the laws against holding mass meetings at night. Curiosity, especially on the part of the women, and calculated proselytizing played a role. To an efficient police force these meetings must necessarily have appeared suspicious. Those people might have applied for permission. To the authorities, there was no great difference between the carousings of the priests of Bacchus and the love feasts of the early Christians. "What for these sacred banquets?" (14, 318). They abolished both.

Such levelheaded, objective research, Lessing explicitly pointed out, ought to be limited by two considerations: the openendedness of philology; and the fact that it does not concern religion itself but deals with natural phenomena that can be investigated within the limits of conjecture based on actual documents.

The openendedness of philology is erroneous. There is only the one passage in Plutarch on the Elpistic philosophers: they declared "hope to be the strongest bond of human life, and the latter without the former to be completely unbearable" (Plutarch, *Moralia,* 668E; 14, 306).

This is paradigmatic of "all accounts that are based solely on the testimony of a single person. You are satisfied with knowing it, repeating it. . . . But in the end there appears, most likely, an intelligent person who connects such a supposed island to some mainland. He does not know more than his precursors but he conjectures more. His conjecture produces a second one, which leads to a third; and if the matter has sufficient importance . . . then, within a short time, there are so many conjectures that the variations perplex the reader far more than he would have been had there been no conjectures at all. Unfortunately, this is the way in which objects of scholarship are infinitely multiplied . . . and whoever has not mastered the full history of all these fleeting phenomena . . . is considered to be totally ignorant about the matter itself. Conjectures and probabilities fill the brain of the man of letters; where could room for truth be found in it?

"We are lucky enough if these excesses of wit and vanity that divert us from the straight path . . . again stumble on the direction of truth, and at long last one discovery grows out of all the conjectures. Then our true science has gone at least One Step further; those who come after us see the labyrinthine alternative, leave it aside and forge straight ahead" (14, 306–07).

Historical inquiry does not infringe upon religion. At the end of his inquiries into the spread of the Christian religion Lessing writes:

"If from all that has been mentioned so far one were to conclude that the Christian religion was propagated and spread by wholly natural means, one must not think that anything detrimental to religion itself might result from this" (14, 331).

An example is the view "among our theologians that Christ himself could not have chosen a more propitious time to come into the world. . . . If Christ himself had awaited the most propitious time, if he had not been content with supporting the great miracle of his appearance by many additional miracles but had also intended to fit it into the natural course of events, why then do we want to lose sight of this natural development in the subsequent spread of Christianity?" (14, 332).

c) *Deliberate pause and deeper reflection:* At age forty-two Lessing becomes fully aware of what he has been practicing since his youth. In probing the contents of Christian faith and actuality, he means to destroy neither.

1) *Concern about having gone too far:* October 9, 1771, to Mendelssohn: "But is it really right . . . to occupy oneself seriously with truths in whose constant contradiction we live anyway and for our peace of mind must continue to live . . . and equally those that I have long ago ceased to consider as truths. Yet I have been concerned, not only since yesterday, that, by casting off certain prejudices I may have jettisoned a little too much that I shall have to retrieve. Only the fear that I may, bit by bit, drag all the rubbish back home again has so far kept me from doing so, at least in part. It is infinitely difficult to know when and where one should stop, and for a thousand compared to one, the goal of their thinking is reached at the point where they have become tired of thinking" (17, 346–47).

Lessing never underwent a change or experienced a conversion. His fundamental conviction never wavered. On this firm basis he took clarifying steps, scrutinized critically, made retractions, changed fronts.

The nature of this unchanging component can be made clear only by description.

2) *Remains consciously Christian:* "I have nothing against the Christian religion: rather, I am its friend, and will remain kindly disposed toward it and attached to it as long as I live" (16, 536).

3) *Follows neither the old orthodox nor the enlightened "neologic" theology,* although he gives preference to orthodoxy:

"We are agreed that our old religious system is wrong: but . . . I know of nothing in the world in which human sagacity had been more evident and on which it had perfected itself more than on this system" (18, 101–02). This was no patchwork put together by bumblers, no semi-philosophy; however, the theology of enlightenment, which people now want to put in its place, does deserve these appellations.

Obviously the old theology does battle with common sense; but the new theology wants to bribe it. The old orthodox theology arrogates unto itself much less influence on reason and philosophy than the new (cf. 18, 226–27).

The precedence of orthodoxy Lessing expresses in a simile: "I do not mean that the dirty water that can no longer be used should be preserved: but I do not want it poured out until it is known where one can get cleaner water; I merely do not want it poured out without hesitation, without considering that the baby's bath may then have to be liquid manure. And what else is our newfangled theology, as compared to orthodoxy, than liquid manure as against dirty water?

"With orthodoxy, thank God, we more or less had come to terms; a barrier had been erected to separate it from philosophy, allowing each to proceed along its own way without burdening the other. But what is being done now? The barrier is being torn down and, under the pretext of turning us into rational Christians, we are made into highly irrational philosophers. . . . Consider not so much what our latest theologians reject but rather what they intend to put in its place" (18, 101).

It is understandable that, according to Nicolai, the theologians took Lessing for a freethinker; the freethinkers, however, took him for a theologian.

4) *Basic attitude:* His attitude is astonishing. He lives within something that he no longer considers credible but in which his being senses its roots. Hence his doubting and conserving, his constant inquiring, examining, searching.

Based on the context of what he is discussing, his thinking seems to contradict itself. He speaks about the "abominable edifice of nonsense" (17, 366) and yet is moved to reverence before something in this edifice. He resists all attempts to support this edifice by means of sub- terfuge and deceptive ideas, and yet he shows in what sense it is unas- sailable.

He does not in any way attack Christianity, but does battle for a Christianity that is credible.

In the matter of a credible Christianity he sees the decisive point in historicity, but in turn this too becomes problematic. The solution eludes him. It lies in the future.

"I believe in [the Christian religion] and hold it to be true, to the extent that one can believe anything historical and consider it to be true. For I am unable absolutely to refute it in its historical evidence. I cannot counter the testimony that is cited in its favor: it is possible that there never was any other testimony or that it was destroyed or assidu- ously invalidated. This is all the same to me now that the matter is weighed on a scale on which all suspicion, all possibility, all probability can signify almost nothing when measured against one single genuine piece of evidence.

"This explanation, I believe, should satisfy at least those theologians who reduce all Christian faith to human approbation and dismiss any supernatural influence of the Holy Spirit.

"Yet in order to ease the minds of others, who continue to assume such influence, I wish to add that I certainly believe their opinion to be one more strongly founded in Christian dogma and transmitted from the very beginnings of Christianity, one which can hardly be re- futed by mere philosophical reasoning. I cannot deny the possibility of the direct influence of the Holy Spirit; and I surely do not consciously undertake anything that could prevent this possibility from becoming reality.

"However, I must confess—" Here the fragment breaks off (16, 536).

Theology and philosophy have to be kept radically separate even if this separation is itself questionable and cannot be the final word.

2. Publication of the Fragments

Lessing had the right to publish, without censorship, manuscripts pre- served in the Wolfenbüttel library, a privilege he shared with all Wolfenbüttel librarians. In the long series of such publications, he brought out the first fragment of Anonym, "On the Toleration of the Deists" (1774).

In his preface Lessing speaks of "a manuscript from the Wolfenbüttel library"—but it was Lessing who put it there—"neither have I been able to discover by any means at all how and when it got there"—this is a mystification—"nor does any document tell us how and when . . ." (12, 254)—correct, for Lessing did not deposit any such document.

This first fragment did not attract the slightest attention. Three years later (1777) Lessing published "More from the Papers of Anonym, Concerning Revelation" (12, 303ff.). Since he disagreed fundamentally with its contents, he appended "Objections of the Editor" (12, 428ff.). In 1778 a last fragment was published, "On the Aims of Jesus and His Apostles" (13, 215ff.). These fragments seemed to question the very ground of Christian faith. A deluge of refutations was the immediate response. Interest in this matter went far beyond theologians and spread to the entire educated public. Its high point was reached in the dispute with Pastor Goeze, an event that agitated the German public, but also proved to be a literary event because of Lessing's unique style and his by then established reputation. However, the controversy was cut short when Lessing was forbidden to continue his publishing and his polemics.

The unnamed author of the *Fragments* was the deceased Samuel Reimarus (1694–1768). He had been professor of oriental languages and mathematics at the Johanneum in Hamburg, a learned philologist of great eminence.

To the public he was known as a proponent of the Enlightenment. His *Treatises on the Most Eminent Truths of Natural Religion* (1754) reached a seventh edition in 1798. He was also known for his essay "On the Instincts of Animals."

His approach to religious thought exhibited in these writings corresponds to the natural religion introduced from England. It develops the following theses:

Whoever has vivid knowledge of God has religion. Religion is called natural insofar as this knowledge can be gained through the natural power of reason. It is called vivid insofar as it is operative in practical life. It produces a satisfying insight into the interconnection of things, a voluntary inclination to virtue and a contentment of the soul.

Natural knowledge of God, developed by using Wolff's[15] and Leibniz's concepts, implies:

The corporeal world as such is lifeless, hence has its existence

---

[15] Christian Wolff (1679–1754) was a rationalist philosopher of the early German Enlightenment, influenced by Leibniz.

through an independent, eternal Being. Human beings and animals have their origin neither out of this corporeal world nor out of themselves, but from God. The corporeal world exists for the benefit of the living.

We cognize the attributes of God out of the concept of God through rational inference, and out of his works through experience. Thus the wisdom and goodness of God is demonstrated in his wise arrangement and continuing guidance of the world.

Hence Reimarus opposes materialistic atheism such as that of La Mettrie and the pantheistic atheism of Spinoza. He opposes the naturalist view of man such as held by Rousseau. He turns away from Bayle's arguments against the perfection of the world.[16]

Immortality is proved by the nature of the soul as a simple immaterial substance, by God's providence and justice, by our longing for beatitude.

Religion too serves our happiness; it causes parents to assume the burden of feeding and educating their children. It alone makes it possible for human society to endure. It heightens our joys by curbing our sensuous pleasures and introducing loftier ones. Religion alone can lead to true and lasting contentment.

Basing himself on these fundamentals, Reimarus comes to reject miracles. The result of God's insight can only be his desire to maintain the world in all its actuality and continuity. For if God were to change his decisions, he would have to change his reasons, would have to err now and again. Miracles conflict with the orderly maintenance of nature. The more God performed miracles following his act of creation, the more he would dismantle nature rather than confirm it.

This was as much of Reimarus's views as he had published himself; they were well within the bounds of the Enlightenment as commonly understood. But now came another step. Locke, Leibniz, and Wolff had allowed for revelation, as well as for the thesis "without miracles no revelation." But for Reimarus the denial of miracles *led to the denial of revelation.*

To have worked out this denial with thoroughness, in comprehensive and systematic examinations, was Reimarus's specific contribution. But within the German Enlightenment such a denial was unheard of, and Reimarus kept it hidden. He never published his major work, entitled "Vindication or Apology for the Rational Worshipers of God," though he had worked on it for decades.

---

[16] Julien Offroy de La Mettrie (1709–1751) was a French materialist philosopher and physician; Pierre Bayle (1647–1706), a French philosopher and encyclopaedist.

It is from this work that Lessing extracted the fragments he published. They had been made available to him by Reimarus's daughter Elise, who was a friend of his. The secrecy was maintained even though it was soon rumored that Reimarus was the author. This was known with certainty only after 1814. The entire work, a voluminous manuscript, became known at a time when it had lost most of its interest. A quarter of the material was published in 1850–52 in Niedner's *Journal of Historical Theology*; the rest was reported on in a careful analysis by D. F. Strauss.[17]

The Christian believer accepts revelation. But why is he a Christian? Because his fathers and grandfathers believed in it. No rational person may ground his faith and hope for eternal bliss in such a contingency. The religion of his father could just as easily be false as true. It must be examined with reason and without preconception.

This examination has two aspects: historical examination of revelation in the Bible and fundamental examination regarding the possibility of revelation as such.

A. Historical examination; Reimarus's methods

1) *The criteria of revelation* (already stated by Wolff and many others): Messengers of divine revelation can only be those whose words and actions are in accord with this purpose, and not those who exhibit impure human aims or engage in immoral behavior.

Only those teachings and precepts can be divine which are in keeping with God's essence and serve man's perfection and bliss; those which contradict God's perfections and the laws of nature cannot.

Nor can anything in contradiction to the foregoing be confirmed by means of a miracle. "Vices cannot miraculously be turned into virtues. . . . Anything that by its nature is impossible and absurd; anything that in any other story would be called a lie, deception, violence and brutality, cannot be made rational, honest, permissible and proper by adding the words: Thus says the Lord" (in Pünjer;[18] cf. Strauss, 5, 264).

Reimarus examines the Old and New Testaments in the light of these principles, and is able to prove a number of things: Human beings cannot be admitted as messengers of revelation. This is contradictory and impossible; it engenders moral scandals; in innumerable

---

[17] David Friedrich Strauss, "Hermann Samuel Reimarus und seine Schutzschrift für die vernünftigen Verehrer Gottes," *Gesammelte Schriften*, Bonn, 1877, vol. 5, 229–409.

[18] Bernhard Pünjer, *Geschichte der christlichen Religionsphilosophie seit der Reformation*, Braunschweig, C. A. Schwetschke, 1880.

instances mere mundane matters are taken to be divine phenomena; "the name of God is misused shamefully in a variety of ways . . . the conduct of persons who are represented there as men of God cause nothing but scandal, anger and disgust in honorable and virtuous souls. . . ." "A web of folly, infamous deeds, deception and cruelties . . ." What is named revelation, prophecy, miracle, is "mere delusion, fraud and misuse of the divine name" (in Pünjer, I, 413; cf. Strauss, 5, 322).

2) *The historical origin of the Scriptures:* They came into being gradually, achieved wider recognition by accident, were only later taken to be the word of God. Even the texts of the New Testament are completely human, occasional writings, only later acknowledged to be canonical. Hence they are in need of historical interpretation.

3) *Crucial importance of setting Jesus' teaching apart from that of the Apostles:* Jesus said, "Repent, the kingdom of heaven is near"; His are noble, divine teachings valid for all times and all peoples. Bound up with his teachings are Jesus' intentions to establish the kingdom of heaven, a kingdom of this world with worldly power and glory. He never aimed at introducing a new religion.

4) *The defeat of the plan by Jesus' death:* In the exigency of miscarried hopes, the disciples created a new system.

The Resurrection is invented. Because of its contradictions, the testimony of the disciples falls apart; the testimony they sought in Old Testament prophecies is as worthless to them as the traditional Jewish interpretation of Scripture. Now quotations picked out from the Old Testament are made to prove that Jesus had come to atone through His suffering and death for the sins of the whole world. The disciples abducted the corpse and fabricated events: resurrection, ascent to heaven after forty days, imminent return to sit in judgment.

To the beautiful, rational ethic of their master they appended—accommodating themselves to human weakness—all kinds of impenetrable mysteries and wonder-working supports. The result: "Now observe . . . whether the entire system of Apostolic Christianity does not, from beginning to end, rest on nothing but false doctrines, that is, on doctrines that form the basis and substance of this religion, the very basis on which it must stand or fall" (in Pünjer, I, 414; cf. Strauss, 5, 389).

B. *Fundamental examination*

To the historical and historico-critical examination, proof is added that revelation as such is altogether impossible. Three instances:

First, revelation could be granted in its immediacy to all man-kind—a perpetual miracle and counter to divine wisdom. Second, it could be granted to specific persons; in this case divine revelation would have to be accepted on the basis of human testimony, which is unreliable. Hence this way too seems counter to divine wisdom. Third, it could be granted to only one people at certain times, mediated by specific persons. The miraculous element remains, for in this instance, too, revelation is fraught with uncertainty, not only because anyone's clearest cognition is necessarily obscure and incomprehensible, but because there are always false prophets and the testimony of tradition is merely human. And it is incompatible with God's goodness and wis-dom. So, too, is pretending that belief in this revelation is the indispens-able and only means to blessedness. Rather, the means thereto are revelation in nature or natural religion.

Why did Lessing publish the Fragments?

1) Did he consider their content to be correct and true? He thought so only with regard to historical facts, and even there he was still ques-tioning.

2) Because of his wish to oppose Christianity, indirectly, slyly, under cover? Not at all. He wanted to further truth by bringing into discus-sion matters that had been thoroughly investigated. A great error, car-ried through consistently, is more conducive to truth than thoughtless acceptance on faith of something traditional, accustomed, proper, and considered the hallmark of personal goodness. The presupposition for such a path to truth is honesty in the will-to-truth that arrives at truth necessarily by way of error.

3) Lessing therefore proceeded critically, sifting out what was cor-rect and what does or does not follow from it.

He is far from the univocity of the Enlightenment and from the simplistic certainty of its thinking precisely at the point where it errs radically. What Lessing himself really thought has to unfold itself to us by and by. Certainly he did not reject Spinoza as an atheist. He had his own doubts about a personal God. But Lessing was more inclined toward orthodoxy than toward the enlightened rationalizations in the-ology, which in their halfheartedness seemed dishonest to him.

The one thing certain is that Lessing intended to forge ahead, in-quiring, thinking, testing in public discussion, always seeking to be taught himself. That was his decisive motive.

Reimarus may have offered historically correct insights; more im-portant, he posed historically meaningful questions. He also exhibits a philosophy of Enlightenment which in the religious sphere strikes us as superficial, displaying an unequivocal complacency that was never radically shaken, showing a naïve lack of critical sense, a childlike acceptance of the notion of a personal God and personal immortality.

Following these paths and repudiating this childlike acceptance with an equally naïve criticism leads to total unbelief. Critically separating what one is proving from what one is not, as Lessing does, leads to increasing clarity in a religious faith that, while unable to profess any creed, is unshakable nonetheless, as is Lessing's faith. It is an extraordinary deepening of faith itself.

Both paths lead beyond Reimarus—into the void or into depth.

Why did Reimarus keep silent and Lessing publish?
As a reliable and extremely well-informed scholar, as an honest thinker, as a serious and pious man, Reimarus was impeccable. He was not, however, a fighter, nor a reformer, and as a result was cautious. Lessing too was cautious, in keeping with the times.

Lessing's publication was a courageous act. He dared to do what Reimarus did not dare. He assumed a burden that did not endanger the anonymous dead author—indeed, no one but Lessing himself.

Lessing became aware of this. He justified Reimarus's silence but in the "Seventh Anti-Goeze" distanced himself from the attitude underlying this silence. "The anonymous author was a man so careful that he wished to avoid vexing anyone with truths; but I refuse to believe in such vexation. I am staunchly convinced that it is not the truths that one only presents for examination that foment a raging religious fanaticism among the ordinary masses, but, rather, those that one intends to translate into action.

"The anonymous author was such a clever man that he wished to avoid causing himself or others distress by an all-too premature publication. I in my frenzy risk first and foremost my own safety, which I do because of my belief that opinions, if they are soundly based, cannot be made public early enough in the interest of mankind" (13, 186).

Lessing would agree with the unnamed author if "only the laudable modesty and caution of the anonymous author were not buttressed by so much confidence in being proven right, so much disdain of the ordinary man, so much mistrust in his era!"

Anonym, "holding his manuscript ready . . . for the use of understanding friends," did not destroy it.

"Or do you also believe, Head Pastor, that it is of no consequence what reasonable people believe in private provided the rabble, the dear rabble, nicely remain on the track on which the clergy alone know how to guide it?" (13, 186).

3. Problems faced by Lessing in the critique of Reimarus's Fragments

Lessing is far removed from the world of the Enlightenment and its simple clarity, and from the naïve certainty of its thinking, which errs radically where it supposes self-evidence.

Reimarus, in his philosophy of the Enlightenment, considers some historically significant problems. Yet with regard to religion he is without care or ambivalence, in no way shaken to the roots; he uncritically, like a child, believes he possesses self-evidently the personal God and personal immortality through rational knowledge. But to follow such uncritical enlightenment while also uncritically rejecting such self-evidences will lead to complete unfaith. On the other hand, distinguishing critically between what can and cannot be proved will lead, as in Lessing, to greater clarity in philosophic faith, a faith unable to commit itself to a confession yet unshakable in the depth of faith itself. Both paths lead beyond Reimarus: either into the void of the ungrounded intellect, or into the profundity of reason.

Lessing, in his search, also considers certain problems, but he does not solve them. He points to them with great decisiveness, yet his trenchant formulations must not keep us from noting that, when it comes to essential issues, everything is left open. By rejecting what is false, he opens spaces which he permeates with his basic attitude, but which, toying with various designs, he furnishes neither with rationally known content nor with a confession of faith.

Turning to the main problem areas within which Lessing's discussions take place, let us call to mind those pertaining to history and those belonging to revelation.

A. The problem of history

1) *Truth is suprahistorical.* Insofar as this thesis is valid, Lessing formulates it as follows: "Religion is not true because the Evangelists and Apostles taught it: rather, they taught it because it is true." And still stronger: "Even what God teaches is not true because God wants to teach it: rather, God teaches it because it is true" (13, 127).

Insofar as we seek truth in reason, we mean the truth that is eternal, suprahistorical, independent of history. But we live within history. We do not possess the truth that is absolute and indifferent to history.

This suprahistorical truth, grasped perhaps in history in its rudiments, is the truth which would be wholly present only in complete reason. But it would also constitute the end of history, since everything could now be completed. Because completed reason need no longer find its actualization in history, it is itself no longer historical.

The question of the truth that is historically grounded and actualizes itself historically is challenging because of our human situation: we live historically, must live in time; no matter what we think and do, we cannot but move within history. On the other hand, the idea of eternal, suprahistorical, unhistorical truth is no less compelling and inescapable. It is present for us at least in forms of atemporal correctness in their literal meaning, existing in actuality, and, as such, standing as symbols for suprahistorical absolute truth.

There is a world of correct propositions which are acknowledged as facts, held in common, considered timeless; this world is the only one revealed to us in scientific progress. But there are a number of historical assertions of absolute truth, of juxtaposed claims to revelation that are, in effect, "accidental truths in history." Some assert the claim of being the exclusive and only truth, insisting on their primacy; viewed from the standpoint of primacy, other absolute claims are acknowledged as partial truths and preliminary stages and are appropriated as such.

But Lessing tends as strongly toward reason as suprahistorical and unhistorical truth operative in history and self-creative in its limitless progress, as he does toward historic truth in the basic form of our temporal existence, from which we cannot separate ourselves without sinking into emptiness.

2) *What is the source of our knowledge of historic truth and its claim to absoluteness?* It rests on testimony. Measured against the universal validity of reason, this is a weak foundation.

In the first place, testimony is only historical, which reduces it to probability; it lacks the certainty and reliability of mathematical insight. It needs to be examined by comparing the actually available testimonies, an established method in historical research. How can historical knowledge be based on the study of documents and artifacts? What can be reliably known in this way? What degree of certainty can be achieved? What is the nature of this certainty? For one thing, it is a matter of the difference between the truths of reason (as in mathematics) and those of fact (for example, saying that the sun will rise again tomorrow does not present incontrovertible certainty, as does saying that $3 \times 3 = 9$). Then again we deal here with the difference between the truths of natural events, the laws of which can be established by repeated observation, and the unique, unrepeatable truths of history.

In the second place, however, in dealing with testimony of a revelation, the object witnessed to is of a nature that cannot be seen in a universally valid manner—it is present only to faith; for faith, an "accidental" revelation is absolute in its fundamental quality. Not even the eyewitness can experience any empirical proof of the revelation: to the believer, this revelation is present through an act not repeatable by other eyewitnesses or by mankind in general. No matter what the moment—whether while revelation happens or in the hearing of the testimony—there is no compelling reason for accepting the truth of what is believed.

3) For both of these reasons Lessing states that *"contingent historical truths . . . can never become the proof for necessary rational truths"* (13, 5).

If a historical truth lays claim to the absolute nature implied in the assertion that eternal bliss cannot be grounded on any other foundation than on faith in it, the *situation becomes desperate;* the certainty of rational cognition can never be achieved in this fashion. To mingle the two results is a self-deception and destroys both simultaneously. It is impossible to get from the one (reason) to the other (faith in the absolute truth of history). This is the "nasty wide ditch" across which Lessing, as he confesses, cannot jump, no matter how diligently he has tried to do so. "If anyone can help me across, I hope he will; I ask him, I implore him. He will earn God's blessing for this" (13, 7).

No irony is implied here, since Lessing does indeed see an existential problem at this point; and yet there *is* irony, in that he himself confesses to his inability to make the leap without, however, considering it to be the loss of his eternal salvation. This very transition from demonstrated truths to the truths of history, from valid conceptual cognition to metaphysical contents of faith was a topic in his last conversation with Jacobi, shortly before his death. Jacobi had argued against Spinoza: "I believe that there is an intelligible personal cause of the universe." Lessing, anxious to hear how he manages to do so, receives Jacobi's answer: "I get out of it by means of a *salto mortale;* and you don't seem to find any particular pleasure in standing on your head." Lessing: "Don't say that; as long as I don't have to do as you do. And you will eventually come to stand on your big feet again." Later on, Lessing told him: "Altogether, your *salto mortale* appeals to me; and I can understand how someone with a thinking head on his shoulders can stand on his head so as to move ahead. Take me along if you can."

Jacobi: "If you would only step on this 'springy' spot that tosses me onward, it would happen by itself." Lessing: "But even this would require a leap which I can no longer expect of my old legs and my heavy head."[19]

4) Through his questioning Lessing has touched on *the problem of historicity* scrutinized by reason, and by his pointed formulations has raised a challenge that cannot be brushed aside. He started what was continued by Kierkegaard. The problem defies solution: thinking it through has the purpose of deepening the consciousness of Existenz.

5) *Is Christian faith historic certainty or rational certainty?* Lessing discusses the question. One of the two, after all, ought to be its distinguishing quality. But on consideration it seems that certainty cannot be found along either of the two paths. If Christian faith elects to base itself on historical testimony, then firm ground for the desired salvation cannot be reached on this path.

Hence, Lessing concludes in this context, the truth of faith cannot be grounded, proved, or guaranteed from anything extraneous to it; it is self-assertive. Therefore, understanding the Bible should follow this principle: "The written traditions ought to be explained out of their inner truth, and no written traditions can lend a religious text any inner truth if it has none."

Consequently, all Biblical texts have to be examined in the light of the very faith within which they originated. We cannot claim "inspiration" as their origin, as an article of proof. "Religion is not true because the Evangelists and Apostles taught it: rather, they taught it because it is true" (13, 127).

To this corresponds the following historical fact: The truth of faith is present before it is objectivized in word, scripture, or dogma. The Christian faith predates the New Testament. It can exist independent of the Bible. The Apostles and the first Christians had no written word to ground their faith on. It was "a span of time in which Christian religion . . . had taken hold of a great many souls, though not a single letter had been written of all that since was handed down to us." It took a long time before the first of the Evangelists and Apostles put anything down in writing; "and a very long time before the whole Canon was put together." No matter how much depends on these Scriptures, "the whole truth of Christian religion cannot possibly be said to rest on them." Hence, Lessing thinks, "there is an equal possibility that everything written by the Evangelists and Apostles might be

[19] *Hauptschriften zum Pantheismusstreit zwischen Jacobi und Mendelssohn,* ed., with introduction, by Heinrich Scholz, Berlin, Reuther and Reichard, 1916, 80–81, 91.

lost again while the religion they taught still endures" (13, 121, 117, 118).

6) *From using the Bible* and appropriating it through interpretation, *a veracity results* that need no longer defer to inspired absolutes. For an understanding that grows out of faith makes us see that the Bible obviously contains more than material relevant to religion (cf. 13, 110). Such study rejects the erroneous "hypothesis that the Bible is equally infallible as regards this 'more'" (13, 112).

The wrong use made at various times of the Bible, Lessing calls Bibliolatry (cf. 16, 470ff.). "Luther himself more than once called the Holy Scriptures God. . . . I find Luther more offensive by far . . . when he says that the Holy Scriptures are Christ's spiritual body, and puts his seal on such a crudeness with his ingenuous 'verily.' And now the opposition is charged with having declared that the entire Bible, bereft of the witnessing of the Church, is worth just about as much as Aesop's Fables! It would hardly be possible to find stronger terms for characterizing the two most extreme points of deviation" (16, 472).

7) *Biblical research and the search for assurance of faith* are two separate matters. Biblical research treats the Biblical texts in precisely the same way as other historical documents, inquires into the origins of individual texts (for example, the origin of the Gospels), the intention of the authors, the sources at their disposal. Lessing took part in this endeavor. Two main questions engaged his interest:

(a) The differentiation between the religion of Jesus and the Christian religion: Lessing considered it a foregone conclusion that Christ was the man Jesus, that He had been a real human being. The problem was whether Jesus was more than human. The religion for which Jesus was human in thought and in practice, and the religion for which Jesus was the Christ, that is, more than human, and which made Jesus the object of a cult—these two religions cannot coexist in one and the same person.

Hence Lessing arrives at this differentiation: The religion of Jesus is contained in the Gospels in the clearest and most precise expression. The Christian religion, on the other hand, is "so wavering and ambivalent that there is barely a single point with which two people have associated the same thought, for as long as the world has existed" (16, 519).

Because Jesus' goal differs from that of His disciples, many contradictions in the New Testament texts can be reconciled by proving that there has been an intermingling of both sources.

How did the Christian religion come into being? Not through Jesus, who was not its founder. Jesus was not a Christian. The founder of this religion is not a person but a historical process, the evolution of the Church.

(b) The origin of revealed religion: Lessing attempts to differentiate between "natural religion" and "positive religion" (cf. 14, 312–13). Natural religion defies all definitions. When Lessing writes: "To recognize a God, to seek to create the concepts most worthy of Him, to consider these most worthy concepts in all our actions and thoughts," and that "it is incumbent on each person, and he is obligated to the extent of his powers" (14, 312) to do so, he merely opens a door. He never specified what these most worthy concepts are.

Hence natural religion, seen historically, finds itself in a twofold position: It is innate in man, prior to all history, or at the very beginning, as the precondition of all history, and it stands at the end as the completion unattainable in time. It is immediately present in every human being, linked to the humanity of each, and it can be attained only through the progression of history, through the mediation of a tremendous process.

How does religion operate as "positive religion"? By what means does positive religion come to be? The measure of a man's capacities and hence his natural religion differs from that of other individuals. Hence natural religion cannot be practiced in common. It is not enough to conform in regard to certain matters and concepts. Only when the founder of a religion has imparted to conventional matters the same urgency and necessity as to those recognized by natural religion is communal practice made possible. This communally shared, formed, revealed religion is positive religion.

However, the inner truth is as great in one positive religion as it is in any other. All positive (revealed) religions are equally true and equally false: equally true insofar as it was equally necessary everywhere to produce agreement in public religion; equally false since the essential core is weakened and suppressed. "The best revealed . . . religion is the one which contains the fewest conventional additions to natural religion" (14, 113). Lessing compares the relationship of natural to positive religion with that of natural law to positive law.

In the course of development natural religion is never objectively present as a communal religion. It is the rule intrinsic to each person corresponding to his capacities, and therefore not adaptable to a communally acknowledged and practiced standard. That rule may unite all men in the idea, but only by bringing natural religion to bear on the positive religions. In our communal life we are dependent on positive religion. An individual cannot isolate himself from the community of men on which he depends at every moment, by which and for which he lives.

(c) Lessing constantly presses on beyond the objectivity of the patrimony—Biblical texts, the Church, the dogmas—toward the origin, where truth and the criterion for truth is anchored. Natural religion is prior in origin to revealed religion, as is the religion of Jesus to the Christian religion; the Christian religious faith precedes ecclesiastically formulated faith. In the original primacy everything is simple, immediate, true—to be attained, however, only in the future, in the fulfillment at the end of history.

8) *Historical cognition of Biblical texts,* their quality and value as testimony, and the historical knowledge which today is labeled the history of religion—these Lessing considered important. But with regard to the weight of such knowledge for faith, he declares most decisively that such cognition can neither ground nor refute faith.

Faith cannot be affected by historical or practical objections to Biblical texts. The Bible is not the religion. The "objections against the letter and against the Bible" are "not equivalent with objections against the spirit or against religion" (13, 115).

By taking this position Lessing opposed the orthodox as well as Reimarus. The orthodox say: The Christian faith is true, hence the Bible is true in all its parts. Reimarus says: The Bible is untrue in many parts, hence Christianity is untrue. Lessing opposes the presupposition shared by both opponents by declaring: The Bible is not Christianity, hence attacks on the Bible are not in themselves attacks on Christianity.

To take a particular instance: this way of thinking is evident in belief in the resurrection of Christ. Reimarus says: This resurrection, furthermore, is not credible because the reports of the Evangelists are contradictory. The orthodox say: Christ's resurrection must be believed absolutely for the reports of the Evangelists do not contradict each other. Lessing says: Christ's resurrection may well have happened even though the reports of the Evangelists contradict each other (cf. 13, 22).

By limiting the weight given to historical testimony (it cannot be made to carry the full load since, even in the best of circumstances, it can merely attain a high degree of probability), Lessing also denies that faith as such can be grounded in historical testimony and that the questionable nature of such testimony can subvert it.

He maintains radically that no faith can be grounded in testimony and no tenet be founded in it. "If on historical grounds I cannot raise an objection to Christ raising the dead, do I for this reason also have to accept as truth that God has a son of the same substance?" (13, 6). Because "I cannot counterpose any credible testimony to the resurrection of Christ," must I therefore change "all my basic ideas about the nature of the Godhead accordingly"? (13, 7). That would constitute a leap from historical truth into an entirely different order of truths.

B. *The question of revelation*

Lessing does not deny revelation; neither does he declare himself openly for it. He discusses its possibility and consequences, and refutes only the latter, if he considers them wrong.

When Reimarus thinks that he has proved the impossibility of a revelation that is well-founded so all mankind can believe it, this cannot be taken as proof that revelation is not possible at all. "Would God withhold this blessing from all mankind because he could not let all men, at the same time and to the same degree, take part in it?"

Historically we know of many revelations. Lessing strongly rejects Christianity's claim that its revelation is necessary for the salvation of all men. "Woe to mankind if in this administration of salvation only one single soul is lost. All must participate in the bitterness of the loss of this single soul because each one could have been this single one. And what bliss is so consuming that it does not risk being tainted by such association?" Hence, according to Lessing, it has "never been the generally acknowledged tenet of the Church" that an identical revelation is necessary for the bliss of those who "cannot attain a grounded knowledge of it" (12, 437–38).

We should, rather, assume that "what brings salvation in the various religions must always have been the same . . . but that men did not necessarily . . . connect . . . the same concept with it" (12, 446).

Revelational faith can have considerable substance and yet, looked at from another perspective, appear deficient. In the Jewish belief in God, immortality does not play a role; the Christian sees this as a deficiency, but Lessing sees in this faith of the Jews something unique: "Let us also confess that it is heroic obedience to obey the laws of God merely because they are laws of God and not because he has promised to reward . . . those who obey . . . now and in the hereafter; to obey them though one may totally despair of future reward and not be so very certain of the temporal one either.

"Would a people, raised in this heroic obedience toward God, not be destined, would it not be qualified before all others to be the instrument for carrying out special divine intentions? If the soldier rendering blind obedience to his superior was also utterly convinced of that superior's good sense, tell me if there is anything that his superior might command him to do that goes beyond the soldier's willingness to undertake" (13, 423).

These are considerations of an observer of historical phenomena. But can revelation be even thought of as possible or, because it runs counter to truth, has it to be rejected altogether as a delusion? Lessing does not believe in rejection but approaches the problem with critical and differentiating scrutiny and with an eye on its consequences:

If "there can be and must be revelation, and the right one is discovered, reason should accept this as one more proof of its truth rather than as an argument against it—provided it contains elements that go beyond rational conceptualization. Whoever wishes to cleanse his religion of its suprarational components might as well have no religion at all. For what is a revelation that does not reveal?" (12, 432).

If there is revelation, then "a certain capture of reason by the obedience of faith" rests on the "essential concept of revelation." For "reason surrenders, and its submission is nothing other than the admission of its limits, once it is assured of the actuality of the revelation" (12, 433).

However, Lessing does not clearly determine the mutual relationship of reason and revelation. "The transition from mere rational truths to revealed ones" is "extremely awkward." What has precedence, reason or revelation? He writes: "Whether there can be revelation, or whether it is necessary for it to be, and which one of so many offered as such is the true one can only be decided by reason." Hence reason is the ultimate criterion of truth. Yet a few pages farther on he writes: "Revealed religion does not in the slightest presuppose a rational religion: rather, it includes it" (12, 432 34). Revelation is that which encompasses.

This ambiguity is part and parcel of the historicity of truth for us in time. As individuals and in history as a whole we move toward the maturing of reason. Reason can never relinquish freedom as such but, aware of its particular limits, it may temporarily "surrender" itself. For the time being, captive, as it were, it sees profound truth in the actualities of revelation, a truth which, as yet, is beyond its comprehension, but progresses along with reason in its state of "surrender." In analogy with one's childhood and youthful years, maturity is attained by listening with an attitude of piety to authority, relinquishing the right to be a wiseacre, to merely personal opinion. One follows obediently, provided that matured and self-certain reason remains unharmed. It looks up to authority, submitting itself to the voice of immemorial tradition.

4. The development of Lessing's ideas

A. The actuality of religious faith that Lessing considered incontestable in any questioning

Inquiry into what is historical has no limits, and is not conditional on its congruence with faith.

But the consequences drawn from historical knowledge do not correspond to the assumptions of the Enlighteners or their opponents, the Orthodox. Faith is neither grounded nor destroyed by them; a religious truth alive and present is immune to historical inquiry, even if its results are pragmatically accepted as correct within the meaning and limits of empirical research, and acknowledged by believers and unbelievers.

Lessing expresses the nature of religious truth in various ways, mostly by parables, since this truth of confession to a creed does not lend itself to adequate expression in direct statement. In what way is it present to us?

1) *The eyewitnesses compared to us.* The eyewitnesses of the miracles, of the resurrection, of the prophecies seem to have been in a preferred position: They did not need to depend on historical testimony as a basis, which, as with everything historical, is not so absolutely certain that they safely could base their eternal salvation on it. They saw with their own eyes, they had bodily presence.

But this is not true. What an eyewitness thought he saw did not need to have been universally valid and may not have been really there.

We are in a better position than the eyewitnesses of the past. They "only had the foundation before them on which—convinced of its safety—they dared to build a large edifice. We, by contrast, have before us this great edifice already built. What fool would dig around inquisitively in the foundations of his house merely to make sure of the soundness of the foundation? . . . I am all the more convinced of the soundness of the foundation since the house has been standing for such a long time, a proof that the witnesses of the laying of the foundation lacked" (13, 29–30).

One of Lessing's parables: The temple of Diana of Ephesus "in all its glory." "Now let us assume it was found, in ancient reports, that it rests on a foundation of coal . . . of brittle, crumbly coal." They begin to argue about the coal, what kind it was. "Oh, those arch-fools who would rather argue about the varied texture of the coal than admire the splendid symmetry of the temple!" "I praise what stands above ground and not what lies hidden beneath! . . . Its function is to carry . . ." "That men are so averse to rest content with what stands before them! Here is a religion that, by preaching the resurrection of Christ, has been victorious over the pagan and the Jewish religion." "Not much different . . . with regard to miracles . . . after all, they were not performed for us Christians alive today. Sufficient that they had the power of persuasion they were supposed to have! . . . But to found the truth of religion on the historical probability of these miracles—can this be considered correct intelligent thinking?"

"He who believes he may prove the excellence of the building solely by means of abolishing the scaffolding cannot be greatly interested in the building itself. . . . I shall not allow this preconception of the scaffolding to keep me from judging the structure itself according to the established rules of sound architecture.

"When will they stop trying to suspend nothing less than all of eternity from the filament of a spider!—No; scholastic dogmatics never inflicted such deep wounds on religion as historical exegesis now inflicts on it daily" (13, 30–31).

Another parable: A great palace in a great empire, a palace of immeasurable circumference and very singular architecture: The architecture "appealed . . . through the admiration excited by simplicity and greatness . . . its durability and comfort made it well suited to its purpose . . . from the outside it seemed somewhat confusing; from inside everywhere light and cohesion."

Much quarreling, most heatedly among those "who had the least opportunity to see much of the interior of the palace. For they thought that they had various ancient ground plans in their possession . . . which each interpreted . . . as he pleased."

"Only a very few countered: 'What are your ground plans to us? . . . It is enough for us to discover at every moment that the most benevolent wisdom fills the whole palace and that, issuing from it, nothing but beauty and order and prosperity are spread throughout the whole realm" (13, 94–95).

The others, "who put their trust in one or another of these ground plans . . . claimed that their antagonists were the very arsonists who set fire to the palace itself."

Once, the voices of the guards shouted: "Fire in the palace!" What happened next? Each (outside the palace, in his own house) "rushed to get what he considered his most precious possession—his ground plan. 'Let us at least save just that!'"

And now, their various ground plans in hand, they argued about where the fire was, where it should be doused, quarreling with each other.

"While these busybodies squabbled this palace might really have burned down—had it been aflame in the first place. But the frightened guards had mistaken the northern lights for a conflagration" (13, 95–96).

In this parable Lessing does not have in mind "the commotion aroused by the Fragments." He specifies: "I intended to portray the whole history of the 'Christian religion through it'" (13, 96, note).

Lessing does not personify Christianity, attributing to it good and bad characteristics. He surveys the ages, he sees calamity, folly, crime. He sees the actual substance of life, all the good, the deep significance, the piety maintained throughout the centuries, and to his own day, in his parental home; he sees this as a cohesive force, keeping everything from collapsing into neglect, into chaos, into nothingness.

What is there in the West is Christianity and all that relates to it. What precisely this is cannot be determined. But in its substance it is good. As long as it is good, it cannot be shaken by rational objections or historical inquiries.

2) *Not historical origins but the content of faith exercises a powerful attraction.* What obliges me to believe in the teachings of Christ? "Nothing but these teachings themselves, which, however, eighteen centuries ago were so new, so alien to the whole range of truths known at that time, and so impossible of incorporation into them that nothing less was required than miracles and fulfilled prophecies to attract the attention of the masses to them.

"But to attract the attention of the masses to something signifies helping common sense to get on the right track.—It did arrive there; it is on the track. And those whom it has brought onto this track, to the right and left . . . they are the fruit of those miracles and fulfilled prophecies.

"Seeing these fruits before me ripening and matured, should I not be allowed to satisfy my hunger with them? . . .

"What do I care if the ancient myth is true or false: the fruits are excellent" (13, 8).

What once played a big role—miracles, prophecies—need not do so for us any longer. For what in those days contributed to the acceptance and dissemination of the faith no longer is the ground of faith for us. This ground of faith cannot be settled historically.

3) *Believing without knowing.* Question: "Why have there been so many and good Christians who neither could nor wanted to explain their faith in a rational manner?" (13, 342).

What "do the hypotheses and explanations and proofs of some person matter to the Christian? For him, Christianity is simply there, something that he *feels* to be fully true and in which he *feels* fully blessed.—When the paralytic experiences the beneficial jolts of the electric spark, what does he care whether it is Nollet or Franklin[20] or neither of the two who is right?" (12, 428).

4) *Cognition and practice of faith.* The moral life is sustained by faith and not by cognition of faith.

May 30, 1749: "The Christian religion is not a finished product which one ought to take from one's forebears in trust and in faith. True, most people inherit it from them as they do their money. . . . As long as I see that one of the noblest commandments of Christianity, *to love one's enemy,* is not better observed, I continue to doubt that those are Christians who claim to be such" (17, 18).

This does not mean that Lessing considered the cognition of faith to be invalid. It ought to assume its proper place, ought to be taken seriously, but should not make any false claims. Whenever it is a question of the theory or the practice of faith, practice takes precedence.

"Herrnhuter."[21] On the theological battle within the Protestant sects, Lessing remarks: "One only weakens the other, one side compelling faith through proofs and the other one supporting the proofs through faith; nowadays, I say, a true Christian has become so much more of a rarity, through this perverse way of teaching Christianity, than he was in the dark times. Our cognition shows us to be angels, our lives prove us to be devils" (14, 160).

In the ironical dialogue "The Testament of John" (1777), Lessing refers to a report by Jerome: John the Evangelist, in his old age, had repeated at every gathering only the following words: "Children, love one another"; and to the question why he always said the same words, he had answered: Because it is the commandment of the Lord, and if this alone were to happen, it would suffice. Lessing wanted those divided by the Gospel according to John to be united by the Testament of John. This is the subject of the discussion with the theologians. The

---

[20] L'Abbé Jean-Antoine Nollet (1700–1770), a French physicist; Benjamin Franklin (1706–1790).

[21] "Thoughts about the Herrenhuter," an essay written by Lessing in 1750 (14, 154–). The Herrenhuter were a Mennonite sect that arose in the 1720s in the region of Prussian Saxony where Lessing was at home.

theologian posits the thesis that Christian love is the Christian religion only insofar as "only that is true Christian love which is founded on Christian doctrines." Even if it is far more difficult to practice Christian love than to accept and confess Christian doctrines, Christian love by itself would not help, for one does not become a Christian merely by practicing love. When Lessing points to the words of Jesus: "Whoever is not against us is for us," the theologian answers: He is identical with the Jesus who says at another place: "Whoever is not with me is against me." And Lessing closes the exchange: "Yes, indeed! By all means; here I am silenced.—Oh, you alone then are a true Christian!—And well read in the Scriptures, as is the Devil" (13, 16–17).

This is a radical antithesis, in relation to which Lessing—as a young man as well as in his maturity—clearly takes one side: Is it the knowledge of faith or the correct confession of faith that is necessary for salvation, or is it the way he lives his life? The decision lies not on the side of confession, not in the proofs and rational conclusions based on theory, not at all in doctrine, but in the practice of one's life. All his discussions seem to serve the purpose of preserving the space for this practice.

Exchange between the orthodox and Lessing. In the ironical mode, indirect conclusions: Contradictions have to be examined as to place and weight (as, in a different way, in the case of contradictory testimonies to the resurrection).

You do not prove, you only demonstrate.

The decision lies in practical application, hence not in rational inference, not in proof, not in theory, not in doctrine.

Thus, the true meaning of the critical debate between Lessing and orthodox theologians is limited to keeping the space open for practice.

The radical antithesis to this would be that cognition of faith is the heart of the question, the heart of eternal salvation.

Perhaps only one thing is arrived at: Existence in the world is mysterious and the more deeply we progress in our world-orientation, the more mysterious it becomes. It is disingenuous to declare revelation to be absolutely impossible, even though the mere attempt to define it fails; the very fact that it is expressed gives it substance, makes it a tangible reality in the world. "What God speaks out of the ground prior to any world"—this sentence itself is merely a cipher.

But the limitary consciousness of what is undefinably possible keeps the possibility of revelation open but prevents making it comprehensible; this calls upon us to question, to take soundings, to examine and listen to what appears in the world with such a claim.

5) *The actuality of the faith of Biblical religion.* It is not that Lessing

determines the essence of Christianity and then proceeds to judge it as being either good or bad. Instead, he sees both throughout the ages: calamity, foolishness, crimes, but also the good: the profound meaning as well as the piety through the centuries and in his own time (in his parents' home), holding all things together; the actual life-substance preventing collapse into neglect, chaos, nothingness.

In the West the actuality of faith is Christianity, Biblical religion, and whatever is connected with it, that is, almost everything. What this actuality of faith is cannot be determined. Insofar as it is the substance of good it cannot be shaken by rational scruples or historical inquiries.

Lessing is neither theologian nor pastor nor churchman. He is an independent human being, a unique individual who addresses himself to the unique individuals in his large circle of readers.

But what does he believe in? What is the position from which he sees his opponents? There is no single position that can be considered his final one; he constantly experiments with positions. The only validity, for him, lies in the movement toward truth.

5. Lessing's path

A. The battle against Goeze

Only once did Lessing depart from a style of polemics that was often sharp but served communication and open critical exchange. This happened in his dangerous public battle against Goeze. There are explanatory antecedents to how this radical and abrupt change in Lessing's polemical tactics came about.

Lessing had no intention of entering the fray against orthodoxy when he published the *Fragments*. His aim was, rather, to steer the debate against the blinkered enlighteners in the direction of questioning reflection by means of his "Antitheses." However, what he did not intend and what took him by surprise was that many of the representatives of orthodoxy passionately attacked him—which Goeze also did in the end. To them, Lessing's "Antitheses," in their defense of Reimarus, seemed even worse than Reimarus himself. At first Lessing responded in his accustomed style. But with the intrusion of Head Pastor Goeze his style, his inner attitude, and the meaning of his polemics changed radically from one moment to the next.

Before that, theological-philosophical questions were the main focus. These questions continue to be present, and even find, in part, their clearest formulation; but now they are displaced in importance by a combative style in which Lessing purposely does not shrink from the use of ruthless tactics. Let us take a look at the way this battle is fought. Where there is struggle that no longer intends communication because communication has been recognized as impossible, injustice is being committed. If you set yourself up as judge, you yourself will commit injustice by losing sight of what was at the heart of the struggle. Now the question becomes: Who started it, who broke off communication? A question that also can be answered unequivocally only in rare borderline situations.

From Lessing's perspective this is how it started: He asks the Head Pastor for a correction. "What I said was that even if it were impossible to do away with all the objections which reason is so busily raising against the Bible, religion would yet remain untouched and undiminished in the hearts of those Christians who instinctively have reached an inner feeling for its essential truths. . . . I am said to have said, that objections against the Bible are unanswerable." Goeze must have acted precipitously, and Lessing addresses him: ". . . those who most readily act hastily are not the worst people. For, most of the time, they are just as ready to admit their undue haste. And the admission of precipitousness often teaches us more than cold calculated infallibility." He expected Goeze to respond with an explanatory correction. "However, without such an explanation, Reverend Sir, I have to let you go on writing—just as I have to let you preach." But before this request was printed, Lessing had to read new "calumnies" and wrote: I "am as though destroyed!" Together with the "request," he published his "conceivable letter of challenge," announcing that even the "tone, which I might permit myself to use with Pastor Goeze in the future"—will differ from what he would have preferred as proper. He closed: "Go ahead, Pastor, write to your heart's content: I shall write, too. If I allow you to be right in matters concerning myself or my Anonym when you are not right: then I would have to abandon my pen altogether" (13, 99–101, 103).

Four motives for Lessing's anger:

1) *The defamation of Anonym*

Lessing knew Reimarus and knew his work. Even prior to the Goeze controversy, he protested against the "accusation that Anonym willfully refused to recognize a truth which he actually recognized . . . an accusation that transforms a man so completely into a devil" (13, 211). If one assails the works of "this conscientious and laconically precise man," "if one speaks of warmed-over hash," then he, Lessing, would like to "advise, as a friend, to soften the shrill tone a little." For this work attests to thorough erudition and intellectual power. The justice owing to him as a person is of a nature different from the justice of the cause. The latter may be considered doubtful, the former is not. Lessing rejects the accusations of "willful obduracy, intentional callousness, calculated schemes, lies" (13, 23), but even at this stage he prefers to keep silent and refrains from tit-for-tat scolding. However, as far as the substance of the matter is concerned, a critical discussion is justified, provided it matches the will to truth which animates the anonymous author even where he might be in error. The way in which the treatise is read and interpreted reveals the character of the reader. Hence he is against Goeze: Whoever is able to twist a passage against his better judgment and conscience is capable of almost anything; he may "give false testimony, fraudulently attribute writings, make up facts, may consider any means justified if they serve to prove them" (13, 172).

2) *Being calumnied as non-Christian and a destroyer of religion*

Goeze queries ". . . what kind of religion he understands by the term 'Christian religion,' and let him point out to us the main articles of the religion which he professes and whose great friend and champion he boasts of being" (in Schmidt, II, 294).

Lessing at first reacts furiously to this kind of interrogation: ". . . who gives the Head Pastor the right to issue orders . . . to the librarian, to summon him publicly to respond to a question which presupposes that he cannot respond to it satisfactorily?" (13, 331).

But the question also puts him in a quandary. Lessing feels himself to be a Christian. He does not want to be driven from his Father's house (cf. 13, 155). He wants to write against Goeze in a way "that won't let him get anywhere by calling me un-Christian" (February 25, 1778, to his brother; 18, 265). But Lessing's Christianity is of a kind that does not lend itself to identification with a particular creed. The religion he means, the authentic religion—predating the written texts of the New Testament, and the natural, or rational, religion which is positioned in the origin and at the end of history, and as such is contained in the Christian religion but not identical with it—cannot be evidentially established in a universally valid way, and for all time.

Since he is now required to state what he actually understands by Christianity and what he professes, he reacts inconsistently—since he cannot give an answer to either—if he replies at all. Thus, at one time he comes up with traditional professions of faith by which he means to convey his understanding of Christianity; he does so deliberately, for tactical reasons. He states these in a letter to Elise Reimarus (August 9,

1778): "I want to present him [Goeze] with developments that he surely does not expect. Since he has now made a slip of the tongue and wants to know not what of the Christian religion I believe but what I understand by the Christian religion: this puts me in a winning position . . ." (18, 284). But Goeze had asked about both.

Lessing rebelled against usurpation by churches and against Christian dogmatics, which claim to be entitled to ask, to inquire, and to decide who is a Christian. The Bible belongs to everyone. He does not understand it as a book subject to authoritative interpretation. If you understand it and, true to tradition, know yourself sustained by it in the basic orientation of your life, you can decide independently whether or not you belong to Biblical religion. The churches then are shown as merely mundane institutions, of which there are many, organized by human beings. They can expel you. But that does not confer any decision on the actual Biblical faith which each individual chooses on his own responsibility, and then, secondarily, and inconsequentially, knows himself to belong to a church. No one and no court and no creed can formulate with finality or reliably define the nature of Biblical faith. Each person can only live and speak out of this Biblical faith and be guided by it.

Lessing's weakness in objectivizing the debate arises from his own positions. His natural religion of reason and his original Christian religion as it existed prior to the Bible and prior to dogmatics are intangible ideas or intangible actualities. These, in their temporal appearance, assume the objectivity of contents of faith, creeds, ritual forms and behavior. Natural religion is contained in Biblical and revealed religion; both are divided by revelation and both are undivided through reason. They are divisible only in thought; historically they are one, divisible only at the end of time when only the one truth, the religion of reason, appears in completed form, suspending history itself in eternity.

There is a limit in Lessing which precludes a truly decisive battle. He neither is nor did he consider it his task to be the reformer of Biblical religion who would give a new, credible actuality to religion's mode of historic revelation.

3) *The tendency toward limiting public debate*

Lessing considers the principle of subjecting public debate to censorship in order to shield the general public from harm and from endangering their salvation as blocking the path on which truth can manifest itself. Truth can be attained precisely by way of error, as the differing positions correct themselves in spiritual struggle.

To protect the people against "poison" amounts, instead, to keeping them in unfreedom. The untruth of power which imposes such censorship by force keeps the people fettered in the untruth of the limited and fixed ideas imposed upon them.

4) *The tendency to use the power of the state and the threat of material harm against the opponent*

Lessing sees the underlying intention in Goeze's attack on him not in the will to destroy the freedom of belief, the human freedom of inquiry, of thought, and of searching, but in Goeze's invocation of the powers of the state in the interest of his victory. To be sure, Goeze did not accuse Lessing before a government agency, but he saw it as the duty of the Christian ecclesiastical authorities to protect religion by banning writings harmful to the faith. On the reason cited by Lessing in justifying his publication of the *Fragments,* Goeze writes: "[Lessing's] approach to the Christian faith is comparable to having 'fragments' printed in which the prerogatives of the noble house which he serves, the honor and innocence of the former great and irreproachable ministers of the same, and even that of the august ruler were similarly impugned as are . . . the truth of the Christian religion, the honor and innocence of the holy Apostles, and even of our eternal King . . ." (13, 156).

An examining university official (Wittenberg) alluded to an imperial law that made actions such as Lessing's punishable. Lessing, he pointed out, deliberately played Catholic traditional thinking against Protestant thought.

In view of all the risks he had taken, Lessing was eager to defend himself. "For once I must live with the world; and want to live with it." And: The world pays more attention "to what one appears to be than to what one is" (13, 34).

In Brunswick, Lessing was deprived of the freedom from censorship due to him as ducal librarian. He was forbidden to publish further fragments, nor could he continue his polemical attacks against Goeze. To be sure, this was not done at Goeze's explicit behest but was based on the stance represented by him. Goeze, for the moment, was victorious on a practical level; Lessing, however, won the spiritual battle in the opinion of cultured Germany in the classical age.

B. Neology and orthodoxy

Neology was the name of a theology that meant to adapt the dogmas, the miracles, the understanding of Biblical texts to modern scientific thinking in order to preserve faith as modern orthodoxy. What is untenable was relinquished, miracles were made comprehensible, dogmas were propped up by reason. Orthodoxy, on the other hand, was the name given to the theology that insisted decisively on the truth of traditional faith, on the truth of Biblical texts, which rejected all accommodation. It appeals solely to God's revelation and rejects all rational proofs in favor of that which is suprarational, as well as all refutation, which it considers invalid.

Lessing participated in this theological battle. His tactics have continued to shock all parties among the theologians and the Enlightenment group. We would expect that Lessing, as enlightener, would be drawn to the enlightening neologists, the great names among the theologians of his age. He did just the opposite. He fought, always and unconditionally, against neology. We would expect that he, as enlightener, would have to reject orthodoxy. But he has had high praise for it, though his writings contain judgments both for and against orthodoxy. Let us look at this more closely.

To his brother, in a letter of March 20, 1777, he wrote that he had preferred "the old orthodox (basically tolerant) theology to the newer (basically intolerant) theology" only because "the former clearly lies in conflict with common sense" whereas the latter "would prefer to bribe it" (18, 226–27). This clear division suits him: on one side, absurd orthodoxy which completely disregards common sense; on the other, pure reason which does not engage itself with orthodoxy at all, since it has to leave it untouched. Both ways are honest.

Neologic theology is the dishonest mingling of revelational faith and reason. "Instead of speaking of reason as held captive by obedience to faith," this theology pontificates about nothing "but the close ties between reason and faith." "Faith has become reason confirmed by miracles and signs, and reason has turned into rationalizing faith." These theologians want to "raise up reason and put it to sleep by denouncing the adversaries of revelation as adversaries of common sense!" They impress the people who would like to have reason, but do not (12, 42f.).

To combine philosophy with revelation is impossible. A Christian philosopher is neither Christian nor philosopher.

For the purpose of battle Lessing interprets his position as friendly toward orthodoxy: "I get along with my evident enemies [the orthodox] the better to guard myself against my covert ones," that is, the neologues (to his brother, March 20, 1777; 18, 227).

Lessing's wrath is targeted at dishonesty and self-delusion, at inconsistency and compromise, at ecclesiastical-political cunning, at accusations of heresy. He derides the newfangled theologians who content themselves "with a sweet quintessence" of Christianity and dodge "any suspicion of freethinking," preferring "to prattle nebulously about religion with fine enthusiastic verve" (8, 127).

Lessing the enlightener gives us even more of a surprise. He is in league with orthodoxy not merely as an effective tool in polemical situations but in a serious sense that remains, however, curiously inconclusive.

For example, if with regard to the miracle of the passage through the Red Sea rational explanations are offered which do away with the need for a miracle, these are countered by objections that make the entire event appear totally impossible. But the position of the orthodox is rendered unassailable by his simple statement: "But what if . . . the entire passage was a miracle?" This puts the orthodox above the fray. "You may shrug your shoulders at his answer . . . but you have to leave him where he stands" (12, 441–42).

Here is a man sticking to his principles, who wants to speak and act with consistency. "This consistency, which allows us to predict how this man will speak or act in a given situation, is what makes him a man and gives him character and steadfastness."

This manliness, this character, and this constancy "correct, in time, even the principles." For it is impossible for such a man to act "for a long time according to principles . . . without realizing that they are false" (12, 442–43).

These exalted advantages of the orthodox man are utterly lacking in half of neologic orthodoxy, "a certain cross-eyed, limping orthodoxy, not on a par with itself." This one "is so disgusting" (12, 442–43).

Lessing advocated orthodox Christian education. A writer on pedagogics, following the principle of proceeding from the easy and comprehensible to the difficult, had advocated teaching a child "to begin loving Jesus as a pious and altogether holy man, as a tender friend of children" (8, 124). This, Lessing rejects most decisively:

"Does this intend making the mysterious concept of an eternal savior easier to understand? Actually it means doing away with it . . . it means making the child into a Socinian [22] until it can grasp the orthodox dogma. And when precisely is it able to grasp this? At what age are we more able to comprehend this mystery than we are in our childhood? And since it is a mystery, would it not be fairer to imbue willing childhood with it right away than to await the age of recalcitrant rea-

[22] Socinianism was a rationalistic theological movement that denied virtually all the supernatural tenets of Christianity.

son to do so?" (8, 125). The intended facilitation is thus "a maiming" and "invalidating of the difficult truth" (12, 124).

Since Lessing does not himself profess the content of orthodoxy, this judgment strikes us as strange. Does he mean to pass on as truth to the children and the people in general what he himself considers to be untrue? By no means. Lessing does not declare revelation—though he does not believe in it—to be untrue. In his childhood he experienced something that stayed with him as an irreplaceable core of truth even though for him all denominational religions have become invalid. He retained his awareness of this mystery. You can comprehend it solely as a boundary, but should not miss experiencing its content. Is the child more open to experience, more ready for the imprint of the unforgettable ciphers, for receiving contents that reason cannot dissolve? If its education starts with false enlightenment, the child will be denied all substance unless it partakes of precognitive actuality, unless it learns about Abraham, who speaks with God directly; about Moses on Mount Sinai, the only human being who dares to encounter God and to whom the eternal Commandments in their gripping simplicity are communicated, so that man must feel cast out if he breaks the divine laws; about God in the burning bush, in the soft rustling of the breeze; about the prophets who carry the voice of God and proclaim His commands; about the servant of God; about Jesus who by His death takes all human suffering on Himself, and so on. Fairy tales take hold of the child in the region between actuality and fable and convey inexhaustible images to his impressions. For the child, these sacred apparitions are a gripping actuality, charged with a seriousness that brings forth fear and reverence. Without this ground of substance acquired in earliest childhood Lessing foresees rudderlessness. On questioning him further: Is it right for nonbelievers to impress on their children what no longer is part of their own belief?, he leaves us without an answer. We are left with the position that Lessing neither denies nor accepts what he does not believe—for he wants to see transmitted without untruthfulness what is indispensable on humanity's path.

Neologic theology and freethinking are both in a quandary when it comes to Lessing, and driven to reinterpretation.

The adherent of neologic orthodoxy would prefer as adversary a dogmatic rationalist, whose clearly stated position he can attack, to a man who seems to have no fixed position at all. In the latter case, he would not confront an absolute truth with traces of his own way of thinking; to him, Lessing is incomprehensible and hence seems much more dangerous. He is bound to misunderstand such a man, to extract a variety of statements in order to buttress his neologic orthodoxy. But what truly disconcerts him is his sense of another faith confronting him, arising from another origin and imparted by a different way of thinking. The adherents of neologic orthodoxy have in common with freethinkers that they are dogmatic, which keeps them from understanding how Lessing's mind works. That his kind of thinking is denounced by theologians as un-Christian, anti-Christian, atheistic, and nihilistic is testimony to their willfully blind unrest. Rationalistic freethinkers, on the other hand, perceive only something that to them looks like crypto-theology. They are blind to the entire philosophy of three millennia.

We may ask: Does Lessing intend to salvage revelation? While he does not believe in it, he cannot bring himself to deny its possibility. Does he intend to salvage Christianity? For his own person he never clearly defines in what sense he is a Christian. But in parrying the attacks of his antagonists, he passionately states that he is a Christian.

What then does he aim at? Maybe to go on, for the time being, living with the others in the "palace" or its surroundings, engaged, however, in constant examining, searching, and reaching out.

CHARACTERIZATIONS

1. Lessing's position within history

Lessing belonged to a world that must have exerted a constricting and stifling influence, the German world of the mid-eighteenth century, the world of the small absolutist states, with the Prussian king, Frederick the Great, outright contemptuous of all men and of Germans in particular. When the question arose whether to appoint Winckelmann or a Frenchman who is now considered unimportant, Frederick preferred Winckelmann at a lower salary, saying, "For a German . . . this is enough."[23] In an essay Frederick wrote on German literature he rejected it wholesale. He himself was not fully proficient in German or in French, but his style of life was altogether French. Lessing's ambiance was also that of orthodox Protestantism, which believed in the letter of the Scriptures, and of an enthusiastic pietism; a world of German pusillanimity which considered everything non-German by this very fact as more important, valid, relevant—and, it must be admitted,

---

[23] Johann Joachim Winckelmann (1717–1768), preeminent classicist of the eighteenth century, art historian, and pioneer archaeologist, was never appointed in Frederick's Berlin.

in those days often rightfully so, but also mistakenly, since one failed to recognize the great ones of one's own nation. But not all was gloom. Philosophical thinkers could point to the great European thinker Leibniz, who, to be sure, wrote in French and Latin but also produced some essays in German and professed loving the German language. He represented the "spirit of thoroughness" later praised by Kant. In Lessing's world Leibniz stood among the very great who performed the intellectual task of working out the transition to modern thinking, with personal integrity and fidelity.

But everything, even the good, was, as it were, transposed into smallness, even if not downright pettiness.

And yet it was a culture which in the following decades was the nurturing ground for classical German literature, by virtue of which Germans came truly into their own. And today we continue to be truly German by our classical heritage, whereas Luther, in his aftereffects, proved a calamity for the Protestant portion of the German people, and Bismarck's empire, a political episode, still haunts us, holding in the bondage of fictitious beliefs the perplexed spirits who no longer know what they are as Germans.

It was Goethe who first opened the door to genuine liberation and freedom in the era of German classicism, filtered from the plethora of Western ideas.

Lessing stands as a forerunner, a trailblazer, a liberator who himself did not enter the land prepared by him. Yet, being the harbinger of transition is proper to all times and all men, according to the historical point of view under which they are seen, and including even those who are seen as having attained classical completion.

Each age and each human being is "immediate to God," and lives for the present and for his own best.

Lessing's greatness resides in his unwearying endeavor to work things out, which set an example for all time, and of particular relevance, perhaps, for today.

This working things out has another side: Lessing's world is that of the Enlightenment, an intellectual movement of the European upper classes, modified according to national temperament and condition, earliest in England, followed by France, then Germany, and spreading beyond.

Grounded in the lofty thoughts of modern philosophy since Descartes, Hobbes, Spinoza, Leibniz, the Enlightenment was impelled by the development of the sciences, by the tendency toward what is natural and therefore valid, and by what is cognizable through reason, to be that which can and ought to guide our life (natural religion, ethics, law).

Out of the notion of progress develops the will to remake and to change, not only details but also the whole of our human condition: we believe ourselves knowing and acting in harmony with a necessary process taking place anyway (the "enlightenment of the intellect," a shallow yet still powerful notion).

The masses hardly participated in the Enlightenment. After all, they could neither read nor write.

But among the educated it took hold of all classes, not only the bourgeoisie, which fought for more freedom and rights, but also among the aristocracy and the churches. The reforms of Emperor Joseph II in Austria, the abolition of the Jesuit Order by the Vatican, the despotism of Frederick the Great and the violent nature of his rationally calculated state, which was rejected by German philosophers as being "mechanical" and which sacrificed individuals to its political goals—all tended in the same direction.

2. The relationship between Kant and Lessing

Kant's *Critique of Pure Reason* appeared a few weeks after Lessing's death. Neither felt a close kinship to the other. Kant quotes Lessing with respect—he learned aesthetics and religion from him.

In his later years Lessing deleted a youthful caustic epigram against Kant. Seen objectively, here were two Germans who overcame and went beyond the halfhearted and shallow Enlightenment of reason to the true enlightenment, which is the medium and presupposition of the philosophy of Existenz. Both are "critical," a term recurring time and again in both.

But such criticism is not destructive: its method is differentiation, the drawing of lines, elucidation, a purification and liberation, "making the ground firm enough to build on," "making room for faith," bringing awareness of their negating, purifying, defending, elucidating significance.

3. Lessing judged by the great

Statements about Lessing's influence were made by great philosophers (Mendelssohn, Hegel, Schelling, Schopenhauer, Kierkegaard) and by historians (Zeller, Brockhaus, Schmidt). Almost all great Germans of the age immediately following Lessing's acknowledged their debt of gratitude, not so much for what they learned through him or for what is teachable—though, for that too—but for having been educated by him by educating themselves from his example. Nearly all of them credited him with character, reliability, honesty, and loyalty, and also manly courage.

KIERKEGAARD

Jaspers held Kierkegaard along with Nietzsche "to be the [two] most important thinker[s] of our post-Kantian age." The influence of the two on Jaspers's thinking is evident in many ways. His juxtaposition of the Christian Kierkegaard with the atheist Nietzsche in his protophilosophical *Psychologie der Weltanschauungen* (1919) inaugurated what was to be called "existential philosophy." Another juxtaposition of the two can be found in *Reason and Existenz* (1935), the initial statement of Jaspers's later philosophy.

Jaspers's reception of Kierkegaard, even more than of Nietzsche, served to define his critique of modernity (*Man in the Modern Age* [1931]), as well as his conception of the "Great Awakeners" as the type of philosophers that arose in reaction to the nihilistic tendencies of modernity. In *Philosophy* (1932), his first main work, Jaspers characterizes Kierkegaard as the one "who—shaken to the roots, squarely facing Nothingness—philosophizes out of love of Being as the other possibility." The fundamental redirection of philosophy which Jaspers effected in light of his reception of Kierkegaard is filled with terms, concepts, and phenomena which preoccupied Kierkegaard and his pseudonyms, for example, Existenz, choice, decision, time (historicity, the instant).

Considering all these facts and the seminars and lecture courses on Kierkegaard he taught in his forty years as professor, one would expect Jaspers to have published a definitive interpretation of Kierkegaard per se. But, aside from three lectures on Kierkegaard for the general public, one of which appeared in English ("The Importance of Kierkegaard," *Cross Currents*, 2/ 1952), this was not the case. Jaspers hesitated to write on Kierkegaard, as can be seen from the beginning of this chapter; he used to say: One cannot write on Kierkegaard without making a fool of oneself. However, he felt obliged to include a major treatment of Kierkegaard as the key figure among the Great Awakeners within the typology of the Great Philosophers. At the time of his death only small portions of the projected work had been written down in more or less finished form; these are presented here in the sections "Kierkegaard's Life," "The Works," "Modes of Thought, Problems Posed, Main Themes." The last section, "The Stages," containing Jaspers's interpretation of the writings which form Kierkegaard's central philosophical thought, is more fragmentary. While much of what has been selected for inclusion in this section is in the form of précis, in some cases consisting of mere outlines and notes, the section itself is systematic and coherent. For the sake of clarity, a few passages have been expanded in translation.

The chapter "Kierkegaard" contains many of the terms with which readers of the standard translations of Jaspers's philosophy are familiar. However, a few reminders are in order. 1. The German *Existenz* is retained in English for Jaspers's concept of human actualization within the individual's temporality by virtue of his risk, freedom, decision. The word "existence" is used for Jaspers's concept *Dasein,* meaning man's being-there-in-the-world as an object among objects. 2. "History" stands for *Geschichte,* its adjectival correlate is "historical"; "historicity" is *Geschichtlichkeit,* the corresponding adjective: "historic." 3. "Sublate" is *aufheben* in the Hegelian sense.

In the following text Kierkegaard is quoted, wherever possible, according to standard English translations, though occasionally with some modification. In other instances quotations from the German translations used by Jaspers have been translated into English. All sources are listed in the bibliography.   —LHE

I approach the presentation of Kierkegaard with some trepidation. Next to Nietzsche, or, rather, prior to Nietzsche, I consider him to be the most important thinker of our post-Kantian age. With Goethe and Hegel, an epoch had reached its conclusion, and our prevalent way of thinking—that is, the positivistic, natural-scientific one—cannot really be considered as philosophy.

Because Kierkegaard does not draw conclusions or lay down tenets, he is not a didactic thinker, but an awakening one. He does not leave us with a knowledge that clearly tells us what is what, but casts us back on ourselves. We—as single individuals—have to work for our salvation, to think in the spirit of truth and be brought by Kierkegaard into a state of unrest, but not to be guided by him.

Kierkegaard is the co-creator of the space of modern thinking; as a concomitant he also introduces the possibility of a confusion previously unknown.

He is concrete and forceful, poetic—without ever having written a poem—and capable of the most sublime speculation. He exerts a powerful attraction and yet, through disconcerting, apparently incomprehensible abstractions, he can repel us just as powerfully. We come to believe that we do not know with whom we are really dealing.

From the outset the question arises: *Can Kierkegaard be taught?*

Teaching is indirect communication. You tell what the truth is. It is a doctrine. In doctrinal components it arranges itself into a system. It can be learned and learned by rote. Truth can be acquired as an objective reality. It has meaning for "consciousness-as-such." But is the true exhausted by this? Teacher and pupil are incidental cases of consciousness-as-such. All are objective and wholly impersonal. Kierkegaard emphasizes that he does not lecture: he "experiments."

Kierkegaard anticipated his fame and from the outset thought with horror of what would become of his thought. "When my books will come into fashion, I shall be misunderstood. . . ." But even worse, he will serve as teaching material: I shall "leave behind a not inconsiderable intellectual capital; and, alas, I also know who will be my heir, he, the figure that is so tremendously repellent to me, but who, after all, has so far inherited everything that is superior, and who will continue to inherit it: the academic instructor, the professor. And even if the 'professor' were to read this, it would not stop him, his conscience would not feel bothered, no, he would include this in his teaching. . . . But even this belongs to my suffering, to know this and to continue quite calmly in my efforts . . . whose profits in one sense of the word the 'professor' is to inherit" (Haecker,[1] II, 293–94).

The nature of the 'professor' is as follows: he no longer is a philosopher endowed with moral force and a strong character, as was the case in early antiquity; instead, remunerated as an employee, he is harmless and ineffectual, as he was in the Roman Empire. Since he is a eunuch, he fits well into this characterless world. All he wants is to conform to it. What lies outside his specialized field, he ignores (cf. Gottsched,[2] 134–41).

[1] *Die Tagebücher,* ed. and trans. by Theodor Haecker. Innsbruck, Brenner, 1923.
[2] *Sören Kierkegaard, Buch des Richters,* ed. and trans. by Hermann Gottsched. Jenna/Leipzig, Diedrichs, 1905.

The imitation of Christ is alien to him. However, he is a professor learned in the destruction of someone else. His business is not suffering but studying suffering. Thus he lives off the sufferings of the glorious ones. But even worse: he robs them of the seriousness of their lives, he robs them of their impact by serving up the sufferings of others as interesting knowledge.

Ever since the time of Socrates' struggle against the Sophists, who took money for their teaching, the academic vocation has faced this dilemma. Kierkegaard launched the attack with renewed earnestness. How can a person respond if he is himself a professor?

He has to submit to the same criterion, with the result that there can be no self-satisfaction, that time and again a sense of ambiguity attaches to his actions, that a pull toward the never-attained honesty is experienced. The possibility of a devastating judgment has to be admitted. There should be no evasion by glib talk and the art of objective distancing, with the purpose of remaining untouchable. A person has to know in what sense he is speaking in each particular instance. Kierkegaard perpetually keeps each one's conscience aroused.

But this is no reason to simply negate the task of the academic vocation. This task is indispensable, and not just as serving the survival of civilizing tradition preparatory for one's life. In this vocation existential actualization can take place, as may be seen in Kant and Max Weber. Nietzsche too was a professor.

Kierkegaard himself once felt this task to be a positive one. In his early years, he had seriously thought of becoming a professor himself. (Rasmus Nielsen[3] got ahead of him.) At the crucial moment he decided against entering this profession, just as he did when it came to the ministry and to marriage. This "no" of his will be our subject later on.

The fact that Kierkegaard wrote and published, and did so not casually or occasionally but by exerting all his energies in a grandly planned and, in retrospect, even more grandly deliberate continuity, means that he invites everyone to examine his work, even the professors. Because he himself exposed his work to the public, and in the posthumous publications bared even his private self in its reality, he has to put up with being publicly interpreted, analyzed, appropriated, or judged. By means of his work Kierkegaard wanted to help the "individual." But he cannot determine in advance in what way the individual wants to or can be helped. In accord with his own intention, we may hold on to the independence of the individual. To the very last he asserted that all he wanted was to arouse attention. But what results

[3] Rasmus Nielsen (1809–1884), professor of philosophy, was Kierkegaard's friend.

for the individual thus alerted and how he thinks and deals with it as "professor" is up to him and no longer up to Kierkegaard.

This means that all interpretation of Kierkegaard amounts to unintended self-revelation.

Thus there is a certain tension in any attempt to include Kierkegaard in the teaching of philosophy and in philosophizing. But this task appears unavoidable in view of the importance of his work and his being. In our own age the following is obvious:

a) Any imitation of Kierkegaard has proved to be ridiculous. He is unrepeatable, since what he saw in himself was the exception. Whoever has put on the trappings of Kierkegaard—beginning with his physician's speech at his graveside down to modern rhetoric of indignation appropriating statements and phrases of his—strays away from Kierkegaard.

b) What becomes of Kierkegaard in someone else's interpretation is no longer Kierkegaard. Even though you might not have become what you are without him, you may not cite him as your authority. But if you have experienced his impact, you are entitled to a full debt of gratitude to him.

c) Attempts to reconstruct Kierkegaard's philosophy or theology in the form of a system or a doctrine have always failed. We can see from his own intentions that such a project is doomed.

The task of presenting Kierkegaard as an integral whole has so far not been accomplished. What can be achieved successfully is the following:

a) A study of his life and work in their reality. Interpreting him leads to the limit where tangible interlacings of meaning may be gathered into a totality of meaning that, having been presupposed, is then found. Historical research along proven lines is helpful here as elsewhere, by throwing light on factualities.[4]

To make Kierkegaard as a whole the object of historical research is pointless and detracts from the task of appropriating him individually.

b) By his use of pseudonyms Kierkegaard distanced himself from almost all of his configurations of thought, making them the content of fictitious thinker-personalities. Actually, however, the thinking of all the pseudonymous characters conforms to a common system of categories. It is Kierkegaardian thinking (which originated in Hegel and has to be understood in its departures from him). All the pseudonyms have studied philosophy.

---

[4] Jaspers's note: I am particularly indebted to the relevant writings of Emanuel Hirsch.

Moreover, some of the pseudonyms are not really that. Johannes Climacus, who develops Kierkegaard's body of metaphysical concepts, was given this pseudonym at the last moment and on publication still carried Kierkegaard's name. Anticlimacus was chosen because Kierkegaard did not feel himself adequate in comparison to this character; this pseudonym was later retracted.

It is possible to abstract the structures of thought, methods of thinking and categories which run through the pseudonyms and to put them in doctrinal form. In the texts themselves, however, we find a mingling consisting of constructs having the varied tenor of cool comprehensibility, of passionate concern, of stalwart faith and demand.

Can a portrayal of Kierkegaard be enlarged beyond the foregoing? And by an interpretation that reproduces the movements of thought which are to be taught not as content, but as stimulus to repetition in one's own thinking? Kierkegaard would thus be made present as "the genius of reflection." But thinking is not overcome by confutation, or by a return to immediacy, or through the abandonment of lucid awareness, but through an intensification of thinking into dialectical endlessness.

Properly understood, these movements of thought have existential character. They lend themselves to differentiations: first, existential thinking in the actuality of Existenz itself; this is purely historic and cannot be taught; second, existential thinking as thinking that arouses attention and summons possible Existenz; third, existential thinking as thoughtful self-transformation in acts of thought and their repetition. The second and third modes might possibly be reproducible.

Translated into the thinking of supposed existential facts, all modes of existential thinking are inverted by neutralizing the thinker himself.

KIERKEGAARD'S LIFE

1. The story of his life

Kierkegaard (1813–1855) lived in Copenhagen, at that time a tranquil city. It was still surrounded by the old fortifications and not yet affected by the modern Industrial Revolution. The members of society knew one another and met regularly in church and theater; their lives were open to scrutiny in street and marketplace.

Kierkegaard's father was a rich wool merchant, fifty-nine years old at the time of Sören's birth. Kierkegaard's mother was his second wife, the former housekeeper. Kierkegaard never mentioned her in his writings. Others described her as a "good, dear little woman." She died in 1834. Martensen's mother related that she "never saw any human being as deeply saddened as was S. Kierkegaard when his mother died. . . ."[5] Although his mother seems to have had no influence on Kierkegaard, his entire behavior suggests the overwhelming importance his father had for him. At a very tender age he was permitted to be present during the long-drawn-out discussions and reflections passing between the aged father and his friends. He was brought up in a sphere of stern Christianity centered in the suffering of Christ, with the premise that truth means permitting oneself to be derided and killed. He listened to talk about sin and grace without comprehending their meaning. Later he would say that Christianity was too heavy a burden for the child to carry; and to the question why he believed Jesus to be God, he answered: Because my father told me so. "From him I learned what a father's love is, and thus I came to comprehend the love of the Divine Father, the only thing that is unshakable in life, its true Archimedean point." But then came the terrible other: "I knew or suspected that the only man whom I had admired because of his strength and power was wavering" (Haecker, I, 155, 198). To be sure, his father stood before him "and said: Poor child, you go about in silent despair. But he never questioned more closely, alas he could not, for he lived himself in silent despair" (Dru, 483).[6]

On Kierkegaard's birthday in 1838, the father, who died shortly thereafter, revealed to him certain secrets which dreadfully shocked the son. We do not know what they were; in any case they did not involve the cursing of God on the Jutland heath when his father was a poverty-stricken shepherd boy. It may be conjectured that he confessed to rape of the housekeeper, whom he then married and who became Kierkegaard's mother.

Kierkegaard began his academic studies in 1831, first studying philosophy for a year, and then theology.

There were many clashes between the young man and his father. He later reported on his life as a student: "I played around in life, tempted by a great many things and often by the most radical opposites; and, what was even worse, I found myself in errors and, alas, even on the path to perdition."[7] April to June 1836 was a time of

[5] Hans Lassen Martensen, *Aus meinem Leben, Mittheilungen,* trans. by A. Michelsen. Karlsruhe/Leipzig, H. Reuter, 1883, 53.

[6] References to Dru are to *The Journals of Sören Kierkegaard,* ed. and trans. by Alexander Dru. The figures refer to journal entries, not to pages.

[7] Quoted from Torsten Bohlin, *Sören Kierkegaards Leben und Werden,* trans. by P. Katz. Gütersloh, C. Bertelsmann, 1925, 37.

dissipation.[8] He ran up debts—for books (380 thaler), at the tailor (280 thaler), at the pastry shop (235 thaler), at the tobacconist's, and so on. Father and son entered into an agreement by which Sören's debts were paid and an annuity guaranteed to him corresponding to the salary of a higher government official. In 1837 Kierkegaard moved into his own apartment (cf. H81).[9]

In May 1837 he met Regine Olsen for the first time, quite by accident, and immediately wrote in his diary: "merciful God, why should that inclination awaken just now—Oh, how I feel that I am alone— Oh cursed be that arrogant satisfaction in standing alone—All will despise me now—but thou, O my God, take not thy hand from me now—let me live and improve myself—" (Dru, 118, 119).

Three years later, in September 1840, he became engaged to this young woman, who was ten years his junior. But the next day he knew that he had taken the wrong step. There followed a year of indescribable suffering. He was unable to reach the decision to marry. He tortured the beloved girl. She could not understand his withdrawal and held fast to him with all the means at her disposal. Finally he bluntly broke off the engagement, in October 1841. But he remained faithful all his life to the woman he deserted, "no husband can be more faithful" (Dru, 389). He constantly reflected on her, wrote his first writings for her, deeded her his literary estate. All this will be discussed later.

Kierkegaard attended the university but did not take his examinations in 1835, as would have been normal, but seemed on the way to becoming an eternal student. He did not pass his state examination in theology until July 1840; in 1841 he passed his master's examination with the thesis "On the Concept of Irony with Constant Reference to Socrates." However, he did not become a pastor, but, instead, a freelance writer. In 1843 he achieved instant fame in Copenhagen with poetic, critical, and religious writings.

Following his father's death in 1838, he came into possession of considerable capital. He lived in a large apartment with servant and secretary. He liked to have all the rooms heated and lighted. In several rooms—he enjoyed walking around in them—there were writing desks equipped with ink and paper. He was surrounded by an extensive library (at the auction after his death, 2,197 volumes were listed).

He could be encountered on the streets talking with workingmen and market women, with acquaintances and friends, with all and

[8]Cf. Emanuel Hirsch, *Kierkegaard Studien.* Gütersloh, C. Bertelsmann, 1933, I, 33.
[9]References to H are to Johannes Hohlenberg, *Sören Kierkegaard: A Biography.* Trans. by T. H. Croxall.

sundry, a habit continued in the theater and at the opera, and on excursions into the environs. On solitary trips into the countryside he liked to travel fast, without sparing the horses. On these forays he dined elegantly, and the coachmen received large tips. On Sundays he went to church. Occasionally he made trips to Jutland, and he repeatedly journeyed to Berlin.

This life independent of the norm of professional and social obligations, as the life of a free-lance author who paid for the printing costs of his books himself, was possible only because of his inherited wealth. Kierkegaard was always aware of this. At the outset, he spent money extravagantly; later on, cautiously. To be sure, he could at any time have become a country pastor. He abandoned this last opportunity when he began his strife with the Church. On his deathbed he said how wonderfully everything in his life had worked out: now, that everything he had wanted to say had been said, he had spent all his money, with just enough left for his funeral expenses (cf. H89). Indeed, this is the way it was.

2. His illness

Kierkegaard's uncle and a nephew of his were psychotic; his father suffered from melancholia and a brother from depression.

In school Kierkegaard was teased because of his odd appearance, but he felt himself to be immeasurably superior to his peers. In regard to his childhood he said later, "I was already an old man when I was born." [10]

Starting in September 1835, at age twenty-two, Kierkegaard showed symptoms of depression. His condition was unstable. Its phases can be recognized and described on the authority of his own statements, primarily in his diaries.

Many verdicts on his abnormal psychological states, made by contemporaries, have come down to us. Regine Olsen once told him that to her he appeared crazy. He is described as "the fantastic man," [11] on the occasion of a festive dinner, where he bubbled over with merriment, but from one moment to the next was seized by a taciturn, brooding mood. He loved to spoil children, but his excess of deference to a young niece attracted attention. Five days after Kierkegaard's death, the journalist Goldschmidt commented that the "bitter and passionate" element, especially in his last writings, came "from his illness

[10] Walter Lowrie, *A Short Life of Kierkegaard,* 42.
[11] Henriette Lund, quoted in Dru, Appendix I, 558.

which had, for a long time, influenced his extraordinary talent."[12] Bishop Martensen judged similarly.

A great many phenomena experienced by Kierkegaard were documented by him. I quote a few:

1838: "Sometimes there is such a tumult in my head that it feels as though the roof had been lifted off my cranium, and then it seems as though the hobgoblins had lifted up a mountain and were holding a ball and festivities there—God preserve me!" (Dru, 186).

1851, when the manuscript of *The Sickness unto Death* was to be picked up by the printer: "I did not sleep quietly that night. Also it seemed to me that some other person talked to me or that I talked to myself. . . . I cannot say which words were mine and which mine in the other person. I remembered these words: 'Look, now he desires his own destruction.' . . . I can also remember the words: '. . . it in no way concerns' (but I cannot remember for certain whether it was 'you' or 'me') 'that [State Councillor] Olsen is dead.' I can remember the words but not for certain the pronoun, you—or I could wait for a week or so. I can remember the answer: 'what does he imagine?' In the morning I was quite confused . . ." (Dru, 1220).

Moods and psychological states ranging to extremes:

1837: "I live constantly on the borderline of the fortunate and of the desolate Arabia" (Gottsched, 79).

1837: "It seems as if I were a galley slave chained together with death; every time life stirs, the chain rattles and death makes everything decay—and that takes place every moment" (H & H, 5, #5256, 106).[13]

1838: "There is an indescribable joy which enkindles us as inexplicably as the apostle's outburst comes gratuitously: 'Rejoice I say unto you and again I say unto you rejoice.'—Not a joy over this or that but the soul's mighty song. . . : 'I rejoice through my joy, in, at, with, over, by, and with my joy' . . . a joy which cools and refreshes us like a breath of wind, a wave of air from the trade wind which blows from the [groves] of Mamre to the everlasting habitations. May 19, half-past ten in the morning" (Dru, 207).

1839: "The foreground of my life is cloaked altogether in the darkest melancholy and the mists of the deepest brooding misery . . ." (Gottsched, 17–77).

[12] Quoted in O. P. Monrad, *Sören Kierkegaard. Sein Leben und Seine Werke.* Jena, Diederichs, 1909, 132.
[13] References to H & H are to *Sören Kierkegaard's Journals and Papers,* ed. and trans. by Howard V. Hong and Edna H. Hong.

1847: "And thus I live, even if, at isolated moments, not without attacks of melancholy and yearning, essentially day by day in the most blissful enchantment" (Gottsched, 90).

1851: "Oh, how inexplicable, I feel so indescribably glad and calm and confident and overwhelmed" (Dru, 1229).

1854: "[J]ust as a seasick person feels completely indifferent toward everything on account of exhaustion and nausea . . . you can also become completely indifferent because of a sense of blissfulness that makes you oblivious to the world's demands, so that you refuse to lift a finger in order to fend it off, or to make the tiniest step to escape it—the blissfulness being so indescribable" (Gottsched, 106).

Kierkegaard's loneliness. Kierkegaard was acquainted with many people, was sociable, paid visits, had an uncanny knack for relating to almost everyone in conversation. But: "I can say quite literally that I have never, in my whole life, talked to a single person in the way two people usually talk to each other—I have always kept my innermost being to myself, even when speaking more confidentially; and I have never been able to speak truly confidentially" (Gottsched, 83).

1854: "I have a particular task and it has never occurred to me that anyone else could share it with me, or that there was anything to gain by association . . ." (Dru, 1344).

When Kierkegaard's friend Emil Boesen said to him as he lay dying, "how much in your life has turned out wonderfully well," Kierkegaard answered: "Yes, I feel very glad and very wistful about this; for I cannot share this joy with anyone" (Haecker, II, 414–15).

Kierkegaard constantly experienced significations and intimations of meanings in things, which became clear to him.

1839: "Curiously enough there is something that has often made me anxious, the fact that the life I was living was not my own, but, without my being able to prevent it, identical with another person, and that I only discovered it each time it had been lived up to a certain point" (Dru, 284).

1843: "No one will find in my papers the slightest information (this is my consolation) about what really has filled my life, no one will find the inscription in my innermost being that interprets everything and that often turns into events of prodigious importance to me that which the world would call bagatelles and which I regard as insignificant if I remove the secret note that interprets them" (H & H, 5, #5645, 226).

Such writings are supplemented by numerous descriptions of the pseudonyms, obviously based on Kierkegaard's own experiences. I shall not render them here.

Kierkegaard's physical appearance. Shorter than average, of slender build, with thin legs, a slightly hunched back, somewhat round-shouldered and with thick, frizzy hair, he could look almost impertinent because of his slightly turned-up nose. His complexion is sometimes described as fresh, at other times as yellowish. The blue eyes are clever, lively, and supercilious, mixing kindness and malice. His quiet convulsive laughter shook his body. In conversation he was incomparably charming. All this is reported by his contemporaries. Another person, Zahle, wrote shortly after Kierkegaard's death:

"Kierkegaard was almost like a caricature. Under his low, wide-brimmed hat one could see the big head with the shock of dark brown hair . . . the expressive blue eyes, the yellowish-pale complexion and the sunken cheeks with deep furrows down to his mouth, which was expressive even when he was silent. He held his head somewhat bent to one side. His back was slightly hunched. Under his arm he held a cane or an umbrella, the brown coat was close-fitting and buttoned tightly around his thin frame, the weak legs seemed to carry their burden with difficulty but they could take a lot and carried him out of his study into the fresh air when he took his 'people-bath.' . . . Up to now (1856) there is no portrait of Kierkegaard, but his contemporaries will not forget what he looked like; and especially no one who heard him preach will forget the voice that was extremely weak but surprisingly expressive. I have never heard another voice that was able to modulate to that extent even the slightest nuance of expression." [14]

Kierkegaard was always aware of his physical condition.

1837: "I can't be bothered to do anything, I won't walk—it tires me; I won't lie down . . .—I won't ride—it is too violent an exercise compared to my apathy; I only feel inclined to drive to let a number of objects glide past me while I am comfortably, evenly shaken . . . to feel my own languor" (Dru, 131).

1839: "Slight, delicate, and weak, denied in almost every respect the physical requirements in order to be able to pass for a complete man as compared with others . . ." (Dru, 1335).

1849: "It is sad and melancholy that much which is simply explained as pride and the rest, is quite simply lack of physical strength . . ." (Dru, 1015).

1850: "Give me, or if you had given me, a body when I was twenty: I should not be like this . . . what I lack is the animal qualifications where being a man is concerned" (Dru, 1105).

1851, when Kierkegaard gave a sermon: "I suffered greatly beforehand from every kind of exhaustion, as always when I have to use my

[14] Theodor Haecker, *Essays*. Munich, Kösel, 1958, 615–16.

physical personality. . . . On the Monday I was so weak and feeble that it was terrible." He could not preach. "Then I grew really ill. The unhappy, agonizing pain which is the limit of my personality began to make itself terribly felt, a thing which had not happened for a long, long time" (Dru, 1225).

1853: "To be strong and healthy, a complete man with the expectation of a long life—well, that was never granted me" (Dru, 1287). He was convinced, from an early age, that he would live to be only thirty-five. He did, however, reach forty-two.

In 1830, having enlisted in the Royal Life Guards, he was mustered out on the third day as being physically unfit for service (cf. H & H, 302, note 54).

Kierkegaard's death. In the autumn of 1855, over a few weeks, Kierkegaard had been getting progressively weaker. At one time he slipped off the sofa, another time fell in his room. On October 2 he collapsed on the street, could not walk, and was taken to the hospital. "I have come out here to die."[15] He died on November 11. Coughing up blood, paralysis, and urinary incontinence suggest pulmonary as well as spinal tuberculosis, but this cannot be certain on the basis of the medical records.

The diagnosis. The diagnosis of the mortal illness and the diagnosis of the lifelong psychological state are independent from one another (apart from a certain correlation between a constitution prone to tuberculosis and one prone to schizoid disorders). It is unimportant whether we call the latter manic-depressive, schizophrenic, or schizoid. Kierkegaard's "melancholy" lacks the symptoms of inhibition which characterize the depressive phases of cyclothymia. Phenomenologically it is closer to the schizophrenic state than to the manic-depressive. But there can be no doubt about a powerful endogenic factor that has to be considered as pathological and that cannot be explained in psychological terms; it is, rather, a natural process, and as such not meaning-related. In Kierkegaard, this natural process does not have the character of a progressive, irreversible degenerative process leading to a terminal condition. It might have come to that if he had lived longer, but there are no signs pointing in that direction.

3. His productivity

I use this word to denote an original, non-derivative factuality.

In his youth Kierkegaard seemed to be an eternal student, ardently engrossed in literature and music, in German Romanticism and philo-

---

[15] Henriette Lund, quoted in Dru, 5561.

sophical speculation, in theology; but, able to assimilate everything, he was, in fact, embarked on a tumultuous intellectual development, as his journals, starting in 1834, when he was twenty-one, attest.

His productivity was a basic state of mind, at once a matter of suffering and fecundity. A virtually boundless imagination was able to conjure up a profusion of images. An equally boundless reflection led early to the banishment of all naïveté. As a poet he was driven to think; as a thinker, to poetize.

It was productivity of such exuberant, driving force that it became unendurable if not subjected to the rigorous discipline of a regulated daily task. Once the scheduled time for actual writing had come, everything was set down in finished form.

"Most of what I have written I have spoken and listened to a great many times, often perhaps twenty times. On the other hand, most of what I have written . . . has been composed *currente calamo;* but that comes from my finishing everything while walking about" (Gottsched, 83).

But this productivity also rejected all demands made by the world. Any kind of other activity or profession would have inhibited the stream and hence was felt to be intolerable.

1849: "Producing was my life. I could deal with tremendous melancholy . . . with anything . . . if only I was permitted to produce. Then the world assailed me, a mistreatment that would have made anyone else unproductive—it made me all the more productive; and nothing . . . had any power over me, if only I was permitted to produce" (Gottsched, 91).

This independent force of productivity had its phases of waxing and waning. His publications extend from 1838 *(From the Papers of One Still Living)* to the year of his death, 1855 (when the issues 1–9 of "The Instant" were published). The summit of his productivity as far as volume and variety are concerned was reached in the years 1841–46; the least productive period was in years 1851 to 1854.

4. His self-investment with meaning and his decisions

The external progress of Kierkegaard's life, the state of his illness, and his productivity are three realms of fact which he transformed into a single grand meaning. Kierkegaard's essence is not determined by these factualities but by what he made of them.

From his earliest state of awareness to his very end, he questioned himself about his task, about his purpose in the world, made his decisions, carried out his intentions, but in such a manner that the questioning reflection did not arrive at some finality. He kept on listening to the voice that guided him along his path and that opened to him a new understanding of the stretch behind him.

His biography, his experiences, his productivity were to him tremendously exciting events, which he pondered and transformed, interpreted and described in almost infinite variations throughout his entire life. The externally factual—at times intentionally hidden by him, even from posterity—is not to be taken as the structural or limiting frame imposed on his nature; instead, the obverse applies: it is the basis for his free decisions and the content of his insights, which endure independently of the biographical facts, though gained by him only through them.

The biographical seems merged into an all-embracing objectivity but does not become something that can be mastered by study; it is not a step in progressive cognition of things. Rather, it becomes a philosophical actuality, a throwing-open of possible spaces of existing, and an orientation within them for others; something vicarious, as it were, and a sacrifice.

This high degree of constant self-reflection and autobiographical assurance, this assimilation of everything into a possible knowledge, is not the vanity of self-observation or egocentric curiosity or exhibitionism. To classify it as introversion is superficial and trivial. This whole life is a philosophic reality, always of both subjective and objective concern. Its significance is the indissoluble linkage of person and cause. This thinking is not a game of idle preoccupation but, as Kierkegaard names it, existential thinking.

A. *Kierkegaard as a youth*

The seriousness with which Kierkegaard even in his youth considered life, worshiping "the unknown God" (well before the later so-called religious breakthroughs), is shown in the diaries of the twenty-two-year-old:

1835: "I have looked in vain for an anchorage in the boundless sea of pleasure and in the depth of understanding. I have felt the most irresistible power with which one pleasure reaches out its hand to the next; I have felt the kind of meretricious ecstasy that it is capable of producing, but also the ennui and the distracted state of mind that succeeds it. I have tasted the fruit from the tree of knowledge and often delighted in its taste. But the pleasure did not outlast the moment of understanding and left no profound mark upon me.

"The thing is to find a truth which is true *for me*, to find *the idea for which I can live and die*. . . . I certainly do not deny that I still recognize an *imperative of understanding* . . . but it must be taken up into my life. . . . That is what my soul longs after. That is what I lacked . . . to base the development of my thought upon—well, upon that which grows together with the deepest roots of my Existenz . . . through which I am, so to speak, grafted upon the divine, held fast by it even though the whole world falls apart.

"The man who has no inward hold on life cannot keep afloat in life's storm . . . only when a man has understood himself in that way is he in a position to carve out an independent existence. . . . I shall now try to fix a calm gaze on myself and begin to act in earnest. . . . And so the die is cast—I cross the Rubicon!" (Dru, 22).

This decision of 1835 was followed by the year that is most questionable, the year of the so-called excesses, the year of debts, of dissipation, of what Kierkegaard later interpreted as the darkness of the most sinister secret of his guilt.

B. From poetry to Being

Kierkegaard's productivity allowed him to see all the configurations of human possibilities which he himself could not actualize. He constructed them so graphically that they became more powerful than if they had been based on his own experience. In this openness to everything that he himself could neither be nor become, in wanting "to read solo the original text of the individual," human Existenz-relationship (S/L, 554),[16] he was incessantly driven farther, never leaving himself in peace or granting himself peace. When he asks, what should I do? what is imperative for me? he does not find an answer, whether in intuition or in cognition. Both inhabit his imagination, exist in possibility, and are not actuality.

Existence that does not enter the world nor makes the transition from possibility to actuality, remains speculation, fantasy, poetry. To counter this lostness and to arrive at the seriousness of the actual—this is how Kierkegaard sees his task, to be tackled by his tremendous flood of productivity: not to arrive at a solid standpoint or at a tranquil way of being, but, instead, to persist in going beyond to a depth in which God is found and is actual.

In his joy in productivity, his fantasy of the possible, his intuition

---

[16] References to S/L are to *Kierkegaard's Concluding Unscientific Postscript*, trans. by David F. Swenson, completed by Walter Lowrie.

of poetic images culminating in speculative thinking, this self-torment is included. It shapes his productivity and gives it direction.

Discipline in such productivity is imposed for yet another reason. "I could sit down and keep on writing day and night, for there are enough riches. If I were to do this, I would explode, however. But if I learn submission, do my work as a strict duty, hold my pen properly and write each letter with care, then I can do it."

The poet's existence is distinguished by the distance it keeps from what it sees. It subsists in despair. But because this despair includes the conception of God, it becomes the "most eminent poet-existence" (L208).[17] In its torment, God is its only consolation; yet it loves this torment and is not willing to give it up.

The thinking of the religious is also poetry: "He who became unhappy in love, and therefore became a poet, blissfully extols the happiness of love—so he became a poet of religiousness. . . . But to accept [his torment] in faith, that he cannot do . . . here is where the self ends in obscurity. But like that poet's description of love, so this poet's description of the religious possesses an enchantment . . . not possessed by any description by a husband or a Most Reverend. What he says is not untrue . . . his representation reflects his happier, his better ego. With respect to the religious he is an unhappy lover, that is, he is not in a strict sense a believer; he has only the first prerequisite of faith, the despair, and with that an ardent longing for the religious" (L209).

Hence productivity is by no means good in itself. When, in 1849, the decrease in his productivity and the new breakthrough of his will to Christian Existenz itself converge, Kierkegaard sees his task in a new light:

1849: "Now I must give up producing; I no longer have the means to do it . . . now I consider it my duty to become unproductive and must apply ethical means to prevent me from becoming productive" (Gottsched, 91).

Kierkegaard had such thoughts in rudimentary form from the very beginning; later, in 1839, he wrote about himself: ". . . melancholy, soul-sick, profoundly and totally a failure in many ways, one thing was given to me: a pre-eminent intelligence, presumably so that I should not be quite defenseless" (Dru, 1335). But he also knew what he was lacking when he succeeded in making a "salto mortale into a purely spiritual existence," namely, a "body and bodily preconditions" (Dru, 681). As early as 1835 he wrote: "That was what I lacked in order to

---

[17] References to L are to *The Sickness unto Death*, trans. by Walter Lowrie. Rev. Doubleday Anchor Books ed.

be able to lead a complete human life and not merely one of understanding . . ." (Dru, 22).

In 1848 he said it outright: "From a Christian standpoint . . . a
poet's existence is sin, it is the sin of poetizing instead of being, of
standing in relation to the Good and the True through imagination
instead of being that, or rather existentially striving to be it" (L208).

C. From reflection to action

Reflection shows possibilities, moves within an endless dialectic, does
not come to a halt, consumes the thinker. It comes to an end not
through itself but in the act of faith and in the act of action. Only in
this way does the thinker enter into actuality.

Total consciousness of truth is conditional upon reflection. Acting,
however, presupposes faith. If he had had faith, Kierkegaard said later,
he would have risked marriage with Regine Olsen. Solely through faith
can the leap out of reflection be accomplished and reflection controlled.
For Kierkegaard this leap is the problem that keeps him in a state of
unrest. His reflection is untiring. It never stops. The innocence of immediacy eludes him. But it is also denied to him for another reason:
without the dialectic of reflection, innocence is aesthetic, because it is
mere immediacy.

Reflecting is like poetizing. It separates us from actuality instead of
binding us to it. This was Kierkegaard's experience. Hence he wanted
to believe and to act, to enter into actuality, to become actual himself.

To bring this about determines the way in which Kierkegaard gives
meaning to his life. His unconditional earnestness imposed a dual demand on him: limitless reflection, without which no truth achieves purity
or clarity, and action, without which actuality cannot come into being.

From this results the picture of Kierkegaard's acting and not-acting, his constant hesitation, and the manner of his acting.

His earnestness will not allow things simply to happen and take
their course; to prepare his decisions he needs to reflect on all possibilities with utmost thoroughness.

Once he does act, the momentum of the moment is certainly liberating, but is followed immediately by reflection and a new interpretation of what he has done and what is to be done further. His failure
is inherent in the action itself. One day after his engagement he
knew that he had made a mistake: the marriage is impossible. Several
times he decided to enter the ministry, but in such a way that the
actualization is immediately sublated through new reflection.

Hence we can note as characteristic: first, the continuation, whatever the circumstances, of literary productivity, this action through the word, though always in new, deliberately formulated configurations; second, a constant recurrence of negative decisions—to marriage, to professional career, and to Christian proclamation (as apostle, as martyr, as reformer); and finally, in the actions themselves, against the *Corsair,* against the Christian Church, attack, negation, no reconstruction, founding, establishing. And he is aware of all this by his reflection, by his great honesty.

Two things result from his living, in fact, outside the real world, without any ties, without relating to the world:

He wants to live and fulfill his existence, but cannot; and so transforms it into imaginative fiction, related inwardly to actuality. And he interprets his lack of worldliness in a religious sense, as the consequence of Christian faith, but of an imperfect faith, since he does not become a "witness to the truth" in his understanding, nor a martyr or blood sacrifice.

Let us look more closely at three of his decisions, their character and consequences.

D. Regine.

1) *Engagement and separation from Regine Olsen.* In May 1837, when he first met Regine at the Rördams', Kierkegaard was smitten forever. On the same day he wrote in his diary: ". . . I thank thee, O Lord, that . . . thou didst not let me go mad at once" (Dru, 118).

More than three years passed before the engagement. One and a half years earlier, on February 2, 1839, Kierkegaard wrote in his diary: "You sovereign of my heart [later he added: "Regina"] . . . Oh, can I really believe the poet's tales, that when one first sees the object of one's love, one imagines one has seen her long ago, that all love like all knowledge is remembrance . . .

"Thou blind god of love! Wilt thou reveal to me what thou seest in secret? Shall I find what I am seeking, here in this world, shall I experience the conclusion of all my life's eccentric premises, shall I fold you in my arms—or:

"are the orders: 'FURTHER'?"   (Dru, 259)

"My one consolation is that I could lie down and die and then in the hour of my death admit to the love which as long as I live I dare not do, and which makes me equally happy and unhappy" (Dru, 349).

1840, a few weeks before his engagement: "Altogether it is my misfortune that at the time when I went about pregnant with ideas I was frightened by the ideal . . . and therefore reality does not answer to my burning desires—O God, grant that that should not also be the case in love, for there too I am seized by a mysterious dread of having confused an ideal with reality . . . until now that is not the case" (Dru, 333).

1849: "Even before my father died I had decided upon her. He died (Aug. 9, 1838). I read for my examination. During the whole of that time I let her being penetrate mine." At the time of the engagement (September 10, 1840), Regine was seventeen years old; Kierkegaard, twenty-seven. "The next day I saw that I had made a false step. A penitent such as I was, my *vita ante acta,* my melancholy, that was enough. I suffered unspeakably at that time" (Dru, 367).

Thus the period of the engagement turned very soon into the process of dissociation, which lasted one year. We can trace the ups and downs right into the details of the shifting moods, the feelings of happiness, the high spirits, the demeanor. We have Kierkegaard's letters— seriously meant, to be sure, but often artificial.

On August 11, 1841, Kierkegaard returned the engagement ring with the words: "In order not to have to try out any more what is bound to happen, and what, when it has happened, will give strength as strength is needed, so let it now happen. Forget above all else him who writes this; forgive a person who, whatever else he could do, could not make a girl happy" (H103).

She supplicated. She said it would be her death. Kierkegaard changed his tactics in order to detach her from him: he affected a humiliating indifference, an icy aloofness. He thought she would now despise and hate him. "It was a time of terrible suffering—to have to be so cruel and at the same time to love as I did. She fought like a tigress. If I had not believed that God had lodged a veto, she would have been victorious."

The attempted dissolution did not succeed. Regine held fast to him, no matter what Kierkegaard could say or do. "And so, about two months later, it broke. She grew desperate. For the first time in my life I scolded. It was the only thing to do" (Dru, 367).

On October 11, 1841, Kierkegaard brought the engagement to a decisive end. He left the Olsen house to go to the theater, returned on the following day for the last time. To the father, who pleaded with him, he declared his unshakable decision.

On September 29 he passed his master's examination. Two weeks after having dissolved his engagement he went to Berlin for the winter in order to attend Schelling's lectures and to write.

1842: "my relation to her was always kept in so vague a form that I had it in my power to give it any interpretation I wished" (Dru, 383).

Let us look at Kierkegaard's interpretations of his actions as they appear in his *Journals,* writings, and documents. His love and his rupture were spun by him into the insoluble entanglements of the unending interpretations of his incapacity, without relinquishing the thought of the possibility: It might have been if. . . .

2) *Comment.* We may judge that Kierkegaard did not know what he wanted. For a whole year he tortured a helpless girl with the confusion of his contradictory possibilities. He acted in a morally irresponsible manner, exposing the girl to what in bourgeois society is a scandal. In view of such behavior, as speedy a separation as possible seems mandatory. It is natural that the girl should marry someone else.

In the face of such appearances, bourgeois propriety prevails: leave things be; do not intrude; it is best to forget. Even for those immediately concerned and especially for outsiders it would be indiscreet to probe into the darkness of intimacies.

To pursue such matters in depth is considered unprofitable, at best, relegated to the sphere of psychiatry. If you consider yourself medically knowledgeable, your likely reaction would be: This story is, after all, nothing out of the ordinary. Kierkegaard must have been sexually abnormal. It is said that he was impotent or homosexual—a possibility, but impossible to prove.

Established evidence: From the outset, the whole relationship evolved on a spiritual plane. 1849: "Perhaps she never really loved me as much as she admired me, and perhaps I have never loved her in an erotic sense; I can, however, truthfully say that the amiable child moved me in the finest sense of the word" (Gottsched, 38).

In her old age Regine said that her love for Kierkegaard had been a spiritual love. Only once during the time of the engagement had she suddenly realized: My God, you are supposed to marry him.

It has been advanced: As with so many sick people like him, Kierkegaard was deceived about himself and had attempted the impossible counter to a hidden better knowledge; as a result he had to break things off. Occasionally men in this predicament, about to get married, commit suicide since they see no other way out of their moral and physical situation. Kierkegaard fictionalizes this possibility in his *Repetition.* But in his diaries too are passages such as the following:

"How often I have been on the point of fanning her love into a fire, not into a sinful love" and then "to put an end to my young life then and there" (Dru, 383).

After "all the humiliation she must have suffered from sympathetic relations and friends I long to give her this proof of my love . . . that I . . . turned back to her. . . . And indeed, if I did not abhor suicide, did I not feel that all such virtues were but shining vices, then I should turn back to her—in order then to end my life, a plan which unfortunately has been all too long in my mind . . ." (Dru, 377).

Such a subsumption under moral and medical categories limits itself to a condemnation of Kierkegaard or to the motivation of his biological impotence, supporting a tendency to single out one fact as the substance of actuality and dismissing everything else as matters of secondary importance, as self-deception and deceit, obfuscation and sublimation.

In observing what Kierkegaard thinks, understands, and subsequently, in his writings, makes objective as insight, we notice that a *factum brutum* may well be at play, but the person affected by it is faced with a becoming that is boundlessly understandable yet never understood, or, differently expressed, to a transcendence that opens up infinite understanding and manifests itself in an ongoing becoming.

There is meaning in the torment, but it is a hidden meaning. Kierkegaard's struggle reveals something which eludes definite grasp. But this veiled significance motivates the endless interpretations of himself and his beloved to such a degree that one cannot imagine even an ideal perfection of two "exceptions" encountering each other, who, by virtue of the absurd and the impossible, find the faith of joining in marriage in the world of the "universal."

What is the meaning of such a phenomenon? I cannot tell; it moves us in a strange and compelling manner, tormenting and touching us, not unlike the effect of all of Kierkegaard's work and life.

The biographical actuality becomes the illumination of being-human in its possibilities.

Kierkegaard recognized his guilt: "I carried you with me out into the stream" (H228). He ventured into a region where he did not belong.

But he also sees her guilt: "actually her self-love. She misused my melancholy, she believed one could frighten me so that I would give in" (Gottsched, 25).

3) *Up to Regine's engagement to Fritz Schlegel.* After Kierkegaard dissolved the engagement, Regine became his constant inner problem. Whatever he wrote was intended also for her as possible reader, and

his works took their impetus from the upheavals of this engagement and disengagement. Their purpose is to set her at a distance, by making her lose her trust in him and bringing her to despise him (as through the "Diary of a Seducer"); then, again, to enlighten her regarding his true motives (the secret of his reserve). He knows that he must not revive her attachment to him, and for this reason overt communication is no longer permitted: he has to persevere in the deception. She is to console herself, is counseled to marry another man. But Kierkegaard never ceased to regard her as belonging to him, never was able to forget her (cf. H112). Immediately after the rupture (1842) he fantasized in a letter to Boesen: "And do you not believe then that I long to give her this proof of my love . . . that I, the most inconstant of men, turned back to her . . . for who loves like a dying man, and that is really how I have thought of it each time I devoted myself to her, and to live with her in the peaceful and trusting sense of the word never occurred to me. That, indeed, is enough to drive one to despair" (Dru, 377). In his letters he used wording such as "since, after all, I consider the relationship as over only in a certain sense" and "in case I return to her."[18]

The sentence "Had I had faith I should have remained with Regine" (Dru, 444) needs to be completed with: If she had had faith, she would experience as exception not only me but also herself. She would remain true to me as I am to her—just in case it is possible for us, in the end, to actualize our marriage in this world.

Kierkegaard does, in fact, think in this way. Her question "Are you never going to marry?" he answers with cynical humor: " 'Yes, perhaps in ten years' time when I have sown my wild oats; then I shall need some young blood to rejuvenate me.' That was a necessary cruelty" (Dru, 367), for "if I had not done it, would she now be engaged? No" (Gottsched, 23).

But Kierkegaard considered the other possibility. If she had intended, for herself, as for Kierkegaard, to be the exception and not to get married, "if it had been truth in her case and hence permitted, then the idea would have had to originate with her and become clear to her. . . . She desired the union with me with her whole passion. After that came the idea that the two of us would agree not to marry each other or to remain unmarried. But whereas this was perhaps quite the proper thing for me, for it was original with me, in her case it would have been derivative. . . . But only the original relationship to God is the

---

[18] *Sören Kierkegaard und sein Verhältnis zu "ihr,"* ed. by Raphael Meyer, 75.

justified exception." If it "had been truth, things would have gone differently: she would not have said a word about it to me but, in her own relationship to God, would, out of her own origin, have decided not to get married and perhaps would have done the right thing in this way" (Gottsched, 27–28).

Thus Kierkegaard's love for Regine ran on two tracks: he wanted separation and freedom for her; he wanted the faith of the exception in which he commits himself to her and she, as this singular woman, remains faithful to him, this singular man, as his own.

His actual behavior corresponds to this. On Easter Monday, April 16, 1843, Regine nods to him several times in a friendly manner during the evening service. Kierkegaard, who did not know as yet about her engagement to Schlegel, interprets this to mean that, in spite of everything, she does not consider him a deceiver, is certain of his secret love instead, and is attempting a reconciliation. He traveled to Berlin in a great hurry and wrote *Repetition*.

4) *After Regine's engagement to Schlegel.* In 1843 Regine became engaged to Fritz Schlegel; publication of the banns was in October 1847, the wedding on November 3. He was her first love, even before Kierkegaard, and she had now returned to him. Kierkegaard was deeply shaken: "I was near to losing my mind in those days" (Dru, 444). Later, however, he judged: "The truth came out when she married, of which I strongly approved and for which I have thanked God" (Gottsched, 27).

But Kierkegaard must have felt disappointment at first. Contrary to earlier writings connected with Regine, *Repetition* and *Stages on Life's Way,* a work still related to her, contain passages of an almost malicious character, considering that Regine would have read and understood them.

Kierkegaard considered *Either/Or* to be a "good deed" done for her sake, with the intention of freeing her from him once and for all and opening up for her the possibility of another marriage. Now, however, presupposing that an inner tie to him continued to subsist, we cannot help perceiving an occasional voicing of his contempt for her because of her faithlessness.

She had implored him in the name of God, of Christ, of his father, to remain with her. Had this been merely empty prattle while Kierkegaard felt the import of her words weighing down on him like a terrible burden and understood them to be related to her religious attachment, which also bound her to him?

1846: "A young girl . . . put a murder on my conscience at the most solemn moment, a troubled father solemnly repeats the assurance that it would be the girl's death. Whether she was merely a chatterbox· or not does not concern me" (Dru, 600).

Secretly he had waited for a partnership in being-an-exception, though acting in ostensibly opposite ways. Now he saw her as faithless.

Here, then, is the situation: Kierkegaard is determined to be faithful. But she must not know this. She must be free to contract another marriage. Everything is arranged by him in such a manner that she regains her freedom. His writings intend to propel matters in this direction. But in the very same writings there are intimations of the contrary, most strongly in *Repetition*. Hirsch has proved that this work was already completed when Kierkegaard learned of Regine's engagement to Schlegel. As a result, he mutilated and altered it. By this new fact the work had lost its meaning. Hirsch believes that in *Repetition* Kierkegaard intended to convey to Regine that it needs "a faith of inconceivable quality to reconvert the accomplished sacrifice [Jaspers's interjection: "in *Fear and Trembling* this imagery appears in many variations; it arises from the depths of a relationship to God incomprehensible to an outsider"] into a new possibility in life on earth. It would be possible for them to find each other again on earth [Jaspers: "the repetition"] only if she [Jaspers: "and he"] had this faith. With these two works Regine was supposed to be confronted with a renewed choice in her interpretation of this relationship." [19]

In the original version of *Repetition,* the young poet is driven to his death (by suicide) because of the impossibility of repeating his relationship to the young girl. This was omitted in the revision (six pages were torn out and destroyed), but can still be adduced with certainty by a few crossed-out passages of the manuscript that has survived.

This new version ends quite untragically with the jubilation over the renewed productivity of the poet ("she has got herself married"), and with icy remarks by Constantin Constantius on the female gender.

And now a few examples of what Kierkegaard was capable of writing in the first moments after Regine's engagement to Schlegel became known to him. In his literary works he could push to the extreme what in his *Journals* he treated with moderation.

Constantin Constantius writes: "So far as the other sex is concerned I have my own opinion, or rather I have none at all since I have very seldom seen a girl whose life could be construed in terms of a category. Generally a woman lacks the logical consistency that is necessary if one

---

[19] *Gesammelte Werke in 36 Abt.,* ed. by Emanuel Hirsch, 4, Abt. IX.

is to hold a human being in admiration or in contempt. She deceives herself before she deceives another, and therefore one has no scale to judge her by."[20]

"She did not get to the point of screaming, and that is a misfortune. There must be some crying, that is a good thing . . . and then afterwards she has nothing to cry for, and quickly forgets" (ibid., 138).

In the first version, this passage, which was later eliminated, obviously because of its excessiveness, read as follows: "One has to let a girl scream herself out, provoke her to scream, and she will forget all the more quickly. Once one has done this one merely has to make sure to strike the iron while it is hot. There is no instant where a girl is more inclined to seize upon a new love than when she has lost a love at what she calls the loss of her life. Then it is sufficient to put a man at her arm. She will take him even if he were a man bought in an ironmonger's shop" (H124).

But Kierkegaard's emotional upheaval over Regine's bond to Schlegel in no way altered his basic relationship to her:

"I can say truly: She was the beloved, the only one, I loved her more and more, she was my beloved when I left her, and I do not want to love another one" (Gottsched, 29). "No husband can be more faithful to his wife than I am to her" (Dru, 389).

Kierkegaard felt himself bound to Regine for all time and eternity. This he expressed in various ways.

a) Even after her engagement to Schlegel, Kierkegaard continued to see the relationship in a double light. He reflected on Regine's marriage with conflicting feelings:

1849: "Giving her . . . an explanation could become dangerous for her, could destroy the illusion of her marriage, could become dangerous for me, could alter my relationship to God. And even if this were not so, then there is one more consideration, namely, that for Schlegel, of whom one has to be very careful" (Gottsched, 29–30).

1849: "Schlegel is surely an amiable person, I really believe that she feels quite happy with him: this girl, however, was an instrument on which he does not know how to play, she possesses chords which I knew how to draw from her" (Meyer, 115).

1849: "She can beautify Schlegel's life to a high degree, she can make him happy, he will adore her and thank her. It is possible that she retains an inner pain because of her relationship to me; but he will perhaps idealize her precisely in the deepest sense, and the relationship

---

[20] *Repetition*, trans. by Walter Lowrie, 141.

will correspond truly to her nature, in which there was, after all, so much pride" (Gottsched, 30–31).

As late as 1851 Kierkegaard wrote: "But I cannot speak to her. No . . . I could get to know too much. Perhaps she has put me out of her mind, after all—and then I could . . . ruin everything by speaking with her. Perhaps the whole marriage is a mask, and she is more passionately attached to me than before" (Gottsched, 43).

b) He did not leave her in peace once and for all. Even after her marriage he longed for clarity between the two of them, here in this life. He wanted her to know the truth of his feelings for her.

State Councillor Olsen, Regine's father, had died in 1849. Shortly thereafter Kierkegaard wrote Regine a letter enclosed in a letter to Schlegel, who was to decide whether to hand it to Regine or to return it to Kierkegaard. Schlegel decided to return it. The letter to Regine contained the following:

"Cruel I was. . . . Quiet have I kept. . . . Marry I could not, even if you were free, I could not marry. Meantime, you have loved me as I you; I owe you much—and now you are married. But I proffer you again what I can and dare, and ought to proffer you—reconciliation.

"In any case, as from the first so to the last, I am, Yours honorably and entirely sincerely, S. K." (H226–27).

In the many drafts for such letters which were never sent, he writes: "Thank you, oh thanks. Thank you for the time you were mine. Thank you for all which I owe to you. Thank you, my alluring teacher, for your childlike simplicity which taught me so much" (H228).

c) In 1851 he dedicated *Two Discourses* "To one unnamed whose name some day will be named, both this little work, and also my whole literary work from its very beginning" (H230). Earlier, the first two edifying discourses (1843) were dedicated to "the individual," and this was repeated and confirmed. (Whether "unnamed" is male or female cannot, in Danish as in English, be known.) As regards the philosophical meaning of the matter, "the individual" referred to is Regine.

d) In a little rosewood cupboard, which had been crafted according to his design—based on the memory of something she had said: if only she were allowed to live in a little cupboard in his house!—Kierkegaard kept two copies of each of his writings, one for her and one for himself, and wrote: "To her and my dead father—to the noble wisdom of an old man and the lovable innocence of a woman, who were my teachers, all my books shall be dedicated."

e) In his last will Kierkegaard left all he possessed "to my erstwhile fiancée, Mrs. Regine Schlegel." He concluded with the sentence: "What I wish to express is that to me an engagement is as binding as a marriage, and therefore my effects belong to her just exactly as if I had been married to her" (H226). Schlegel refused to accept the will at his wife's behest because "it seems to be based on an understanding to which she cannot in any way agree" (January 14, 1856; Meyer, 146).

His intention regarding his last will remained unchanged and was expressed in various ways through the years:

November 1849: "It is my unchanged will that after my death my writings are to be dedicated to her and my deceased father. She is to become part of history" (Meyer, 142).

Aware of his historic importance and the great influence he was certain to exercise in the future, he firmly intended to make her share in his place in history. As long as people would talk about him, they were also to talk about Regine. "Since I am involved with her, let it accord with the highest standard. Let everyone know, let her be transformed into a triumphant woman earning full satisfaction for the humiliation she suffered by my breaking the engagement" (Gottsched, 44).

1849: "She must be upheld in the role of my lover . . . for me she is the beloved 'to whom I owe everything' . . . thus history shall accept her . . . my life will then express that she was my only beloved. My life as author shall accentuate her life. And if not now, then she will understand me in eternity" (Gottsched, 36–37).

Kierkegaard and Regine saw each other for the last time on March 17, 1855, one day before she left for the Caribbean with her husband, who had been named governor of the Danish West Indies. Regine tried intentionally to meet Kierkegaard on the street, and said to him, as they passed, in a soft voice: "God bless you—may things go well with you" (Meyer, viii). He responded with a greeting. Henriette Lund describes the same scene, also on the basis of Regine's account: she had greeted him as she passed. Not knowing about the trip, he had "pulled the hat off his head with a highly dismayed expression, while also passing by."

5) *Regine after Kierkegaard's death*. When she was informed of the contents of the last will, Regine wished merely "to receive a few letters and a few small objects found in the estate of the deceased, which she assumed had formerly belonged to her." For this reason she wrote to Henrik Lund, Kierkegaard's brother-in-law. When she received what she had requested, her interest grew. Since, as she wrote on May 12, 1856, it was his wish "that I would receive everything after his death," she now wanted to know everything, asked that he keep back nothing

of "what you might have for me, orally or in writing. . . . God tempts
no one; if it were not His Will that I get to know what I know now,
it would not have happened; even though there was no explanation
between us since he said good-bye to me . . . I surely expected one
after his death, even though, I must confess, not exactly in the form in
which I received it" (Meyer, 146, 148, 149).

September 10, 1856: "You write that he mentioned me during his
illness; I am most anxious to know what he said about me; for, to be
sure, I found information in the papers bequeathed to me regarding
our relationship which put it into a different light, a light in which I
myself have seen it at times . . . mostly my modesty kept me from
seeing this in our relationship . . . but what I felt with certainty was
that an unexplained point remained between us that would have to be
clarified at some time in the future. Short-sighted person that I am, I
wanted to put it off until the tranquillity of old age, for a strange
thoughtlessness led me never to consider that he might die. . . . That
is what I hoped to be able to deduce, if I knew what his last words
about me were; for in my estimation his papers were all written several
years ago. . . .

"Strangely enough, I believed I recognized myself in a dedication
to an unnamed woman . . . from the moment when I saw it for the
first time and onward. I would like to ask you also if you can enlighten
me on this point. At that time his intention was to please and to honor
me, which indeed it did by his famous name" (Meyer, 151–52).

She was afraid of the limelight: "Well, as far as I am concerned
there could never be any question but that I could do without it. But
since his death, it has seemed to me as if it were a duty I had neglected
from cowardice; a duty not only toward him but toward God, to
Whom he sacrificed me, whether he did it from an innate tendency to
self-torment . . . or whether, as I think, time and the results of his
work have shown, from an inner call from God" (H231).

"The information you could give me most likely will not change
my decision at this time, which you will be able to understand is based
on consideration for my husband and his position; but I feel an urge
to clarify things as well as possible for myself, I no longer want to
postpone things in secrecy, I have had enough of such in this life. . . .

". . . but I would be very ungrateful if I did not call myself happy,
indeed, as happy as only very few; for it has been repeated often that
a happy marriage is after all the most important thing in life, and
Schlegel and I are so good for one another that we make each other
rich; to a certain extent I also have to thank him for this" (Meyer,
152–53).

Schlegel died in 1896, Regine in 1904. She survived Kierkegaard by half a century.

Kierkegaard invented his Regine. She, however, as a pure, natural soul, understood none of this. She completed her path through life granted to her with Schlegel, cherished her memories of Kierkegaard, and finally in her old age was somewhat proud that she had once been loved by someone so eminent and famous, loved to such a degree that he remained faithful to her up to the time of his death.

"You see, Regine, there is no marriage in eternity; there Schlegel as well as I will be happy to be together with you" (Meyer, viii). This sentence the aged Regine liked to repeat after Schlegel's death. No longer did it offend her.

5. *The fight with the* Corsair

In 1845, conscious that he had completed his literary work, Kierke-gaard again considered entering the ministry. But he could realize the "universal" of a professional life as little as he could that of marriage.

His life had to take a new direction. His human existence was not to remain uncommitted and free from risk. He had to act, to provoke danger and suffering. The meaning of his published writings de-manded the confirmation of their truth through the public character of the act. The inner suffering demanded complementation through exter-nal suffering. The first step, as carefully thought through as everything touched by Kierkegaard, was the fight with the *Corsair*.

This was a weekly paper appearing in Copenhagen, published and written to a great extent by M. A. Goldschmidt, whom Kierkegaard described as "not without a certain talent" (H, 172). In this scandal sheet all things and all people were ridiculed, private personality traits exposed, scandals uncovered. Whoever had a skeleton in his closet was made apprehensive. But the wider public found this approach in-triguing and relished the ironic, aggressive, angry tone, though no one would admit to it. This was when the first small-town publishing ven-tures were started, among people who knew each other; it was the first time this new dimension of newspaper publishing made its appearance, causing great excitement and enormous success. Privately people called it a disgrace but publicly no one dared to stand up to it. Even the Church remained silent.

In this paper, Goldschmidt spoke of Kierkegaard as a kindred spirit. His writings were praised. Goldschmidt treated the spirit of aes-thetic reflection and of irony and the playful wit in Kierkegaard's writ-ings as allied in character to his own.

But P. M. Möller—in the spirit of such a new press organ—had written in *Gaea* about the "Stages" by which Kierkegaard "puts his bride on the experimental torture rack in order to dissect her while still alive, to torture her soul out of her drop by drop."[21] Most likely this became the occasion for Kierkegaard to put a notice into the daily paper *The Fatherland* toward the end of 1845 which read: "Would that I might get into the 'Corsair.' It is really bad for a poor author to be so singled out in Danish literature, that . . . he is the only one who is not abused there" (H167).

The *Corsair* responded immediately, on New Year's, 1846. Thereupon Kierkegaard said, this time too, his old wish had been fulfilled of always having the laughs on his side. He had asked to be insulted by the *Corsair,* and the paper was very accommodating and fulfilled his wish. "One can engage the 'Corsair' to abuse, just as one can engage an organ grinder to make music" (H168).

But now the *Corsair* set Kierkegaard up for ridicule week after week, commenting on his personal appearance and exposing his private life. Caricatures that are effective even today made fun of his trousers, tailored of unequal lengths, of the way he carried his cane, of his features and his hat. One caricature shows him on Regine's shoulders. The *Stages [on Life's Way],* they wrote, are "an extremely skillful experiment . . . now we know how you trained your girl" (Niedermeyer, 456).

Another caricature shows him standing in the center of the universe, his cane under his arm: heaven and earth, sun, planets, and Copenhagen revolve around him, "who stands silent in the center and does not even show gratitude for the honor by taking off his hat" (Niedermeyer, 459).

The consequence of this was that ordinary people on the street stared at him and laughed; street urchins derisively called "Either/Or" after him—everyone suddenly saw him the way he was caricatured in *Corsair,* as a ridiculous figure. On the street, in the café, wherever he went, people stared at him.

Kierkegaard did not keep the laughs on his side. Copenhagen now laughed at him. He kept silent. Up to this time he had relished walking about the town, conversing with all and sundry; now he felt discarded, grinned at now and ridiculed to death by those around him. He suffered unspeakably. He was hypersensitive to begin with. Now he, who had no position in society, no office, no profession, no friends, had been

[21] Gerhard Niedermeyer, "Sören Kierkegaard und der Corsar," *Zeitwende,* II, Munich, 1926, 453.

robbed of the only thing that kept him aware of living with others. Suddenly he saw how things really stood. He came to despise people.

This experience confirmed his knowledge of truth: Truth is suffering, just as Christianity is actual only where people are suffering for it. What had been knowledge became actual for him. Up to then he had suffered only inwardly; now his suffering assailed him also from outside.

He realized that he was the only one to dare take up the cudgel against baseness and took upon him the unanticipated suffering, since everyone else remained silent. This he came to interpret as his personal atonement, as a gift from God, as the suffering incumbent upon the Christian.

This experience he now took as the occasion for a new version of his task: perhaps he should actualize in public battle what true Christianity is. He had used the incognito of the aesthetic writer so far. Now he entered into the incognito of a figure of ridicule demolished by sneering derision.

He felt compelled to go further. He who is uncommitted cannot remain a writer. He constantly asked himself what it was that God wanted him to do. He had to risk without restriction the suffering coming from outside. It is not enough to write poetically about Christianity. Action is what is called for. Always in preparation, always hesitating, always ready for the leap, his will to action finally came to a head in his attack on Church and Christendom, an attack that was bound to destroy completely his existence-in-the-world, because he had closed the door to the ministry for himself and his inheritance was spent.

6. The attack on the Church

In 1846 Kierkegaard still had a long way to go to reach this point. The first step was his new productivity as an author. From the initial aesthetic productions, and later from his indirect communication in his literary works and his attempts at the logic of faith, he proceeded to religious writing and direct communication. To be sure, all of his production up to then had run parallel with "edifying discourses." But now, in *The Sickness unto Death* and *Training in Christianity,* it evolved into his true task.

With these works Kierkegaard waged the battle against the Church only indirectly. He hoped that he could move the leader of the Danish Church, Bishop Mynster—who was his father's pastor and to whom, in memory of his father, he was attached, whom he revered and did not wish to attack—to confess that the Church is an attenuation of New Testament Christianity and an adaptation to the world. Mynster remained silent.

Meantime, the tension within Kierkegaard increased. The problem of the martyr, of the witness to the truth, asserted itself. In what guise, he asks, would such a Christian appear today? He knows himself not to be such, but something inherent in his life bears affinity to this role. He, Kierkegaard, points in that direction.

Waged at first indirectly, without aggressiveness, the battle for the truth of Christianity in Christendom turns, in Kierkegaard's second step, into open battle.

When Bishop Mynster died (January 30, 1854) and Martensen, who was to be his successor, lauded the deceased as a witness to the truth, a change took place in Kierkegaard. He was no longer inhibited by his reverence for the living Mynster, nor was he to be satisfied with an admission that true New Testament Christianity had been diluted in adaptation to the secular world, something he had vainly hoped for from Mynster. Kierkegaard turned radical. Only New Testament Christianity itself, without attenuation or accommodation, can call itself true.

Once more, after hesitating and procrastinating, Kierkegaard, in December 1854, opened his battle against the established Church, a battle whose ardor increased steadily in a series of pamphlets, unique in power and consistency, and developed into the greatest sensation. First he directed his attack against Martensen, now a bishop, but widened it soon to a fundamental questioning of the then prevailing ecclesiastical and Christian spirit, from which true Christianity had disappeared. He attacked the fraudulence of contemporary Christendom not from the standpoint of modern enlightenment but based on the truth of New Testament Christianity as he understood it. Ten months later, at the height of the battle, Kierkegaard died.

7. *Sickness and meaning*

He asked himself: Is this sickness curable? Is it to be identified with sin or is it precisely not sin? Repeatedly he relates that he raised this question with his physician and explains why.

1846: "Although no lover of confidants, although absolutely averse to talking with others about my innermost self, I nevertheless think and thought that it is the duty of man not to skip such a factor as that of seeking the advice of another man, only it must not become a foolish confidence but a serious and official communication. I have therefore consulted my doctor as to whether he thought that the discord between the psychical and the physical could be resolved so that I might realize the universal. He doubted it. I asked him whether he thought that acting through my will my spirit was capable of reforming and transforming that fundamental disproportion; he doubted it; he would not even advise me to set my whole will power in motion, of which he had some idea, lest I should burst everything asunder.

"From that moment I made my choice. That sad discord, with its attendant suffering . . . I have always looked upon as my thorn in the flesh, my limit and my cross" (Dru, 600).

1848: "Yet it consoles me to have spoken to my doctor. I have often felt anxious about myself for perhaps being too proud to speak to anyone. But just as I did so earlier I have done it again. And what had the doctor really to say? Nothing. But for me it was important to have respected the human authority" (Dru, 749).

If Kierkegaard is to acknowledge human authority, it has to prove itself.

Kierkegaard does not assume "as many physicians do, that melancholy is a bodily ailment, though for all that, remarkably enough, physicians cannot cure it; only the spirit can cure it, for it lies in the spirit" (A.H., 500).[22]

In this non-medical understanding of illness, Kierkegaard can go beyond all limits. 1855, in the hospital: "The doctors do not understand my illness; it is psychic, and they want to treat it in the ordinary medical way" (Dru, 549).

Kierkegaard told his doctor of the higher meaning of his fatal illness. The doctor's entry in Kierkegaard's medical history after he was admitted to the hospital reads: "He considers the illness to be fatal. His death, he claims, is necessary for the cause whose solution has used up all his spiritual powers, for the sake of which alone he has been active, and for which he believes that he is exclusively destined; this explains the conjunction of his keen thinking with such a frail body. Should he live, he would have to continue his religious struggle; but this would then flag; whereas, if he died, it would maintain its strength and, as he believes, its victory."

But Kierkegaard never said that the elicitation of meaning was the concern of physicians, nor did he consider the spirit's task of overcoming

---

[22] References preceded by A.H. are to *Either/Or: A Fragment of Life,* abridged and trans. by Alastair Hannay.

melancholy by making it transparent to itself before God a medical matter. The very thought, not to mention action as spiritual adviser, presupposes categories and ways of thinking that are medically incommensurable. Of the physician, Kierkegaard expected only an awareness of his limits and an openness to the other, but not that he should think and act in the direction of that other.

What possibilities he saw in his illness he expressed again, for example, in 1849: "There is no sense in suffering as I suffer and then doing nothing, if one's life is all the same to be entirely without significance. But here is the mystery, the significance of my life corresponds to my suffering" (Dru, 981).

Hence: illness has a meaning. Kierkegaard interprets it for himself in various ways:

a) *Illness as precondition of his productive spirituality.*

1846: "This is how I have understood myself in my entire literary work. I am in the profoundest sense an unhappy individuality which from its earliest years has been nailed fast to some suffering or other, bordering upon madness, and which must have its deeper roots in a misrelation between soul and body; for (and that is what is extraordinary) it has no relation to my spirit. On the contrary, perhaps because of the strained relation between soul and body, my mind has received a tensile strength that is rare" (Dru, 600).

"I have looked upon it as the high price at which Almighty God sold me an intellectual power which has found no equal among its contemporaries. That does not puff me up for *I am already ground to dust*" (Dru, 600).

1849: "Do you think that if you were perfectly healthy you would easily or more easily become perfect? On the contrary . . . To lead a really spiritual life while physically and psychically healthy is altogether impossible. One's sense of immediate well-being at once runs away with one. In one sense the life of the spirit is the death of immediacy. That is why suffering is a help. . . . Good health, an immediate sense of well-being is a far greater danger than riches, power, or position" (Dru, 954).

If this is the case, then relieving the illness, if such were possible, would be a questionable matter altogether.

1849: "Yes, if my suffering, my weakness were not the condition for my intellectual activity, I should naturally try again to tackle the problem quite simply medically" (Dru, 981).

b) *Kierkegaard's interpretation of his abnormal states.* Kierkegaard was able to interpret for himself his ever shifting emotional states (if he does not simply consider them to be results of illness, that is, as givens) as an incapacity for being actual (actuality stands in the shadow), especially as the disposition to translate everything he experiences immediately into recollection by means of reflection, or into possibility; he is able to interpret his mood shifts as the expression of his failed attempt at becoming transparent to himself, as sin, as vicarious suffering, as insurmountable isolation and withdrawal (no one understands him), as inner contradiction (he harbors the opposite in his soul at the same time). I shall cite just a few instances.

c) When *Kierkegaard appeals to the medical authorities,* he wants to liberate himself from a ruinous confusion. 1849: ". . . that I saw as guilt and sin what perhaps was nothing but unhappy suffering, mere temptation after all" (Gottsched, 94).

But then again there is a curious interplay of two elements: the meaning of Christian suffering as the expression of the truth of Christian Existenz, and the meaning of his suffering through illness—Kierkegaard's melancholy as expression of his Christian truth, both as penitent and as someone who has been pardoned.

Kierkegaard lets the moralist in *Either/Or* interpret melancholy (cf. A.H., 499): Melancholy is the sin of not willing deeply and inwardly. To will in this way one has to be transparent to oneself. Immediately enmeshed as one is in the affairs of the world, one yet has to collect oneself, as it were, from this dissipation. If the movement of the wanting-to-become-transparent-to-oneself is inhibited and repressed, melancholy sets in. To the question what is making him so melancholy, the melancholic has no answer. He does not know. For as soon as he knows what melancholy is, it is lifted. In this it differs from sorrow, which is not lifted when its cause is known. The sin of melancholy can never be lifted completely. Even the person whose life takes its course in quiet, peaceful, healthy motion will always retain traces of melancholy. The deeper reason for this lies in original sin, which makes it impossible for human beings to become wholly transparent to themselves. People whose souls are not familiar with melancholy have no intimation of metamorphosis.

d) *Kierkegaard understands his illness by interpreting it* like the other realities of his life, but all of them in interconnection, such as money: "It is essentially owing to her [Regine], to my melancholy, and to my money that I became an author" (Dru, 748). "In a certain sense my whole misfortune lies in this: had I not had means it would never have been possible for me to redeem the terrible secret of my melancholy. . . . But then I should never have become the man I have become. I should have been *compelled* either to go mad or to break through. As it is I have succeeded in making a *salto mortale* into a purely spiritual *Existenz*. But then again in that way I have become completely heterogeneous from mankind in general" (Dru, 681).

In the same way he understood the pathological element in his relationship to his father and to Regine Olsen. Both have "educated" him. Through them he came to comprehend his life's task, a task which, over the years, he discerned with increasing clarity and finally exclusively in his stressing the true meaning of Christianity according to the New Testament. "Truly, the cause of religiosity and especially Christianity can surely use a solitary person; but what a lengthy history my education has, and how strangely dialectic it is!"[23]

Everything is God's tool.

His father: "My father too was terribly unjust to me in his melancholy—an old man who put the whole weight of his melancholy upon a child, not to speak of something even more frightful, and yet, for all that, he was the best of fathers" (Dru, 681).

e) *The fusion of illness and Christianity.* In Kierkegaard this has strange consequences. He discusses the twofold possibility: to confirm, based on his Christianity, the others, the healthy ones, in their happy state, or, in Christian suffering, to disturb them in their happiness.

1846: "Without being able to appeal to revelations or anything of that kind, I have understood myself in having to stress the universal in a botched and demoralized age, in making it lovable and accessible to all others who are capable of realizing it, but who are led astray by the age to chasing after the unusual and extraordinary. I have understood my duty like the man who, himself being unhappy so long as he loves man, desires only to help others who are capable of being happy" (Dru, 600).

But when Kierkegaard wanted to emphasize the demand of New Testament Christianity, namely, that truth is suffering and being put to death, he considered things differently.

1853: "Now, for better and for worse, I live in the isolated cabin of melancholy—though I may rejoice at the sight of other people's joy and may sanction it from a *Christian* point of view. . . . But when I step forth from my horrible suffering and I come out among happy people, I thought I might have the melancholy joy of confirming them in their enjoyment of life. Oh, but if I have to preach mortification and that to be loved by God and to love God is to suffer, then I have to

---

[23] *Sören Kierkegaard Verhältnis zu seiner Braut,* trans. by E. Rohr, Leipzig, 1904, 87.

disturb others in their happiness, I cannot have the melancholy joy of rejoicing in their joy, the melancholy love of thus being loved by them. . . .

"If anyone can prove to me from Holy Scripture that to be loved by God and to love God is compatible with enjoying this life: I shall accept this interpretation from God's Hand with unspeakable thankfulness . . ." (Dru, 1287).

f) *His solitude is caused by abnormality:*

1848: "Remaining in the painful prison of my isolation, in a profound sense cut off from communication with other men . . ." (Dru, 749).

1849: "My misfortune, or the thing that made my life so difficult, is that I am strung a whole note higher than other men, and where I am and what I am about does not have to do with the particular, but always also with a principle and an idea" (Dru, 928).

1845: "But if it is true that I have no right to compare myself to others in order to glorify and praise myself, but only in order to keep the ideal before me, it is equally true that I have no right to compare myself to others in order to despair over myself, for there again I must keep to myself and the truth . . ." (Dru, 550).

g) *Interpretation of his becoming different:* Kierkegaard felt himself to be constantly in motion, in a change of his condition up to opposite extremes, in transformations of his whole way of life, in discovering anew what his task is.

1848: "My whole being is changed. My reserve and self-isolation is broken—I must speak." Shortly thereafter: "No, no, my self-isolation cannot be broken, at least not now" (Dru, 747, 749).

1851: "Something new was born in me: for I now understand my duty as an author in quite a different way, it is now dedicated in quite a different sense to the direct spreading of religiousness" (Dru, 1225).

"I constantly feel as if something new is moving within me" (Gottsched, 96).

h) *Interpretation of the negative decisions.* The illness serves Kierkegaard to interpret his negative decisions.

He cannot take over an office. 1849: "I cannot because I am not an ordinary human, am melancholy to the point of imbecility; while I can hide it as long as I am independent, it makes me unfit for office where not everything is determined by me" (Haeker, II, 94).

His external appearance is deceiving, is a mask. 1850: "In personal encounters I am a lighthearted merrymaker" (Haecker, II, 142).

8. His greatness: interpretive transformation
of the actuality of his illness

An attitude of rejection of Kierkegaard may be based on the following grounds: he is ill, and therefore has no validity for us, either in his nature or in his thinking; he is eccentric, takes the wrong paths, which block his progress and in which he gets mired; he moves in extremes, uncommitted, in an empty, merely negating restlessness; whoever follows him is in danger of ruining his own life. Against Kierkegaard can. be argued the virtues of health, the will to live, reasonableness, all that is positive. In rejecting him, we are reassured in our natural instincts, in the given of a supposedly known, in unassailable personal health.

But what is Kierkegaard's actuality? Into his life enters an alien element, a sickness growing out of its own ground, which nonetheless becomes his own being because he is able to give it meaning, a meaning he finds and experiences with growing wonder and thankfulness as the work of Providence.

Devastating fear and incalculable joy, breakthroughs to newly experienced certainty of faith and task—familiar phenomena from an external psychiatric point of view—these play a role in his life; in such a manner, however, that they are not mere factual data; though incomprehensible for us, he himself accepts them and endows them with meaning. Never mind that he experienced them at first as strange and senseless; Kierkegaard appropriated them and read into them a meaning that thenceforth determined him.

His notes testify to the difficulty and endlessness of this process; they manifest to what extent everything became excruciating and had to be questioned again and again, how remote from any madness was the capacity for mastering this madness while constantly touching its limits.

1839: "The sad thing about me is that my life (the condition of my soul) changes according to declensions where not only the endings change but the whole word is altered" (Dru, 252).

The question of "illness and meaning," "schizophrenia and meaning" might be discussed as follows:

Does Kierkegaard imbue his originally schizophrenic experiences so convincingly with meaning that the reader ceases to notice the schizophrenic nature of their presentation? Do they become comprehensible in an objective sense, multivalent and dialectical? Does all that is sick in Kierkegaard become the material of a meaning, so that it ceases to have the character of mere sickness?

Is being laid bare on this schizophrenic ground an attribute of spirituality as such, which as a rule remains so inhibited and constricted that it is hidden? Such as the contradictory and dialectical element in the radicalism of its actualizing consistency?

This is not to say that "the healthy individual" is without contradictions. But he is either untouched by them and leaves them be, or employs them appropriately to gain advantages in life in an unconsciously purposive manner. In no case does he seriously act from the contradictions. In an intellectually gifted schizophrenic, however, a dialectical seriousness may assert itself and take over the entire life of the psyche in a manner not possible in a healthy person. Is this the only way to unseal the riddle, the riddle of finding everything questionable, this radical knowledge of impermanence and foundering, this inner reversal? Is it only in this way, within the limitless dialectic of possibilities, that the intuition of the different ways of life and the language of transcendence reach clarity in an all-sublating scope?

If that is the case, the following would be valid: only in contact with such actuality does one become "initiated." And then it becomes evident whether or not human beings desire this kind of knowledge.

The two ways of looking at Kierkegaard's existence, namely, that of the givens of sickness and constitution and that of the freedom of interpretative dialectics taking things to extremes, are juxtaposed in his actuality. Decisive here is that, first, the natural force of the illness did not gain the upper hand but was kept within limits, and, second, it was met by the energy of a spirit which, in the process of understanding himself, managed to preserve the person from being overpowered by the sickness which imposed on actual life so much suffering of loss and defeat. Kierkegaard achieved this by transmuting what was sick into his working material, erasing thereby its independent power.

There is another way of viewing this problem:

Schizophrenic episodes are metaphysical experiences, visions that assume shape in art and poetry. Or they are seen as exposure of the human abyss and its possibilities, of what is normally hidden but no less actual.

From this angle, health is perceived as the great concealer, the power of distraction, the blindness, the drifting into uncharted misfortune; whereas illness, by its obvious mischance, shows the misfortune inherent in man as such, the volcano on which man lives.

If we try this approach, then deceptive truisms and self-satisfied attitudes are demolished; the eerie enigma of mental illness and the way it can manifest itself in certain cases—not in all, and perhaps only in rare ones—finds its justification. But that is not the final truth.

The fact that we admit, even demand, this viewpoint does not imply that we as well as Kierkegaard set up against it the value of human achievements, human actualizations, human happiness, human tragedy—liberating and fulfilling in an exemplary manner, and imparting to human beings the exaltation of love.

With all of Kierkegaard's greatness, we cannot help feeling pity for him and a strong sense of strangeness; he does not elicit love.

We have to relinquish understanding him completely. We cannot come to grips with his enigmatic natural constitution, since Kierkegaard himself in a grandiose, almost incomprehensible manner transforms it into meaning, nor can we construe a comprehensible interconnected whole which would illuminate the parts. What we are left with is, on the one hand, a disparate multiplicity of meaning and, on the other, radical contradictions; both are deliberately set down on principle, but, all the same, defy understanding.

This perception of his life and personal character must be kept in mind as we study Kierkegaard's thoughts and meaning-configurations, their marvelous simplicities, their illuminating power, their recollection of what is essential, but also their strange somersaults, instances of self-destructiveness, dead ends, and violence. The two cannot be separated.

In all this it is Kierkegaard's greatness that, understanding himself as an exception, he did not make himself into a universal. He did not claim to be an example, a signpost, but, humbly subordinating himself to the universal, merely wanted people to pay attention. He did not make use of himself to do violence to others.

It is Kierkegaard's greatness that he not only interpreted but in interpreting transformed his actuality. The consuming equivocalness of illness and sin is changed into the great unequivocalness of the meaningful as such; nothing incomprehensible, outside the naturally given, is allowed to persist; only the depth of the divine sets a limit to understanding, a limit that constantly shifts into the infinite.

As a result, Kierkegaard engaged in constant self-criticism, never found an end to his desire for self-transparency, was unwavering in his honesty, and never established as his possession a final understanding of himself. He never surrendered to the endless spiral of his reflections or to the dishonesty of sophistries advantageous for his assessment of himself.

The infinite play of interpretations so confusing to the reader is held together by his seriousness, undeviatingly directed toward the one thing that, however, never becomes known.

The pathological nature of his constitution and of the most extreme experiences of his mental conditions when they come over him in bodily and psychological immediacy are transformed into meaning in such a high degree that it stands virtually unexampled in its concreteness.

Hence, Kierkegaard's illness has to be kept constantly in mind as he is being interpreted, not, however, in order to use his sickness as explanatory basis or to interpret something negatively as rooted in sickness. Our position, rather, should be that everything accessible to us is "objective" in the broad sense that it is universally understandable and carries weight for every individual in his becoming himself.

Everything articulated by Kierkegaard has a meaning independent of his illness and cannot be understood more clearly by a knowledge of his illness. But insofar as all of Kierkegaard's thinking is objective and subjective at the same time, and everything is grounded also in his personality, we cannot set aside the picture of his nature that emerges when we understand the meaning of what he has thought.

THE WORKS

1. Introduction

Kierkegaard burst upon our age through his life as well as through his thought. The thinker refers us to what he has thought, the thought refers us to the thinker. What he lived and shows us in the *Journals* is as essential as his work. His not-acting reveals as much as his acting.

The seemingly random life of an idler and invalid actually was a process of the highest discipline and concentration. His work testifies to the seriousness of this life in a richness and multifariousness of meaning that is almost overwhelming, a seriousness whose dramatic final act could not be ignored by the public.

A variety of answers presents itself to the question of what his work, regarded as a meaningful structure, represents as a whole:

It understands our age and thereby reveals what is.

Spurning the deceptive sense of safety and security in our intuition of world history, in the aesthetic enjoyment of spiritual life, in the actually existing, and in tradition, it manifests that life is a serious matter: each individual as such carries his own responsibility.

He makes us aware by indirect communication without showing us the way.

So it might appear that Kierkegaard has nothing decisive to communicate. But does he not want more than being the harbinger of disaster; and does he not say it? His clear and firm intention is philosophical and religious. As philosophical: he wants to read again "the original text of the individual, human existential relations." As religious: through the progress of his at first aesthetic literary work, he wants to "deceive into" Christianity, as it were. But philosophically he refuses to present a doctrine. Religiously, he keeps repeating that he is not a prophet of Christianity, not a believing Christian, has no authority; even in his final attack on the Church, he asks for nothing but honesty, does not claim to found Christianity anew, to rebuild or to reform it.

His work is suffused by the polarity of philosophic and religious interests. Both interests draw from the torrent of his overwhelming productivity. His philosophical will to insight and his Christian will to faith are both of extraordinary force. But neither of them declares itself with finality; time and again they are forced into indirectness, hesitate and again pounce, are present and again denied for the sake of simple honesty.

If we wish to hold fast to this ultimate positive guideline of Kierkegaard's, we have to give up all pretense of the univocal in his life and work. Nor must we allow ourselves to be deceived by the impression of consistency emanating from the totality of his work, created as it is by his retrospective self-understanding. The lack of the univocal coupled with the depth of the problems presented and the passion that informs the work of his thought are what constantly excites us anew. Kierkegaard is an awakener, not a leader.

An overview

Kierkegaard's greatest literary and philosophical productivity is concentrated in the four years 1842–46. Between his thirtieth and his thirty-fourth years, the following works came into being: *Either/Or, Repetition, Fear and Trembling, The Concept of Anxiety, Philosophical Fragments, Stages on Life's Way, Concluding Unscientific Postscript.* Of equal and perhaps greatest importance, though later, is *The Sickness unto Death.*

If, following the aesthetic-literary works, the religious writings constitute the second group and his religious polemics animate the third, we must not forget that Kierkegaard's aim throughout is to alert us to the underlying religious intent of all his *literary* writings. Starting with *Either/Or,* all his writings are accompanied by edifying discourses, the former published under pseudonyms, the latter in Kierkegaard's name.

The structural coherence of the chronological sequence of his works is astonishing. The divisions represent substantive modifications of goals as well as turning points in his personal life. Each work seems to have its subjectively proper place as well as its irreplaceable value.

No work of Kierkegaard's may be claimed to be his main opus, in which he can be found in his entirety. Each one exhibits his nature but taken by itself would be misleading.

As we study these writings, our admiration grows for the total organism which develops, initially unconsciously but constantly accompanied by planning and reflection. In retrospect, determined by Kierkegaard's self-understanding between 1848 and 1851, each of his writings seems to fall into its particular place as though by necessity, each grouping seems finished and complete, and—even though Kierkegaard died at the early age of forty-two—the sequence of his works builds to a meaningfully complete, finished whole.

The sureness—the result of extraordinarily concentrated reflection—the steady beat, as it were, of the steps, and their meaningful progression, seem to us as though guided by an encompassing significance. We can well understand why Kierkegaard, at rest after all the unrest, should wonder at the inexplicable rightness of this progression, in which he sees, with infinite gratitude, the workings of Providence.

The literary form

Under this heading we have to differentiate the published works, the literary remains, preliminary drafts, and miscellaneous papers; the journals; the letters.

Kierkegaard kept journals from 1834, his twenty-first year. Their content deals with his cogitations and personal affairs. He reworked them. Many thoughts in them were transposed into the published works. Crucially important ones are found only in the journals. The continuous self-reflection and self-interpretation in them is irreplaceable, as is the originality of his daily self-contemplation and thinking. Unfortunately, out of the eleven volumes, only excerpts have been translated.

Kierkegaard's letters are less numerous and do not constitute an essential part of his writing.

In real life, however, he was utterly unable to engage in communication. He was aware that he could never open himself up completely, that he could not fully confide in anyone, that he always held something back. His ability to establish rapport with people, to captivate on his walks and in social settings by a word, a look, by no means signifies readiness for communication. "He had a peculiar manner to greet someone from a distance with a glance. It was only a flicker of the eye,

and yet it expressed so much. His glance could express infinite gentle-
ness and amiability but also something provocative and teasing.
Through a glance at a passer-by he could irresistibly 'establish rapport'
with him, as he expressed it. Whoever encountered this glance became
either attracted or repelled, embarrassed, insecure or provoked."[24] It
was an "art of psychological experimentation," and understood as such
by Kierkegaard himself.

Interesting as their contents often are, and subtly formulated, the
letters still strike us as contrived, especially those to Regine. They lack
spontaneity (except for some passages in the letters to Boesen). From
an infinitely rich sensitivity, from an extraordinary agility of thought
and feeling, issues a stiff humaneness.

From the outset, the *Edifying Discourses* were intended to testify
under his own name to the religious concerns about which Kierkegaard
lets the pseudonyms speak; but according to his own statement voiced
by Climacus, they are not Christian discourses at all. Not only are they
not sermons, since they were written without authority, but they utilize
"merely the categories of ethical immanence and not the doubly reflected religious categories in paradox." Kierkegaard wanted to see
"how far one can go being edifying with purely philosophical means"
(*Philosophische Brocken,* 329).

Later on, Kierkegaard also wrote "Christian" discourses.

2. The pseudonyms

Most of Kierkegaard's writings were published under pseudonyms. He
speaks in his own name in the *Edifying Discourses* and the *Christian
Discourses,* in the last writings of his attack on Christendom, in elucida-
tions of his writings, and in his self-interpretation. His voluminous
journals appear in part like a great trial arena from which much is
taken over into the pseudonymous writings, in part like spontaneous
confidential messages from Kierkegaard himself.

But, as with the diaries, it is, ultimately, impossible to draw a clear
line of demarcation between him and his pseudonyms.

What he says directly also stands within the space of his reflection.
What is said by the pseudonyms is equally the outcome of Kierkegaard's thought, expressed by pseudonymous mouthpieces. It is he who
invents these thinkers.

---

[24] Hans Bröchner (1820–1875), "In Memory of Sören Kierkegaard" (cf. H,303). A professor of
philosophy in Copenhagen and a friend of Kierkegaard, he wrote this article after Kierkegaard's
death.

Some of the pseudonyms are close to Kierkegaard; others are less so. He himself differentiates: *"The Concluding Unscientific Postscript* is not an aesthetic work nor is it, in the strictest sense, a religious one. Hence it is voiced by a pseudonym; but I have named myself as the editor, which I did not do with any of my merely aesthetic writings. . . . Then came the two years which produced only religious writings, under my own name. The time of the pseudonyms was over."[25]

He composed some of his works as written by himself, and only at the end, based on reflection, did he introduce a pseudonymous author (for example, Climacus and Anticlimacus).

Can a clear and sharp line of demarcation be drawn between thinking presented as fictive and Kierkegaard's own thought?

This is most clearly answered in borderline cases. What John the Seducer says is not said by Kierkegaard. What Climacus and Anticlimacus say can be quoted to a great extent as the expression of Kierkegaard's thinking, and initially was written as such. The play of opposites by means of pseudonymity is for Kierkegaard of crucial importance. He is neither the unbelieving nor the believing author. He wants to be both but only by way of pseudonyms.

The criterion may be found in what he says in his own name: in all the *Edifying Discourses,* self-interpretations, the "Attack upon Christendom," the *Journals.* Yet even there we find differences, we find the searching, experimenting Kierkegaard.

In his literary works Kierkegaard dares to think through and give shape to what was experienced by him as possibility or realized, perhaps, in tentative ways; in making use of explicit literary invention he can venture to the utmost extremes and vent his inner emotions and agitation without identifying himself with them. The inventing of the pseudonyms frees him from a responsibility—which he bears nonetheless, because, or insofar as, they are his poetic inventions.

Kierkegaard asks us to allow his writings to stand as they are. If we wish to quote them, he demands that not he but the pseudonym speaking be quoted.

3. Survey of the exposition

As we try to get hold of Kierkegaard's mode of thinking, of the questions he poses, and of his projects and subject matter, the fundamental difficulties faced are the following:

---

[25] *Sören Kierkegaards agitatorische Schriften und Aufsätze 1851–1855,* ed. by A. Dorner and Chr. Schrempf. Stuttgart, F. Fromann, 1896, 393.

a) Kierkegaard rejects being an object of teaching, yet we want to teach him. How can this be reconciled?

1) By recapitulating his lecturing, which raises the question what such lecturing meant for him at the time.

2) Whatever is said by anyone has to be said in the objectifying mode, so also by Kierkegaard. This has to be stressed.

3) Kierkegaard does not aim at direct, but at indirect, communication. In recapitulating the objectifications, we set ourselves the task—in accord with Kierkegaard's intention—of cancelling what tends to objective fixation. But this process of reproduction is itself not indirect communication, but speaking about Kierkegaard's thoughts, a view from the lower position of rational comprehension to the higher one, up to the borderline where the thinker's thoughts are his inward action.

4) We can speak in direct communication about indirect communication, which Kierkegaard himself cannot escape doing. We can observe and discuss the methods by which indirect communication, by deliberately projecting itself, also destroys itself.

We are faced with the abiding substantive situation that philosophy of Existenz cannot be thought in a mode leading to a systematic doctrine consisting in propositions under which one can subsume instances. This means that existential philosophy cannot be taught in the form of a doctrine that lends itself to recital and examination.

b) In speaking of the development of Kierkegaard's thought, do we take into account his personal development? No, that is an entirely different subject.

We can speak of a development on the part of Kierkegaard in terms of new beginnings in the way he formulates his task (which structures the entire organism of his writings chronologically), and in terms of tracing his thoughts from brief initial sketches to full development and elaboration.

But the structures of his thought are so pervasive and coherent that to a great extent it is possible and proper to gather them from all his productive periods, from the brief span of the initial twenty years and from the still briefer span of the immensely productive last six years. Even in the early journal entries prefigurations of his last thoughts can be found.

c) What should be the arrangement of his thoughts?

The problem is how to order the sequence of topics so that they may be appropriately surveyed in the absence of any system.

1) Such a survey could be organized following the chronological

sequence of the writings and the way they are grouped. This would make sense in a literary discussion, which takes Kierkegaard's creative process as a chronological guideline and considers each work as an isolated unit.

2) We could take as the organizing principle the goal expressed by Kierkegaard, in his self-understanding, with such extraordinary retrospective clarity. From this perspective all his works would be understood and judged as means to this end. Concurrently we might ask whether other goals Kierkegaard set for himself actually assert themselves, though they are not specifically objects of reflection.

3) A starting point might be made of the "exception," the negativity and sacrificial nature of Kierkegaard's existence, leading to the perception of the seriousness in this incomprehensible aspect that eludes us; we could inquire into it and discover what points to this seriousness in and through the objectifications and configurations of his thinking. Out of Kierkegaard's intention and interpretation, we might arrive at comprehension of the meaning of his thinking in our age, whose special character Kierkegaard was the first to discern. And with his influence as our guide, we could tackle the criticism that may properly be raised against him, as it is against any human action.

Each of these approaches, and maybe some others, follows from one principle. Each may lead to a clear overview from its particular viewpoint. But none of these paths is the only possible and the only correct one. Whoever concerns himself with Kierkegaard will try them all and will on each of them arrive at the limit where it manifests its inappropriateness.

MODES OF THOUGHT, PROBLEMS POSED, MAIN THEMES

1. Signa of Existenz

Introduction. In this presentation of the signa of Existenz, the Christian aspect will initially be set aside and precedent given to what challenges, awakens, brings to consciousness, becomes existentially present, to the exclusion of specifically Christian faith or belief in Jesus as God become man in a dogmatic Christian sense.

Also set aside is the historical question of whether thoughts such as Kierkegaard's would have been conceivable without the background of Christian faith, thoughts that keep, and perhaps even increase, their persuasive power and effectiveness outside that faith. Their historical origin does not limit their appropriation to the Church and dogma based on that origin, particularly since precisely such claims were rejected and opposed by Kierkegaard without reservation.

Kierkegaard's intention. 1846: "My merit in literature is that I have set forth the decisive determinations of the whole of the compass of Existenz with such dialectical clarity and so originally as has not, so far as I know, been done in any other literature, neither have I had any books to help me . . ." (Dru, 607).

Kierkegaard repeated the content of this journal entry in a statement of the same year in which he admits to being the author of the pseudonyms. The importance of the pseudonyms "absolutely does not consist in making any new proposals, any unheard-of discovery, or in forming a new party, in wanting to go further, but precisely on the contrary, consists in wanting to have no importance, in wanting (at a distance which is the remoteness of double reflection) to re-read solo the original text of the individual human Existenz relationship, the old text, well known, handed down from the fathers, to read it through yet once more, if possible, in a more heartfelt way." He added: "And oh, that no half-learned man lay a dialectic hand upon this work, but would let it stand as it stands" (S/L, 554). But we cannot bow to this wish of Kierkegaard's when his thoughts are to be discussed. We would have to keep silent and ignore all that concerns his literary activity.

Kierkegaard's task seen in comparison. The mystery of existence in which we find ourselves is that of being-human. This focal point preoccupies philosophical thought from Augustine's "quaestio mihi factus sum" (*Confessiones,* X, 50) to Kant's formulation of the meaning of philosophy, that is, to show man's position in the universe and man's tasks.

The particular historically common doctrines of what man is, the so-called anthropologies, furnish no adequate answer. Some of these anthropologies proclaim the doctrine of man as a being having his place midway between angels and animals; then there are the doctrine of the soul that structures thinking, feeling, and willing; the doctrine of man's conscious and unconscious, and the interplay between these two realms, its borderlines and transmutations. Common to those and other doctrines is the belief that they objectify man and know in principle what man is. In this assumption, I am what I know about man and am the instance of a universal. But, instead, the principle is: Man is more than he knows of himself, not so much in the sense that as knowledge progresses more will subsequently be known about him, but that he can be certain of this "more" prior to and beyond all cognition, without ever actually knowing it.

Kierkegaard's greatness consists in transcending anthropology to reach a different ground of man's self-assurance as possible Existenz.

What man is, is not at all a self-evident fact. Kierkegaard frequently quotes Socrates (*Phaedrus,* 230a) that he cannot as yet "know himself" and discover "whether I really am a monster stranger than Typhon, or a simpler, gentler being who by its nature participates in something divine."[26]

Some of Kierkegaard's attempts to arrive at self-assurance through thinking will be offered here as examples.

Our task, however, must not be to twist Kierkegaard's thoughts into a system which he did not intend and which would contradict their meaning.

What should be made clear is that each attempt—in a combination of concepts specific to each—sketches an illuminating thought which calls for other such sketches.

We shall try to reproduce each complex of thoughts by itself. To be sure, they are interconnected. They interpret each other. Their relatedness makes it possible to have each taken up into the other. But each such connection is again found only in individual movements of thought, so that a sequence is the way to present them. No simulacrum of a system is called for. Let every thought complex be taught, if it can be. Since what is being discussed here is to be imparted and not passed over in silence, the directness in teaching is unavoidable but must be put in its subordinate place.

2. *Immediacy; consciousness; spirit; freedom; anxiety*

a) Suspension of *immediacy*: Immediacy simply is but has no knowledge of itself. It does not question itself, it is there, it lives, it experiences. We may also call it the unconscious.

As we find ourselves existing, we are no longer merely immediate, but are out of an immediacy, related to it.

Immediacy is darkness. There is in the first place the sensuous immediacy that can never become spirit but remains, under the constant intrusion of the spirit in us, the darkness that cannot be lifted; second, the immediacy of the spirit itself, the germ of the spirit, come to itself in spirit and transformed into self-understanding; third, a new immediacy out of a different origin, arising only in the suspension of sensuous

---

[26] Quoted according to Kierkegaard, 6, 34.

and spiritual immediacy, yet itself always consciousness and spirit, the immediacy of faith as the new ground that receives us when all immediacy disappears, and dissolves as it becomes conscious.

The path of existence or of the spirit becoming conscious of itself is the venture of never-ending illumination, of unceasing reflection in which we in our awakening actually come to ourselves but in a way that entails the risk of losing ourselves and along with this the unconsciously living immediacy.

At first we live by unquestioning immediacy; we can also live authentically but not by simply cancelling this immediacy, something that can be achieved only by the limitless process of becoming conscious and by reflection for which there are no limits. Kierkegaard calls this faith. "Faith then becomes the new immediacy, and one which never can be sublated in Existenz since it is the highest immediacy and its sublation would reduce a man to null and nothing" (S/L, 310). An existing individual cannot continue to exist if he were to sublate all of his immediacy. "Although one reads hundreds of times: Immediacy is sublated—one never sees a single statement about how a person manages to exist in this manner."[27]

Everything is called "immediate"—even that which has become conscious as spirit—provided it has darkness as its component, a darkness in need of being surmounted by illumination in order to allow existential authenticity; this darkness represents seduction for possible Existenz, if it wants to remain within it.

If, ultimately, faith is called the new, other, immediacy, this becomes possible only on the basis of sublation of all immediacies, which brings with it a new darkness, of a principally different kind, to be illuminated in a different manner.

Immediacy is sublated by consciousness and by the clarity prepared by consciousness. Consciousness illuminates the universal and the spheres of all that can be thought. It makes possible the self-being of the thinker. "The more consciousness, the more self; the more consciousness, the more will, the more will, the more self" (L, 162).

To deny oneself to consciousness and to reflection means to remain mired in misunderstood immediacy, purposely blind and bereft of self.

b) *Freedom:* As we step out of immediacy we find freedom. Or, freedom takes this step. Both the venture of clarity and the clarity itself are freedom.

---

[27] *Stages on Life's Way,* ed. and trans. by Howard V. and Edna H. Hong.

Now merely living from day to day constitutes guilt. Freedom opens up the way to guilt in various ways. Every step we take within it has to be accounted for.

But to live only from day to day is also not a possibility for man. Man can forfeit his freedom but he cannot not be free, that is, live without responsibility.

Freedom and unfreedom presuppose each other and cannot be explained by any antecedent in the world. Unfreedom in itself constitutes guilt.

It is impossible to maintain that freedom begins as *liberum arbitrium* that can choose good just as well as evil. "To speak of good and evil as the objects of freedom reduces both freedom and the concepts 'good' and 'evil' to finiteness. Freedom is infinite and originates out of nothing. Therefore, to want to say that man sins by necessity makes the circle of the leap into a straight line" (T/A, 112).[28]

The good cannot be defined. The good is freedom. Only in freedom can there be the distinction between good and evil, a distinction that subsists only *in concreto*.

If one thinks the distinction could be determined abstractly, then freedom changes into something else, into an object of thought. "If freedom is given a moment to choose between good and evil, a moment when freedom itself is in neither the one nor the other, then in that very moment freedom is not freedom but a meaningless reflection," confused thinking (cf. T/A, 111, 112).

c) *Anxiety:* The possibility of freedom feels the impetus toward the actuality of freedom. In logic, says Kierkegaard, one can simply say that possibility leads into actuality. "However, in actuality it is not so easy, and an intermediate term is required. The intermediate term is anxiety . . ." (T/A, 49).

Anxiety is the intermediate determinant: from possible Existenz to actual Existenz (to become Existenz at all); before the decision in the particular instance—out of the possibility, which is comprehensive and still comprises opposites, to actuality, which is one or the other, finite and definite and irrevocable.

It is a qualitative leap. Anxiety does not explain it, nor does it justify it.

Anxiety is a determination neither of necessity nor of freedom. It "is entangled freedom . . . but not entangled by necessity but in itself" (cf. T/A, 49). This entanglement comes to consciousness as anxiety. "As

[28] References to T/A are to *The Concept of Anxiety,* trans. by Reidar Thomie and Albert B. Anderson.

soon as the actuality of freedom . . . is posited, anxiety is lifted" (cf. T/A, 96).

What kind of anxiety? In the state of innocence, of ignorance, there is peace and quiet, to be sure, but ". . . there is simultaneously something else that is not contention or strife, for there is indeed nothing against which to strive. What, then, is it? Nothing! But what effect does nothing have? It begets anxiety. . . . Dreamily the spirit projects its own actuality; but this actuality is nothing, and this nothing is what innocence always confronts." It is said: "Be not anxious over anything." Anxiety is "the enormous nothing of ignorance" (T/A, 41, 44).

The spirit's very possibility lures forth its intimation before which anxiety arises. But the intimation "disappears as soon as one seeks to grasp for it, it is a nothing that can do no more than alarm" (T/A, 42).

Fear refers to something definite. Anxiety has no object. "It is freedom's actuality as the possibility of possibility . . ." (T/A, 42). Freedom is anxious before itself.

Freedom is spirit: "the less spirit the less anxiety" (T/A, 42).

Anxiety does not contain sensuous desire as such but the urgency of the possibility of freedom. Hence the linguistic usage: a pleasing anxiety, a strange anxiety, a bashful anxiety (cf. T/A, 42).

Kierkegaard observes children: Their anxiety is not yet guilt because they are innocent. It is not suffering that cannot be brought into accord with the blessedness of innocence: "One will discover this anxiety intimated more particularly as a seeking for the adventurous, the monstrous, and the enigmatic. . . . This anxiety belongs so essentially to the child that he cannot do without it; though it causes him anxiety, it captivates him by its pleasing anxiousness" (T/A, 42).

Kierkegaard's interpretation of Adam: It is not the prohibition that awakens the desire. In that case Adam would have had prior knowledge. "The prohibition induces in him anxiety, for the prohibition awakens in him the possibility of freedom. What passed by innocence as the nothing of anxiety has now entered into Adam, and here again it is a nothing—the anxious possibility of *being able*. . . . Only the possibility of being able is present as a higher form of ignorance, as a higher expression of anxiety . . ." (T/A, 44, 45).

The threat "You shall die" is not grasped by Adam. "The terror is simply anxiety. Because Adam has not understood what was spoken, there is nothing but the ambiguity of anxiety. . . . Innocence is not guilty and yet there is anxiety as though it were lost" (T/A, 45).

Anxiety may be compared with dizziness. "He whose eye happens to look down into the yawning abyss becomes dizzy. But what is the

reason for this? It is just as much in his own eye as in the abyss. . . .
Hence anxiety is the dizziness of freedom which emerges when . . .
freedom looks down into its own possibility, laying hold of finiteness
to support itself. Freedom succumbs in this dizziness" (T/A, 61).

3. Self-being

The self is not existence, not an object, not something which I have
and which I am as I am.

"But what is the self?"

In the first place: "The self is a relation which relates itself to its
own self . . ." (L, 146). Man is not yet himself as synthesis, as relation,
for example, of freedom and necessity, of the infinite and finite, of the
eternal and the temporal, of soul and body. These are always relations
between two factors. Only when the relation relates itself to itself is
this relation the positive third, and this is the self (whereas the relation
between two factors is termed a negative unity).

Second: A self, a relation which relates itself to its own self "must
either have posited itself or have been posited by another" (cf. L, 146).

The human self is such a derived relation. In its relating itself to
its own self, it relates itself to another: "By relating itself to its own
self, and by willing to be itself, the self is grounded transparently in
the Power which posited it." The self, "in being itself and in willing to
be itself, is grounded transparently in God" (L, 147, 213).

Let me explain this:

a) *What am I myself?* To this question no answer is given by way
of psychological reference to my disposition, my faculties, my being-
thus, or by reference to the universal being-human that is identifiable
on a physical, psychological, or anthropological basis; nor by reference
to the unconscious that can be unlocked, or to the history of my life as
something not yet fully worked through, as something unknown; nor
by the sociological reference to me as a civic person endowed with
rights.

Instead, the self assures itself only by transcending everything objectively known or that can be objectively known, reaching to the origin
in the Encompassing. "When an individual considers himself aesthetically, he becomes conscious of this self as a multiple concretion inwardly determined in many ways, but in spite of all the inner diversity
it is all still his nature; everything has just as much right. . . . His soul
is like soil from which there springs all kinds of herbs, all equally
entitled to strive . . ." (A.H., 52, 59).

b) *The self is dialectical.* It eludes our determination. It is the one and the other. In the relation of the two factors to each other, it is the relation to itself, and this it is transparently only in relation to the power which posited it. No moment of this dialectical whole can be left out without robbing the rest of its support.

To want to know the self objectively is an evasion of actual self-assurance. Instead of willing oneself in one's being-granted-to-oneself, instead of listening in limitless openness, instead of inner action toward becoming oneself, I cling to a knowing, an "ought," an ideal, a program.

We would like to take hold of self-being as an object of our knowledge and productivity. Then we would be having it, and we could assure ourselves of possessing it by objective signs and guarantees, could watch over our self as though it were a thing. But the self is dialectical. I never know whether I am. If I use only my intellect, with its urge to know and cognize and determine, I fall into the abyss.

Because the self is dialectical, because it is impossible to know what it is in order to want or not to want it, every definite tenet concerning the self is in the first place wrong, and, second, a means of escaping self-being by rational means through pseudo-knowledge and pseudo-wanting-to-know.

c) *The more consciousness the more self.* "Properly speaking, immediacy has no self" (L, 86). Consciousness, will, self are an intensifying whole.

The self acquires its measure through consciousness. The self, whose measure is man, progresses from ignorance to consciousness of the self and is intensified within this knowledge. But a new measure is that this self stands in the sight of God: "What an infinite reality this self acquires by being before God! . . . What a finite accent falls upon the self by getting God as a measure! The measure for the self always is that in the face of which it is a self . . . each thing is qualitatively that by which it is measured." Hence: "The more conception of God, the more self; and the more self, the more conception of God. Only when the self as this definite individual is conscious of existing before God, only then is it the infinite self" (L, 210, 211).

d) *The concrete self.* The self signifies the following contradiction: the universal is posited as the individual. "Although there have lived countless millions of such 'selves,' no science can say what the self is without again stating it quite generally. And this is the wonder of life, that each man who is mindful of himself knows what no science knows, since he knows who he himself is . . ." (T/A, 78, 79).

"The most concrete content that consciousness can have is con-sciousness of itself . . . the self-consciousness that is so concrete that no author, not even the one with the greatest powers of description, has ever been able to describe a single such self-consciousness, although every single human being is such a one. This self-consciousness is not contemplation. . . ." The self together with self-consciousness cannot be something completed for contemplation, because it is in the state of becoming. "This self-consciousness, therefore, is action, and this action is in turn inwardness . . ." (T/A, 143).

The consciousness of an infinite self "is really only the most abstract form, the most abstract possibility of the self. . . ." (L, 201). It would detach the self from the power which posited it, and from the necessity and limitations of a definite self with its specific gifts, dispositions, these determinate conditions. Mistakenly it would like to create itself out of the infinite possibility of self, in the form that it desired.

The concrete self, on the other hand, is actuality and limitation and can see its task only in the self granted to it.

This task is again dialectical: "But to become oneself is to become concrete. But to become concrete means neither to become finite nor infinite; for that which is to become concrete is a synthesis. Accord-ingly, the development consists in moving away from oneself infinitely as one's self becomes infinite, and in returning to oneself infinitely as one becomes finite" (cf. L, 163).

e) The person who knows that he can be a self knows thereby that there is *something eternal* in him. ". . . next to God there is nothing as eternal as a self . . ." (L, 186).

". . . to be a self is the greatest, the infinite concession made to man, but at the same time it is eternity's demand upon him" (L, 154).

Man cannot shed the eternal. "He cannot cast it from him once and for all, nothing is more impossible; every instant he does not possess it he must have cast it or be casting it from him—but it comes back. . . . And the relation to himself a man cannot get rid of any more than he can get rid of his self . . ." (L, 150).

This then is the paradox: The self is not; it is in the process of becoming; and the self is eternal self.

f) *Despair:* That man is and is not eternal self, becomes eternal self, and casts it off—that is the origin of his despair.

1) Despair "is related to the eternal in man." It is "the disrelation-ship in a relationship which relates itself to itself" (L, 150, 148).

It is not a natural given, such as in the disrelationship of body and soul. It is there as long as the self, in relation to itself, does not want to be itself, does not ground itself, transparent to itself, in the power that posited it. Expressed differently: man is desperate when he leaves the basic structure of his Existenz (that is, grounding himself transparently in his relation to himself in the power through which it is posited). "Every human Existenz which is not . . . grounded transparently in God but obscurely reposes or terminates in some abstract universality (state, nation, etc.) or in obscurity about itself takes its faculties merely as active powers, without in a deeper sense being conscious whence it has them, which regards its self as some explicable thing, whereas it is to be understood from within: for every such Existenz—whatever it may achieve, be it most amazing, whatever it may explain, be it the whole of existence, however intensely it may enjoy life aesthetically—every such Existenz is nonetheless despair." (L, 179).

2) Anxiety is the state of possibility preceding freedom. Despair is the state in face of the loss of the eternal self.

The anxiety of spiritless immediacy can be recognized by spiritless certitude, despair by enchantment and seduction of the senses. When the enchantment ceases, "when existence begins to totter, then too does despair manifest itself as that which was at the bottom" (L, 177).

Happiness is not a determinant of Existenz. In the most secret, hidden recesses of happiness dwells anxiety (as the possibility of freedom) and despair (as the incongruity of the self of mere existence with its eternal self grounded in transcendence) (cf. L, 158).

3) The possibility of this despair (of the sickness unto death) is man's advantage over animals (cf. L, 148). "One cannot at a given moment decide anything about a person who is not saved by the fact that he has been in despair. For in case the condition comes about which brings him to despair, it is at that same moment manifest that he has been in despair throughout the whole of his previous life" (L, 157).

"Despair, just because it is wholly ambiguous, is in fact the sickness of which it holds that it is the greatest misfortune not to have had it—the true God-given fortune to get it, although it is the most dangerous sickness of all, if one does not wish to be healed of it" (cf. L, 159).

4) There are various possibilities of despair:

(a) Despair at not being conscious of man's capacity of being a self: despairing ignorance.

(b) Despair that knows it is despair:

(1) Despair at not willing to be oneself: despair of weakness; despair of worldly things or something of this world; despair of the eternal or of oneself. This would be the only possibility of despair if I had created myself and would like to get rid of myself.

(2) Despairingly willing to be oneself. The self, in its dependence, cannot attain balance or rest through itself: the despair of defiance.

Despair at not willing to be oneself (of not willing to be rid of oneself) and despair at willing to be oneself (detaching oneself from the power that posited me) are together a statement to which "basically all despair" can be reduced.

The contradiction is resolved (cf. L, 153). One statement results from the other, and vice versa:

The self which man despairingly wills to be is not his self but a willed one; and the self which he despairingly does not will to be is the concrete self (cf. L, 201).

In both, the eternal self posited by the power through which I am has been denied, and so has despair, in turn changing dialectically from the one to the other: into the infinite negative self, into the concrete self which I happen to be.

Does "the self" have the same meaning in all the statements? No. Because it is dialectical, it brings confusion into the discussion. It is always elusive; every discussion can, in principle, be turned around immediately and become open to misunderstanding.

There is the eternal self, which keeps disturbing us.

There is the concrete self, which I just happen to be, with its specific traits and situations.

There is the negative self, which in its formal infinity wills to bring itself forth according to its will: the infinite self (cf. L, 201, 202).

5) There is the clear-cut defiance. The clarity of the spirit takes a twofold direction: out of immediacy to reflection and freedom; out of relation to itself either to true relation or to disrelation, that is, either in the leap to the ethical and religious, or as transparency in the despair of defiance.

The "more consciousness the more intense the despair. . . . The devil's despair is the most intense despair, for the devil is sheer spirit, and therefore absolute consciousness and transparency; in the devil there is no obscurity which might serve as a mitigating excuse; his despair is therefore the most absolute defiance . . ." (L, 175).

When consciousness is at its minimum, the despair is least; indeed, it is almost as if it were questionable whether one is justified in calling such a state despair.

6) Man cannot destroy his eternal self; he can merely ruin it.

We can "demonstrate the eternal in man from the fact that despair cannot consume his self, that this is precisely the torment of contradiction in despair. If there were nothing eternal in a man, he could not despair" (L, 153).

"It is not only the greatest misfortune and misery to be in despair, no, it is perdition" (L, 148).

4. Existenz and time

Reading time off the face of the clock is an objective process. We think of time guided by a line as the chronological time of events, of history. We experience time at every moment, remember and work through what has been, await and plan what is to be.

If we want to grasp the present, it has already become past. We experience time in various ways, as moving quickly, as sluggish; in judging time in this way, we deceive ourselves. We describe and observe the psychological experience of time.

But Augustine's words keep their validity. "What is time then? If nobody asks me, I know; but if I wish to explain it . . . plainly I know not" (*Confessiones,* XI, 14).

We have concepts and representations of time, can differentiate them, but we do not precisely hit the center where all are connected, that is, what time itself is. And yet we speak about time as if it were one and had only one meaning.

If, in order to grasp time itself, we give preference to one concept of time or one notion of time so that we derive all concepts of time as originating from there, we merely engage in mental construction. To give priority to physical, objectively real time, or to experienced subjective time, or to biological (life-shaping) or historical time constitutes arbitrariness. Whenever we think about time, we have to make use of some sort of notions and concepts by which time is present to us.

Decisive for assuring ourselves of the existence in which we find ourselves is to keep in mind that we cannot escape time. To be sure, we may think timelessness, such as attaching an enduring and valid meaning to what goes beyond time. We think of eternity, which comprises all time without itself being time. In the fullness of the moment we experience a presentness in which all time seems to have been obliterated. But all this we experience, after all, within time which remains the inexorably moving arena or the path on which all that takes place which, according to its content or substance, points beyond time. What we are is in the process of becoming. Nothing is without reference to temporality.

This may seem a matter of indifference. Time belongs to the universalities of form and matter which, because they are always present, are just as much a matter of course as the air we breathe, the forms of thought in which our consciousness is always related to objects, the light and the darkness which surround us.

Kierkegaard, however, made it matchlessly clear that time is not at all a matter of indifference, but that, in its universality as well as in our inability to transcend it, it is infinitely essential, since it is not only phenomenon and field of activity but constitutes our nature as Existenz. But what this means is not at all simple. No definition, no mere knowledge can lead to it; it can be reached only in thought on the part of Existenz, to which thought expressed in sentences is merely a signpost.

Any time that we can define, think, and treat objectively is a determinate time, as it were, external to us, kept at a distance insofar as we relate to it.

In order to express that we mean time in itself and that our being is bound to it, we might say: The nature of Existenz is time. But this statement does not address what its content seems to signify, for in thinking it we have, as thinking beings, taken a position outside it, namely, that Existenz itself is time.

To what extent and in what sense the content of this statement is true can be clarified only by way of thoughts and images in which our being-time, the import of our temporality, is brought to mind in a way that, in the forms of the separation of I and time, the identity of I and time is yet palpable, or by which it becomes manifest that separating ourselves from time lets us fall into the void; the identity, however, becomes clear only in the specific configurations proper to Existenz and time.

Here Kierkegaard is extremely inventive in producing illuminating ideas.

a) *The conception of time as such:* We do not merely become and happen but become conscious of time. What is commonly shared and universally valid is objective time in its determinability, that is, that which concerns indifferent time.

Time can be represented as a line; as an empty regular progression; as past, present, future; as an objective happening that I comprehend subjectively as more filled or more empty, as longer or shorter, and which I estimate correctly or deceptively.

I can describe how time is experienced and lived, can determine the deceptions through a comparison of the subjective estimations with the real objective passage of time, and can examine them by varying the conditions of the conception of time.

But who or what relates to time in such an objective manner, deals with time as with something that is reliably measurable, that is more

or less at our beck and call, and becomes an aspect of cognitive thinking concerned with natural events?

It is consciousness-as-such, in which and as which everyone is equal
to any other one, everyone is replaceable by any other one. Kierkegaard, however, asks about what I myself am and can be.

To speak about this, notions and concepts of time are needed, time
experienced and lived through, not, as it were, in detachment but in
connection with the substance of possible self-being. This approach creates new and specific difficulties in intelligibility, since, to objective
opinion, it is a verbal absurdity, yet at the same time, by doing without
all objective intuition of time, it challenges the self that is illuminated
by it.

Objective investigations of time impel cognitive effort by the riddle
it poses. Existential utterance imparting thoughts about time elicits, by
the questions it poses, the possibility and concern of self-being.

However, what time *is* as essential for our consciousness of Existenz
and the forces that impel it is not clear-cut, but varies greatly in the
oppositions of modes of Existenz. If we call these modes standpoints,
then this statement of Kierkegaard's applies: "The conception of time
is decisive for every standpoint at all."

The standpoints in Kierkegaard are the "stages": "In the same degree that time is accentuated, in the same degree we go forward from
the aesthetic, the metaphysical, to the ethical, the religious and" (insofar
as time is emphasized as a paradox) "to the Christian-religious"
(S/L, 265).

In this whole series we find the one great alternative: to live outside
of time or to submerge oneself in time; to live abstractly in possibility
and in the universal of the timeless or to execute the "leap into life"
(A.H., 71, fn); to place time over against ourselves as an other or to be
time ourselves.

The aesthetic stage, says Kierkegaard, constantly runs aground
against time so that the aesthetic suspends itself in time. The ethical
stage is the very first to point to the importance of time: "To be capable
of becoming history . . . is the significance of temporality and finiteness" (cf. Dru, 467).

b) *To exist means being contemporaneous with oneself.* We desire to
be contemporaneous with great men and great events. This is an aesthetic desire.

Everyone likes to live in his imagination a good bit ahead of himself "beyond what he is in action and actuality . . . the majority of men
are like a wagon from which the locomotive has run away—they are

so far ahead of themselves, they are so far behind their actuality" (cf. Dru, 697).

But one thing matters: "Being contemporaneous with oneself . . . "(and so neither in hope nor fear of the future, nor in the past) is to understand oneself and be at peace, and that is only possible through one's relation to God, or it is one's relation to God" (Dru, 700).

But past and future lie in presentness. Existing, being temporal, is recollection and hope. Presentness does not become comprehensible or actual in itself to itself: it must be understood backward and lived forward. The consequence of this is "that life can never really be understood in temporality simply because at no particular moment can I find the necessary resting-place from which to understand it—backwards" (Dru, 465).

The ethical standpoint sees two errors: "those who live mainly in hope, and those who live mainly in recollection. Both exhibit an incorrect relation to time. The sound individual lives in both hope and recollection, at one and the same time, and it is only through this that his life acquires true, substantial continuity. Accordingly, he who adds hope to recollection is saved from seeking the substance of his life in the past." For him, who adds recollection to hope, the present moment "is increased by his remembering one in the past" (cf. A.H., 465, 466).

Not being identical with one's time manifests that existing is not simply a temporal happening. It is as if we were manipulating time and getting lost that way, since we are wasting it. Time can be a human being's "worst enemy," as shown in the expression "killing time"—and, conversely, that one is bored *to death*. It could be the psychologically correct rejoinder of a suicide in the last moment before he shot himself: "with this shot I kill time" (cf. Haecker, 236, 237).

If the contemporaneousness with oneself is disturbed, then this constitutes a reduction of Existenz; if it is suspended, then this constitutes the loss of Existenz.

c) *External and existential relation to time.* "When in a written examination the youth are allowed four hours to develop a theme, then it is neither here nor there if an individual student happens to finish before the time is up. . . . Here, therefore, the task is one thing, the time another. But when time itself is the task, it becomes a fault to be finished before the time has transpired. Suppose a man were assigned the task of feeding himself for a day and he were finished by noon with his food: in this case his celerity would not be meritorious. So also when life constitutes the task. To be finished with life before life has finished with one is precisely not to have finished the task." Here it is "the most dangerous of all experiences to have finished one's task too quickly" (S/L, 146, 147).

Existing temporally is no mere becoming that happens by itself, develops, unfolds, matures, and dies. What man becomes as possible Existenz is up to his Existenz. "It is a lack of sense as to what spirit is, and moreover it is a failure to appreciate that man is spirit, not merely an animal, when one supposes that it might be such an easy matter to acquire faith and wisdom which come with the years as a matter of course, like teeth and a beard and such like. No, whatever it may be that a man as a matter of course comes to . . . one thing it is not, namely faith and wisdom." On the other hand, it is easy "with the years to go from something. And with the years one perhaps goes from the bit of passion, feeling, imagination, the bit of inwardness, which one had, and goes as a matter of course . . . under triviality's definition of understanding of life" (L, 192).

d) *Time and eternity.* What is existentially essential is to gain eternity within time.

For inwardness is "eternity or the determinant of the eternal in man." Whoever "has not understood the eternal correctly, understood it altogether concretely, lacks inwardness and earnestness" (T/A, 151).

What is Existenz?

"Existenz is the child that is born of the infinite and the finite, the eternal and the temporal, and is therefore a constant striving" (S/L, 85).

What is eternity?

Eternity and time are incommensurable. For endless duration is not eternity, because for one thing it does not exist, and then because it would be merely time, and endless boredom at that (Lessing).

What is timeless is the status of what is logically valid, of the cognitive object, of consciousness as such. Timelessness is not eternity. Because it is without time, it is also without actuality.

Whoever has not correctly understood the eternal does not arrive at earnestness. Such deceptions are:

1) "Some deny the eternal in man. At the same moment 'the wine of life is drawn.' . . . A person . . . may continue to deny the eternal as long as he wants, but in so doing he will not be able to kill the eternal entirely" (T/A, 151–52).

To be sure, one preaches the moment. Eternity is done away with by all the moments. ". . . this denial of the eternal may express itself . . . as mockery, as prosaic intoxication with common sense, as busyness, as enthusiasm for the temporal . . ." (T/A, 152).

2) "Some conceive of the eternal altogether abstractly. Like the blue mountains, the eternal is the boundary of the temporal; but he who

lives energetically in temporality never reaches the boundary. The simple individual who is on the lookout for it is a frontier guard standing outside of time" (T/A, 152).

3) "Some bend eternity into time for the imagination. Conceived in this way, eternity produces an enchanting effect. One does not know whether it is dream or actuality. As the beams of the moon glimmer in an illuminated forest park or a hall . . . the mood is always the same: Am I dreaming, or is it eternity that is dreaming of me?" (T/A, 152; cf. Nietzsche's "noontide").

Or one conceives eternity simply as an object of imagination, as in the statement that art is an anticipation of eternal life. But poetry and art are merely a reconciliation in imagination. "They may well have the sensitivity of intuition but by no means the inwardness of earnestness. Some paint eternity elaborately with the tinsel of the imagination and yearn for it" (T/A, 153).

4) "Or eternity is conceived metaphysically." The pure I is to become eternal self-consciousness. "He talks about immortality until, at last, he himself becomes not immortal but immortality. . . . Considering the ridiculousness of this, what Paul Möller said is true, that immortality must be present everywhere. But if this be so, the temporal becomes something quite different from what is desired" (T/A, 153).

The Existential Meaning of Duration of Time:

The existing thinker is constantly striving. This does not mean "that he has a goal in the finite sense for which he strives, nor that he would be finished once he had attained it; no, he strives infinitely, is constantly becoming . . . as long as he exists he is becoming. . . ."

Existing is ". . . pathetic because the striving is infinite, that is, it is directed toward the infinite. . . . It is comic, because such a striving involves a self-contradiction. Viewed pathetically, a single second has infinite value; viewed comically, ten thousand years are but a trifle just like yesterday when it is gone; and yet the time in which the existing individual lives, consists of just such parts. If one were to say simply and directly that ten thousand years are but a trifle, many a fool would give his assent and find it is wisdom; but he forgets the other, that a second has infinite value. When it is asserted that a second has infinite value, one or another will possibly hesitate to yield his assent, and find it easier to understand that ten thousand years have an infinite value. And yet, the one is quite as hard to understand as the other. . . ."

What is to be understood becomes evident only when one is "so infinitely seized by the thought that there is no time to waste, not a second, that a second really acquires infinite value" (S/L, 84, 85).

There is neither knowledge nor objective certainty of the eternal.

The eternal is a matter of venturing forth (Socrates), a venture in faith. The passion for the infinite in the process of venturing is the truth.

The believer anticipates the eternal only by risking the process of becoming, by risking temporality.

The existential present of the eternal becomes clearer for Kierkegaard in his development of the meaning of "moment" and "repetition."

THE *STAGES* (FRAGMENTS)

1. Introduction

Approaching Kierkegaard through the Stages. Proper understanding of Kierkegaard can be gained only by appropriating his total output: only from this encompassing view can a specific item find its meaning and place (insofar as we apply the scaffolding of the doctrine of stages). For example: Reading the "Diapsalmata" [in *Either/Or*], we might be puzzled and ask: Does Kierkegaard mean this? Only when reading them as the observations of an aesthete do we realize: The thinking in these aphorisms displays the aesthetic attitude toward life. That domain is presented not by means of description or criticism but by exposing its way of thinking.

But taking the doctrine of stages as a completed and fixed structure and the details unequivocally as simple progression would be misleading. Moreover, the individual writings cannot be pigeonholed systematically within a whole. They would immediately shatter it. When Climacus characterizes "the contemporary movement (sic!) in Danish literature," his remarks hit the mark only with regard to certain aspects. He is unable to integrate these writings systematically; they always contain something more and different.

In *Either/Or* the religious makes its appearance (within the second stage as the third); in *Fear and Trembling* and *Repetition* Kierkegaard adds Religiousness B.

A complete separation of the ways of thinking, categories, and topics is intended but not carried through.

The doctrine of stages as a whole becomes transparent only when seen from the last stage. From the outset, the scheme of Kierkegaard's doctrine of stages is determined by the goal of Christianity.

Kierkegaard lets the stages be explicated by their pseudonyms, each from his own standpoint. Nonetheless they always follow the same gradation: the transition from one stage to the next takes place by means of a leap that is always one-directional.

In each instance the true outlook is gained from a later stage while looking at an earlier one.

The stages are possible attitudes toward life taken by the individual within existence. They cannot be determined adequately as objective worldviews but have to be presented as existential behavior. There is no position outside; rather, from each standpoint—that is, a stage— the view corresponds to what is portrayed in each instance.

In progression with the stages, the signa of Existenz assume new meanings.

The stages stay the same throughout, becoming only more or less subdivided; there is a minimum of 2, a maximum of 5 or 7.

This does not lead to conflicting positions; it is, instead, the specific point of view that determines the objectification of the stages. For Kierkegaard after all cannot alter it: He too must, as the speaker, speak in objective and general terms. But what is objectified is a verbal expression and is relative. Consequently we grasp the doctrine of stages only by its externals if we rely on numbering the series of stages.

Deeper penetration is reached if we pay attention to the analogical form of the stages which is common to them:

a) There is always a leap between the stages. Not a gradual transition, not a becoming and growing, but a decision. Only the first stage comes to be by itself, as it were, as immediacy. The decision leads to a second stage and turns the first stage, should it again be the choice, into something essentially different: what, as immediacy, presented a possibility, now is perdition should it be a matter of deliberate choice. Between the stages there is an either/or. Theoretically, in observation, everything is combinable, "you can have it both ways." Existentially, however, I have to choose and take a stand, whether I like it or not, either by my own decision concerning myself or by someone else's decision: choosing perdition, or immediacy, or rationality, or the ethical, or the religious.

b) Each stage has contradictory elements. The world of existence can nowhere be smoothed into harmony. Contradiction cannot be eliminated. The dialectic is ever-present. It can only be a matter of the form that it takes. Disregarding the contradiction leads to ridiculousness. The comic, irony, and humor play a decisive role at the limits of the stages. In them, indirectly, another is revealed. Mere contemplation ("speculation") evades contradiction, solving it in its own way, and, by the same token, also Existenz and inwardness. Illumination of Existenz can deal with contradiction, but differently in each case, according to its own standpoint.

Immediacy, that is, the *Aesthetic* finds no contradiction in existing;

existing is one thing for it, contradiction something else, outside it-self.

The *Ethical* acknowledges the contradiction but draws it into its self-assertion.

Religiousness A understands contradiction as suffering in self-destruction, though "still constantly within immanence" (S/L, 474).

c) Distinguishing between the spheres is the pre-condition for avoiding a state of comic confusion. Kierkegaard separates the "categories" of each sphere; paying full attention to them prevents the confusion which divides life itself, or Existenz, from being merely a confusion of thought.

d) Distinguishing is obviously difficult since what looks similar objectively can indeed be considered identical viewed from the outside, while actually it is absolutely different. So, for example, the Aesthetic and the Religious. In the stages, therefore, one stage frequently has for Kierkegaard the significance of creating the articulation in order to preserve what has thus been divided from being, in turn, confused with another stage.

The ethical stage above all fulfills this function. We are partially justified in saying that in explicating the Aesthetic and the Religious Kierkegaard was deeply involved; when it comes to the Ethical, he sometimes exhibited a pathos reminiscent of Kant, sometimes an irony, as though it were, after all, nothing authentic. In any case, Kierkegaard's involvement here is the weakest. It is most alien to him. Whereas in his own existence he had analogous experiences within the Aesthetic and Religious, in real life he sidestepped the Ethical, that is, the actualization of the universal.

There is no direct leap connecting the Aesthetic and the Religious; the mediating stage is the Ethical. The questionable nature of the Ethical, however, rather than permitting backsliding into the Aesthetic, makes possible the leap to the Religious; and here the categories of the Aesthetic reappear with another significance; the proximity and the absolute distance of the Aesthetic and the Religious, the Ethical as the in-between serving as articulation.

The objectification of the stages. We seem to attain a philosophical knowledge of what Existenz is. At each step of our exposition we can document this knowledge by quotations from the pseudonyms, particularly from the *doctrine of stages* itself: the configurations of Existenz are a progression—from the aesthetic stage by way of the ethical to the religious, and in the last-named from humane rational religiosity to paradoxical Christian religiosity (Religiousness B). Within this progression the leap from the one to the other configuration takes place through existential decision, which in the last stage attains to truth. The stages are forms of life with specific categorial systems.

It has been advanced that by this method it is possible to construct Kierkegaard's philosophy as a system for living. Thus he would obtain a place among the founders of doctrines in the history of philosophy. It is a doctrine which Kierkegaard expressly allows the pseudonym Johannes Climacus to excogitate, and it forms the title of one of his works *(Stages on Life's Way),* which exhibits configurations of these stages in their respective modes of thinking. This, however, concerns only one of the objectifications, namely, forms of direct communication, which not even Kierkegaard's will to indirect communication could altogether do without. But, should we take this specific direct communication for the subject matter itself, we are bound to miss Kierkegaard's meaning. For what we are faced with here is not a recognition of various stages and then choosing among them, nor does the sequence of stages constitute a necessarily ascending development, nor do they promise, from an outside position, assistance in clarifying our view with regard to human possibilities.

Historicity is an example of the inescapability of objectification in verbal expression and the necessity of suspending objectification in the appropriation of the meaning that is expressed. Through Kierkegaard we become aware of the fact that what is historic, hence altogether temporal and therefore particular and singular, may yet, in its Existenz—provided it is authentically historic—for this very reason also partake of eternity. This may sound simple, as though we were on the firm ground of knowledge, but it is also paradoxical. Something has been articulated which abrogates itself. Looked at as a doctrine, the following becomes evident: No universal factor has been expressed which would allow a particular instance to be justified in its historicity. There are no universal criteria by which what is historic Existenz can be validly determined through the subsumption of one instance under a category of Existenz. Existenz is neither an objectivity nor a subjectivity that could be recognized as such. Hence speaking about it can have only the meaning of intimation through signs. The altogether historic lies beyond all reason; it becomes palpable in the clarity of concepts beyond objectivity and becomes conscious when thought founders. The very unfathomableness of Existenz is to illuminate it for consciousness, offering it protection, confirmation, and encouragement in its temporal actualization.

As a result we find ourselves dealing with a conceptualization not based on determinate objects but concerned with means of expression that powerfully illuminate fundamental existential acts or experiences of choice, of guilt, of willful blindness, and of manifestation in the world and of transcendence. Insofar as they appear to be universal, these existential concepts are comprehensible only if filled with unique historic content, which, however, does not come about in the way applicable to concepts of objects and sensible configurations in the world which owe their intelligibility to verification. What happens, rather, is that the relation of universal and particular falls away and what remains as the meaning of thought is the power to illuminate and to give depth to each unique historicity. Such concepts awaken Existenz rather than teach knowledge. It becomes not a matter of being-thus but of being-able-to-be.

A choice restricted to contemplated alternatives, as it is intimated in cogitating on the stages, is substituted for the existential choice of the actual human being. Mere thought, being all-inclusive, does not need to make a choice.

If anything in Kierkegaard comes close to a doctrine that embraces the entire thinking and gives it design, it is the doctrine of the stages.

It is by this doctrine that the entire pseudonymous production acquires unity: "I was concerned to present, if possible, the different stages of Existenz in *one* work—and this is how I look at the whole pseudonymous production" (Haecker, I, 265). Kierkegaard's doctrine of the stages can be regarded as an analogue of a system.

Kierkegaard does not build an edifice but penetrates into human possibilities of life and lets them speak. Concepts are merely one avenue of approach among many.

Kierkegaard cannot—since this is impossible—but think in universal terms; and thinking in universal terms always means thinking systematically. Therefore all that is fundamentally conceptual shapes itself, against his intention, into systematic form.

The stages—aesthetic, ethical, religious—as world views to choose from are not to be considered after observing and testing them. Instead, they are actualities of life, existential configurations of man.

The human being who passes through the stages (and Kierkegaard thinks that the history of each individual man is a history of this passing-through) does not proceed from one stage to another as from a wrong to a right cognition, from a wrong to a right view of the world. Rather, man transforms himself by entering another stage. These stages are not locations of objective knowledge but basic attitudes of subjective Existenz.

2. The aesthetic stage

The aesthetic stage receives its characterization from two sides: Kierkegaard lets the aesthete speak in the first volume of *Either/Or*, and gives voice to the different configurations of the aesthetic attitude toward life in the first part of *Stages on Life's Way* ("In Vino Veritas").

The aesthete as seen from the ethical standpoint is presented in Judge William in the second volume of *Either/Or*, and in the second part of *Stages*, in the section "Some Reflections on Marriage."

The aesthetic stage and art. The aesthetic stage is a form of human existence expressed as attitude toward oneself and to things. As such, it is initially not identical with the "aesthetic" concept in the sense of being "artistic." The visual arts and poetry have their share in this stage, but as spiritual objectifications which Kierkegaard considers in their relevance to one's attitude toward life.

Multifariousness of the aesthetic stage and of its movements. The aesthetic stage, however, is not in the least homogeneous. Kierkegaard gives no importance to univocity in his systematic schematism, which serves merely as guideline. In order to grasp clearly and concisely his intended meaning in each instance, and not to be put off by contradictions in the wording, one has to keep this multiformity foremost in mind.

On the one side, the aesthetic stage is immediacy, the state of Being antecedent to decision. It represents possibility, germination.

On the other side, straying away from existential Being, hence perdition, means evasion, enjoyment, the endless curiosity of the intellect — refusal of commitment.

Each aspect in its turn has a variety of forms and each form has its specific processes. The process, which always encompasses the leap — there is no transition, only decision — accordingly goes in two directions: out of immediacy by way of reflection and choice to the Ethical and the Religious; and out of Existenz by way of despair into the abrogation of Existenz — into the trivial.

In the first instance man retains his possibilities, though not yet aware of them; in the second instance, he carries the limitless abundance of the spiritual, which to him has become a matter of indifference.

Thus the aesthetic existence is, on the one hand, immediacy that is possible Existenz and, through reflection, leads Existenz into the Ethical. On the other hand, in the abstract thinking of a system, in the aesthetically emotional intuiting of all things, it is devoid of Existenz, obliviousness of self, and loss of self.

Negative determinations of the aesthetic stage. Not taking anything seriously, boredom, changeable moods, arbitrariness, lack of continuity: indifference to the consequences of one's actions, extensive and intensive changeability, neglectful inattention. Life maintained in suspension. Refusal of any fixed state. Fear of being mired; aphoristic style; restlessness; aesthetic both reflectedly and unreflectedly. Percipient only of chance and using it for enjoyment. Rejecting significance. Despair. Faced with alternatives for acting: regretting both. The art of breaking off. No repetition. Only the first experience [in love] is valid. Man as seducer. Delight in the other's first love. Fleeting contact with actuality, remaining without consequences. "Recollection" as technique.

All this is presented as though establishing a theoretical system of principles and their consequences: Their style of expression: literary works, treatises on aesthetics; the erotic seducer; the poet as seducer; the harmful seducer.

The aesthetic individual speculates about the psychological relationships which, for him, always are the decisive factor; they are the ultimate beyond which his knowledge does not go. Hence the psychological determinations, all of which become "aesthetic" by the way in which they are used: the difference in abilities; the effect of "recollection," of contrast; the importance of immediacy.

Persisting in psychological observation is aesthetic, as is all persisting in observation. Our judgment of things, our way of acting are determined by this psychological observation, achieving by this method "isolation" and formalization of function.

On boredom. How much in Kierkegaard is unerring astuteness, hitting the nail on the head! What excellent observations in individual instances! It is easy to become fascinated and succumb to the belief that, indeed, this is the way it is. What seemingly magnificent independence he exhibits—what wealth of experiencing, brilliant and altogether unique!

What consciousness of the loftiness of spirit in contrast to the plebeian position of rationality, of primitivity, and of the vapidity of half-measures!

To relocate boredom allied with nothingness into the ground of the temporal world—what a playful myth of speculative thought! Man diverted from his existential problem and from his decisive choice in the either/or, from the transcendental ground of his unique self-being, in which his being is granted to him as a gift, and from preparing himself to receive the gift.

3. The ethical stage

A. Women's emancipation

Kierkegaard's lifetime coincided with the first glimmerings of the emancipation of women, which he did not understand socially or legally, only in the "spirit" that animated it from the outset and continued to permeate it throughout its entire progress, aside from the undeniably positive aspects it represents. Kierkegaard is not concerned with societal issues and the extension of human rights of the individual, but with the individual's existential significance.

In today's view the reaction might be: irritating and boring. The stage sets have merely been exchanged. The meanings predicated are edifying, unconditional; existentially, however, everything is in a state of confusion. Substituted for the idea are reflection, blueprint, rationalization. The appeal is to whatever instincts are present. Freud has his day. And in the intervening time, emancipation was accomplished.

1) *Society's economic transformation.* Instead of being a "home economist," woman is drawn into the economics of profit. This proves to be the decisive process, in which the fight for equal rights becomes a material and personal one: equal pay for equal work, equal opportunity in education and training, unhampered competition without discrimination, financial security, equal status in marriage. This necessary and inevitable development, however—no matter whether desired or not—was substructured by ideas that cannot be reduced to a single principle. Certain types of women and men, though by no means all, created the ideology; what was happening anyway became the result of their battle for rights, acquired the pathos of justice, the single-mindedness of the battle for fairness in material conditions.

2) Beyond that we are faced now not with social and legal institutions but with principle and the unconditional, with the idea of *woman with regard to the sexual question:* equal rights for male and female. Traditional ties were loosened, but no new ties substituted. The question is raised: What now is woman; what is man?

This battle concerns definite and relative matters, and extends to "social institutions" and mass phenomena. At stake here are the unconditional, the question of self-being, of understanding or not understanding oneself—and matters infinitely more complicated for women.

What Kierkegaard saw coming has happened: woman is abandoned to man. Traditional practice no longer sets unconditional rules, as did Church and custom. As for emancipation as sociological phenomenon and emancipation as content of faith, only the last-named is the object of Kierkegaard's attack. The fact that he did not include economic problems or sociological matters in his foresight contributes to making some of his formulations so startling. He has in mind only the unconditional, the fundamental, the deceptions and confusions, the general mixed state of what determines Existenz.

The emancipation of women has brought about equalization. The process itself is experienced as agonizing.

Here as everywhere in this century, substantial elements are vaporized, at the expense of women's possibilities. Attendant phenomena:

a) Spiritual achievements of women, in the sciences, art, creative work, which remain scanty. Splendid singular specimens commanding respect and exuding energy. But the male response still is: "all due to our erotic interest."

Possibly this erotic interest is conscious of its eternal essence as authentic Being. This erotic interest may find further illumination through Kierkegaard, but this is questionable.

However, this is not what is at issue here, namely, the material and legal emancipation of women: their liberation is an inescapable historical process, comparable to democracy in politics. What is new is the evaluation, the emphasis which the self-being of the individual gives to facts and goals.

b) The sexual uncommittedness of the male is countered by woman's demands for the same erotic freedom. But there remains an ineradicable heterogeneity: the consequences.

3) *Emancipation is a configuration of positivism.* It does not go beyond what can be grasped by the intellect, it is set in time and passes with time, its duration is relative, is bounded by relativities; its satisfaction is that of the moment, lies in the advantages gained by "achievement." "Absoluteness" is conspicuously absent. But what is absoluteness?

B. Spirit and sensuality

Everywhere in the conditions of Existenz a contradiction is present: in the world regarded as existence there is no perfection. In the erotic sphere we run into the dissociation of sensuality and spirit, of flesh and spirit.

Our initial reaction is to balk at this. Our wish is for harmony. Reflection produced the concept of original sin to deal with it, through which sensuality first becomes truly sensuality. Once this has been thought it cannot be rescinded; all one can do is to master the situation relatively, overcoming reflection through reflection, but not without soon seeing the contradiction reappear in altered guise.

First, we are faced with the historical legacy of the West: the diabolization of sensuality, and unbreakable bonds and taboos, the "bourgeois" mentality.

Concomitant deliberations lead to the urge toward liberation:

1) Sociological interconnections: Man's need to be certain of his own progeny, and his wish to bequeath to his own children his rights and his property. Relation between property, family, and marriage.

This is clearly expressed in Demosthenes: "Mistresses we keep for the sake of pleasure, concubines for the daily care of our persons, but wives to bear us legitimate children and to be faithful guardians of our households" (*In Neaeram,* 122).[29]

Hence arises a clear separation of entirely immanent satisfaction of needs. Where the marriage bond becomes a historic reality, we also find property, inequality among human beings, long-term concern for our own spiritual as well as blood substance: emphasis on education, discipline, family cohesion, loyalty. In actual fact, abolition of all property rights equals dissolution of the family. But Demosthenes' standpoint also equals dissolution of the family, though not without a tinge of asceticism—without family implying concepts such as loyalty to first, exclusive love, eternity, historicity. This can come about only out of transcendence, for otherwise pragmatic justification is open to discussion and can therefore also be repudiated, since it lacks unconditionality.

2) Positivist considerations: the "sexual question," that is, sexual gratification prior to and outside of marriage. Obvious consequences: Precisely at the time of strongest sexual drive, marriage among the bourgeoisie is impossible because of lack of means of subsistence. (There is, however, marriage within the working class.) A convention [of restricting sexuality to marriage] is assumed that never actually existed; see the institution of prostitution. Present-day custom has changed to openly admitted long-term relationships. Contraception: "My body belongs to me." See Lindsey's[30] optimistic and idealistic phraseology—but these are fading superficialities, based on the shallow presupposition that life is something that lends itself to appropriate management.

Eudaemonic goals: Tranquillity, satisfaction, marriage, children. No

---

[29] Trans. by A. T. Murray.
[30] Benjamin Barr Lindsey (1869–1943), American jurist, educator, and author. Among his books is *The Companionate Marriage*. New York: Boni and Liveright, 1927.

event, whatever it may be, is to be considered more than a mischance that can be corrected. Result: there are no unconditional demands. Instead: sowing wild oats, though preferably discreetly, taking life such as it is in its crude reality. Appeasing all parties to circumvent serious consequences. If a girl gets pregnant at an inconvenient time, is single and without independent means of her own, there are plenty of childless couples willing to adopt: Lindsey always has many more presumptive parents seeking children than unwanted children up for adoption. In short: no seriously challenging decisions are ever called for, nothing takes place that attacks life at its roots nor anything that is the wellspring of Being.

3) This is mentioned merely to point out what is altogether outside Kierkegaard's concern. Positivist premises have their consequences in law, social welfare regulations, and medical therapy. In none of these does one find anything unconditional; everything is relative, bound to circumstance, including compassion, the alleviation of suffering. This implies shirking decision-demanding situations, treating human beings as though they were pitiable animals with no individual Existenz—do not exist out of their own ground.

Legal consequences: Marriages must be open to dissolution even if only one partner desires it. Grievance: a loveless union loses its truth. What this amounts to: The authorities are simply informed of matrimonial vows and subsequently of their dissolution (Kierkegaard). The positivist outlook: Who profits more in such arrangements, the man or the woman? If the partners are young and wage earners, the answer might be both equally. But as the couple advances in years, the commonplace situation occurs: As the woman reaches menopause, around her mid-forties, the man looks for a younger companion. Sexuality interpreted as a positive, life-enhancing force takes this direction. The law, therefore, implies: After two decades of marriage, the male partner is entitled to a younger woman.

To this we may respond: "Well, since this is what is actually happening you have to be able to adjust to it, to make sacrifices."

I will not pursue this further: the pathetic emphasis on truth, on objectivity, used nowadays as a cover-up for real motives. What is truth? Mostly it is a self-serving choice of a segment cut out of a living whole, with its history and possible meaning. Almost always, what it amounts to is sophistry. There are always "good reasons" for the human being who wants to follow his urges and break through the bonds that, all things considered, gave him substance to begin with.

Legal problems are problems that apply to the public at large; thus we have to expect practical, customary, indeed vulgar solutions.

In the presence of certainty in the existential actuality of marital love, legal bonds would be entirely unnecessary, but this can never be assumed to be certain. Therefore only sophistry and untrue, unacknowledged hidden motives want to shirk legality: it is the indisputable bond I desire on entering into actuality. What is seriously intended calls for legal confirmation. As an individual at the point of decision, I am not guided by what "is done" by the masses; instead, I act out of my origin and my being myself, at the same time acting in accordance with the universal.

In Kierkegaard it is a matter of the individual in his possibility. With him the disparity between sensuality and spirit is not a troubling and inhibiting distortion brought about by untruthful social order or by bourgeois prejudices. Kierkegaard does not concern himself with this level. For him, the disparity cannot be reconciled; it is part of being-human.

Every form of Existenz is regulated by a discipline; only people without existential consciousness go through life dedicated uniquely to their own cause, satisfying their sensuality as the occasion arises, with no committed choices, without memory, living merely in momentary concerns or pleasures.

The relation of man and woman in the three stages: the Aesthetic: the art of seducing, of breaking off, of variety, of stimuli, of the interesting; the Ethical: bonding through marriage in the positive decision for the one and only; the Religious: destruction of marriage.

None of this is a matter of necessity. Every form of Existenz has its being in the world, siding with evil or good, or choosing Being beyond the world.

Positing a "sexual question" as though it were solvable misjudges a basic human situation. To be sure, the social and legal regulation may be solvable, rules and instructions regarding hygiene and the like may be devised, but all this aims at practical ends and is peripheral to Existenz, relevant and useful only for superficial gratifications, valid only relatively in a life of existential bonding.

The sexual question is essentially insolvable: in each case it depends on the unique fate of each individual, who, in his freedom, may master it or be defeated by it.

C. Does marriage constitute truth for Kierkegaard? The only truth?

He sees it as the pattern of an idea, not as something objective and palpable to be put into practice identically by everyone. Rather, it is the explication of an unconditional whose ground cannot be demonstrated and whose reason cannot be given. It is the consequence of freedom—not of the vacuous freedom of something that can be willfully chosen but of the substantial freedom of Being itself as existence through "decision."

Is the pattern thereby "untrue idealism"? The standpoint and meaning of such debates have to focus explicitly on this question.

1) The debates are not concerned with determining an actuality. In no instance can such actualities be subject to objective proof.

Nor do they offer instructions for social ordering, for legal assessments, for objective claims.

They attempt an illumination of possible actuality; they are meant as a call for examination, not by way of objective investigations of a Being outside and independent of me, but by the process of becoming conscious of my own authentic being, whose most original impulses come to awareness in this process or fail to do so.

2) Such debates do not have as object instructions regarding my personal conduct; they are not in the nature of counselling. For instance:

a) The question whether to marry. Kierkegaard lets Socrates answer: "Marry or do not marry—you will regret both." Why? Because the very question proves that the inquirer does not know what he is talking about.

b) I am perplexed. The marriage has become torture. Living together is impossible. Should I get divorced? It was based on an error. Continuing the marriage would be an untruth; and so on.

There are endless such instances: children or no children, special difficulties, special justifications. In regard to this Kierkegaard argues:

Was it love? What is love? Is eros possible? It is a term for something different. Intoxication through erotic charms; shared interests; equality of social position, of social importance; compatibility of certain traits of temperament or else attraction between complementary opposites, and so on; psychologically explicable bases of a sympathy that, however, lacks an unconditional character, for it fails to encounter transcendence. It is not really I myself who feels committed, but an insubstantial I aloof from the real one.

And further: what is truly meant by saying that living together is impossible? Signs of mental illness? Another possibility: emotional entanglements, excessive reactions, complexes—traceable to the egocentricity of both. A contrary response is possible: Having committed myself to an unconditional decision I am responsible for the other one; as I cannot separate myself from myself, I cannot separate myself from this other.

Whoever seeks counsel and offers arguments has already abandoned the unconditional stance, the apriority—he "poetizes," puts himself, as it were, on the outside of himself and outside the life which by his decision was his life. He takes back into finiteness and relativity what, if it truly exists, is infinite and absolute as well as the presupposition for his life. Whoever seeks counsel has already decided on breaking away, or wants to satisfy his urges, repudiating the idea of absolute obligation. He wants to evade responsibility by means of arguing, by a show of good will, of reasonableness, by way of endless talk, enjoyment of a sense of self-importance in both the talker and the one who listens and advises. (Max Weber's contempt for spreading out one's innards.)

Wherever the unconditional (decision, resolve, choice) finds expression we no longer seek advice—or, rather, if we do, then only on relative matters. I myself cannot know objectively, hence no one else can tell me what is really at stake and whether my decision is authentic.

c) Problem: I have loved; it was a mistake. Now here I stand, disappointed, despairing. The first love has evaporated. Are all possibilities closed to me? Or are there new possibilities?

This is not an objective, unambiguous problem. Again there are only a series of possibilities:

(1) Factually there is ruination. Destroyed innocence, especially on the part of the woman. Everything has changed. The new love is no longer what it ought to have been. Life is under a pall. The outcome, perhaps, a negative decision. Impossible to foresee what possibilities of authentic Being remain. Not the same as before. I am responsible for what happened. I am guilty. What happened is ineradicable, forever an element of my being. Only the aesthete forgets.

(2) It was not love to begin with. It was imagination and erotic bemusement. But do I know this? A matter of calling authentic self-being into question. Accepting responsibility for my self-deception. Is this to be looked at as an anticipatory experience? Something I could not have avoided? Or is it guilt? Does it bring me in touch with transcendence? Is seriousness in an unconditional sense involved? Has it been the other who misunderstood herself and do I remain faithful to her (or him)?

(3) Might even the suitable erotic devotion be merely an anticipation? Not an actual decision, not yet binding. However that may be: the sensual has no place in the determination of the spirit. This kind of separating out always occurs where the sensual is not,

simultaneously, symbol of the unconditional. Absoluteness: whoever lusts after his neighbor's wife. The sensual exchange of glances, the kiss, the pressure of hands—in all this the non-sensual touching of the spirit is possible, an accepted convention. The pathos of symbolism, by which sensuality is saved, as it were, for the one and only; interpreting him and being in turn evaluated by him gives meaning and depth to sensuality itself. This was done away with entirely in polygamous sexuality and lives on only as Dionysian-naturalistic symbolism of an original pantheism.

Argumentation *ad infinitum,* and inevitably with ambiguous results. This is necessary. Why? Philosophy can only aim at clarification, it cannot furnish incontrovertible proof.

In Kant: Appearance and being-in-itself.

Existence in suspension. Infinite orientation in the world and unconditional actualization out of freedom.

The world: Communion of an eternal Being with itself.

In Kierkegaard: Possibilities. Contradiction. Leap.

Not contained in this is: Assumption that the objectively correct can be realized in time. This "correctness" pertains only to the radical immanence of a world that has to be put right.

Consequently also the exclusion of a single objective truth that is correct for everybody. But preserving the possibility of communicating—indirectly—the experience of the unconditional.

In the case of eroticism and marriage, this signifies:

The unconditional is outside the sphere of rational foundation.

Universality does not apply here. There is only *this* love, the one and only—an inner attitude of expectation of the exalted moment of decision.

The idea of marriage cannot be brought to finite conclusion.

The yardstick of More or Less does not apply here. Either love is or it is not. There cannot be an objective yardstick—the participants alone decide.

Belonging to a different order of things:

Considerations of material ends and worldly prudence applied to what is not unconditional: legally, aesthetically, and so on. Relative concern for rights, especially those of the woman.

The pressure exercised by societal demands: monogamy as constraint.

Additional questions: Should one force one's own faith on everyone? Pressure and constraint that lend gravity to life. Suffering, claims, friction.

Questions for the individual person, as to where eroticism does or ought to break through any kind of bonds: in encounters left to chance, or through legal stipulations, or as symbol and consequences of spiritual affinity.

What is truth? Objectively nothing and everything.

The idea of marriage? Unimaginable in the absence of the presupposition: the decision born out of love itself in the mutuality of a historic community of two.

The promise of unspeakable happiness—but against it the freedom of abstaining, of waiting, of coming to a decision, of the obligation to oneself.

No one may say: "I deserve this" (cf. Max Weber).

No one may say: "It is not my fault. I just happen to be different. I never met the right person. I wanted to marry but was deceived in the other."

But surely: There is no worldly arrangement which guarantees that all shall go well, that everyone will be happily married, will realize the possibility and actuality of his or her positive decisions and actualization in time. Nowhere is the world a finished whole. Everywhere one meets antinomial structure. Perfect marriage itself is only an ideal and, like any ideal, does not become mundane actuality in ideal form. It can never be self-enclosed; rather, as historic process, it includes guilt and straying, reunion and assimilation—completion in transcendence, and within time the elements of danger and the tension of decision which integrates the difficulties. It is life, not finished Being. Being is only in the shared relation toward transcendence.

It is foolish to aim objectively for the ideal marriage. Impulses arise from actual persons, but there is no such thing as guiding example and absolute correctness.

If in a concrete instance I want to know what is and what the possibilities are, then I ask the wrong question. The answer has always to be: objectively, anything is possible.

The deceptive train of thought here is that concepts destined only for illumination and the sketching out of possibilities are perverted into generic terms of an objective being.

Consequently one arrives at the explicit contradiction: the first love does not need to be the first love.

But the questioner appears dubious. Instead of asking about tangible matters of this world, his questions aim at the unconditional.

Only one thing matters: What has actually been done and happened will be retained by the existing person. This will take on a meaning which may, perhaps, change in the course of one's life. Whoever is authentic will be so through the "decision" that is unconditional because there are no reasons for it; it expresses, instead, that a being is itself and does not stand outside itself or keep itself in uncommitted detachment, poeticizing, as it were, reflecting on itself in universal terms, in mere factuality, rather than drawing its actions from its very own ground and the historic reality of its existence and becoming one with something unconditionally: This I am, or I do not exist.

Consequently: neither using arguments to justify and express something that is factually the case; nor, in an about-turn, giving reasons for everything and yet keeping all possibilities open for yourself; nor purposefully bringing something to completion once you believe you have reached full insight into it. Instead, this leaves only the possibility of illumination, enabling self-being to come to itself by way of existential decision. The end does not consist in acquiring knowledge but in a quiet readiness or a quiet decision that cannot become completely objective. Philosophizing has no scientific result, but, if it results in anything at all, it results in what the Greeks called "knowing oneself."

D. The limits of marriage

Kierkegaard does not absolutize marriage.

He throws light on the limits of marriage, frequently giving a comic touch to the husband's contentment and his marital bliss; he opens up the possibility that marriage is impossible. The unconditional nature of marital love may assert itself even in situations when no marriage results. Kierkegaard heaps ridicule on the "poor husbands" in their various guises.

True, Kierkegaard can speak wholeheartedly and positively about a person who loves:

"Love involves a transfiguration, a spiritualization, which lasts his whole life long. In him there is a union of all the factors that ordinarily are dispersed . . . he is a harmony . . . which . . . echoes through his whole life."[31]

This is how he speaks for the husband. Kierkegaard himself knew only longing for this possibility. In himself he realized only the aesthetic and the religious aspects, as well as the negative decision. He lacked the experience of marriage (all the more astonishing is what he is able to say about it); the concreteness of difficulties is lacking: that

---

[31] *Either/Or: A Fragment of Life*, trans. by Walter Lowrie, II, 37.

both partners are human beings, given to faltering, nervous reactions, perhaps succumbing to mental sickness. The relativities of daily life, the actuality of battle. The unconditionality of self-being in the context of being-together.

When Kierkegaard speaks about marriage, there is always lightning on the horizon.

Kierkegaard has an impressively multifaceted grasp of the aesthetic possibilities of eroticism as they are affirmed by the aesthete, and equally as seen ethically as cause for despair, exemplified by the breadth and multiplicity of his descriptions.

4. *The religious stage*

A. *Twofold faith as consequence of the mode of historicity*

Religiousness B represents something not universally human, something not attainable to every individual by his own efforts. Instead, it is conditional upon being given by God. It cannot be brought about by an effort of will or arrived at by means of reason.

What does this mean? And what are the consequences?

1) A sense of paradox which expresses the fact that the Encompassing of being-human understands paradoxes "rationally" even in the form of paradoxes.

Faith as a sense of paradox: seeing the absolute as manifest once and uniquely here in time.

Faith as the Encompassing in which we are assured of Being.

2) Either an absolute historicity or multiple historicity in communication.

If God is a singular God and manifests Himself in the world only once, the consequence is a historicity that is absolute, exclusive, unique.

The one all-embracing historicity as line of vision in the communication of manifold historicities.

The fundamental decision, however, implies:

Either it is historic in the sense of the multiplicity of each unconditional Existenz in communication;

Or it is seen as singular absolute historicity;

Or if understandable only for faith—as the God-given condition not granted to every human being—then a rift results:

Is it understandable only for faith itself, for the condition that God may give or deny?

In that case, there is a radical rift between believers and all those who do not share this belief, an impossibility of reciprocal communication about essentials, silence instead of debate. All that remains possible is witnessing, one-sided proclaiming. But since we deal here with rhetorical statements and assertions, these are also subject to human investigation regarding their meaning, presuppositions, and consequences.

"Hatred for father and mother and beloved who do not believe."

B. *Passion is the will to eternal bliss*

But what is eternal bliss?

"Presentness." The eternal forms the background transverse to time, in time beyond time, which Kierkegaard calls "immanence."

Eternal bliss is grounded in the faith in Something, and is dependent on this faith.

This eternal bliss is the future.

Is it that which is present without any visible world, without any actualization in the world, and which, therefore, rests on a life consisting of a series of negative decisions?

Then why is there the world? What is the purpose of the world? Can it be insignificant that we find ourselves in the world merely as something which we have even without the world, and within the world counter to it, that is, our Existentz and eternal bliss?

What is "eternal bliss"?

It is an other, located in the future which is not here yet but is desired passionately as the only thing that matters, that is needful—that is reached through a faith rooted in the decision of passion; it is not brought about by it but is given by God as the instrument of faith, as the capacity of faith.

It concerns the individual as individual, isolating him in the world; it constitutes his overwhelming interest, to which he sacrifices everything because everything is unimportant compared with this eternal bliss.

It [eternal bliss] exists only in the hope of a future, a suprasensible, eternal future, toward which we look throughout life and at the hour of our death.

Its presuppositions and consequences are:

First, making light of time, time regarded not as the phenomenal character of existence but as the nothingness of existence. This view excludes the fundamental attitude that sees the eternal in time as historicity, transverse to time (humanistic religion, Religiousness A).

Second, judging all nonbelievers as being sinners who do not want to believe. This in itself is considered the greatest sin—whereas what is in question here is an incapacity for believing.

Third, not meaning the actualization in the world by a clarity that intensifies it: "Nothing existed before God." Instead, an emphasis on rejection of worldly actualization, on the necessity of living counter to the world, of being excluded, because the believer excludes himself; suffering and the existence of a martyr.

The manner of Kierkegaard's own "speculative thinking."

The fundamental difficulty in our comprehension of Kierkegaard, which may make us feel confused and angry, is explicitly and repeatedly emphasized by him and inherent in the nature of the matter.

We are given the task to think, are led onto paths of thought and into speculative constructions which are inescapably objective, but with this thinking we are to think the unthinkable.

If this dialectic develops the unthinkable as the absurd and expresses it in a series of categories which by their contradictoriness are immediately burst asunder for operative thinking, if this dialectic captivates at one moment and then strikes us like a trick which, once discovered, can be utilized with ease, a trick that serves to establish Christian positions though their truth is precisely that they are irreplaceable, then, alongside thinking, the possibility of raising objections disappears. Every objection is confirmation, since it is actually itself an expression of the absurd, proof that contradictoriness belongs to its nature.

Thought pursued in this manner is, as faith or as a mark of faith, the condition of eternal bliss.

This dialectic of the absurd carries within it a unique consistency of content (the series of fundamental categories: God in time, moment, sinner, rebirth, faith, eternal bliss), provided there is no reciprocal contradiction in a nexus of absurdities, in all the negation of what can be thought and of all actualizations in the world (all of them seductive by dint of their objectivity).

The question is: What is the actuality of faith, this passion for eternal bliss, in the negation, the No that is expressed in the dialectic of the unthinkable? There is no alternate way to grasp it objectively (unless, on another level, as "sickness"); according to Kierkegaard, faith is both certain and uncertain, that is, it is again dialectical, something positive that is knowable only by way of the negative.

In reading Kierkegaard, we feel we are, as it were, constantly caught in a trap: we are called upon to think, and then find ourselves ensnared immediately by objects and concepts.

But you are not supposed to think objectively. The only thing objective we encounter (Religiousness B) is the absurd. The non-absurd objective, however, is indifferent toward Existenz, seducing us to believe that in possessing knowledge we have all that matters.

But the absurd itself becomes something objective, an "outside-of-me," in actual fact an object of speculative thought in which the content of faith, the basic wellspring of action, the inner attitude are to become clarified.

C. Religiousness A

As Johannes Climacus, Kierkegaard differentiated between two kinds of religiousness: A and B.

He demonstrates that the third stage, the religious one, is the humanly universal, and sets it in contrast to the specifically Christian.

Religiousness A has all the earnestness that is not satisfied in the pure ethos of the ethical stage. The ethos is presupposed, is itself supported by the Religious, cannot be separated from it. (It is God who gives us history, who gives me to myself as a gift in becoming myself, who sets me my tasks in the situations and events occurring in my lifetime, and who speaks to me—always ambiguously, never with finality.)

This humanistic religiousness apprehends: God; the fundamental experience of existence regarding God as the absolute telos; suffering; the totality of the consciousness of guilt.

This religiousness goes far beyond the so-called deism of the eighteenth century, which knew God as creator of the world who then lets its mechanism run and withdraws His attention from it; who guarantees the moral law which is comprehensible even without Him, and for which God is only the guarantor by His existence, not by any effective interference.

5. Dialectics and infinite reflection

The dialectic thinks opposites and their mediation (Kierkegaard says "meditation") in a synthesis.

However, by dialectic Kierkegaard posits a thinking that disrupts rather than unites, that holds firmly to a thinking that accepts the insoluble, incomprehensible. This "qualitative dialectic" does not understand, but brings to mind the absolute paradox, which is the absurd. Keeping this in mind means to break with the intellect and its ways of thinking (to execute the *sacrificium intellectus,* going beyond the intellect and thus sacrificing it); losing the last ground of immanence, and, placed in the exigency of Existenz, to exist by virtue of the absurd, eternity at one's back.

Christian faith, for Kierkegaard, means doing just this.

Infinite reflection makes use of dialectic.

In the history of philosophy, dialectic thinking is always the play of opposites and contradictions, and consequently: either the semblance of deception, the playing with mirrors to prove the opposite through tricks; or the lucid presentation of the opposites in order to penetrate and solve them: either as avoidable illusion, or within a whole completing itself (the one *and* the other, both moments of a whole), or demonstration in the clarity of insoluble antinomies.

In Hegel the dialectic, in its varied applications, was the principle of understanding of all Being and existence. Kierkegaard learned his dialectical skills from Hegel:

Any definite statement carried to its ultimate conclusion arrives at the opposite.

In the world everything that is seems to turn into its opposite because it is temporal.

In dialectical argument a concept ceases to be a firm intellectual notion but becomes the movement of opposites returning into themselves.

Time is the existing concept.

Dialectic is that which agitates, infuriates. It robs us of the calm of stability. This was the reaction to Socrates. It makes us feel duped. And, indeed, it lends itself to deception. Kant still refers to it as the logic of appearance. But if by the most strenuous efforts the deceptive illusion is kept at bay, it is the truth in which all the stability of worldly existence becomes unsettled: it is the means of authentic philosophizing, either as impulsion in existence beyond existence; or as the destruction of all objectification and dogmatization of a transcendence; or as abyss and limit situation in which man is awakened to himself.

Dialectic never takes the form of a thesis, but always that of a movement of thought; it never takes the form of a result, but that of a performance; its result is negative for the intellect, positive for an absolute consciousness.

Hence dialectic is deceptive if regarded as mere thinking of objectivities and has its truth instead in the reality of acting and living which by the dialectical process finds its truth.

Dialectic leads us to the decisive either/or, which is not a logical alternative between correct and false but is existentially alternative between historic possibilities.

Dialectic carries with it the incompletion of the objective which may answer to a meaningless relativism and of a life that takes its unconcerned course, or leads to an unconditionality of existing that has the objective incompletion as its condition.

Hence the dialectic method is ambiguous and remains deceptive no matter how it moves. As purely objective movement it becomes a mere game—the carousel of the Hegelians, the almost journalistic witticisms of the Marxists.

Like the realities of individual lives dialectic is implacable, disintegrating, disturbing.

Kierkegaard did not enrich it methodologically; indeed, he diminished its possible acuity; but by applying it concretely he created something historically significant and brought its existential meaning to the fore as against the transformation into purely objective movements of thought posited by the Hegelians.

"Superstitious": each objective fixity is given the character of absolute truth. Hegel earlier, in his *Logic,* mentions "object" as superstition.

Thus there is superstition everywhere: superstition in the sciences, in party politics, in religion—wherever something exists in unquestioned objectivity, in each fixation. Such is the atmosphere of unfreedom: an inability to listen, repetition of the same thing over and over again (Plato on "laws"), tunnel vision; desperate clinging to superstitious belief when danger is palpably imminent; no communication, concentration on the matter at hand. Thus the erotic superstition (also called "the new objectivity").

In contrast to superstition, the historic, which, however, I cannot demand of others since historicity is a matter of one's own decision, is the precondition and ground of infinite deepening; it is never objective and hence not superstition. Freedom does not skip over self-being.

Kant's philosophy, according to his own sense of it, is a constant splitting off of the dialectical. But what constitutes the depth of his philosophizing is precisely the fact that the dialectic always looms as something threatening or as something going on subconsciously.

For Kant, it is contradiction that is absolutely destructive. For him, the following holds true in every instance: contradiction is not possible.

Hence his cogent cognition as philosophy—and hence the solution of his antinomies and the unspoken presupposition that the transcendent too cannot contradict itself.

It is instructive to compare how Kant thinks the antinomies with how Kierkegaard thinks the paradox.

Comparison of

Antinomy   and   *Paradox*

Antinomy	Paradox
Example: Freedom—everything has its cause by necessity.	Example: God takes on the guise of servitude. Eternal truth tied to historic time. Eternal bliss dependent on it.
The contradiction is to be solved through the doctrine of the two worlds. The pathos: There can be no contradiction.	The paradox (the improbable, self-contradictory?) recognized and passionately adhered to.
Necessary because the unconditional has to be thought and cannot be thought.	Necessary where eternal truth stands in relation to an existent Existenz in time.
The unavoidable illusion is discovered and canceled through contradiction.	Experiencing sin through the paradox in passion (untruth of subjectivity), and its redemption through the paradox.
Presupposing reason and incomprehensibility.	Presupposing Christianity.
Humanitas in the world.	World-less transcendence of the isolated soul with God.

The crisis:
a) The historically accessible "fundamental operations" all have their own truth and ought in this sense to be apprehended and appropriated. They are not placed in juxtaposition and cannot be added up. Not only are all of them flawed in their actualization, but they are false in their totality.

We have to question them as to what they can do and their validity—in which area, for which purpose.

In studying these great philosophies, we do not wish to backslide to what precedes their accomplishments and we do not wish to fall prey to their magnificent seductive aberrations.

b) With Hegel ended the attempt at creating conclusive systems, perfected knowledge.

The bubbles blown to tremendous size from the most splendid materials, radiating in all colors of the rainbow, yet paper-thin in their spirituality, suddenly collapsed into nothingness. In conjunction, and perhaps merely as the symptom of the actual crisis, western philosophy entered a state of crisis, of dispersion, into a decline to the lowest antecedent points, into new risks of disunity, and also into a new, unprecedented openness for the depth of Being. Kierkegaard is the great philosopher of this crisis.

Kierkegaard, in full command of the philosophical tradition, thinks out of his own Christian origin, and lives in a world which in its crisis is for the first time made transparent in a truly radical manner, with the consciousness of the era (by contrast, Fichte's characterization of the era is superficial and above all optimistic: the dawn of a splendid new era outlined in his addresses to the German nation).

Kierkegaard performed the basic operation of a reflection that eventually reached an abysmal extreme: from reflection to self-reflection, to infinite reflection, followed by the leap.

He sees reflection in place of immediacy to the degree of infinite reflection—yet all the basic operations as moments of the final basic operation: the leap out of the universal into historicity.

Reflection:
Consciousness raises what is obscure to a content of meaning; self-consciousness is aware of this raising in thought.

Reflection puts the content in question, relates it to something else, leads thought to a turnabout, turns it into its opposite, spins it out without end—self-reflection turns itself back into the I: I am conscious of myself.

I am the observer of myself, behaving toward myself as if I were another; what I observe is not I, but something about me and in me is given to me; as I watch I do not acknowledge the I as being truly myself, only as something that takes hold of me or is given to me; I assure myself as myself, am one with what I know myself to be.

I perform an inward action: a thinking-myself, as if I brought myself forth; this thinking is not incidental but effectual—by my thinking and through the way I think I become another. In relation to the inwardness and analogous to the external a technique is developed, but a magical element is also involved.

Constant reflection is the principle of philosophizing. Nothing should remain unreflected on, nothing should remain alien to thought.

Not just cognizing, thinking, knowing, but consciousness of what is being done with it—and the consequence is: knowledge of what one does, how one does it, of the method.

Thus, in philosophizing, the mark of the will to clarification is identical with the will to truth, which implies: questioning once more everything that has been thought; lifting oneself above everything that has been thought.

Sovereignty of thought, its most radical possibilities, its most extreme experiments. Making myself the question.

Reflection has no limit:

The question about specific presuppositions and, beyond, the question about the significance of what is thought with regard to its necessary consequences for the thinker, and for the meaning within thinking as a whole.

Limitless: infinite reflection, bottomlessness, reflection between one hundred mirrors—infinite interpretability and re-interpretability. What sets a goal to reflection, or gives it support?

The continuity of infinite reflection and the leap.

The obstacle constantly to be overcome (but a mere interruption of reflection).
Getting lost in what is thought, becoming absolute as a symbol, chains of modes of thought, in content, in method.

What is constantly lost and restores itself again.
The abrogation of naïveté, of the unconscious—not feasible, however, in the process of bringing forth in thought. Even in the clarification of the unconscious we are aided by an unconscious element; in the most lucid creation there is a remnant of naïveté. If it were lacking, creativity would get nowhere; the lucid intellect by itself cannot force creation.

But will and proclivity are bent on abrogating naïveté, the unconscious, rather than cultivating it. Philosophizing is the most radical will toward clarification and abrogation of the unconscious. But this very endeavor will, unintentionally, bring it forth anew and intensify it.

Reflection and immediacy as irreconcilable.
Two fundamental motives: to attain immediacy and, proceeding from it, to push reflection to extremes.

Two poles, played off against each other: in place of incomprehensible, obscure, arbitrary, accidental immediacy stand reflection, clarification, illumination.

In place of bottomless, endless reflection which leads into nothingness stand immediacy, origin, actuality, authenticity, presentness.

The question is whether all basic mental operations, since they are paths toward a universal (including the universal of the now known immediacy), become moments in the final basic operation:

Out of the universal, the leap into historicity mediated by the universal, into a historicity no longer represented by the universal, but becoming goal and origin of the philosophy of the universal.

The leap brings man to the source of philosophizing. What is taught is guided by what precedes teaching. What is shown is immersed in a specific mood, may be reliable or unreliable, honest or spurious; in the last analysis, this cannot be demonstrated in the teaching itself: the teaching does not rest on itself alone. Ever since philosophy has become not a knowledge of something but actual philosophizing, it cannot be separated from the personality which carries it out: the unconditionality or ungroundedness of historic Existenz which, to be sure, can never be proven but is always present, not as a matter for examination but as actuality of communication or the lack of it.

Hence the import of the "personality" of the philosopher, the reality of his existence, his acts and his attitude—basically not recognizable, to be sure, in the philosophic contents; danger of false psychologizing. But in philosophy today the private is no longer private; it becomes an element of the matter under discussion. The question arises of the untruth of an Existenz as the source of untrue philosophy, philosophy deriving from the soil of a trivial or crooked or feigned or confused, of an evil Existenz; the importance of insight into the biography and character of the philosopher, to be used not for argument but as an aspect of the whole of a philosophy, and, at that, not a single completed one, since man cannot be completed.

Kierkegaard brings to consciousness the meaning of infinite reflection; he pushes on and on, with nothing to hold on to, and not necessarily in an endless void, but always creating stimulating, novel, surprising positions, what he calls the aesthetic "changeable state of affairs." Where is the correct spot for hammering the nail that will truly support it? Where do we find a firm foothold? Where is the leap into that which overcomes all reflection because it includes it?

Kierkegaard pushes this process of thinking to an extreme. There is no escaping.

But neither is there any logical insight that would help with my infinite reflection. It is the leap which I take but which is made possible for me through something that is not of my own doing.

For Kierkegaard it is faith as Christian faith "because my father told me so"—his negative decisions.

But there is more to be achieved in philosophizing: insight into the necessity for the leap as such—the readiness for it through philosophizing.

You cannot purposefully plan the leap; it may have been taken already and is merely clarified by philosophy.

But the leap has no universal content; in its actuality and content it is historic; it is actuality itself, presentness.

Beginning with Kierkegaard philosophy has an unprotected flank—which, as a matter of fact, was always there.

Since the mid-nineteenth century, philosophizing has a peculiar character; it is the mental climate in which we grew up.

Over against poetic completion stands infinite reflection, in contrasts embodied in great philosophic thinkers: Hegel as counterfigure to Kierkegaard. Reflection is never completed; it merely stops. Questions cannot be laid to rest with finality. The solution for philosophic thinking is not to be found in a rounded whole that would appeal to an aesthetic intuition, as in the case of a transcendent symbolism where wholeness may appear as redemptive even if non-binding. Infinite reflection throws the individual back unto himself in his authentic being rather than granting him self-deceptive satisfaction in the objective totality of a world which, seen philosophically, is only a relative one.

If what is true is something objective for consciousness-as-such, then the intellect requires that it be in the form of a non-contradictory thought. But if truth is a matter of existing out of something unconditional, then it is in its phenomenality historic—that is, temporal—and does not have to be seen objectively as a non-contradictory statement.

Existence as possible Existenz in the medium of consciousness-as-such is aware of both. It knows what is thinkable and valid without contradiction as a mere enclave within existence. It also knows the jolt of coming up against what is not objifiable (or, if it were objectified, would be caught in contradiction) as the ground for Existenz.

Thinking is reflecting. Reflection is the way both to knowledge about the objective and to illumination of the ground of being. Reflection is finite, is relative in its determinacy, relative to things in the world. As such, it is the knowledge of "something."

Reflection becomes infinite when all that is determinate and solid in the world is dissolved. As such, it knows nothing.

Let us see what Kierkegaard says about reflection:

. . . If the individual does not call a halt to reflection, it partakes in the infinitude of reflection, that is, no decision takes place. Hence philosophizing has to be seen as something objectified, imparted: prior to decision, all there is is possibility. Everything firm dissolves. It lets nothing stand.

"One analyzes everything until nothing is left."

Infinite reflection has a twofold nature.

Destructive: inexhaustible in its nature (it can never be concluded); faithless reflection; "the poison of reflection"; reflection degenerating into "dialectical chatter"; a process inherently unable to come to a halt; unable to reach a decision.

As condition of Existenz: without it: superstition—unfreedom in the immediacy of passion; with it: Existenz "runs aground," has a starting point, exhausts itself in decision, in faith.

Finite reflection is relative. It becomes untrue when it aspires to appropriate the absolute in its thinking modes.

In this case immediacy holds more truth than the finite reflection through which it is abrogated.

But there is no way of return.

How does the forward progress proceed?

Endless reflection dissolves the individual thinker. Everything vanishes. But the possibility of this endless reflection is the condition of freedom. Immediate passion is unfree. If endless reflection becomes the medium out of which immediate passion is affirmed or negated, then it can be carried out in freedom. Kierkegaard calls endless reflection infinite reflection, that is, it has a self-related form. This form is called dialectic.

Consequently *reflection has two possibilities:*

As the "poison of reflection" it is something that can never be concluded. It is called faithless. It cannot be brought to a halt through itself. It cannot be exhausted in reflection. "If the individual does not call a halt to reflection, it is made infinite in reflection, that is, no decision is arrived at."

Reflection "runs aground." Either it proceeded from something that gave it substance—is not just hypocritical rhetoric and intellectual game-playing—or it reaches a state of exhaustion when the individual acts out of the origin of its existence, translating his thought into the "decision," into "faith." This is a new immediacy. Reflection does not have its beginning and end through itself. It is a process that serves other ends, or it is destructive as illegitimate autocratic rule.

Original immediacy, once it has been touched by reflection, can no longer simply live out of itself. Once it has been subjected to reflection, its tasks undergo a change. Immediacy no longer battles only with external enemies; it now battles with itself. It now contains its own checks. It has to be taken and affirmed as immediacy, yet immediacy ceases to be what it was. It is now free instead of being merely given.

Infinite reflection equals dialectic.

On the "fiction" of paradoxical faith.
Socrates speaking about the skipper and those whom he has safely transported across the sea: ". . . he does not know for certain whether it might not have been better for the passengers to have perished in the waves" (S/L, 81).

A young woman expecting her lover's arrival would laugh at Socrates; for she would not be so foolish as not to know with complete certainty how splendid it was that her lover had come.

And now Climacus:

"To be sure, such a little damsel is attuned in spirit only to a tryst with her lover in erotic embrace on the safe shore; she is too undeveloped for a Socratic rendezvous with the divinity in the Idea, on the boundless ocean of ignorance" (S/L, 81, 82).

Comment: True: "the boundless ocean of ignorance." But from this does not follow: that the skipper does not know with certainty whether he has done well by fulfilling his task; that the young woman does not know with certainty that the arrival of the beloved is the only thing desirable—that is (and here Climacus's distortion enters in), not in the confined sexuality of the erotic embrace but in love itself.

There are three modalities: the task of the skipper; the bliss of the erotic embrace; the love in the actualization of existence. The first and second are relative goals; the third is itself unconditional. The shadow of uncertainty and the sensing of eternity differ in the three modalities.

In the third, the loss of what has been lost forever, what cannot be repeated in a new love:

In the thought that "it might be better if . . ." the only possible outlook would be that another mode of being is posited as enduring, as future, that another "eternal bliss" is posited, a perspective from which this loss of the unconditional can be considered as possibly good—as the will of God, as the path to eternal bliss, as something other than this world—hence divested of its unconditionality. This is the decisive point: is there for me an other, the other, the wholly other, the winning of which is called "eternal bliss," or does eternal bliss proceed only through actuality in time itself? The following questions arise:

Where is the unsurpassable becoming-present?

Does its loss mean ineradicable sorrow?

Is eternity to be found in the moment as possibility which now has been lost forever, and in the ineradicable sorrow and alteration of life—or somewhere else?

Against the construction of Johannes Climacus and against Kierkegaard's faith we suggest that this is poetical fiction—hence the guilt of refusal, of the "no." It is the "betrayal" of what is human, of the beloved, of the world. Is it not actually a running away, such as that of the suicide?

This is not an excessive position; rather, it is the location of the either/or.

For truth is mere foundering and what is actuality in foundering; it is inseparable from him who founders, is the "nothingness in the face of transcendence." It becomes untrue by being transposed into an other, a worldly actuality; moreover, in its construction by Johannes Climacus, the other moments of the "absurd" become an existential lie, whereas Existenz is that of an individual but an individual who experiences himself as himself and can become himself only conjointly with the other individual.

Justification of the individual in his isolation:

It is the point of departure of an entirely self-destructive life, of a life arranged in such a way that everything done is conceived in a manner that must make it fail.

And now Kierkegaard's suffering from his "betrayal," his renunciation of justification, his conjuring up of the "exception," his finding transcendence, understood in such a way that all negation is based on it since the deity needs "the exception" for its purposes as "a pinch of salt," "a pinch of cinnamon," a corrective.

But there remains: the quiet attendant on the disastrous consequences all this causes in the world, since the absolute No would have prohibited even starting out [on the life as an exception]. Once begun, this could only lead to disaster because of the totality of the No, because of his hopelessness, because of his abolishing hope altogether, and because of his incapacity for achieving betterment in the world. Kierkegaard himself realized this in thought and in action, and he experienced it in its dubiousness when he regarded himself justified by God's call, while simultaneously repudiating the justification; hence the ambiguity and uncertainty of his being an exception, which is thought through by him to the last detail.

But in this life as exception there inadvertently occurred, time and again, the opposite, whether in speaking, or judging, or negating, just as a formal lecture will inevitably also be a lesson.

6. The stage of religiousness B: Christianity

Kierkegaard's Conception of Christianity. Characterization and Criticism:

a) It is not incumbent on us to consider Christianity as conceived by Kierkegaard to be *the* Christianity.

b) If Kierkegaard's Christianity is the one and only one, then his thinking would spell the end of Christianity brought about by Christian thinking itself.

c) Where the concepts and clarifications developed by Kierkegaard's thought are penetrating, palpable, and fascinating, they can be appropriated as existential insight regardless of his Christianity.

What happens to Christianity through Kierkegaard's influence?

It is possible that, contrary to his conscious intent, Kierkegaard's indirect communication puts an end precisely to Christianity:

through his interpretation of it as something impossible to actualize in the world, an understanding from which he draws the ultimate conclusions inherent in it;

through the rejection of Church and dogmatics in favor of the individual's being a Christian as a martyr, a witness to the truth.

It is possible too that a transformation of Christianity might grow out of this radical interpretation. This would be brought about through indirect communication, not as purposeful design.

Criticism of Kierkegaard in all his aspects:

He may have understood the unconditional nature of Jesus but have missed the substance of this unconditionality.

Consequently he calls forth seriousness but leaves out the how, the what, or the wherefore.

Man's situation is brought to consciousness, but the solution given is tied to this specific faith which is put in place of the unconditional, steered in the wrong direction, out of this world into another world, in differentiation from the world and hostile toward it, eliminating the task of building within the world. Kierkegaard elicits earnestness most deeply, but by a negation based on the notion of an eternity without time, a bliss without world, a love of God without reality—too great a demand for man, too little for man and his task in the world.

His actual achievement: to bring the human being, the individual, to himself, keeping at him, needling him. To this extent he introduces the condition of truth into the world, with the intent, however, of letting each individual find the truth for himself.

His way to self-understanding is convincing. Any reader of Kierkegaard will also be captivated by his conception of himself: in the last analysis he leaves the Christian faith, as he understands it, open-ended.

Kierkegaard understood himself as called to arouse attention, as gifted with the talent of a policeman whose task it is to uncover fraud, as the will to honesty; but he does not do this by lecturing, proclamation, testimonial.

Consequently he does not show the way, but brings the individual to seriousness, to come to himself, to find himself, and to conduct his life out of his own freedom, not as a follower of Kierkegaard's counseling.

Only at one point does he seem to give direction and show the way to truth: according to his own repeated statements his intention is a religious one—all of his writing is intended to "deceive" into Christianity, away from contemporary deceptions (the premise that we already are Christians).

He poses the question: How do I become a Christian? And though Kierkegaard does not proclaim and does not attest, and explicitly states that he does not want to do either, still he wants to help us find our way to true Christianity.

But what that means for him, in which way he means it, what the consequences would be for us, is not so simple.

Yet the subject is of the utmost importance: for the historically correct understanding of Kierkegaard; for the way in which we philosophize with him or through him; for theology, what has been clarified by him for our knowledge of Christianity and for being a Christian.

No all-inclusive pronouncement can characterize this meaning; we have to see, step by step, what details found in Kierkegaard's writings and life give us an answer, with the possibility that the result will be ambiguity.

Kierkegaard's greatness can hardly be derived from his interpretation of Christian faith, which on the contrary he formulates in a manner that strikes us as the self-destruction of this faith. It is an artful dialectic of unsolved contradictions that discovers in them the truth of God's actuality.

Kierkegaard circumscribes God as the wholly Other, utterly inaccessible to all human capacities and even to the power of human thought, yet he speaks about Him. When he does speak, he, like all philosophers, cannot help but follow the guidelines of this world in his utterance. The human imagery he makes use of in order, for example, to interpret the nature of Jesus' suffering or his indirect communication is thought profoundly and originally.

But the images Kierkegaard uses for God are, as human interpretations, independent of Christian faith. Here he exhibits greatness. Here he bases himself on Plato and on philosophy. His "concepts of Existenz" are meaningful for us without the forced reference to God become man.

How Kierkegaard's Christianity can be understood.

Kierkegaard can be understood in opposite ways. According to Schrempf the subjectivism of Lutheran inwardness alone carries weight. Haecker thinks the opposite in claiming that he was led to Catholicism through Kierkegaard.

What the pseudonym Anticlimacus says is, according to Kierkegaard himself, not said by Kierkegaard but by a consistent radical Christian. And yet what Anticlimacus says corresponds to the ancient position of Christian faith.

What can be said about this?

What cannot be understood cannot be appraised; according to Johannes Climacus the paradox is the expression of this incomprehensibility.

And yet, language produces understandable statements; there are also actions, behavior patterns, ways of life, as well as institutions and their politics. All this is being-in-the-world, hence subject to worldly appraisal.

There have been different kinds of Christian individuals and personages; some attract us, some repel. There is Francis of Assisi and Conrad of Marburg, there are Benedictines and Jesuits, there are Quakers and Calvinist fanatics.

No one can say objectively what Christianity is. What can be said is that it is a phenomenon enduring for almost two millennia, and that it has become so all-embracing and all-affecting that it has lost its specificity: we are all Christians, and also Jews, insofar as we have been nurtured in this Western spirit, and have a relationship to the Bible.

But Christianity as subjectivity—as the truth of subjectivity—was developed by Johannes Climacus and Anticlimacus and by Kierkegaard himself. Most Christians will not recognize themselves in their portraiture. The term "Christian" must not mislead us into considering everything that goes under this name to be identical, except in the indefinite, unspecific, and almost meaningless context of the Western spirit as such. In no way can we accept that Kierkegaard's conception of Christianity is the true one and comprehends authentic Christianity.

What Christianity is cannot be explained or maintained in simple terms, least of all through such negations. It will always be in the nature of a confession of faith rather than a valid statement. The Christianity of someone who calls himself a Christian can be challenged only from the vantage point of a confession of faith. Unchallengeable consensus cannot be established by the historical determination of a uniquely valid Christianity.

If, in the human sphere, the presupposition of mutual communication with the will to understand each other and the fundamental ability to do so is valid, objections may be raised by pointing out contradictions in the declared faith, in the way it is practiced, in the meaning of the faith maintained.

Whoever maintains that the contradictions of the "absurd" are appropriate, and who, therefore, forgoes the identity of understandable meaning, is a person with whom one cannot either argue—one must leave him standing "like a plant" (Aristotle)—or have reliable dealings—for a divine demand rooted in faith in the absurd might assert itself at any time; something will then become fixed in the world that, for a rational philosophy, can never be fixed in time but remains open.

All discourse about Christianity is untenable unless one states explicitly which Christianity is under discussion.

If we affix the term "Biblical religion" to the entire world of human actuality and of thought grounded in the Bible, then such a religion encompasses a multiplicity of confessions (in intellectual history it also includes Judaism and Islam) and has a historically effective form only through these confessions of faith. But through them a human profundity, reliability, and open spirituality became actualized, a religion that interpenetrates and unites by its Biblical core, though this actuality remains unacknowledged.

If it is one of the fundamental spiritual-ethical questions of our age whether and how Biblical religion in its tradition and actuality can continue to be our ground, then a transformation of all of its configurations is unavoidable; no dogma would escape questioning. The earnestness of faith has become the measure and origin for appropriation of what is transmitted to us in the historic garb of the Bible and its interpretation.

Within this exposition of the spiritual situation the question arises:

Did Kierkegaard, by his conception of Christianity, and especially by interpreting it with consistency in the age of greatest reflection, bring about the end of this Christianity, by making its actuality appear impossible in our time—or at least impossible in one form of its realization?

What we are left with: either appropriation of Kierkegaard's concepts dishonestly, for purposes alien to him; or a new reinterpretation—the revival of the community spirit, of a Christianity adapted to the world, concomitant with a weakening and reversal of the demands of the New Testament; or a radical metamorphosis of the historic garb of Christianity, perhaps of all of Biblical religion.

Let us bring to mind once more the significance of Kierkegaard's Christianity:

There is no doubt that the later Kierkegaard sees his intention and the meaning of his work in the question how do I become a Christian, and in the goal of "eternal bliss."

There is no doubt that this meaning is ultimately demonstrated as the central meaning in his public attack on the Church.

However, engaging ourselves in reflection, we must ask in what sense we approach him, in what sense we take impulses from him and learn from him.

What in fact is the Christianity which Kierkegaard has in mind? It is that of the New Testament, as he understands it: Truth is suffering, martyrdom; truth is a paradox; it is the absurd. Christianity manifests itself in negative decisions in relation to worldly matters, such as marriage, career, and so on. Implicit in it is being an exception; its criterion lies in being a witness for truth. Everything else is a watering-down, adaptation, habit, is abrogation, is paganism.

Do I want this Christianity as my own? Do I want this path? Do I consider it to be historically true?

The impulse of honesty issuing from Kierkegaard must preclude obfuscation, must not posit a Christianity different from his as substitute—a Christianity of congregations, of the official Church, of compromise with the world, that is, the Christianity that is generally practiced—and misuse Kierkegaard as presumed guide to this Christianity.

Kierkegaard's interpretation of Christianity is not meant to support ecclesiastic theology, which leads us back to the earlier question:

In what way can Kierkegaard be appropriated if I take him seriously, without simultaneously adopting his explicit goal, that is, the goal of becoming a Christian?

By taking his indirect communication seriously. In the last analysis, it cannot be considered as a purposely planned and directed program of subterfuge and clever mental detours, in which case, once the goal is reached, direct communication would take over; rather, it is implicit, the heart of the matter. Wherever it is genuine, communication is indirect in itself as much as toward the other. It cannot be persuasive via directness. Consequently whatever grows from it is open-ended.

It is therefore possible to understand Kierkegaard's basic thoughts and to appropriate them as "the primal text of individual, human conditions of Existenz," completely divorced from Christianity; as a transformation of philosophy that grows out of his indirect communication, a philosophy that cannot be programmed, in which contrived indirectness falls away and the meaning of teaching undergoes a change. It would no longer be the mere passing on of a content to be learned; it would relinquish the posture of summoning and invoking. Remaining factually indirect, it would also remain in-"comprehensible." There would be no results, but possibilities of finding and understanding oneself. Anyone in search of objective certainties would be disappointed. It would be repulsive if its implicit demands on one's humanity were to become palpable.

There is no doubt that Kierkegaard remains ambiguous. His other intention was:

Fomenting disquiet, arousing awareness, acting as policeman, pointing to the way without actually showing the way that is now open to passage (provided we have grasped the task of becoming a Christian in its problematic nature, or if one lacks the "pre-condition" for faith which, according to Kierkegaard's conception, only God can supply). Becoming serious is what the initial understanding of Kierkegaard most effectively brings about, independent of the diversity of paths actually taken.

In the process of becoming aware of the ambiguity he came to regard himself as "an exception."

Kierkegaard is not setting himself up as "the path"—he knows himself to be unique, responding to a situation of fraudulent Christianity in this world.

NIETZSCHE

Editors' Note

Jaspers's literary remains on Nietzsche consist of over 1,500 sheets of notes, more than on any other of the Great Philosophers. In the absence of an outline, it is not clear how Jaspers had planned to use this material in his treatment of Nietzsche as one of the Great Awakeners. However, over the decades, he published more on Nietzsche than on any other "great philosopher." His major study of Nietzsche first appeared in 1936; it has since gone through several editions and been translated into several languages, in English as *Nietzsche: An Introduction to the Understanding of His Philosophical Activity,* translated by Charles F. Wallraff and Fredrick J. Schmitz (Tucson, University of Arizona Press, 1965). In the edition of 1946, immediately after the fall of Nazi Germany, Jaspers added a new preface, which included the following:

"My book is meant as an interpretation that is valid independently of the time when it was written. Yet at that time, 1934 and 1935, the book was also meant to invoke Nietzsche's world of thought against the National Socialists, who had declared him to be their philosopher. The book grew out of lecture courses in which many a listener understood my quoting Nietzsche's saying "we are emigrants . . . ," a quotation which I left out of the book, as well as Nietzsche's sympathetic words about Jews. . . . Since Nietzsche could, in fact, not become the philosopher of National Socialism, they soon dropped him without a word."

Considering the politically sensitive nature of the very act of publishing the book, it is understandable that Jaspers also left out some material critical of Nietzsche which he had drafted. Other critical drafts about Nietzsche were written in the same period and similarly left out of the following two publications for which they seem intended: a comparison of Nietzsche and Kierkegaard in "Lecture One" of *Reason and Existenz* (original edition, 1935; English translation by William Earle, London/Toronto/New York: The Noonday Press, 1955), and *Nietzsche and Christianity* (original edition, 1946; English translation by E. B. Ashton, Chicago, Henry Regnery, 1961).

Since none of the fragments were designated by Jaspers for inclusion in his interpretation of Nietzsche within the framework of *The Great Philosophers,* the following compilation of critical drafts is presented as a supplement to his definitive treatment of Nietzsche in the books mentioned above.

1. The importance to life of historical consciousness[1]

In Nietzsche contradiction is sublated even where, with tendencies of *dialectic thinking,* he transforms the mere "and also" of two forces into their belonging-together. He does this by means of a constantly moving reversion of the one into the other, so that there is neither the historical nor the unhistorical but only a whole in motion. For a moment the intellect falsely divides this motion into the rigidifying aspects of the exclusively historical and the exclusively unhistorical. The dialectical tendencies pervade the whole of the treatise "The Use and Abuse of History for Life": Nietzsche attaches to remembering as the essence of man the ability to forget as the condition of this life. In consequence, he alerts us to the dangers and abuses inherent in the three historic attitudes that are necessary because they create life and preserve it; and equally to the five ruinous effects of history, their counter-forces. Each time, however, the dialectical reveals itself as a tendency, since the exposition immediately reverts to the "and" and hence does not arrive at the historicity of the actual human being. The consequences, apart from the contradictions, are inescapable obscurities in expression, irrespective of the truth of what Nietzsche intends to convey.

a) If the dialectic were carried through, then, in the turnabout of what is linked together, the deeper ground of this movement would become manifest. In Nietzsche, however, forces of merely quantitative character are made to fill the gap, which in view of their common indeterminateness in monotonous repetition remain vacuous. He speaks, as he does about the forces of nature, of plastic *force,* and of the

[1] This section is a further development of "The Life-Destroying Effect of Historical Science" in Jaspers's *Nietzsche,* trans. by Wallraff and Schmitz, 238, 239.

highest power of the present, both of which are able to master history, of the *strength* of personality, of the great fighters *against* history, and of *youth* as though it were merely a period of life buoyed up by hope, filled with faith in the future and nonchalance. These concepts are not charged with the content from a preceding movement, but are accepted immediately, as though they were known. One has to accept their indeterminateness and their unbounded ambiguity, which receives its meaning only through the reader's comprehension, a reader, moreover, who is not guided by Nietzsche but is free to interpret according to his own subjectivity, even the most brutal and the worst, rather than see in them man's historicity illuminated through a movement of thought in whose dialectic the depth of Existenz becomes palpable.

b) If the dialectic were carried through, the separation of the living human being and history would cease, remembering and forgetting would be moments of the same integrated Being in its movement, and so would appropriation of the transmitted ground; the sense of being out of one's own origin would result, one becoming the appearance of the other. There would be no origin issuing as if from the void, dispensing with historic appropriation, no appropriation that does not lead to the revelation of a present origin; there would not be the actual human being without being historic, or remembering that was not also a forgetting. With Nietzsche, the relation of man to history is like that of life to something outside it that can be used and misused as though it were a material put at anybody's disposal. As we acquire history, we seek the line which divides measure from excess, the limit within which history does not have a ruinous effect; but the significant union in the possible descent into individualizing moments of the whole is not illuminated. Nietzsche does not go beyond the strong instinct which is supposed to sense at which point in time it is necessary to forget, and at what point to remember.[2] He does not see that raising the question of the division of points in time and of the distinction "forgetting and remembering" is itself a descent from the true origin.

Insofar as Nietzsche, by his manner of phrasing, sets man in relation to history, rather than putting him inside history, past and present; he uses history as something in which he is interested only for purposes of present life, as though life in this present existed in itself, and might originate even without history. Rather than seeing that my interest in history concerns me essentially because of my being grounded in

---

[2] *Untimely Meditations,* trans. by R. J. Hollingdale, 63.

history, Nietzsche treats of human life as though it were based on itself and capable of existing without roots in its ground.

c) Insofar as Nietzsche regards existence as a mixture of factors and forces, he recognizes only "more or less." He takes no decisive stand in distinguishing between authentic original movement on the part of historic Existenz in its wholeness, and the down-sliding by which, in momentary isolation and perversely, we find ourselves on a different plane. Thus he does not focus on the existing origin of historicity which, as part of the present, stands within its appropriate ground, but immediately sees the down-sliding in which either what has passed becomes mere object and consequently only of superficial interest or, in bypassing the past, all that remains is mere life. Nietzsche seems to see only the latter. Consequently, it often appears as though he were not urging us toward the ground out of which man's real future grows, but toward a radicalness that lets go of everything in order to begin anew. Under this aspect what is past becomes merely a chain, and deploring this situation signifies: ". . . since we are the outcome of earlier generations," it is "not possible wholly to detach oneself completely from this chain."[3] It may happen that Nietzsche, even when expounding the "uses" of history, is beginning to present a down-slide, rather than origins; for example, when he considers, first, monumental history in the uncritical exaggeration of the human past. To be sure, in existential historicity human beings become exemplary in the manner of their ascent, their possibilities and actualities; but they never become perfection, since man does not become God. In the factual finiteness of their existence, they cannot be saints or sages. Hence persons who are put on a pedestal are henceforth at a distance, deified, untrue, and not actual, fit only to serve the improper practice—soon to be pilloried by Nietzsche—of annihilating all presently existing human greatness in favor of the empty mediocrities who deify greatness for the purpose of denigrating true stature in their world.

2. *Nietzsche and Kierkegaard*[4]

a) In order to arrive at an overview of Nietzsche it might be preferable to try to understand him by juxtaposition with those he comes closest to. He is not really akin to the poets, psychologists, writers, systematic philosophers. No matter how extraordinary several of his poems are, they primarily represent one of the forms of promulgating the philoso-

---

[3] *Untimely Meditations,* 76.

[4] These three fragments were written at different times, presumably in the 1930s, in connection with Jaspers's comparison of Nietzsche and Kierkegaard in *Reason and Existenz* and in his Nietzsche book.

phizing peculiar to him, a matter of "taste."[5] Even though he considered himself close to the French psychologists, essayists, and aphorists, thought in the form of aphorism was not what he aimed for and psychology was merely a means of promulgating genuine philosophizing. Were we to compare his work to Kant's or Leibniz's system, it would become obvious that in contrast to them the system, also, is for him only a means, and not a way to completion, or a possible goal. For Nietzsche, the Presocratics are the mirror in which he looks for himself; but in their homogeneity and certainty, in the greatness of their discoveries, they completely differ from him. His way of thinking might be comparable to the philosophizing of Socrates—whose personality was entirely different; however, the comparison is based solely on parallelism in the spiritual situation, that is, that then as now a majority of systematic philosophies, widely known and referred to but no longer believed, prepared the road that would issue in the new, essentially different system of Aristotle. But the fact that we do not indubitably find ourselves in this situation and that the future Aristotle cannot be glimpsed even as a rudimentary possibility puts this comparison on shaky ground. Nietzsche makes us see the openness of our situation, which appears more radical than ever before. We are on a road, but only by traveling it can we see where it leads. Augustine might seem close to Nietzsche, sharing with him the inner turmoil, but in contrast to Nietzsche he takes hold of a tremendous positive content, on which he elaborates. The solitary philosophers of the Renaissance are comparable to Nietzsche in only superficial aspects.

One thinker alone seems to have affinities with Nietzsche. The question as to what Nietzsche is, is of course not answerable by comparing him with Kierkegaard, but it becomes clearer and more urgent. I have elaborated this comparison elsewhere with regard to what is common to both.[6] This astounding commonality can be traced in conceptual details and images, and also in the larger fundamental characteristics of their thinking. Here I shall add a comparison showing the essential differences against the backdrop of what they have in common.

b) Their *dissimilarity*, all the same considerable, brings out more clearly the intrinsic necessities of each. Kierkegaard is the more trenchant of the two, with a methodically more lucid consciousness. In his different way, he worked through Hegel in true philosophic labor and

---

[5] See *Zarathustra*, Part II, "On those who are sublime."

[6] *Vernunft und Existenz*, Groningen, Batavia, 1935, 5–25; *Reason and Existenz*, trans. with an introduction by William Earle, New York, Noonday, 1955, 23–50, 127–30; see also Ehrlich, Ehrlich, and Pepper, *Karl Jaspers: Basic Philosophic Writings*, 37–53.

arrived at his own thought by his critique of him; whereas Nietzsche takes his point of departure from Schopenhauer and develops his philosophy through his critique of the inappropriate status accorded to Dühring, Teichmüller, F. A. Lange, Spir, and E. von Hartmann.[7] Kierkegaard dealt with the method of indirect communication as a persistent problem; Nietzsche's handling of it was tentative, and posed as a problem only intermittently. In Kierkegaard, pseudonyms were a constant consciously adopted method; Nietzsche uses them only occasionally. Kierkegaard is in full command of every configuration of dialectic; Nietzsche follows dialectic necessities without mastering them. Kierkegaard develops the experimental method in thinking the possibilities of Existenz; Nietzsche merely experiments with it. Kierkegaard's experimental psychology, which aims at the coherence of human Existenz in its possible decisions, becomes schematized in the doctrine of the aesthetic, ethical, and religious stages and unfolds into the encompassing continuity of a thinking that pursues possibility in all its consequences up to the crisis point. Nietzsche's psychology, by comparison, seems short-winded, scattered along various bypaths, forcibly narrowed down. Kierkegaard is decisive in keeping his distance as well as in being master of his possibilities; he is high-minded but with little regard for high-mindedness. Nietzsche, by contrast, is overwhelmed by the thoughts he is suffering, does not keep his distance from, or possess knowingly as real dialectic what he brings forth and suffers; he is less high-minded but strives for nobility and absolutizes it as a value. In Kierkegaard the main thread of the complete opus is evident; the function of each individual work is clearly in its place. By comparison, Nietzsche's individual writings are fortuitous in their configuration. In Kierkegaard the work is completed according to his plan; in Nietzsche the main work founders and remains a shambles.

Much of what in Kierkegaard is grasped in context appears in Nietzsche in passing and is then forgotten or not carried through, or is merely repeated without further development. Whereas Kierkegaard, for example, develops the "exception"—against the universal—in its aesthetic and religious possibilities, Nietzsche remains at the level of simplified antithesis in sentences such as: "Well, there actually are things to be said in favor of the exception *provided that it never wants to be the rule*";[8] "Precisely because he is an exception, [the philosopher]

---

[7] Karl Eugen Dühring (1833–1921) was a philosopher and economist; Gustav Teichmüller (1832–1888), a philosopher; Friedrich Albert Lange (1828–1875), a philosopher and political sociologist; Afrikan Alexandrovich Spir (1837–1890) and Eduard von Hartmann (1842–1906), philosophers.

[8] *The Gay Science*, trans. by Walter Kaufmann, 131, #76.

has to take the rule . . . under his protection."[9] Whereas Kierkegaard reaches out to the individual in his own way, Nietzsche merely touches upon him: "If I ever thought about readers, then always only of scattered ones, individuals sown over centuries." Whereas Kierkegaard developed "crowd" and "public" three-dimensionally, Nietzsche's "mass," "herd," "people" remain wholly one-dimensional foils.

Kierkegaard altogether has greater depth: we see here the difference between someone thoroughly grounded in theology, and another drawing on philology, poetry, literature, and the sciences. The degree of tension in both is measurable by the criterion of how the Christian paradox compares to the absurdity of the eternal recurrence—the concepts from which their thought processes arose. Nietzsche, to be sure, has his own particular richness, absent in Kierkegaard; there is more of the world in him. Though he lacks Kierkegaard's persistence, unremitting deepening, and compellingness, he offers the many-faceted application of his valuations, the expansion of concepts grasped, and, in his poetic originality, an expression of his sublime metaphysical experiences, unique in their splendor.

c) *Being-an-exception,* a mystery that confronts our entire presentation, would have found its existential actuality anonymously under any circumstance, digging, as it were, its own grave in the world. That Kierkegaard and Nietzsche could gain attention through their work, could gain the leisure and freedom to carry it out, is due to economic conditions. Their visible achievements were possible only under specific sociological preconditions.

When Nietzsche's illness forced him to relinquish his professorship at age thirty-five, the city of Basel, where he had taught, granted him an annual pension of 3,000 francs for six years, without any obligation to do so, and the pension was continued after the six years were up. This generosity on the part of the citizens of Basel made Nietzsche's work possible. He did not have to battle for his day-to-day livelihood. By utilizing to the utmost the role of exception, he grandly justified the situation of complete freedom made possible for him in the bourgeois world. When Nietzsche writes, in *Zarathustra,* "A free life still remains for great souls. Truly, he who possesses little is so much the less possessed: praised be a moderate poverty!"[10] he speaks from the situation of his own life. Nietzsche knows the freedom secured by a financial minimum which, provided he is willing to live modestly, allows for that leisure which is the precondition for his extraordinary

---

[9] *The Will to Power,* trans. by Walter Kaufmann and R. J. Hollingdale, 416, #893.
[10] *Thus Spoke Zarathustra,* trans. by R. J. Hollingdale, 77.

creative effort; but he also knows the incontrovertible fact that everything depends on this minimum: there is not such great discrepancy between having 300 or 3,000 thaler per year than there is between having 300 thaler or nothing.

Nietzsche fully suffered and grasped the threat of possible dependence, and the dependence inherent in independence. When he sensed that he would have to relinquish his professorship because of his illness, and was obsessed by the awareness of his task as the basis and center of his existence, for which he was willing to sacrifice everything, he played the lottery. Once he had been granted the pension, he stopped trying his luck. "Have broken off relations with Hamburg (after the 35th failure)," he wrote to Overbeck (cf. letter to Overbeck, April 11, 1879).

The loss of his professorship had its counterpart in setting him free for his real work. Although Nietzsche's serious illness ruled out an eventual return to teaching, he had scruples that his early retirement might be seen in a dubious light, while at the same time he considered with horror the prospect of being forced again into the distractions of an appointment, which would hinder him in the accomplishment of his true mission. Hence one can understand his fear that he might be perceived as "leading a life of idleness" (to Overbeck, Oct. 21, 1881). Overbeck, the loyal friend who collected the pension payments in Basel and handled all money transfers, was repeatedly suspected by Nietzsche of harboring expectations that he might resume gainful employment. Thus Nietzsche, in reporting to his sister his excellent state of health, added: "What I am writing to you today is confidential. . . . Please write Overbeck with some circumspection. Strange! he seems to assume that the citizens of Basel give me the pension for being ill and not for getting well; there is no lack of hints that, in the latter case, I would have to look for a position immediately. In that case everything would be lost that has now been achieved. . . . I write to Overbeck only on my bad days—as, incidentally, I usually do to others as well; —there is therefore much moaning in my letters. On my good days I do not waste my time on correspondence" (Jan. 22, 1882).

To make the most of his limited means—a part of which was later used to cover printing costs—money had to be budgeted with constant forethought and care. Nietzsche saved with deliberate strictness, "so that I can live on it for a considerable period of time after the 6 years are up . . ." (to Overbeck, Sept. 1881). He calculated precisely in choosing localities, rooms, board, in order to live as cheaply as possible and yet meet the most urgent hygienic conditions needed to enable him to work. That his fingers turned blue with cold every winter (a constantly recurring complaint), that his taste and his fastidiousness were sorely tried by the least lack of cleanliness—all this he bore calmly. However, when, in a boardinghouse in Nice, he was charged an exceptionally low price, he commented: "All the other guests pay more. . . . By the way: torture for my pride!!!" (to Overbeck, Nov. 12, 1887).

To the very last, Nietzsche's approach to money was an intertwining of realism and fantasy. Because of his impecunious friend Gast,[11] he again played the lottery, speculating about the use to be made of the hypothetical jackpot: they would both be enabled to observe life with more irony; for, in order to be creative in the areas of their talents, irony was needed. "All right—for this is the logic on earth—half a million, the premise of irony . . ." (to Gast, Feb. 1, 1888). When the publisher Fritzsch offered to sell him, for 11,000 marks, the publishing rights to his works, which Fritzsch owned, Nietzsche wrote to Overbeck: "Basically, this matter is a stroke of luck of the highest order: I become the sole owner of my writings at a time when they become saleable. . . . Problem: how to get hold of 11,000 Mk at this time? . . . I could as last resort borrow money for the first time in my life, since my 'solvency' should become not inconsiderable in the next few years" (Dec. 22, 1888). Möbius sees in this the typical symptom of paralytic megalomania ("even the million is there").[12] Nietzsche, however, out of an insight nobody else shared at that time, had indeed calculated correctly in this "madness."

It is not Nietzsche's existential being-an-exception, but its effect and tangibility for us that were contingent on economics. In presenting his life out of philosophical interest, we look for instances of this being-an-exception; in the last analysis, it proves to be the same continuous event that cannot be reduced to any single phenomenon. We perceive it in three ways: in the process of his intellectual development, in his friendships, in his illness.

3. Characterization and critique

A. Critique of contents[13]

The consequences of Nietzsche's lack of methodical, concrete knowledge and, with it, of a consistent critique arising from it, are initially of no great import.

He is apt to indulge in positivistic fancies: "Urticaria: now regarded

[11] Peter Gast (1854–1918) was a composer and devotee of Nietzsche.
[12] See P. J. Möbius, *Nietzsche,* Leipzig, J. J. Weber, 1904, 178.
[13] This fragment was written in connection with a section of the same title in the concluding chapter of Jaspers's *Nietzsche.* In German see 417–18; in English, 420ff.

as an illness, seems to have been originally a defense mechanism of the skin, against insects and such. . . ." "The differences in temperament are perhaps predominantly conditioned by the different distribution and volume of inorganic salts than by anything else. Bilious people are deficient in sodium sulfate; melancholiacs lack potassium sulfate and potassium phosphate; phlegmatics are deficient in calcium phosphate. Enterprising natures have an oversupply of ferric phosphate." Socrates' daimon was perhaps the effect of an ear infection that he misinterpreted.[14]

We encounter the same attitude in Nietzsche's sociological judgments: apart from his grandiose insights, all reality factors are ignored in his development of nomothetic fantasies; his wholesale judgments fascinate us merely by virtue of their expressive power, while what is formulated with such plasticity often reveals itself as devoid of concreteness. We find him attributing utopian possibilities to the planning intellect in a technical and progressive frame of mind: "Surely the world would have progressed infinitely further if instead of chance the human intellect had been permitted a free hand; it would also have saved billions of years."

Since even Nietzsche's basic concepts deteriorate into naturalistic conceptualizations, bringing about momentary confusion, it is essential to apply critical correction to the whole.

Thus, in laying a foundation for eternal recurrence, Nietzsche enters upon paths that not only run counter to the laws of physics but also, by misunderstanding the character of scientifically provable insight, destroy the content of his thought. Thus he arrives at fanciful naturalistic interpretations, carrying through the notion of the possible creation of a human race through a process of breeding, deliberately planned by the rulers of the earth. He even forgot his own simple demand, namely: "If mankind is not to destroy itself through such conscious universal rule, it must first of all attain to a hitherto altogether unprecedented *knowledge of the preconditions of culture* as a scientific standard for ecumenical goals.[15] Mainly, out of the premise of a positivistically inclined planned guidance of the entire fate of the world, he radically misunderstood the limits of all technological planning, and confused making with creating. To set demands theoretically, without the means of implementation, creates the urge to want what cannot be achieved by willing but, to the contrary, would be destroyed by a willing too precisely focused on it.

---

[14] *Human, All Too Human*, trans. by R. J. Hollingdale, 68, 120.
[15] *Human, All Too Human*, 25.

However, neither deficiency of knowledge with regard to substance nor failure of realistic criticism matters within the entirety of his philosophizing. No one can base himself on Nietzsche's isolated pronouncements, counsel, plans. But just as his concrete realistic insight in comprehending factualities was stronger than his propensity to be deceived (as can be shown in a thorough biographical analysis), so the power of his visionary eye for true reality and the actual course of things outmatched his inclination to precipitous knowledge about the whole. The fact that this inclination intrudes at all points calls for objective criticism and correction on the part of the reader who inquires into Nietzsche's approach to knowledge. What is important to stress here is that the substance of Nietzsche's philosophizing is never anchored in these contents as such.

Primarily it is Nietzsche's contents, together with his value judgments, that often become questionable. His eye for human substance does not seem reliable, even though his ranking of [forces and creations of the spirit are] accurate and often illuminating. He perceived deviations and confused them with the original, for example, in the case of Christianity, of philosophy, of almost all ideas, of the idea of God itself. It seems to be of little importance, however, that next to his convincing value judgments there should be others: his overrating of Byron's "Manfred," his exaggerated praise of the *Mémorial* of St. Helena, his adoption of the hypothesis that Shakespeare's plays had been written by Bacon. But the important examples of his misjudgment point to his insecurity. Even if the lack of restraint of the later period and the decline of his critical faculty narrow his view and let him make use without qualms of an interpretation that fits his context precisely at this point, there continues to remain intrinsic to his very nature this ability to astonish.

We should not forget that Nietzsche's unmasking of things and the negations resulting from this process are the aspect most easily accessible to the reader. But if we ask what is the real motivation in Nietzsche's own will and valuation, it becomes less important whether or not he has given the right interpretation to what he rejected in its historic uniqueness—for instance, Christianity; what the other that he attacks is itself can, in its historicity, be critically restored, in opposition to Nietzsche, without destroying the meaning of Nietzsche's thought as it applies to lapses of what is historically original. Uncritically adopting Nietzsche's rejections without consideration of the underlying substance comes easy, for all negating discourse can then be fueled by it. To criticize this distortion is not a criticism of Nietzsche; instead, it rescues Nietzsche from the misuse made of him.

B. Nietzsche's limits[16]

The Question of Nietzsche's Limits: We can step into the purgatory that
Nietzsche prepares for us. But we can also ask what is lacking in his
work and nature that seem like failure, regardless of all the grandeur
of his thoughts—what it is that runs parallel with his thinking like a
primal untruth.

I think we have noticed that Nietzsche, from the very outset, had
deprived the Christian impulses that infused his thinking with so much
passion of their proper Christian contents. But no other original contents become visible in their place. His guileless approach to possibilities
of thought and realities is no longer supported by the inherited ground
and not yet supported by a new historic one. His thinking seems to
grow from a transitional moment of groundlessness, which, indeed,
may prove to be a dead end.

We run here into questions that help to determine our being-
human: whether the *metamorphosis* (not *pseudometamorphosis*) of the
Christian tradition—attempted as early as the fourteenth century—is
today still possible; whether mankind's lack of grounding is now recognized all the more profoundly, and man's leap to transcendence is still
his challenge; whether man's imperfectibility in time forces him to advance by riveting his eye on authentic perfection; whether, through all
the fragmenting of Being, the unity of the One is still palpable;
whether the limitless demand of truth retains its transcendent ground
and thus its absolute force. Because of our Western origin we glimpse
a unique possibility of true, undisguised *humanitas,* which can get lost
through our lapses as well as by our turning away from our history
and the authority of our tradition; in Nietzsche rudiments of the desire
to preserve that tradition are still evident, but alongside the predominantly emergent aspect of its loss. This, to me, seemed linked to the
absence of the Christian contents, absent even in his Christian impulses.
This loss seemed all the more disastrous because Nietzsche was mostly
unaware of the hidden soul of the Christian West, which chose neither
the path of the world-less Jesus nor that of a Christianity which transmuted to worldliness.

In the following we shall try, by means of examples, to elucidate
more tellingly how this absence of ultimate origins is manifested in
Nietzsche's work. To be sure, it gives us pause to express such percep-
tions applied to the entirety of someone's thinking. To some readers

[16] This section consists of two fragments planned to be part of *Nietzsche and Christianity* but
deleted by Jaspers.

they may appear evident, to others not convincing at all. The impression might be created of presumptuous familiarity with the thinker, a reflection that exposes the speaker's own weakness. Presentations such as this one should always be seen as mere possibilities. Their intention is to make the psychic eye attentive; everyone has to decide for himself, according to his nature, to what extent he will be persuaded. Objective observation and analytic intellect alone are not by themselves convincing; they are only the means to personal expression. In this spirit I shall attempt to offer a few hints toward a characterization of Nietzsche.

Lacunae in Nietzsche's perception and experience: Is it possible to identify and point out Nietzsche's blind spots, as it were, in his vision? What primal forces and powers are missing, so that they remain inoperative for him? And what, therefore, does he persist in seeing only from the outside, psychologically and therefore in its shortcomings?

To me, it appears that the terms "love," "reverence," "authority" have a content that Nietzsche passes over. To be sure, he speaks about love, about reverence, about authority; but for him the words do not signify what can be contained in them. In moments when the soul is fatigued we may not miss their reverberation in Nietzsche; all the more so since, given his manner of speaking of them, it is almost natural to understand them the way he does, "emptied" of meaning. To exemplify, I am selecting passages from his writings where he seems to associate a maximum of content with these terms, in order to highlight what actually has been lost.

1) *Love:* "The principle of love derives from the little Jewish community: it is a soul of the more passionate kind that glows here: . . . this was neither Greek, nor Indian, nor Germanic. The song in praise of love that Paul composed is nothing Christian, but a Jewish outburst of the eternal flame that is Semitic. If Christianity has done anything essential psychologically, then it is *that it raised the temperature of the soul* among those colder and nobler races that were then on top. . . ." [17]

Love is understood here as a rise in temperature and as passion of the soul. Indicated, to be sure, may be something other as also belonging with love, but love's concept itself is grasped in an astonishingly shallow manner. St. Paul's hymn to love seems alien to Nietzsche, to the point of incomprehensibility. Nietzsche does not know the clearsightedness of love, but constantly speaks about its power to blind; does not know its relation to transcendence, but only its psychological reality of temperament and drive; does not know its fulfillment garnered from

[17] *The Will to Power,* 106.

historic ground, but sees in it a will to power; does not know the existential elation it engenders, and reduces it to creative activity. He has no eye for Christian charity, which is not identical with softened, sentimental humanitarianism. He does not know the possibility of a unique, exclusive love between man and woman, nor the loving struggle of limitless open communication. For him, as for all emphatically modern persons, these are unrealities, illusions, comparable to the One and Only God. The knight of the Middle Ages—that idea which unites manliness and love, courage in battle and readiness for self-sacrifice, activity within the world and Christianity, an idea growing from the depth of what to this very day is called "chivalric"—is apprehended by Nietzsche as merely a miscreation caused by calamitous Christianity. For him, chivalry is nothing but "the conquered position of power."[18] It takes love to know love; hence Nietzsche's world and history lack authentic love.

How this registers in his consciousness is deeply moving. He speaks about "death with open eyes"; he composes *The Night Song,* "the song of a lover": "A craving for love is in me. . . . Light am I: ah that I were night! . . . But I live in my own light, I drink back into myself the flames that break from me. . . . Many suns circle in empty space: to all that is dark they speak with their light—to me they are silent. . . . Ah, ice is around me, my hand is burned with ice!"[19]

It is not an empty soul deprived of the capacity for love which speaks in Nietzsche, not the vulgar blindness to actualities, indifferent to itself, but the deep sorrow of someone incomprehensible to himself. With his receptive nature, with his unmatched sensitivity of response, he experiences desperately that nothing decisive speaks to him or through him to others.

But this does not mean that this sorrow predominates in him at every moment. It has no inhibiting influence, nor does it produce critical questioning in his thinking. His pronouncements, therefore, are written with utter disregard for context or obligation. He knows that one may not simply say everything that comes to mind, he knows the responsibility of every thinker writing for the public and has given this thought profound expression; and yet he cannot put it into practice because of the lack of rootedness in the origin of which he is aware at times, and at such moments he seems to get lost, as it were, and has no guide in his thinking. Hence we find occasionally in this noble man statements that perturb.

[18] *The Will to Power,* 58.
[19] *Thus Spoke Zarathustra,* 126, 127.

2) *Reverence:* "There is *an instinct* for rank, which is . . . already the sign of a high rank; there is a *delight* in the nuances of reverence. . . . The . . . loftiness of a soul is put to a perilous test whenever something passes before it that is of the first rank but not yet protected . . . by the awe of authority . . . the commonness of some natures suddenly spurts up like dirty water whenever some sacred vessel . . . is carried by; and on the other hand there is an involuntary falling silent . . . which reveals that a soul *feels* the proximity of something most worthy of reverence."[20]

Nowhere in Nietzsche is reverence a basic attitude toward Being in its transcendence, nor is it the awe before the Being in all that is, nor the glance toward the possibility in all existence; it is merely the recognition of rank.

It is sufficient to be reminded of Goethe's threefold reverence to feel the narrowness in Nietzsche. Goethe's three religions, which for him are one, comprise the reverence before that which is above us, before that which is equal to us, before that which is beneath us. The last-named is, for him, the specifically Christian one: What "would be needed so that we would not consider the earth as something beneath us and claim a higher place of birth, but also to acknowledge lowliness and poverty, derision and disdain, shame and misery, suffering and death as part of the divine; indeed, to revere and learn to love even sin and crime not as obstacles but as promoters of the holy!" It is that "last-named religion which grows out of what is beneath us, that reverence of the offensive, the hated, the shunned. . . ."[21]

Nietzsche, by contrast, gives unequivocal expression to what cuts him off from such reverential feelings—namely, "that we find that which has been reverenced as God not 'godlike' but pitiable, absurd, harmful; not merely an error but a *crime against life.*"[22] Whereas Nietzsche correctly perceives the degeneration of value-feelings arising from *ressentiment,* all too often, and also in this case, he missed the essential elements in reverence, without which the perceived corruptions by *ressentiment* would not have been possible.

3) *Authority:* Nietzsche questions what the basis is of the tremendous power wielded by Christianity for two millennia. What is the basis of the power of analogous orders in the world? He answers: It is the herd instinct submitting totally to an authority. "Indeed it is the greatest relief and benefit for endangered, vacillating, fragile, weak

---

[20] *Beyond Good and Evil,* trans. by R. J. Hollingdale, 183.

[21] *Wanderjahre,* Book II, Chs. 1–2, Jubilee Ed., XIX, 183, 191.

[22] *The Anti-Christ,* in *Twilight of the Idols and The Anti-Christ,* trans. by R. J. Hollingdale, 162.

herd-animals to get an absolute commander, a bellwether: their ultimate demand of life is to be rid of the ceaseless agitation which commanding oneself brings with it." Eventually the habituation of men to
authorities becomes for all of them a deeper need for absolute authorities. The more original, independent, creative a person is, however, the
less does he need authority: "The high regard for authority increases
relative to the decrease in creative powers."[23]

It is in keeping with such a psychological basic understanding that
Nietzsche neither acknowledges an authority nor claims to be one.
Even though, according to his conviction, his inspirations are, qua revelation, the most tremendous event in the course of millennia, he rejects
their revelational character. "Do I speak like someone to whom it has
been revealed? Then despise me and do not listen to me. — Are you
still such as need gods?" Even at the end he declares: "I do not want
'believers,' I think I am too malicious to believe in myself, I never
speak to masses . . . I have a terrible fear I shall be pronounced *holy*.
. . . I do not want to be a saint, rather even a buffoon . . ."[24]

But with his characteristic ingenuousness Nietzsche recognizes that,
owing to the nature of the average and mass-bound human being, order and discipline are necessary, and these are made *possible only
through authority*.

Authority can only exist by means of the spirit. Spiritual powers,
Nietzsche says, manifest themselves in the world as mighty pomp in
order to impress and subdue man. Going to extremes is called for. But
the presence of spiritual powers even such as Christianity can be justified only as long as it is a necessary presence: "Superfluous Christianity:
there where extreme measures are no longer necessary! There everything becomes false, and every word, every Christian perspective turns
into tartuffery and blandishment."

But even spirit needs authority in order to become actual; by itself
it is impotent. Of the Bible, for example, Nietzsche says: "Such books
of profundity and ultimate significance require for their protection an
external tyranny of authority, in order that they may achieve those
millennia of *continued existence* which are needed if they are to be exhausted and unriddled."[25]

Nietzsche wants to comprehend the *sociological* process of the
founding of authority, the *methods* of the founders. Using the Code of
Manu as well as Christianity, he makes it clear that the means of secur-

---

[23] Ibid., 163.
[24] *Ecce Homo*, trans. by R. J. Hollingdale, 126.
[25] *Beyond Good and Evil*, 183.

ing authority for truth are fundamentally different from those that would be used to prove it. No reasons are ever given, only commands: You shall! The most knowledgeable stratum of society, the most experienced, declares the experience to be conclusive and sets up the final laws. The period of trial and error belongs to the past; experimenting beyond it is to be prevented. Hence a double wall is erected: most important, *revelation,* that is, the assertion that the reason in these laws is not of human but of divine origin, is outside history, a gift, a miracle; then, *tradition,* that is, the assertion that the law has existed since time immemorial: the forebears lived it.

The train of thought confirming the authority of revelation counters possible critical questions posed by the intellect, a train of thought that Nietzsche characterizes as the "priestly syllogism" and develops in the following sequence. The priest argues:

"There are questions whose truth and untruth *cannot* be decided by man; all the supreme problems of value are beyond human reason.

"To grasp the limits of reason—only *this* is true philosophy. . . .

"Mankind cannot of itself know what is good and what is evil, therefore God taught mankind his will.

"To what end did God give mankind revelation? Would God have done anything superfluous?"

The "priest does *not* lie; the question 'true' or 'untrue' doesn't *arise* in such things as priests speak of; these things do not permit of lying at all. For in order to lie, one would have to be able to decide what is true here. But this is precisely what mankind *cannot* do; the priest is thus only God's mouthpiece."[26]

Then again Nietzsche discovered phenomena in authority which if looked at superficially, psychologically, and sociologically are perceived correctly. His insights appropriately characterize externalized authority; they are serviceable for self-examination regarding those of our impulses which urge us to preserve and acknowledge authority. If, in concord with Nietzsche, I regard authority as a clever contrivance for the purpose of breeding or for safeguarding stability, if I see in my attitude toward authority nothing but obedience and habituation, a relinquishing of inquiring thought, then the truth of authority becomes questionable—it is then only the fixed objectivity of a mere finiteness.

Genuine authority to which we willingly defer goes beyond this fixed character. To be sure, authority is bound to forms, institutions, offices, insurmountable barriers; but in the realm of the spirit it

[26] *The Anti-Christ,* 174.

manifests itself from the very beginning as historically present truth, laying the foundation for the soul that nourishes our life today. Authority meets us coming out of a space of stillness, the battleground on which the deepest innermost struggles are fought, but where truth prevails only provided the full extent of the historic ground is perceived here and now, reaching back to the "knowledge shared with creation" (Schelling), not rationalistic knowledge, not knowledge of something, but knowledge reaching full awareness of what is expressed in the sentence: "For other foundation can no man lay than that is laid . . ." (I Cor. 3:11).

It is reverence which attunes us to authority. We feel awe; we do not judge lightly that which speaks as essence and soul. We know ourselves tied to what has been given us in historic tongue as the truth of human Existenz. We do not rashly espouse the brilliant flashes of mere intellect or the never wholly reliable mood of the moment; we distrust them where they doubt what has been reverently glimpsed. Valid truth, for us, is thinkable only within the sphere of critical method and in the interrelation of all methods. We accept as true only that which in us is experienced as faithful and reliable, as a constant in our feeling. Authority guides us from the very first awakening of our consciousness, even though what constitutes authority withdraws, as it were, from that which is finitely comprehensible; but its voice comes to us all the more authoritatively from everything that arouses reverence.

Love, reverence, and trusting oneself to authority exist conjointly. They are almost equivalents.

They are easily understood through their frequent perversions, always correctly stigmatized in Nietzsche's psychologizing: *Love* becomes pliability, becomes blindness, or is reduced to bodily desire, which, to be sure, may well be its substratum but ought not to be its substance— regardless of whether it is the sexual instinct, the parental instinct, the élan unleashed by the community of existence and of interest, or it is perverted into the desire for belonging at any price. *Reverence* for authority turns into fear, becomes submission to whatever prevails publicly—to success, wealth, posturing, show. Confidence in *authority* becomes obedience devoid of critical understanding, prostration before what is powerful in the world, merely because it is established, emotion with an empty soul, habit without living content.

Nietzsche's works are suffused with a certain climate that, in spite of all his enthusiasm and passion, has an icy quality. It may, to be sure, convey to the reader a sense of cleansing, paving the way for truth— something we search for and to which we want to expose ourselves;

but then it is found to be something that not only does not warm us but also threatens to snuff out our real life. Because of what is missing, everything may become questionable. But to learn about Nietzsche's struggling is deeply moving, a struggling which toward the end he would like to deny but which still draws us to him even when we are repelled by his apodicta—whether true or false—because they are declarative. It is distressing to see Nietzsche's persistent bent for rejection, how rarely he perceives the truth of the origins, focusing overwhelmingly on falsifications and deviations, always seeming compelled to pejorative interpretation.

4. The genius of the heart

In conclusion, we are inexorably led to the question: What do we gain by engaging with Nietzsche? Admittedly, we can never expect a result. Indeed, if our aim is to arrive at definite positions, if we expect the sort of substance which can be made the matter of argument in order to establish what is true, Nietzsche is not the man to turn to; only isolated propositions of his will serve the purpose. In Nietzsche we soon find the opposite of what he has said elsewhere; we do not find a decision. He is the bearer of a truth different from that of positions and decisions: what he offers is the breadth of all that is possible, his having ventured forth on all paths; hence the openness of vision which soon excels the content to be found in him.

If we do not succumb to the temptation of taking Nietzsche's statements in their bluntness to be absolute, we shall be drawn into the vortex because of him. We shall be drawn into trains of thought of unaccustomed profundity and shall also, again and again, come up against statements that in isolation display a startling shallowness. We shall feel the magic emanating from a noble soul, and here and there feel confronted by an emptiness which makes us think that what is most essential eluded us.

Wanting to arrive at a definitive position with regard to Nietzsche would be a mistake. He is an exception, not an example. He does not stand for a doctrinal system. Rather, he is the indicator of a change in orientation, testing the waters, shaking things up. Nietzsche is wholly concerned with the effect he will have on us as he touches us with his thinking. He wants to awaken, to bring about, to arouse, not to teach and even less to force anything on us. He speaks *about himself* when he speaks of the genius of the heart that can do this:

"The genius of the heart . . . whose voice knows how to descend

into the underworld of every soul . . . to whose mastery belongs knowing how to seem— . . . the genius of the heart who makes everything
loud and self-satisfied fall silent and teaches it to listen, who smooths
rough souls and gives them a new desire to savour— . . . the genius
of the heart . . . who divines the drop of goodness and sweet spirituality
under thick and opaque ice . . . the genius of the heart from whose
touch everyone goes away richer, not favoured and surprised, not as if
blessed and oppressed with the goods of others, but richer in himself,
newer to himself than before, broken open, blown upon and sounded
out by a thawing wind, more uncertain perhaps, more fragile . . . but
full of hopes that as yet have no name . . ."[27]

If we are affected by the Nietzsche who is this "genius of the
heart," and if, in these electrifying sentences, we still sense the absence
of that which truly sustains life—when we feel that, essentially, it is
the *"genius"* of the heart that is speaking and not the depth of the soul
as the historic ground—then, it seems to me, we understand Nietzsche
in the way in which, according to his own intent, we are to appropriate
his thinking.

[27] *Beyond Good and Evil,* 199, 200.

Philosophers in Other Realms

Editors' Note

Jaspers distinguishes three main groups of Great Philosophers: Paradigmatic Individuals (Vol. 1), Philosophers Proper (Vols. 1, 2, 3, 4), and Philosophers in Other Realms (Vol. 4). In Volume 1 he explains the inclusion of the last: "Since our book is devoted to philosophy, they are not at its center. But such is their importance for philosophy that something must be said of them if we are not to take too narrow a view of philosophy and ultimately reduce it to the exclusive preserve of rationality." In the introduction to the German original of Volume I of *The Great Philosophers,* the only one published in his lifetime, Jaspers presents the following outline for the projected third main group:

Philosophers in Other Realms

in Literature	(Greek tragedians. Dante. Shakespeare. Goethe. Hölderlin. Dostoevsky)
in Science and Scholarship Natural Science	(Kepler. Galilei. Darwin. von Baer. Einstein)
Historians	(Ranke. Burckhardt. Max Weber)
in Political Thought Theorists	(Macchiavelli. Morus. Locke. Montesquieu. Burke. de Tocqueville)
Uncritical utopians	(Rousseau. Marx)
in "Bildungswille" and Literary Criticism	
Humanists	(Cicero. Erasmus. Voltaire)
"Bildungswille"	(Shaftesbury. Vico. Hamann)

German Humanism	(Schiller. Wilhelm von Humboldt)
Critics	(Bacon. Bayle. Schopenhauer. Heine)
in Life-Wisdom	
Literary Wisdom	(Seneca. Xuang Tzu)
Skeptical Independence	(Montaigne)
in Praxis	
Statesman	(Ikhnaton. Asoka. Marcus Aurelius. Frederick the Great)
Monks	(Francis of Assisi)
Professionals	(Hippocrates. Paracelsus)
in Theology	(Me-Ti. Mencius.—Paul. Tertullian.—Malebranche. Berkeley)
in Teaching of Philosophy	(Proclus. Scotus Erigena. Wolff. Erdmann)

The literary remains contain notes and fragments on most of the figures listed; in some cases these are voluminous, in others as little as one page. There are notes and fragments on some figures not included in the above scheme, who apparently were to have been included if the project had come to fruition, for example, contemporaries such as T. S. Eliot and Saint-Exupéry. Jaspers published interpretive essays on only two of the figures mentioned, Goethe and Schopenhauer. The German edition of this volume contains fragments on the following realms and figures:

Philosophers in Poetry: Dante, Shakespeare
Philosophers in Science and Scholarship: Einstein, Max Weber
Philosophers in Utopian Political Thought: Marx
Philosophers in "Bildungswille" and Literary Criticism: Voltaire, Cicero.

The three chapters presented here (Einstein, Max Weber, Marx) consist of notes for Jaspers's lecture course Philosophy of the Present, which he presented at the University of Basel in the Winter semester 1960/61, his last year of teaching.

Philosophers in Science and Scholarship

EINSTEIN

MAX WEBER

Editors' Note

Hans Saner, the editor of the German edition of this book, introduces this sub-part as follows, in part paraphrasing Jaspers, in part quoting him:

"Jaspers wanted to bring out 'the basic nature and claims of modern science,' in particular 'its perverted relation' to philosophy; in this way he meant to show that philosophy is the impulse of science, but is not itself scientific. And science is as such not philosophy; on the other hand, '*that* there ought to be science, the *idea* of the scientific attitude, and the *idea of the unity* of all the sciences: all that is philosophy.'

" 'From this we derive the meaning of the university: By virtue of philosophy it is the cosmos of the sciences, but in such a way that philosophy itself is represented at the university in its many configurations, in the multiplicity of the spiritual forces that prevail through it.'

"The fundamental nature of philosophy is clarified to the degree that the fundamental nature of science is clarified. [With the rise of modern science] philosophy has 'entered a new atmosphere'; in a certain sense it must 'begin anew,' knowing that 'philosophy regarded as science is untenable; philosophy without constantly being mindful of science is mischief; philosophy has its own origin and its own substance' which it can reach only if divested of the 'veil of scientific universal validity.' "

Jaspers had planned to divide the type of "philosophers in science and scholarship" in two, discussing several main figures in modern natural science and some leading scholars in the *Geisteswissenschaften* (the humanities). The following chapters on Einstein and Max Weber are representative of this division. Jaspers brings all that he had previously written on the redefinition of the relation of science and philosophy necessitated by the rise of modern science to bear on his discussion of Einstein. Similarly the chapter on Max Weber reflects Jaspers's earlier appraisal of him as "the Galileo of the *Geisteswissenschaften,* as well as Jaspers's own pioneering work in the methodology of *Verstehen,* which a later generation came to know as "hermeneutics."

EINSTEIN

Editors' Note

The material on Einstein consists of notes Jaspers composed for his course "The Philosophy of the Present" at the University of Basel in the winter semester of 1960–61. They were not arranged by him for presentation in *The Great Philosophers,* and have here been put in the most cogent order. Of interest is a collateral work by Jaspers, *The Future of Mankind,* translated by E. B. Ashton (Chicago, University of Chicago Press, 1961).

1. The modern image of the universe; the philosophical significance of physics

For the contemporary human being, it is of considerable consequence to find his place in what is now known of the cosmic world—a knowledge which in the last half century has experienced a tremendous intensification and deepening.

Consequently, I begin with cosmology and physics. Today this area of knowledge has an exciting impact on human consciousness; it is the great event of this age, manifesting matters that in their magnitude as natural phenomena make man shrink to become but one living being on a tiny speck of dust in the cosmos.

Physics is at the same time the origin of the upheaval of knowledge and of the power which threatens the very existence of humanity. For the outcome of this knowledge is the atom bomb. It forces human beings to a radical reversal, if mankind is not soon to be destroyed. The time allowed it to prepare for this reversal may be a few decades, perhaps less. The aggregate political condition of the world has already changed.

Our topic is modern science, its meaning and consequences for our fundamental philosophical knowledge.

Within natural history, the research of the last seventy years—by the degree of the transformation and not just the increase in our knowledge—has risen to an unprecedented level within the history of the sciences. We witness here a knowledge-creating process comparable to the beginnings of exact science with Copernicus, Kepler, Galileo, Newton, not so much because it encompasses the principles of scientific investigation as such, but because only now do the spiritual consequences become apparent in total clarity and these consequences, namely, the fate of all human life on earth, make themselves inexorably felt.

2. What is the main issue for those concerned with present-day philosophy?

In the realm of atoms, things ceased to be representational. Space, time, causality, and substances were no longer valid as they had been in our previously *accessible* world. The representational models of the tiniest particles and most minuscule waves had their assured position. They might contradict each other as representations, but they complemented each other as models, each being merely the guideline for the always mathematically founded theses, but not these theses themselves. Niels Bohr spoke about the complementary nature of representational models. Both are true. They come to the fore according to which experiment is performed and according to the underlying theoretical blueprint.

In the atomic as well as the cosmic realm, appropriate representation has given way to several models which cannot be combined into a total representation, into a picture of the world of matter.

Through mathematics and measurement a world has opened up to us which becomes operable in the hands of man without his knowing intuitively what it is. Human beings were able to transfer the energy of the sun to the earth by releasing it out of matter (uranium) present on earth.

This does not mean, however, that classical physics has lost its validity. What transcends its sphere has, by experimental procedures, to be brought within its sphere.

As in ancient times, man has to operate manually in a world of familiar physics, so that the machinery constructed by him actually produces what would otherwise remain mere mathematical speculation.

The ingenuity of the experimenters is no less important than that of the theoretical investigators. The experimenters, however, always remain within the space of classical physics. Mathematical speculation transcends it.

It resembles magic when by the hand of man something is opened up that no human hand will ever be able to grasp. But it is not magic, because the acting, thinking, and imagining behind it become transparent in the process—even in contradiction, even in the determination of incomprehensible factualities (the "cosmic constants").

Man can do and does more than he comprehends; he does not do it by means of magic, but rationally and comprehensibly, founding himself on the nature of things.

Once they have actually been materialized, no prior calculations can predict their consequences—disastrous in the case of the atom bomb. This is fundamental to all experimenting that reveals unexpectable consequences. It is the genius of the scientist to notice the significance in the expected.

3. The significance of this cognition

All the foregoing refers to knowledge available to the general public in excellent popularizations written by the great scientists themselves, though clear in their full scope only to the expert.

But here we ask about the significance of this cognition, what it really effects, what it means, how it enters into our fundamental knowledge. With the development of scientific research, cosmology lost much of its interest; what still satisfied Kepler became obscured, since it was not really scientific.

Knowledge of the cosmologies of the Greeks, those that dominated the Middle Ages and those that reappeared during the Renaissance was interesting only from a historical viewpoint. As cognition it had collapsed.

Only with the possibility of penetrating the universe by observation, to confirm or refute projections via observation, did cosmology become again interesting. Now it had and continues to have a fundamentally different character: that of research extending into infinity, of renunciation of a conclusive world-picture. It was the rebirth of a new cosmology out of the principles of scientific, methodical research.

But the impulses toward a cosmology based on speculative intuitions and the conjuring up of marvelous possibilities do not cease.

Pure science, which had to find itself through development and even had to give up such beautiful notions as Kepler's celestial harmony, must maintain itself constantly in the face of such intrusions.

Either we are here confronted with new scientific insights, to be verified or rejected by observation, and which disclose new facts and interrelations, or what is pointed out to us is a phantom, comparable to that earlier chimera the *perpetuum mobile*.

4. Einstein as representative

Einstein summarizes his work as follows: "Positing of the theory of relativity, combined with a new conception of time, space, gravity, equivalence of mass and energy. General field theory (not complete). Contributions to the development of quantum theory."[1]

He was the central figure among the research scientists who established modern natural inorganic science on a new foundation—a turning point that has been compared to the huge advances made by Copernicus and Newton.

Attention has been focused on him as on no other contemporary scientist.

Throughout his long life Einstein conjoined his scientific research with a search for the meaning of such science. He commented on political problems, religion, Judaism, Zionism, on timely matters of universal concern. As a result of his unique fame, his voice made itself heard. Attention was paid to whatever he said, the premise being that a man of such outstanding scientific achievements had something essential to say about everything. Without himself laying claim to be an authority, Einstein became for many a sage and prophet of his time. His pronouncements, no matter how imposing, convey the self-contained image of a man with a personal approach and worldview.

5. Einstein's cognition of nature and his philosophical worldview

There is no objectively necessary relation, valid for everyone, between this cognition of nature and a worldview expressing itself philosophically, religiously, historically.

The purely scientific state of things is not by itself philosophy or the element of a philosophy; rather, as is everything else that exists, it is merely an object for philosophical reflection.

But the scientist is not simply a human being; if scientific research is a vital necessity for him, he is a philosopher—in the sense, to be

[1] Carl Seelig, *Helle Zeit—Dunkle Zeit. In memoriam Albert Einstein.* Zurich/Stuttgart/Vienna, Europa, 1956, 9.

sure, that every human being qua human being is a potential philosopher. But in his case this sense is heightened by the fact that his thought, via his research and beyond his research, forms a whole, expressing an attitude toward life and a way of thinking.

Such a research scientist is, then, a philosopher, perhaps a type of philosopher prevalent among scientists in his field, a representative, as it were, a personal phenomenon, as every philosopher of rank has to be and, as such, deserving of regard and elucidation.

By the nature of his research he belongs to an impersonal field of science to which he has made lasting contributions by his achievements, discoveries, and the results in the process of progress; in the future these will be permanently attached to his name, not because of an intrinsic necessity, but to honor him.

The presence he projects as philosopher is such that we do not get close to him by discussing objective, tangible subject matter, but, rather, by accepting or rejecting, by responding to states of mind, motivations, aspirations, and the measure of depth or superficiality in his relation to the actuality of human beings, the world, and transcendence.

6. Einstein's intellectualistic approach

Under discussion is the meaning of science. Einstein has no doubts about this. It is a matter of indifference how the correctness of cognition was gained. For the process of science, the person of the scientist is irrelevant.

Einstein, however, knew that experiencing the meaning of research or faith in the goal, that is, the discovery that simplicity is the source of the infinite diversity of rationally structured nature, determines the humanity of the scientist, who, after all, is a human being. In Einstein's simple language: "This, as it were, religious attitude of the man of science is not without influence on the total personality."

This faith was Einstein's "cosmic religion." A critique of it cannot be scientifically cogent. All it can do is circumscribe what is contained in this cosmic religion and what remains beyond its horizon.

In Einstein's productive constructions it is a matter of pure intuition of the mathematic structures of the cosmos, of the beauty in simplicity, of the harmony in infinite richness.

By comparison, the world of men, the world around him, and history, appear to him chaotic; in self-defense he insists on reason, the mathematical intellect, rational order.

Something analogous is noticeable in Einstein's approach to politics:

pragmatic thinking along the path and consciousness of something unconditional toward which the path leads; behavior in a given situation
adjusting to circumstances and variety of conditions, and faith in a goal.

Such faith applied to politics is not as clearly expressed by Einstein
as the cosmic religion within natural science. But the analogy seems
clear to me:

The element that determines meaning and which is designated in
science "cosmic religion" is not cognized explicitly but acknowledged
to be a matter of faith; in politics it is interpreted more casually: why
a war is "worthwhile" or perhaps not worthwhile.

Such pragmatism in politics has its limit in what is seen as worthwhile. There is, however, an unconditional truth, which is decided by
the will of an individual, by what he conceives as the purpose of his
life, which kind of life he considers worthwhile, what he really wants.

So we have to speak in philosophical terms of all that is not accessible to scientific thinking: of the cosmic religion which stands above all
that is personal and provisional; of what is motivated by personal desire
in the men and women making concrete decisions and overrules pragmatic considerations.

Only in asking this question, that is, what is worthwhile, does the
taproot of judgment, of valuation, of response to events and actions
taken become evident.

In the matter of "being worthwhile," the same intellectual calculus
is given absolute status as is done in cosmic religion—as though it
were clear and evident to all and sundry. . . .

7. The limits of Einstein's philosophical position

No wrenching experiences characterize the foundation of Einstein's
life. He knows neither the wrathful God nor the God of love, only
what he calls God allegorically: the harmony of the laws of nature, the
cosmic religion.

Many intelligent judgments were made by him, ruled by moderation, but seeming superficial by their very reasonableness, out of touch
with the real driving forces, with no appeal to anything other than
reasonableness, within a horizon displaying only the givens, political as
well as social. He takes as his witness the Old Testament, without
sensing the adamant grandeur and power of faith that are at its origins—no trace of Job.

His insight into the basic phenomena of human existence was
decent, and to the point, but severely limited.

This self-contained stance, which allows its own contradictions to operate in a meaningful way, does not grow into a wholeness of its own, clear to itself. Imposing in his truthfulness and independence, he might easily infuriate us at the same time because of all that remains beyond his horizon. But our indignation is silenced because he is unpretentious; what you see is what he is; he does not set himself up as an example, as guide.

A phenomenon representative of the age? But what would the age he is supposed to represent be? He lived in this era, and by his discoveries raised it to its high rank of progression in the natural sciences.

Under the conditions of his era and his own discoveries, he replicates an ancient form of living, untragic, indeed incapable of tragedy. He knows no defiance of divinity, no Jobian revolt, no angry God.

An anecdote may be cited as typical:

When, in 1938, I, with my Jewish wife, wished to escape from Germany, a friend of ours who knew Einstein from his Berlin days visited him in Princeton with the purpose of discussing the creation of a position for me there. Einstein replied in approximately these terms: "When I read Jaspers, it affects me like listening to a drunk; well, Hegel affects me the same way. It surpasses my comprehension. I don't want to ruin his reputation, but I cannot recommend him."

It was crisp and clear and irreproachable—as was everything about Einstein.

MAX WEBER

Editors' Note

Jaspers's published writings on Weber consist of an early tribute:
"Max Weber, Eine Gedenkrede von Karl Jaspers" (Tübingen,
Mohr, 1922, which also appeared in *Aneignung und Polemik,* Munich, 1968, 409–23), and, later, an evaluation of Weber's meaning
for modern thought in general, *Max Weber. Deutsches Wesen im
politischen Denken, im Forschen und Philosophieren* (Oldenburg,
G. Stalling, 1932; in English: "Max Weber as Politician, Scientist,
Philosopher," in *Three Essays: Leonardo, Descartes, Max Weber,*
translated by Ralph Manheim (New York, Pantheon, 1964, 187–
274).

A Characterization

1. Introduction

In reporting on Max Weber's political thought, I claimed that it is
not philosophy.

In an earlier lecture I reported on Max Weber's science, saying that
this too is not philosophy.

My reasons are:

a) Philosophy which does not become political is not genuine philosophy. In political thought and in one's attitude toward concrete situations, human beings have been tested by their philosophy. This has
always been the case.

b) Philosophy that ignores the sciences, does not direct itself purposefully toward the sciences, or does not manifest itself in science is
not genuine philosophy either. This has always been the case.

Today, however, politics and the sciences have gone through a
change of such radical nature that it is seen clearly only against the
background of the profound rupture in world history.

I did not choose as my topic the philosophical writings of our era, but philosophy of the present time in its existential gravity; not the "hobbies" of tedious and diligent conceptual games, but the thinking that engages our possibilities, as individuals and in the world, in our nations and in mankind.

Now follows a subjective statement:

To me, Max Weber appeared as the true philosopher of the age, the philosopher who did not express his philosophy directly, but whose life and thought were based on it.

Such an assertion cannot be proven to be universally valid. Some may object that, biased by my attachment to him, I exaggerate his greatness. For my part, I think that these commentators have not really studied Max Weber.

I myself can only stress the continuity of my view of Weber over the past fifty years, the fact that throughout that long period I did not philosophize without keeping him in my mind, without asking myself what would he say. I made his basic position my own—not in the sense of continuing his sociology and furthering sociological research, but in the sense of bringing this philosophizing to consciousness.

I have been under his influence since 1909.

When he died in 1920, I felt as if the German world had lost its heart, and as if it were no longer possible to continue living as before.

I expressed this in a speech at the memorial service organized by the Heidelberg student body shortly after his death, and in a booklet I wrote in 1932.[1] This was at the time—shortly before the National Socialists seized power—when speaking of the German people became that appalling din which prompted me to choose the subtitle "The German Character in Political Thought, Science, and Philosophizing"—as a parrying thrust against it. Subsequently I deleted the word "German," reducing the title to *Max Weber as Politician, Scientist, Philosopher.*

Objectively, the following topics of discussion present themselves:

a) Fame and historical influence.

Nowadays fame can be very considerable and at the same time very ephemeral. Once a person has died he is quickly forgotten. For anyone who has lived with awareness through half a century, it is startling how completely names once resoundingly famous have faded entirely.

Historical influence begins with a spiritual rebirth after death. All that is merely personal or peripherally interesting has been sloughed

---

[1] *Max Weber, Eine Gedenkrede;* see Editors' Note to this chapter.

off. Personal contacts no longer exert influence. For the new generation, the work alone is relevant.

In this sense, Weber, in contrast to most of his contemporaries, has come to life again. It is also remarkable that interest in his work is arising and growing in America and England.

b) Showing what one sees.

This may serve as another avenue of approach. After concentrated reflection and remembrance, intuiting, as it were, his spiritual personality and linking it with his actually increasing though admittedly still very limited impact on the world—primarily based on a perception of his achievements in the social sciences—if someone sees greatness, he should show it and give his reasons for it.

c) Weber as a contemporary (at least for people my age).

No one can tell what effect may be in the offing. I believe I can see it *will* come, of necessity, but whatever the outcome, Max Weber was representative of a basic quality of our age, true, honorable, and valid for a long future.

2. Weber's place in philosophy today

In view of the questionable nature of philosophy today, at a time when it is despised and tolerated only as a bow to tradition—a time, in fact, when philosophy needs to be reborn—and in this transitional period that boasts its attachment to whatever is tangible and spreads its illusions and assertions abroad pushing true philosophy to extinction without creating anything cogent and valid, the phenomenon Max Weber has a chance of exerting considerable influence. His philosophical effectiveness derives from the very fact that he does not attempt to create a new persuasive and valid framework, that he dispenses with addressing us from a center that has philosophy as its primary source; this applies to the entire scope of his thinking in all its creative, intellectual intensity, in the humanities, history, sociology, the ways of his political thought, and to the actuality of his life and private existence.

With Weber, philosophy manifests itself in its concrete effects, in the sciences, in politics, and in practical life.

In this way they assume a character differing from the accustomed one, but one that has always been theirs in all great philosophy. The sciences, politics, and practical life today often become lost in their concreteness, in their ultimately aimless advance, in the mere "onward," in their hustle and bustle—lacking as they do a philosophic center.

3. The sciences

Up to the present, causal-empirical analysis was almost always limited by the transformation of relatively justified principles of research into absolute ones; and almost always kept within research itself, since research and valuation, knowing and willing were not separated. Such analysis was almost always seen as construction of what authentically is.

But Weber advanced research in sociology and history to such a degree and heightened the demands on investigative work to such an extent that those coming after him hesitated to follow him on this path.

They prefer to circumvent his work, which lies on the path like a block of granite that has to be climbed with utmost exertion and toil of reasoned research in order to glimpse from its top the right way. In this circumvention, they get lost in the multiplicity of wrong tracks, closed in, boundless, and dead ends.

The important question here is: Can science reach to a height that is out of reach for those coming after?

The only promising road to cognition is linked to the will of such supreme personal effort.

To see this even when the effort proves unsuccessful is good in itself; moreover, the criterion of knowing what one is doing may, after all, serve those audacious and capable enough to proceed on the royal road, by preparing the stepping-stones.

This is the great divide for every modern sociologist and historian: Does he appropriate or circumvent?

Weber is distinguished by the absence of anything sensational or symbolic, of catchwords, of overpowering prophecy.

What has been forgotten is Weber's personal attendance at congresses, his participation in debates at plenary sessions of a political character. But how few comprehended the subject matter, which he believed he comprehended—in modesty, without noise—in his far-reaching work.

His life and work were indissolubly intertwined. This presupposes in him, considering the nature of the subject matter, the following: He practiced specialization as an objectively valid activity with intrinsic value. Yet it was something relative for him, something that provided resources without itself becoming an absolute. He experienced it as a profession which he exercised with ascetic seriousness, but, though he gave it his energetic effort, he did not abandon himself to it altogether. Things have to be dealt with, by whom is a matter of indifference. Hence the validity of his statement "What I don't do, others will."

Regardless of whether it concerned scholarship, investigative research, or political insight, everything was a matter of concrete concern for him. A man can only become an authentic personality if he focuses attention wholly on the matter at hand; if he intends to become such a personality in any other way, no matter how hard he tries, he will rotate around himself and become empty.

We might ask: Did a great Existenz express itself in the research? Or was it the effort of relentless thinking that brought this Existenz into being? But there is no either/or here. The one is as true as the other.

Weber was a man in whom the personal formation developing from cognition and original experience translated into such an interlocking knowledge that no more magnificent image of a contemporary philosopher could be imagined. For a philosopher is that human being who steadfastly thinks and cognizes by focusing on the ground of Existenz, always referring to an unspoken absolute while always expressing himself in the finite.

4. Politics [2]

a) No one disputes *Weber's understanding of politics,* evident in his sociology. Yet his practical political thinking and acting with respect to historical developments in Germany are controversial. His soundness in evaluating a particular situation, however, is frequently undeniable.

b) The *overall assessment of Weber's political initiatives* throughout the decades: Lack of realism, since the powers and conditions of the period did not even wrestle with him, but ignored or unconsciously smothered him.

Realistic in the sense that they might have served the advance of German affairs beneficially.

This advancement, however, presupposes that the motivations and insights of the authorities as well as of the general population would have been of a nature open and actively responsive to his initiatives.

What concerns us here is not so much any specific proposal, but, rather, his way of thinking about politics, its grandeur, dignity, truthfulness, seriousness; his eye for realities; his faculty of judging; his sensing in present activities their much later consequences.

Weber presupposed a nation at a high level of feeling, thinking, and willing—a nation that did not exist.

[2] The reader is referred to Wolfgang Mommsen, *Max Weber and German Politics;* see Bibliography.

He realized the necessity to further political education, a task Bismarck had conspicuously neglected, so that there was a glaring gap in the Wilhelminian state, which did not have a single representative statesman of stature. Weber himself could not take on the role. Only once, in his inaugural lecture and in a few essays, did he attempt a public gesture, but it was fleeting and not propelled by further ambitions. Not before the First World War, and then only in 1917, did he begin to speak out regularly.

Always, when he spoke warningly, it was not yet too late, but always it soon became too late. He had missed the decisive moment.

From his early years on, he saw the catastrophe approaching step by step, yet he did not want to believe it would happen.

c) *Weber's will to greatness:*

1) His stand *against* baseness, lack of substance, narrowness, against fear, against the unconditional desire for security; *for* high goals in the self-assertion of what a man can be: worthy of existing and testifying to the meaning of being human.

2) His truthfulness when faced with the factual, aware of the limit set on all knowledge, and realizing the risk of basing ourselves on ever inadequate knowledge; his ideas of asceticism and sacrifice, transposed into the actuality of politics.

3) His argumentation, always to be seen against the background of these stern demands on himself and others, to be measured with his yardstick.

On this decisive point he was misunderstood, since others are not that way or wish it this way.

He impressed enormously even those whose natures were alien to his and who hated him for this reason, who found his existence unbearable because it touched their consciences and demanded what they were not willing even to see.

He experienced the smothering power of the mediocre, of those who look for what is practicable. There was a grotesque difference between his nature and this ordinary level.

d) *Weber did not act.* The passion of his thinking, always focused on the moment and the situation and what was decisive in it, did not result in the passion to take action.

1) In his youth, when he was full of vigor, such action never occurred to him. Even though he became a scholar reluctantly, he did become one and devoted his entire immeasurable strength to this profession, feeling this decision to be an either/or. He never considered

becoming a professional politician. It would have been hopeless in any event, because of sham constitutions and his being a commoner. He was not fueled by the powerful energy of revolutionary action and not able to swing the mood of the masses, whose thinking ran along entirely different lines. For political action he would have needed friends and followers and at least the rudiments of an audience among the people.

Nor did he engage publicly in the battle against Emperor William II—his person as well as the system—though the thought crossed his mind, without, however, being seriously considered.

2) Anyway, after he contracted a serious illness in 1898, he would have been physically unable to become politically active.

It appears strange, tragic, and nearly comical to think that someone, somewhere, might consider him for a political role, glimpse for a moment the unfathomably deep intellect animated by high goals, only to end up silently discarding him.

He never experienced his "high noon," was never called to leadership in grand politics, though he offered his services on a modest scale. All his energy was poured into small matters, since great things had been denied to him.

He made no move to advance himself into positions of power, but, instead, acted in ways that made this impossible.

Do we have to regard him, then, as a failure who, all things considered, was unable to counter the simplest intrigues, the antagonism of stupidity, the pressure of mediocrity?

Is he an example of fastidiousness, incapable of decisive action at the right moment?

He embodied insight into German politics, tasks, and possibilities— the truth of the moment that was not understood.

The impression is inescapable that, if his thinking had developed into political leadership, the fate of Germany and of Europe might have been more propitious. Why was this impossible?

Weber restricted himself to his approbation of Naumann,[3] after having corrected him on decisive points. Naumann, open-minded, not vain, with good will toward Weber, failed, however, to understand him at decisive turning points.

Weber's suggestions were as clear and simple as they were impracticable, given the people and the historical conditions.

---

[3] Friedrich Naumann (1860–1919) was an influential publicist and co-founder of left-liberal parties.

5. The total view: the unavailing "and yet"

Weber embodied the reality of thinking to which the myopia, narrowness, indolence, and emotionality of contemporary politics came into view simultaneously. This was borne out by the hindsight of history.

Against him stood, even in historically informed retrospect, the kind of "realism" that considers the "average" to be the ultimate and decisive authority—the type of person whose eye is on immediate success, ignoring its aftereffects.

Is Weber the symbol for the movement toward universal destruction, in view of which the light of the human spirit shines in vain? But why and whence does this light then shine at all?

Is Weber's protest in the face of this reality misguided or, considering his unremitting energetic deployment of spiritual effort, action, and planning, can his "and yet" be seen as ultimately victorious, when its time has come?

Or is what is ultimately valid the melancholy view of history which inescapably draws closer to its end and, as its best, offers the knowledge of men not totally caught up in its movement but able to keep their heads above the waters of the flood?

One is as ephemeral as the other. Each man decides for himself what, for him, is decisive, what he ought to do, what the meaning is of "eternity" and of empty decline.

6. The total picture in the antitheses of "inner" and "outer"

The view:

a) A man who almost always recognized what is politically decisive and articulated it, as it were, into the void of his solitude (for a long time more in private than in public, since his politically oriented literary work is an extremely small part of his total output), expressed it with passion, in fury and bitterness, in worry and terror, and who, all things considered, had no impact on current events.

b) On the one hand the masses, with their freight of stupidity, mired in habit, tradition-bound, thoughtlessly satisfied by slogans and lulled by their unreadiness to know, by a sense of the irresistible, to which they would succumb without a fight; on the other, a man perceived by his colleagues and many of his friends as merely excessive, indeed as sick, a complainer, an inveterate denouncer of all and everything, who is not to be taken seriously, and yet who speaks and knows the truth which could benefit all, who, as the course of events has shown, was right—though not in the manner of a complete pessimist and prophet of doom who turns out to be right—but who has a positive approach, points out ways and necessities, and to the very end never ceases to believe in the possibility of taking the right way.

As cognitive achievement in the sphere of historical, sociological, and political knowledge, his work is unique in our age.

But the human being was more than the sum of his work, in contradistinction to most people nowadays who are achievers; with help from supportive systems, their achievement may easily make them appear greater than they themselves were originally.

Weber's great work cannot be adequately grasped without philosophy but the attempt to articulate this philosophy seems to weaken it; if one were to succeed, one would reach authentic philosophy, in the form of thought that corresponds to our situation.

7. Weber's doubters and opponents

Did this man of unbending factual investigation, of the clearest political thinking of the age, ultimately amount to no more than a dreamer, a utopian?

Did he, who recognized the tendencies of world events, still stand for a lost cause?

He was perceived in this way by a great many, who either rejected him as odd and unbearable, or loved him but complained: Niagara emptying into a washtub. . . .

Weber was in closest touch with every mode of reality; no one has surpassed him in this regard, and very few can even match such realism in its many-sidedness and openness. But his thinking mode goes beyond all realisms, to depths from which human reality draws its humane, constructive, substantive, inspiring achievements, overcoming itself in its actualization.

In appearance and gesture he was true to his original self, never cloaking himself in style and pretense. Protection via conventions and masks was not for him. He was not self-important. The way he was by nature revealed his magic directly and left him vulnerable to all kinds of attack. In him we see a man who was truly human, a man who devoted his thought to everything in the reach of human experience.

8. Weber's philosophy

There is no need to justify my treating Max Weber as a philosopher.

In any definition of philosophy, it presupposes itself; if, as is proper, it is not defined, the thinking individual decides what concerns him as philosophical, what speaks to him, inspires him, and which human being he considers to be, in the elevated sense of the term, a philosopher.

The philosophical traits of Weber's science:

a) The meaning of his logical and methodological discussions is itself philosophical and may even be counted as belonging to traditional philosophy. Hence also may the references to professors of philosophy in his works, such as Rickert.[4]

b) His commitment to actually knowing, cogently knowing: This commitment implies that he would propose no philosophical position masquerading as knowledge with content and object. In this sense he expressly rejected philosophy for himself. Empty speculation and construction of systems were alien to him. He was aware that this kind of philosophy has had its day of greatness, but in fact it is past. He did not deny its possibility but he did not see it in the present. The original impulse of cognition ("the truth is the true," he said at the last, mysteriously, when he was delirious) did not have a random effect. It is important to know what one knows and does not know, what meaning, what sense attaches to this knowledge—hence logical studies.

9. Weber's illness

Can Weber's illness be regarded as a coincidence? His insight into politics was just as clear and true before the onset of his illness as after it. But his philosophical sense deepened,and the breadth of his vision was led into the immeasurable. What would he have been without the illness?

His illness, however, made a full participation in practical politics impossible; he was physically capable of it for only short stretches of time.

Does the highest cognition presuppose illness? Kierkegaard? Nietzsche? Hölderlin?

Weber's illness was fundamentally different: in comparison with those three he was fully "a man," with an originally powerful vitality. The illness attacked him not from the outside, but out of his constitution itself.

[4] Heinrich Rickert (d. 1936) was a professor of philosophy at Heidelberg.

We are inclined to dismiss what is significant by ascribing it to "illness." Weber as a person, his spirit, was in no sense sick. No symptoms can be detected in his work. The illness did not touch his personality, only his physical vitality via neurological functions, and at that not an organic illness but a curable, functional one, unpredictable, subject to fluctuations. In his last years he had regained much of his health.

10. Weber's limits

a) He did not strive after power, did not court leadership; he did not limit himself to the printed word, but waited, kept himself in readiness without actively interfering; he was radically inhibited, conscious of his nerves: "I make mistakes."

b) He refused to formulate his philosophical consciousness and to impart it.

c) Perhaps in science, particularly in thinking through its "freedom from value," he did not quite see through the "positivism" of the humanities; in spite of his appropriate intention to extract ever more clearly what is "a matter of fact" (for example, "the intended meaning"), he did not sufficiently penetrate logically that which is a "fact" in history and in *Geisteswissenschaft* (the humanities).

To what extent may we lump him together with positivism, as Troeltsch did?[5] Troeltsch, though clearly perceiving Weber's greatness, was mistaken.

11. Weber's foundering in his time

He was the heart of Europe; in him appeared the widest and clearest consciousness of actual events, which he objectivized at every moment into the most definitive formulation.

This great man seemed destined to be the representative of greatness in his time, his actual lifetime—if there were no leading politicians to shape it. But in fact Max Weber hardly touched his time. He existed virtually unknown, ineffective—for, measured against what would have been possible and appropriate, what he achieved was a mere trifle. This fact itself seems to be emblematic. The times clamored for "personality" but ignored the greatest they possessed.

To be sure, Weber never pushed himself forward, never reached for anything, did not run for any office. It seems that our age requires

[5] Ernst Troeltsch (1865–1923) was a German theologian, philosopher, and sociologist of religion.

ambitious people to do this. It neither asks nor searches for the men it wants to follow. It seems characterized by the fact that it has no use for great men. For this reason it fails to have them. Here was a man who still drew his authority from the great figures of the past. It was given to him to articulate the nature of his age. It can hardly be doubted that future times will evaluate his works and his life as among the most important phenomena of our age.

Like many others, he was known during his lifetime as an academic, a sociologist; of course, any personal appearance was an event, though rarely fully understood by his audience. Though fascinated, even deeply affected, most listeners forgot—with some exceptions certainly—to consider what he really meant to convey. He lived in splendid isolation, with no craving for a friend, or at any rate for pseudo-friendships, but easily communicated with those he trusted. His simplicity made him open to human concerns, to a sense of friendship, but made him shrink from adulation. He was only marginally aware of what he represented; he lived in relation to objects, ideas, concrete matters, and with instinctive wisdom restricted any self-reflection of a narrowly individualistic tendency.

They had no use for him—not the old monarchy, not the republic. During the war, friends vainly tried through channels in Berlin to secure for him some political office, even if on a subordinate level. He would have been willing to work in Poland. His friends vainly hoped to get him into the Weimar National Assembly; the Democratic party, of which he was a member, made no use of him, either. Of course it is possible to ascribe each individual instance—of which there are many more—to coincidence; also, each separate case has its own causality. But the consistency with which Weber was excluded from politics has its own grandeur that erases indignation.

It seemed ordained that he was to be without immediate effect, testified within his very own environment, the academic world: at a time when honorary doctorates were liberally distributed in Germany, he did not receive a single honorary degree, remaining what he was: doctor iuris.

Most scholars of his acquaintance were afraid of him. His mere existence was like a reproach.

Lately, there has been a change, or there seems to be a change. In Heidelberg, Weber was recently eulogized in a public address by the president of the German Federal Republic[6] as the greatest German he

---

[6] Theodor Heuss (1884–1963).

ever encountered. So, in Heidelberg Weber is now frequently cited as one of the town's greater glories.

If you are attuned to curious coincidences, it may appear peculiar that Providence itself barred him from active influence: the illness inflicted on him, at least from 1900 to 1914, the exclusion from any public and indeed even academic activity.

I cannot say what this signifies. I merely believe that it has a meaning. The consistency, even in the negative sense, the integral nature of the person, the image of his existence without will to power, without trying for a particular form or style, arising in its originality from the mere being of this man—all that cannot be merely coincidence.

Philosophers in Utopian Political Thought

MARX

Editors' Note

Jaspers's full title for this projected subpart of Part Three of *The Great Philosophers* is "Philosophers in Political Critique as Basis for Uncritical Utopia." Under this heading he planned to discuss Rousseau and Marx. A few of his notes characterizing this type of philosopher in general have been published, of which the following are excerpts:

"Utopias, even if presented as 'critical' utopias, derive their deeper meaning from a timeless idea, or else are presented as reverie and playful diversion. Both Rousseau and Marx reject utopian thought, deeming themselves to be above it. Marx regards his thought as proceeding 'from utopia to science.' "

"In the formation of destructive mass movements their effect is negative; such movements arise from other motives and go their own way: French Revolution, Bolshevik Revolution. But the basis of utopian thought is their means of capturing masses of believers, and of debating within the context of 'Enlightenment' or 'dialectical philosophy,' by means of which anything can be justified or refuted."

"Rousseau and Marx differ in their political thought from all previous political philosophers of note: they dwell on the universal, the generally human, the unhistoric, and do violence to all of history as well as to the present and future."

"Their great abstract motivations are justice and freedom, but severed from every historic basis and all actual human society."

"Theirs are powerful spiritual motivations; while they translate their fanatical feelings into sober thought constructs, these are suffused with sentiments of hate and contempt."

Within the framework of "The Great Philosophers" Jaspers projected an elaborate exposition, interpretation, and critique of Marx (including Engels) and the political consequences of Marxist

341

ideology. The presentation was left in a fragmentary state, consisting of notes, including notes for Jaspers's lecture course on Contemporary Philosophy, which he gave in 1961; the following consists of selections from these notes. The reader is directed to Jaspers's collateral treatments of Marx, Marxism, and Communist totalitarianism in *Man in the Modern Age* (1931), *The Origin and Goal of History* (1949), *Reason and Antireason* (1950), and *The Future of Mankind* (1958).

MARX

1. Marx's orientation toward the cause

Marx, whose sole concern was the "cause," that is, humanity in its duration and in world history, as a person facing this cause, is indifferent to himself—in radical distinction from Kierkegaard, and Nietzsche.

The cause is of such nature that it does not itself affect the personality in the sense that the individual, by a constant process of cultivation and self-education, becomes an authentic human being; to the contrary, it allows the personality to lead a strange, perhaps ungrounded private existence which is neither a problem nor a matter of concern, and which is accidental in character.

This view of Marx is not a matter of psychologism but coalesces from actual facts.

2. The elements of greatness in Marx

a) Marx conjures up the prophetic vision of the calamity of modern times, understood in definite, tangible realities: in economic life, in society, in ideology. He sees "man's alienation." He envisages the impetus toward a humanity embodying "rights of man" for all, instead of the human rights declared by the French Revolution. And there are his factual insights in particular, his lucid perception of the diabolical aspect of modern processes of labor and their consequences.

b) Marx transformed meditative philosophy into active politics; used interpretation and cognition as means of action, and cognition as faith.

c) Marx had a monumental conception of history, inclusive of past and future. He praised the achievements of the bourgeoisie in the *Communist Manifesto*. His political way of thinking differed from that of all earlier important political philosophers; it was universal and ahistorical, drawing in all of mankind, by doing equal violence to all of history, the present as well as the future. The great abstract impulses of justice and freedom were dissociated from all historic ground and all actual human community.

d) Marx's language and style: He introduced a new style to philosophical discourse that remains effective and copied up to the present; lively dialectic and striking phrasing; forceful language; passionate accusation conjoined with recognition of necessity as a phase of history; radicalism; propagandistic slogans in which each word hits the target; an agitative style, enriched by knowledge; riddance of "maudlin sentimentality" through the consuming passion of anger, of demands, of sober factuality in which accusatory statements were expressed.

e) Marx's achievement becomes all the clearer if compared with the way in which socialism and communism had been formulated before. He disassociates himself from his socialist predecessors, and his sharpest polemics attack unscientific, merely sentimental methods. He places his faith in the critical intellect, expending immense intellectual effort, as in the research work for *Das Kapital*.

Great intellectual figures distinguish themselves not by a radical rift and an absolutely new beginning, but by how much they build on received tradition. Marx was a voracious reader, a scholar of tremendous application, taking full advantage of the accumulated treasures in libraries, where he unearthed what he needed.

The great innovation he brought about is spiritual—a synthesis, a conjoining of heterogeneous spiritual motifs, integrated into something original that leads and impels.

It has to be looked at and allowed to touch us as a whole.

3. Attempt at characterizing this whole

What is new and indeed also unique in Marx, even within the socialist movements: In hindsight, we can find elements of Marx's theories in earlier socialist writings, but, even so, he was the first to accentuate them and show their importance. To achieve this he intertwined three movements:

a. From utopia to science: Science was the science of a faith, a new prophecy, which consequently became an analogue of dogmatics and theology—Revolution with a "Book" in its hand.

b. From the timeless ideal world to history: For the Socialists, history became the vision of the new economic-industrial age, unprecedented in its comprehensive scope, apart from individual precursors. Consequently history became a matter of a reshaping that would do violence to the total picture, now seen from the horizon of the present—a vision that yielded separate fruitful insights but as a whole was false.

There was a new consciousness of our position within the process of history and the rejection of an absolute yardstick in favor of the historical one.

c. From clamorous demands and unconsidered actions to consciously calibrated politics: Politics, through stirring up the masses, became a new means of activism, with a long-term view, even though infused with impatience and with false expectations for the present.

4. Innovation in Marx

What is new within the whole of Marx's thought is, for one thing, its truly powerful effect. As an important theoretician of political economics, Marx would join the ranks of various others in this field, and perhaps not even measure up to them. As a philosopher, he would be counted among the materialists in the broad sense, devoid of philosophically creative ideas. As a historian, he would be a man of shrewd observations and purely rationalistic characterizations. If his contributions to knowledge were broken down in this way, he would still be considered an important figure, but not of outstanding eminence, and what constitutes the power and greatness of his work would be missed.

But this whole of his achievement is also questionable. Since Marx conjoins scholarly research and activism, science and philosophy, the questions arise: Does this synthesis not bring about confusion? Is the whole not vitiated at the source because its demands exceed human possibilities? And is it not ultimately a calamity, because activism based on what is wrong at its roots can end only in destruction and devastation, intensified if an alleged total knowledge, by using the powers of the masses, leads to total planning? Does the wrongness devolve from a basic philosophical error that is demonstrable? And is this way of erring perhaps typical of an age which, witnessing unique scientific advances, has fallen into a state of scientific superstition, and the abandonment of transcendence, wanting to be able to do and make everything—an age that tends to make man godlike and to consider history the highest authority, the substitute for God?

From this viewpoint we see Marx as a man who, in a Godforsaken world, becomes the prophet, not of God, but, supposedly, of history, a prophet of science, but of science that no longer is true science, and a lawgiver speaking in the name of the knowledge of history rather than as mouthpiece of the deity.

5. Critique of Marx's theory of alienation

a) Marx's thesis: Man's alienation is a historical, transitory phenomenon that can be overcome for everyone; there is no alienation in times preceding ours, nor will there be any after us. This thesis treats a phenomenon as though fully apprehended, ignoring that it belongs to the mystery of being human. It objectifies what can never become wholly an object, and in turn brings about a new alienation.

b) The truth in this Marxian thesis is not centered in the principle he absolutizes—a supposed total knowledge about alienation—but in particular insights, perspectives, and possibilities. Situations arise that follow a regular pattern, that is, consequences of human actions beyond intention or volition which are intuitable in the manner of ideal types. Alienation as a process is brought about through a concurrence of circumstances, through the detachment of our actions from ourselves, as in the case of Wallenstein[1], and the use made of them by others; our acts have their own independent dynamics, that of supply and demand, for instance.

One cannot deduce from man's nature what is bound to the occurrence of such specific circumstances, and without one's being such "nature of man," the image of which becomes intuitable only in individual configuration.

Individual alienation—such as is brought about by mindless work in the machine age or by letting our thinking run headlong instead of remaining master of it—is quite distinct from the principle that private property brings about total alienation from being-human.

c) The radical suspension of all "alienation" as posited by Marx would mean the suspension of man as we know him; a utopian, differently constituted human being would take his place, and that is impossible. What man now is would to a great extent reassert itself. Here the question arises: What is man, what are his "enduring" as against his "historic" characteristics? The question inevitably remains open, both as to fact and as to certain knowledge.

6. Critical remarks regarding Marx's view of the human being

Marx holds that there cannot be slow improvements, but only radical change into a new whole; the new authentic human being is actual only as a whole. There is no evolution toward him; only rebirth through revolution.

---

[1] Albrecht Wallenstein, Duke of Friedland (1583–1634), was a general in the service of the Emperor in the Thirty Years' War.

Alienated man turns into self-possessed man; dismembered man becomes total man. But it is vain to search for a picture of this total man in Marx's later works. Even in his youthful writings such passages are rare; they do not recur later.

This picture is an imaginary point, not filled in and not intuitable, the abstract fiction of a boundlessly happy state, held up as an achievable object of enthusiasm—a substitute for the imageless God.

a) Marx himself does what he rejects: for him, the ground has always to be "material"; hence he rejects "that all human conditions are derived from a concept, from the human being represented in the mind, from what is conceived as human nature, as *man* per se."

And Marx's own concept? He sees man as existing under material conditions, as the being that produces its food.

b) Total man is based exclusively on economics. Result: no interest in immediate alleviations for man as he lives today.

All questions regarding human beings are reduced to questions of economics, totally and exclusively.

As a result, any specific problems carry no weight, as, for instance, those concerning practical solutions, corrections, and improvements of the work process, adjustments of wage levels, organization, or satisfaction in one's work; no consideration is given to organization in specific instances or to the tremendous discrepancies between different kinds of work. Authentic ethical and humane concerns give way entirely to all that is concrete, favoring that totality as against actual man—a monstrous abstraction.

c) Marx's total man is either empty or not at all total. What is man in Marx? Perhaps total man as opposed to abstract man? But Marx's propositions about man are extraordinarily abstract.

d) Marx presupposes the possibility of a perfect human being, as though the concept of the correct organization of the world and of man perfected in it existed. He also attributes to private property all that is problematical and unsolvable in man as such. He does not consider the possibility of practical consequences that actually occur with the forcible abolishment of private property.

e) His vision of the technical age misjudges technology itself in its ineluctable consequences. Marx sees the world-historical significance of technology: the radical reorganization of the means of production with its fabulous achievements in contrast to all of preceding history. But he sees only the tremendous possibilities of production, the mastery of nature, the possibility of liberation from the hardships of existence; he does not see the limits and threats inherent in technology as such.

The only disastrous consequence of technology perceived by him is capitalist exploitation. Whatever the consequences of work with machinery, of the pragmatic division of labor in all kinds of enterprise, they seem to him, where not desirable, to vanish with the birth of the communist system.

His is a romantic view of technology. He sees its promises entirely in the mode of the nineteenth-century belief in progress.

f) Basic critical questions are: What are, for Marx, the salient features in the image of the human being? What is actually achieved by outlining a utopian being? What possibilities, drives, tendencies, dispositions are promised by a plan, a goal, an ideal project, a symbol?

There is the question whether Marx, in the guise of immanent knowledge of man, in his urge toward betterment, in his apparent rejection of all utopias, proud of his scientific socialism, does not himself succumb to an empty utopia: that of the abolition of real being-human concomitant with the ideal stultification of man submerged in society, the abolition of all intermediate stages, of the relationship of man to man, in which I myself identify with the other.

7. Criticism of the theory of ideology

a) If all of history without an underlying idea of eternal truth is moved solely by ideologies (except for technological progress in the domination of nature), why, then, can this new theory not be an ideology?

Because it leaves what is new about it—the salvation, the classless society, authentic man—wholly indefinite; and yet it is not a doctrine about a vision of Being, but only about a movement toward a goal, a goal that is stated only negatively, analogous to negative theology, with God now replaced by the world of history, that is, by man himself; and because, as a classless doctrine, it claims to be applicable to being-human in its total reach.

Yet it is, first, a negative doctrine, the will to destroy, and, second, a positive doctrine absolutizing the process of labor into the being of man as such.

b) Confusion of condition and origin:

We would have to clarify why, if we see merely exposition and superstructure, there is such richness of intellectual development (analogous to the wealth of the organic "imagination" of living things); why there is the perception of unique historic greatness, and its significance for all that follows.

Is not the condition turned into the origin itself? The lower level into the source rather than the agency?

The great truth in Marx lies in his recognizing the conditionality of the growth of spiritual realities ("sociology of knowledge"); plain factuality against abstract unrealistic idealism. But there is also, negatively, the suspension of spiritual openness in favor of a shallow reduction to materiality.

To the latter criticism, the Marxists object: Such openness amounts to the sacrifice of rigor to compromise, to perversion of causality, to decline into half-measures and apathy, to the trivialization of Marxism attempted in bourgeois research. But such objections are not critical discussions based on facts, but defamation based on absolute faith.

c) To be held against Marxist doctrine: Blindness for man's authentic original will to freedom; man's striving to gain space for his possibilities; the idea of freedom that arose in the axial era of history; this freedom in regard to politics as the form of life guaranteeing ordered existence through a sense of community, a system of representation, soliciting the voice of the masses, working through open discussion, compromise, corroboration, and experiment with no presumption of totality—and denigrated by Marxist believers as opportunistic, hypocritical, deceptive, exploitative, and characterized by spinelessness, malice, and stupidity.

d) Blindness for the incalculable rarity and greatness of spiritually creative people, a blindness that is a terrible leveling of intuition.

Summary: Based exclusively on economic grounds and the will of history, the hierarchy of being-human is suspended.

Question: Where is equality and where is it altogether lacking?

8. Critical analysis of the use Marx and Engels make of dialectic and the possible result of such use

Dialectic is meaningful as "structural form" of phenomena, as illumination of mutual relationships, of opposites, and of how realities are brought forth in such interplay.

A cluster of phenomena becomes orderly insofar as it conforms to a dialectic configuration that is comprehensible from inside.

Dialectic is perverted, becomes false, misinterpreted, misused if the following is allowed to happen:

a) When, instead of being the structural form of specific phenomena, it is taken to be the form of the entire process of events, and thought of as the process of genuine actuality, that is, the metaphysics of the total movement of events regarded as being-out-of-itself. When what is thought in dialectic is considered to be Being itself, the method is elevated to conclusive cognition.

b) When dialectic is understood as causality, and its "laws" are treated like necessary causal laws (instead of as the method of searching for more or less far-reaching correspondences between actual phenomena, and the sharp outline of the dialectical movement).

In such a case, dialectic becomes mono-causality: The total happening takes place in the form of turnabouts which are dialectically comprehensible and recognizable as necessary, in the sense of genuine causality.

c) The confusion of taking what is thought dialectically as though it were causal cognition results in expectations of what is to come and in acting on them according to the principle of speeding up the turnabout through intensification of the antitheses. Thus one engages in action in order to produce the turnabout oneself, believing that what is expected to happen can be effected by such action and equally by the application of causal cognition in technology. One expects that out of the radically destructive revolution there will result the abolition of private property, and salvation in the form of total man, the new man as total man.

No criterion is offered for differentiating destructive from productive dialectic.

When, in breeding, organisms are allowed to mate, the outgrowth, according to partially understood laws and within a certain scope for deviations, will be new, deliberately planned living beings.

If, in carrying out a total act of destruction concerning human circumstances, I expect the new man to arise by virtue of a dialectical meaning-relation falsely treated as causality, I in fact execute a magical act. It is the ancient magic clothed in pseudo-science. Faith in this magic grows out of faith in the "causal" reality of dialectical turnabouts.

In realistic analysis, however, we must expect, as the result of the overthrow of an entire existing order without an already constituted order in place that does not need to arouse but merely to unfold, a ruinous accumulation of helpless masses or the despotism imposed by terror, which, for a while, takes the place of order.

It is impossible to study, by means of repeatable experiments, whether and in what way such changes may happen; they have to be studied in the light of actual history, using it as a form of experimentation.

The assertion on the part of Marxists that there is a higher form of knowledge is equivalent to magical thinking.

9. Objections to Marx's economics

If, from the standpoint of theoretical economics, we separate Marx's specific contributions, examining them objectively and empirically, objections arise that have been voiced often enough. They do not amount to demolition of Marx's achievement, but do not withstand scientific investigation via strictly scientific discussion.

Earlier, science developed out of metaphysics and subsequently achieved validity independently of its origin; in the same way so did Marxist thought: out of a doctrinaire origin, namely, immanent faith, scientific insights were garnered which remain valid in their relativity independent of that ground but have also, as that ground has, relinquished a whole world of faith (seen as false and destructive) and have in their turn become a matter of examination and progressive knowledge as against doctrinaire application and subsumption.

Marx sees so-called economic laws as issuing from the nature of private property. With the cessation of private property, they too will cease to be.

But how? If all is common property, then it has to be administered—by the functionaries of a democracy. When it comes to common property, the individual is practically in the same position he is in confronting private capital, that is, without power.

The question here is what means are at his disposal to right wrongs, to reach for justice. Obviously fewer than previously, since he is forbidden to strike, may not organize an opposition when the despotic bureaucracy becomes terrorist, claiming to be the incarnation of the will of the people and of absolute justice instead of acting from the knowledge that we too are human and fallible.

10. Acting and onlooking

Action determined by knowledge can be action in an antithetical form: knowledge as technical applicability in an end-means relation or knowledge leading to a transformation of consciousness, producing a new, non-specific, total mood of expectation.

Marx's way of reasoning allows both to merge into one. Hence the power of its effect on heads that never think clearly. And hence the calamity arising from the confusion of mental operations which, by their very nature, rely on intuition, as though they were based on technically applicable knowledge. All this is most beautifully illustrated in some statements by Lassalle.[2]

If I look at history as though it were a natural process in which I do not take part, then history divides into the automatic happening and the spectator.

However, for history to happen, human beings have to take an active role, since the spectator does not participate; and if all became spectators, history would come to a standstill and there would be nothing left for spectators to watch. Marx's idea of history, which precisely should not be reduced to mere observation, since it calls instead for strenuous activity, can, in analogy to the confusion of intuitive knowledge and technical application, be used in two ways: for passively watching as things happen, or for the justification of activism.

In the first case, the attitude is "why do anything, why interfere; since everything will happen by necessity, why not wait until the time is ripe and brings forth what my own efforts could never bring forth!" This attitude is characteristic of stable periods, periods without catastrophe, revolution, war.

In the second case, the moment in which actual force becomes a possibility, the tendency of Marxist ideas is to justify the use of extreme force as the means of bringing about splendid conditions whose realization may be expected with certainty if the ineluctable movement of history is recognized.

In both cases there is no hint of collaboration to bring about a constructive ordering of actual human existence, which, allowing for all half-measures, injustices, disagreements, still makes possible human fulfillment, in the framework of positive—not destructive—history.

11. The dogmatic faith

The great power of Marxist thought lies precisely in its fundamental wrongness, in the dogma that is not proven and is not subjected to self-reflection, in the fanaticism of certainty.

Hence one's personal belief is dubbed science. This science is confounded with authentic science, from which derives its persuasive power, which then is wrongly transposed to the whole.

This faith presents itself as faith without transcendence, as pure, human science. It does not call itself faith, but shows every feature

---

[2]Ferdinand Lassalle (1825–1864) was a German-Jewish Socialist theoretician and founder of Social-Democracy, who became a rival of Marx for intellectual leadership of the movement.

of other dogmatic faiths: blindness for what is against it, fanaticism, aggressiveness, sophistry, inability to communicate (in personal terms: Marx's break with all who do not simply follow him).

We find here, carried to the highest degree, precisely what is held against the others: dogmatism, fictitious imagination, illusion, dogmatically inspired dreams.

12. Methods of Marxist disputation

Marx was irrefutably criticized in the last century. Why was this without effect? Because this criticism involved something outside its scope, a faith which adopted Marx's thought not so much as knowledge but as speculative thinking. Scientists have wearied of rehashing what was said long ago. The part that is genuine science has meanwhile entered into general science.

For Marxism, the truth is known and can be appropriated. Thinking in regard to truth is principally advocatory, that is, "apologetic" and "aggressive."

One cannot seriously dispute with someone who no longer wants to investigate or think. Something is being presupposed by Marx which, no matter what cognition establishes, will invariably emerge as the result, independent of whether we are dealing with the interpretation of the Gospels or the materialist conception of history.

The dialectic is always right—which lies in the nature of the thing, since it absorbs all contradictions. All opposition becomes proof of one's own truth, the opponent himself being a link in this truth, even though one to be demolished. Dogmatic faith and the absurd are somehow related—therein lies the impossibility of refutation; for where absurdity is not a fault, no debate based on reason is possible, which explains the inability to listen. Whom could one address? Not those in power; they do not debate at all, but merely use everything as grist for their propaganda mill. Not with those who obey; they are convinced that what value they have lies in submission, added to which is the good conscience of being loyal to their cause.

Presuppositions for an exchange based on a shared search for truth consist in suspension of the political will in the give and take of debate; a scientist's unbiased observation, even where it concerns one's own direction of will; scrupulous inquiry into what contradicts us, into facts that are uncomfortable for us.

Thwarting debate: truth conceived not as truth but as self-assertion, not as subject for discussion but the property of a party; unshakable stand instead of perseverance in probing; instead of answering, changing the subject; instead of reasoning, asserting; instead of the truth, the desire to prevail in one's existence and one's "ism."

Psychological consequences: anger, vindictiveness, prejudice; shunning one's opponents, or disparaging one's opponent by accusing him of being motivated by matters unrelated to the topic under discussion.

Marxism almost invariably exhibits these character traits: assuming at once an attitude of attack or defense, creating a supercharged climate, exhibiting a constitutional rage which can become an instrument of manipulation to a point where it can be turned on and off, allowing a person in a complete frenzy to return to a state of utter calm once he has said his piece.

Thus, from the outset, such methods of debate and criticism are imbued with violence, which, in practice, is kept in check only as long as brute force is not at hand.

The method of Marxist criticism: to despise what is opposed to it, to regard it as stupid or vile; to proceed from the matter at hand to the assertion that the opponent is befogged by class prejudice. Scientific examination or criticism is regarded as ideology, thus a position specific to moments of historical development. The greatest denial is reserved for that which belongs or fits nowhere in the ideological scheme of history: it is wholly null and void.

BIBLIOGRAPHY

This Bibliography lists the main primary sources used by Jaspers in his exposition of the individual thinkers. In some cases several editions in different languages were drawn upon to explicate the same thinker. Also included under primary sources are standard English editions used in translating the text; they are identified in the text. Included under Secondary Works are some consulted or referred to by Jaspers.

Descartes

SOURCES:
Oeuvres de Descartes. Ed. by Charles Adam and Paul Tannery. 10 vols. Paris, J. Vrin, 1897–1913; repr., 1974–89.
René Descartes's philosophische Werke in der Philosophischen Bibliothek. Ed. by A. Buchenau and J. H. von Kirchmann. 29 vols. Leipzig, F. Meiner, 1904–.
Briefe 1629–1650. Ed. by M. Bense. Cologne, Staufen, 1949.
Descartes' Philosophical Writings. Trans. and ed. by Norman Kemp Smith. London, Macmillan, 1952.
Descartes: Selected Philosophical Writings. Trans. by J. Cottingham, R. Stoothof, and D. Murdoch. New York, Cambridge University Press, 1988.
Meditations on First Philosophy. Trans. by John Cottingham. Introduction by B. Williams. Cambridge and New York, Cambridge University Press, 1986.
Philosophical Letters. Trans. and ed. by Anthony Kenny. Minneapolis, University of Minnesota Press, 1970.
The Philosophical Works of Descartes. Trans. by Elizabeth Haldane and George Ross. 2 vols. 2d ed., Cambridge, Cambridge University Press, 1931; repr., 1967.

SECONDARY SOURCES:
Cottingham, John: Descartes. Oxford, Oxford University Press, 1986.
Doney, Willis, ed.: Descartes: A Collection of Critical Essays. Garden City, NY, Anchor Books, 1967.
Gaukroger, Stephen, ed.: Descartes: Philosophy, Mathematics and Physics. Totowa, NJ, Barnes & Noble, 1980.
Grene, Marjorie: Descartes. Minneapolis, University of Minnesota Press, 1985.
Jaspers, Karl: "Descartes and Philosophy," in Three Essays. Trans. by Ralph Manheim. New York, Harcourt Brace & World, 1964.
Kenny, Anthony: Descartes: A Study of His Philosophy. New York, Random House, 1968.
Sorell, Tom: Descartes. Oxford, Oxford University Press, 1987.
Williams, Bernard: Descartes: The Project of Pure Enquiry. Hassocks, Harvester Press, 1978.
Wilson, Margaret: Descartes. London and Boston, Routledge & Kegan Paul, 1978.

Pascal

SOURCES:

Oeuvres complètes. Ed. by Jacques Chevalier. 34 vols. Paris, Gallimard, 1954.
Pensées: Texte de l'édition Brunschvicq. Ed. by Ch.-Marc des Granges. Paris, Garnier, 1958.
Pascals Briefe. Trans. and ed. by W. Rüttenauer. Leipzig, 1935.
Gedanken. Trans. by W. Rüttenauer; introd. by R. Guardini. Wiesbaden, Diederichs, 1947.
The Heart of Pascal. Ed. by H. F. Stewart. Cambridge, Cambridge University Press, 1945.
The Miscellaneous Writings of Pascal. Trans. from French edition of M. F. Faugère by George Pearce. London, Longmans, 1849.
Pascal's Pensées. Trans. with introd. by H. F. Stewart. New York, Pantheon Books, 1950.
Pensées. Trans. with intro. by A. J. Krailsheimer. Harmondsworth, Penguin, 1960.
Pensées. Ed. by John Cruickshank. London, Grant and Cutler, 1983.
The Provincial Letters of Blaise Pascal. London, J. M. Dent, 1904.

SECONDARY SOURCES:

Adamson, Donald: *Pascal: A Critical Biography.* Totowa, NJ, Barnes & Noble, 1984.
Auerbach, Erich: "Über Pascals politische Theorien," in *Vier Untersuchungen zur Geschichte der französichen Bildung.* Bern, A. Francke, 1951.
Broome, J. H.: *Pascal.* New York, Barnes & Noble, 1966.
Brunschvicq, Léon: *Le génie de Pascal.* Paris, Hachette, 1924.
Cailliet, Emile: *Pascal: The Emergence of Genius.* New York, Harper and Row, 1961.
Coleman, Francis: *Neither Angel nor Beast: The Life and Work of Blaise Pascal.* New York, Routledge & Kegan Paul, 1986.
Davidson, Hugh: *Blaise Pascal.* Boston, Twayne, 1983.
Goldmann, Lucien: *The Hidden God: A Study of Tragic Vision in the Pensées of Pascal and the Tragedies of Racine.* Trans. by P. Thody. New York, Humanities Press, 1964.
Jens, Walter: *Literature and Religion.* Trans. by P. Heinegg. New York, Paragon House, 1991.
Krailsheimer, A. J.: *Pascal.* New York, Hill and Wang, 1980.
Nelson, Robert: *Pascal: Adversary and Advocate.* Cambridge, MA, Harvard University Press, 1981.
Steinmann, Jean: *Pascal.* Trans. by Martin Turnell. New York, Harcourt, Brace & World, 1965.
Stewart, H. F.: *The Secret of Pascal.* Cambridge, Cambridge University Press, 1941.

Lessing

SOURCES:

Gotthold Ephraim Lessings Sämtliche Schriften. Ed. by K. Lachmann. 3rd edition, 23 vols. Stuttgart/Leipzig/Berlin, Göschen, 1886–1924.
Lessing: Geschichte seines Lebens und seiner Schriften. Ed. by E. Schmidt. 4th edition. Berlin, Weidmann, 1924.
Lessings Sämtliche Werke in 20 Bänden. Ed. by H. Göring. Stuttgart, Cotta/Kröner, 1883–.
Lessing's Theological Writings. Ed. and introd. by Henry Chadwick. Stanford, Stanford University Press, 1967.

Lessings Werke. Ed. by J. Petersen and W. von Olshausen. 20 vols. Berlin/Leipzig/ Vienna, Bong, 1925 – .

Nathan the Wise, Minna von Barnhelm, and Other Plays and Writings. Ed. by P. Demetz; introd. by H. Arendt. New York, Continuum, 1991.

SECONDARY SOURCES:

Allison, Henry: *Lessing and the Enlightenment: His Philosophy of Religion and Its Relation to Eighteenth Century Thought.* Ann Arbor, University of Michigan Press, 1966.

Aner, Karl: *Die Theologie der Lessingzeit.* Hildesheim, G. Olms, 1929.

Arendt, Hannah. *Men in Dark Times.* New York, Harcourt, Brace & World, 1968.

Barner, Wilfried, ed.: *Lessing. Epoche, Werk, Wirkung.* Munich, Beck, 1975.

Bauer, Gerhard, and Bauer, Sybille, eds.: *Gotthold Ephraim Lessing.* 2d ed. Darmstadt, Wissenschaftliche Buchgesellschaft, 1986.

Cassirer, Paul: *The Philosophy of the Enlightenment.* Princeton, Princeton University Press, 1951.

Drews, Wolfgang: *Lessing.* Reinbek, Rowohlt, 1962.

Göring, Hugo: *Lessings Leben.* Stuttgart, Cotta, 1884.

Heller, Peter: *Dialectics and Nihilism: Essays on Lessing, Nietzsche, Mann, and Kafka.* Amherst, MA, University of Massachusetts Press, 1966.

Hildebrandt, Dieter: *Lessing. Biographie einer Emanzipation.* Frankfurt, Ullstein, 1982.

Leisegang, Hans. *Lessings Weltanschauung.* Leipzig, F. Meiner, 1931.

Mann, Otto: *Lessing. Sein und Leistung.* Hamburg, M. von Schroder, 1949.

Rilla, Paul: *Lessing und sein Zeitalter.* Munich, Beck, 1977.

Sime, James: *Lessing: His Life and Writings.* 3rd ed. 2 vols. London, Kegan Paul, Trench and Trubner, 1986.

Kierkegaard

SOURCES:

Gesammelte Werke in 12 Bdn. Ed. by H. Gottsched. Jena, E. Diederichs Verlag, 1909.

Gesammelte Werke in 36 Abt. Ed. by Emanuel Hirsch. Düsseldorf/Cologne, E. Diederichs Verlag, 1950 – .

Sören Kierkegaard, Buch des Richters. Seine Tagebücher 1833 – 1855 im Auszug. Ed. and trans. by Hermann Gottsched. Jena/Leipzig, Diederichs, 1905.

Sören Kierkegaard und sein Verhältnis zu "ihr." Ed. by Raphael Meyer. Stuttgart, A. Juncker, 1905.

Sören Kierkegaard, Zweiter Teil, Die Tagebücher 1832 – 1839. Ed. and trans. by Hermann Ulrich. Berlin, 1930.

Die Tagebücher. Ed. and trans. by Theodor Haecker. Innsbruck, Brenner Verlag, 1923.

Christian Discourses (incl. The Lilies of the Field and the Birds of the Air and *Three Discourses at the Communion on Fridays).* Oxford, Oxford University Press, 1939.

The Concept of Anxiety. Trans. by Reidar Thomie and Albert B. Anderson. Princeton, Princeton University Press, 1980.

The Concept of Dread. Trans. by Walter Lowrie. Princeton, Princeton University Press, 1944.

Concluding Unscientific Postscript to the "Philosophical Fragments." Trans. by David F. Swenson; completed and ed. by Walter Lowrie. Oxford, Oxford University Press, 1941; Princeton, Princeton University Press, 1941.

Edifying Discourses. Trans. by David F. and Lillian Marvin Swenson. 4 vols. Minneapolis, Augsburg Publishing House, 1943 – 46.

Either/Or: A Fragment of Life. Vol. I trans. by David F. and Lillian Marvin Swenson; Vol. II trans. by Walter Lowrie. Princeton, Princeton University Press, 1944.

Either/Or: A Fragment of Life. Abridged and trans. by Alastair Hannay. New York, Penguin Books, 1992.

Fear and Trembling and *The Sickness Unto Death.* Trans. by Walter Lowrie. Garden City, NY, Doubleday Anchor Books, 1941; Princeton, Princeton University Press, 1941; repr. 1954.

For Self-Examination and *Judge for Yourselves!* (and *Three Discourses,* 1851). Trans. by Walter Lowrie (except "God's Unchangeableness," trans. by David F. Swenson). Oxford, Oxford University Press, 1941; Princeton, Princeton University Press, 1944.

The Gospel of Suffering. Trans. by David F. and Lillian Marvin Swenson. Minneapolis, Augsburg Publishing House, 1948.

The Journals of Søren Kierkegaard. Ed. and trans. by Alexander Dru. Oxford/New York: Oxford University Press, 1938.

Kierkegaard's Attack Upon Christendom. Trans. by W. Lowrie. Princeton, Princeton University Press, 1944.

Kierkegaard's Concluding Unscientific Postscript. Trans. by David F. Swenson; completed by Walter Lowrie. Princeton, Princeton University Press, 1941.

Kierkegaard's Writings. Ed. and trans. by H. Hong and E. Hong. Princeton, Princeton University Press, 1987–.

The Lilies and the Birds. Trans. by A. S. Aldworth and W. S. Ferrie. London, Daniel, 1941.

Meditations. Trans. and ed. by T. H. Croxall. Philadelphia, Westminster Press, 1955.

Philosophical Fragments: Johannes Climacus. Ed. and trans. by Howard V. and Edna H. Hong. Princeton, Princeton University Press, 1985.

The Point of View for My Work as an Author (incl. "Two Notes about 'The Individual'" and "On My Work as an Author"). Trans. by Walter Lowrie. Oxford, Oxford University Press, 1939.

The Present Age (with "Two Minor Ethico-Religious Treatises"). Trans. by Alexander Dru and Walter Lowrie. Oxford, Oxford University Press, 1940.

Purify Your Hearts! Trans. by A. S. Aldworth and W. S. Ferrie. London, Daniel, 1938.

Repetition: An Essay in Experimental Psychology. Trans. by Walter Lowrie. Princeton, Princeton University Press, 1946.

The Sickness unto Death. Trans. by Walter Lowrie. Oxford, Oxford University Press, 1941, 1954; Princeton, Princeton University Press, 1941; rev., Doubleday Anchor Books, n.d.

Sören Kierkegaard's Journals and Papers. Ed. and trans. by Howard V. Hong and Edna H. Hong. Bloomington and London, Indiana University Press, 1978.

Stages on Life's Way: Studies by Various Persons. Ed. and trans. by Howard V. and Edna H. Hong. Princeton, Princeton University Press, 1988.

Thoughts on Crucial Situations in Human Life: Three Discourses on Imagined Occasions. Trans. by David F. Swenson. Minneapolis, Augsburg Publishing House, 1941.

Training in Christianity (and the "Edifying Discourse" which accompanied it). Trans. by Walter Lowrie. Oxford, Oxford University Press, 1941; Princeton, Princeton University Press, 1946.

Works of Love. Trans. by David F. and Lillian Marvin Swenson. Princeton, Princeton University Press, 1946.

SECONDARY SOURCES:

Collins, James: *The Mind of Kierkegaard.* Princeton, Princeton University Press, 1983.

Croxall, T. H.: *Kierkegaard Studies.* London, Lutterworth Press, 1948.

Gardiner, Patrick: *Kierkegaard.* London/Oxford/New York, Oxford University Press, 1988.

Geismar, Eduard: *Lectures on the Religious Thought of Sören Kierkegaard.* Minneapolis, Augsburg Publishing House, 1937.

Gouwens, David: *Kierkegaard's Dialectic of the Imagination.* New York, P. Lang, 1989.

Haecker, Theodor: *Kierkegaard the Cripple.* Trans. by C. van O. Bruyn. New York, Philosophical Library, 1950.

Hohlenberg, Johannes: *Sören Kierkegaard: A Biography.* Trans. by T. H. Croxall. New York, Pantheon Books, 1954.

Lowrie, Walter: *Kierkegaard.* Oxford/New York, Oxford University Press, 1938.

————. *A Short Life of Kierkegaard.* Princeton, Princeton University Press, 1942.

Thompson, Josiah, ed.: *Kierkegaard: A Collection of Critical Essays.* Garden City, NY, Doubleday Anchor Books, 1972.

Nietzsche

SOURCES:

Friedrich Nietzsches Gesammelte Briefe. 6 vols. Berlin/Leipzig, Schuster and Loeffler; Leipzig, Insel, 1900 – .

Gesammelte Werke, Musarionausgabe. 23 vols. Munich, Musarion Verlag, 1920 – .

Nietzsche-Register. Compiled by Richard Oehler. Stuttgart, Alfred Kröner Verlag, 1943.

Nietzsches Briefwechsel mit Franz Overbeck. Ed. by C. A. Bernoulli and Richard Oehler. Leipzig, Insel, 1916.

Nietzsches Werke, Gesamtausgabe in 16 Bdn. Hrsg. im Auftrag des Nietzsche-Archivs von E. Förster-Nietzsche. Leipzig, A. Kroner, 1899 – .

Werke in Drei Bänden. Ed. by Karl Schlechta. 4 vols. with Index. Munich, Carl Hanser, 1954 – 56, 1965.

Werke in 11 Bdn, Kröner-Taschenausgabe. Ed. by A. Baeumler. Leipzig/Stuttgart, R. Kröner, 1906 – .

Werke und Briefe, Historisch-Kritische Gesamtausgabe. Ed. by H. J. Mette u. a. Munich, Beck, 1933 – .

The Basic Works of Friedrich Nietzsche. Trans. and ed. by Walter Kaufmann. New York, Modern Library, 1968.

The Birth of Tragedy and The Case of Wagner [The Wagner Case]. Trans. by Walter Kaufmann. New York, Vintage Books, 1967.

Beyond Good and Evil: Prelude to a Philosophy of the Future. Trans. by R. J. Hollingdale. New York, Penguin Books, 1972.

Complete Works of Friedrich Nietzsche. Ed. by Oscar Levy. 18 vols. New York, Macmillan, 1909 – 11.

The Dawn of Day [Aurora]. Trans. by J. M. Kennedy. New York, Gordon Press, 1974.

Ecce Homo. Trans. by R. J. Hollingdale. New York, Penguin Books, 1979.

The Gay Science [The Joyous Science]. Trans. by Walter Kaufmann. New York, Vintage Books, Random House, 1974.

Human, All Too Human. Trans. by R. J. Hollingdale. Cambridge, Cambridge University Press, 1986.

Nietzsche: A Collection of Critical Essays. Ed. by Robert C. Solomon. New York, Anchor Press, 1973.

A Nietzsche Reader. Trans. by R. J. Hollingdale. New York, Penguin Books, 1977.

On the Genealogy of Morals and *Ecce Homo.* Trans. by Walter Kaufmann and R. J. Hollingdale. New York, Vintage Books, 1973.

The Portable Nietzsche. Trans. by Walter Kaufmann. New York, Viking Press, 1973.

Thus Spoke Zarathustra. Trans. by R. J. Hollingdale. New York, Penguin Books, 1969.

Twilight of the Idols and *The Antichrist.* Trans. by R. J. Hollingdale. New York, Penguin Books, 1968.

Untimely Meditations. Trans. by R. J. Hollingdale. Cambridge, Cambridge University Press, 1983.

The Will to Power. Trans. by Walter Kaufmann and R. J. Hollingdale. New York, Vintage Books, 1968.

SECONDARY SOURCES:

Danto, Arthur: *Nietzsche as Philosopher.* New York, Macmillan, 1965.

Hollingdale, R. J.: *Nietzsche: The Man and His Philosophy.* Baton Rouge, Louisiana State University Press, 1965.

Howey, R. L.: *Heidegger and Jaspers on Nietzsche: A Critical Examination of Heidegger's and Jaspers's Interpretations of Nietzsche.* Atlantic Highlands, NJ, Humanities Press, 1973.

Kaufmann, Walter: *Nietzsche: Philosopher, Psychologist, Antichrist.* 4th ed. Princeton, Princeton University Press, 1975.

Lea, F. A.: *The Tragic Philosopher: A Study of Friedrich Nietzsche.* London, Methuen, 1957.

Morgan, George A. *What Nietzsche Means.* Cambridge, MA, Harvard University Press, 1941.

Stern, J. P.: *Friedrich Nietzsche.* Cambridge and New York, Penguin Books, 1979.

Einstein

SOURCES:

Geometrie und Erfahrung, erweiterte Fassung des Vortrags von 1921. Berlin, J. Springer, 1921.

Mein Weltbild. Ed. by C. Seelig. Zürich/Stuttgart/Vienna, Europa, 1953.

Über die spezielle und die allgemeine Relativitätstheorie. 6th ed. Braunschweig, Viehweg, 1920.

Einstein on Peace. Ed. by Otto Nathan and Heinz Norden. New York, Schocken Books, 1960.

Essays on Science. New York, Philosophical Library, 1934.

Ideas and Opinions. Based on *Mein Weltbild.* Ed. by Carl Seelig. New York, Dell, 1954.

The Meaning of Relativity. Princeton, Princeton University Press, 1950.

On the Method of Theoretical Physics. The Herbert Spencer Lecture delivered June 10, 1933. Oxford University Press, 1933.

Out of My Later Years. New York, Philosophical Library, 1950.

Relativity. New York, Crown, 1961.

SECONDARY SOURCES:

Bernstein, Jeremy: *Einstein.* New York, Penguin Books, 1976.

Born, Max: *Einstein's Theory of Relativity.* New York, Dover, 1962.

Frank, Philipp: *Einstein: His Life and Times.* New York, Alfred A. Knopf, 1947.

Infeld, Leopold: *Albert Einstein, His Work and Influences on Our World.* New York, Charles Scribner's Sons, 1950.

Katz, Robert: *An Introduction to the Special Theory of Relativity.* Princeton, D. Van Nostrand, 1964.

Moller, C.: *The Theory of Relativity*. Oxford, Oxford University Press, 1952.

Schilp, Paul, ed.: *Albert Einstein: Philosopher-Scientist*. Evanston, IL, The Library of Living Philosophers, 1949.

Sciama, D. W.: *The Physical Foundations of General Relativity*. New York, Doubleday, 1969.

Williams, L. Pearce, ed.: *The Relativity Theory: Its Origins and Impact on Modern Thought*. New York, John Wiley & Sons, 1969.

Weber

SOURCES:

Gesammelte Aufsätze zur Religionssoziologie. 3 vols. Tübingen, Mohr, 1920–1921.

Gesammelte Aufsätze zur Sozial- und Wirtschaftsgeschichte. Tübingen, Mohr, 1920.

Gesammelte Aufsätze zur Soziologie und Sozialpolitik. Tübingen, Mohr, 1924.

Gesammelte Aufsätze zur Wissenschaftslehre. Tübingen, Mohr, 1922.

Gesammelte Politische Schriften. Munich, Drei Masken Verlag, 1921.

Wirtschaft und Gesellschaft (Grundriβ der verstehenden Soziologie). 2 vols. Tübingen, Mohr, 1956.

Ancient Judaism. Glencoe, IL, The Free Press, 1952.

The City. Glencoe, IL, The Free Press, 1958.

Economy and Society: An Outline of Interpretive Sociology. Ed. by Guenther Roth and Claus Wittich. New York, Bedminster, 1968.

From Max Weber: Essays in Sociology. Ed. and trans. by H. H. Gerth and C. Wright Mills. New York, Oxford University Press, 1947.

General Economic History. Trans. by Frank H. Knight. New York, Macmillan, 1961.

Max Weber on the Methodology of the Social Sciences. Ed. and trans. by Edward Shils and Henry A. Finch. Glencoe, IL, The Free Press, 1949.

The Protestant Ethic and the Spirit of Capitalism. Trans. by Talcott Parsons. London, Hammersmith, 1991.

The Religion of China: Confucianism and Taoism. Glencoe, Il, The Free Press, 1949.

The Religion of India: The Sociology of Hinduism and Buddhism. Glencoe, IL, The Free Press, 1958.

The Sociology of Religion. Introd. by Talcott Parsons, new foreword by A. Swidler. Boston, Beacon, 1993.

SECONDARY SOURCES:

Aron, R.: *German Sociology*. New York, The Free Press, 1964.

Bendix, Reinhard: *Max Weber: An Intellectual Portrait*. 2d ed. Berkeley, University of California Press, 1977.

————: *Scholarship and Partisanship. Essays on Max Weber*. Berkeley, University of California Press, 1971.

Dronberger, Ilse: *The Political Thought of Max Weber: In Quest of Statesmanship*. New York, Appleton Century Crofts, 1971.

Freund, Julien: *The Sociology of Max Weber*. New York, Vintage Books, 1969.

Giddens, Anthony: *Politics and Sociology in the Thought of Max Weber*. London, Macmillan, 1972.

Honigsheim, Paul: *On Max Weber: Collected Essays*. New York, The Free Press, 1968.

Macrae, Donald: *Max Weber*. New York, Viking Press, 1974.

Mayer, Jacob Peter: *Max Weber and German Politics: A Study in Political Sociology*. 2nd ed. London, Faber & Faber, 1956.

Mitzman, Arthur: *The Iron Cage: An Historical Interpretation of Max Weber*. New York, Alfred A. Knopf, 1970.

Mommsen, Wolfgang J.: *The Age of Bureaucracy: Perspectives on the Political Sociology of Max Weber.* New York, Harper & Row, 1974.
————: *Max Weber and German Politics.* Trans. by Michael Steinberg. Chicago, University of Chicago Press, 1984.
————. *The Political and Social Theory of Max Weber: Collected Essays.* Chicago, University of Chicago Press, 1989.
Runciman, Walter F.: *A Critique of Max Weber's Philosophy of Social Science.* Cambridge, Cambridge University Press, 1972.
Sahay, Arun, ed.: *Max Weber and Modern Sociology.* London, Routledge & Kegan Paul, 1971.
Weber, Marianne: *Max Weber: A Biography.* Trans. by Harry Zohn. New Brunswick, NJ, Transaction Books, 1988.
Wrong, Dennis, ed.: *Makers of Modern Social Science: Max Weber.* Englewood Cliffs, NJ, Prentice-Hall, 1970.

Marx

SOURCES:

Marx/Engels: *Der historische Materialismus.* Ed. by S. Landshut and J. P. Mayer. 2 vols. Leipzig, A. Kroner, 1932.
————: *Gesammelte Schriften von 1852–1862.* Ed. by N. Riasanoff. 2 vols. Stuttgart, n.p., 1917.
————: *Werke, Deutsche Ausgabe der vom Institut für Marxismus-Leninismus beim ZK der KPdSU in Moskau besorgten Ausgabe.* Berlin, Dietz, 1961.
————: *The Communist Manifesto.* Ed. by A. J. P. Taylor. New York, Penguin Books, 1967.
Basic Writings on Politics and Philosophy. Ed. by L. Feuer. Garden City, NY, Doubleday, 1959.
The Early Texts. Ed. by D. McLellan. Oxford, Oxford University Press, 1971.
Economic and Philosophical Manuscripts of 1844. Ed. by D. J. Struick, trans. by M. Milligan. New York, International Publishing, 1971.
Karl Marx Reader. Ed. by R. C. Tucker. New York, Norton, 1971.
Karl Marx: Selected Writings. Ed. by D. McLellan. Oxford, Oxford University Press, 1977.
On Revolution, On Press Freedom and Censorship. Ed. by S. Padover. New York, McGraw-Hill, 1971.
The Portable Marx. Ed. by E. Kamenka. New York, Penguin Books, 1971.
Selected Writings in Sociology and Social Philosophy. Ed. by T. B. Bottomore and M. Rubel. London, Watts, 1956.
Works. New York, International Publishers, 1975–.
Writings of the Young Marx on Philosophy and Society. Ed. by L. D. Easton and K. H. Guddat. New York, Doubleday, 1967.

SECONDARY SOURCES:

Avineri, Shlomo: *The Social and Political Thought of Karl Marx.* New York, Cambridge University Press, 1971.
Berlin, Isaiah: *Karl Marx, His Life and Environment.* New York, Oxford University Press, 1939.
Bober, M. M.: *Karl Marx's Interpretation of History.* 2d ed. New York, Norton, 1965.
Carr, E. H.: *Karl Marx: A Study in Fanaticism.* London, J. M. Dent, 1943.
Fromm, E.: *Marx's Concept of Man.* New York, Ungar, 1961.
Hunt, Richard: *The Political Ideas of Marx and Engels.* Pittsburgh, University of Pittsburgh Press, 1975.

Kamenka, Eugene: *The Ethical Foundations of Marxism.* New York, Routledge & Kegan Paul, 1962.

Lichtheim, G.: *Marxism, an Historical and Critical Study.* New York, Columbia University Press, 1982.

McLellan, David: *Karl Marx.* New York, Viking Press, 1975.

———. *Karl Marx: His Life and Thought.* New York, Viking Press, 1974.

———. *The Young Hegelians and Karl Marx.* London, Macmillan, 1969.

Seigel, Jerrold: *Marx's Fate: The Shape of a Life.* Princeton, Princeton University Press, 1978.

Tucker, Robert C.: *Philosophy and Myth in Karl Marx.* New York, Cambridge University Press, 1961.

INDEX OF NAMES